THE BOOK ON ADLER

KIERKEGAARD'S WRITINGS, XXIV

THE BOOK ON ADLER

by Søren Kierkegaard

Edited and Translated
with Introduction and Notes by

Howard V. Hong and
Edna H. Hong

PRINCETON UNIVERSITY PRESS
PRINCETON, NEW JERSEY

Library of Congress Cataloging-in-Publication Data

Kierkegaard, Søren, 1813–1855
[Bogen om Adler. English]
The Book on Adler / by Søren Kierkegaard ;
edited and translated with introduction and notes by Howard V. Hong and Edna H. Hong
p.   cm. — (Kierkegaard's Writings ; 24)
Translation of: Bogen om Adler
Includes bibliographical references (p.   ) and index.
ISBN 0-691-03227-0 (alk. paper)
1. Adler, Aldoph Peter, 1817–1869.   I. Hong, Howard Vincent, 1912–.
II. Hong, Edna Hatlestad, 1913–   III. Title.
V. Series: Kiergaard, Søren, 1813–1855. Works. English. 1978 ; 24
BX8080.A25K5313   1998
198'.9—dc21   97-18083

Production of this volume has been made possible in part by a grant from
the Division of Research Programs of the National Endowment
for the Humanities, an independent federal agency

CONTENTS

CHAPTER IV

A Psychological View of Adler as a Phenomenon and as a
Satire on Hegelian Philosophy and the Present Age
91

ADDENDUM I

The Dialectical Relations: the Universal,
the Single Individual, the Special Individual
143

ADDENDUM II

The Difference between a Genius and an Apostle
173

HISTORICAL INTRODUCTION

The Book on Adler is ostensibly about Adolph Peter Adler;[1] essentially it is about the concept of authority. The book was never published because, in order to diminish emphasis on Adler and to concentrate on the concept of authority, the manuscript was revised by Kierkegaard more than any other of his manuscripts. The present volume is version III, the last integral version. Part of version III (Addendum II) was eventually published, with minor changes, as the second part of *Two Ethical-Religious Essays*[2] (May 19, 1849), of which he wrote, "This little book is very significant. It contains the key to the greatest potentiality of all my writing, but not the one at which I have been aiming. And the second essay contains the most important of all the ethical-religious concepts, the one I have deliberately omitted until its appearance there."[3] The second essay, "The Difference between

---

[1] Adolph Peter Adler (1817–1869), Danish theologian, pastor, and writer. After finishing his theological studies, he wrote a dissertation (in Danish, as Kierkegaard did, by special permission) on isolated subjectivity, *Den isolerede Subjektivitet i dens vigtigste Skikkelser* (Copenhagen: 1840). During the winter of 1840, he gave philosophical lectures at the University of Copenhagen, and in 1841 he was appointed pastor in Hasle and Rutsker on the island of Bornholm. The next year his *Populære Foredrag over Hegels objective Logik* was published. The following year a volume of sermons, *Nogle Prædikener* (Copenhagen: 1843), was published, and in the preface Adler asserted that he had received a revelation in which Christ dictated a new doctrine. He was suspended from his pastorate and eventually dismissed with pension by his ecclesiastical superiors. He then published documents on the affair in *Skrivelser min Suspension og Entledigelse vedkommende* (Copenhagen: 1845). On June 12, 1846, four books by Adler were published: *Studier og Exempler, Forsøg til en kort systematisk Fremstilling af Christendommen i dens Logik, Theologiske Studier,* and *Nogle Digte.* Kierkegaard purchased the first three books on the day of publication and began writing what he called "The Book on Adler."

[2] *Two Ethical-Religious Essays,* in *Without Authority,* pp. 47–108, *KW* XVIII (*SV* XI 49–109).

[3] *JP* VI 6447 (*Pap.* X[1] A 551). See Supplement, pp. 213, 310–11, 330–33 (*Pap.* IV C 99; VIII[1] A 225, 416; X[1] A 625; X[2] A 119, 396; X[4] A 110).

a Genius and an Apostle," is an analysis of the presumed authority of genius and the qualitatively different apostolic authority.

Kierkegaard's consideration of authority in *Two Essays* is an epitomization of *The Book on Adler* and is in accord with what he describes as the movement of the entire authorship:

> *from* "the poet," from the esthetic—*from* "the philosopher," from the speculative—*to* the indication of the innermost qualification of the essentially Christian; **from** the pseudonymous *Either-Or,* **through** *Concluding Postscript* with my *name as editor,* **to** *Discourses at the Communion on Fridays** . . ..
>
> * . . . And a little earlier in that same year there appeared a little book: *Two Ethical-Religious Essays* by H. H. The significance of this little book (which does not stand *in* the authorship as much as it relates totally *to* the authorship and for that reason also was anonymous,[4] in order to be kept outside entirely) is not so easy to explain without going into the whole matter. It is like a navigation mark *by which* one steers but, please note, in such a way that the pilot understands precisely that *he is to keep a certain distance from it.* It defines the boundary of the authorship. "The Difference between a Genius and an Apostle" (essay no. 2) is: "The genius is without authority."[5]

Although an explicit, developed consideration of the concept of authority is not part of Kierkegaard's earlier writing, the theme is by no means absent. Throughout the works, beginning with *The Concept of Irony* (1841), authority on various levels and in various forms is repeatedly represented and discussed. In *The Concept of Irony* (even though Kierkegaard did not regard the dissertation as part of the authorship proper), a variety of concepts of authority constitutes a unifying theme: the authority of Sophistic dialectic,[6] the divine authority of the Delphic Oracle,[7] the authority implicit in Socratic ignorance,[8] the authority of the

---

[4] Under the pseudonym H. H.
[5] *On My Work as an Author,* in *The Point of View, KW* XXII (*SV* XIII 494).
[6] *The Concept of Irony, with Continual Reference to Socrates,* pp. 204–10, *KW* II (*SV* XIII 284–90).
[7] Ibid., p. 172 (227).   [8] Ibid., p. 175 (258).

state,[9] the authority of Socratic irony,[10] esthetic authority,[11] the authority of irony in writers,[12] the immediate authority of Don Juan as a sensate genius,[13] and the constitutive authority of the immediate *I* in its freedom.[14] In *Repetition* (1843), Constantin Constantius discusses the authority of the comic genius,[15] and the Young Man attests to the authority of Job's character.[16] In his concluding analysis of the Young Man, Constantin asserts that if the Young Man had possessed "a deeper religious background, he would not have become a poet . . . and he would also have had a quite different authority."[17] In *Concluding Unscientific Postscript* (1846), Johannes Climacus discusses the authority of the Bible, of the Church, of the test of time, and of speculative thought in the religious sphere.[18] He also touches on the psychological authority of an esthetic philosophical genius,[19] on the confusion of poetic authority with religious authority,[20] on divine authority in religious address,[21] and on the miraculous authority of an apostle.[22] In *Two Ages* (1847), Kierkegaard contrasts the process of leveling in a disintegrating world with levels of authority in an organic society.[23]

Continuing the ascending line of concepts of authority, *Upbuilding Discourses in Various Spirits* (1847) presents the authority and task of parents as analogous to the Lord's authority and task[24] and presents Christ as the one of preeminent authority.[25] This is repeated in *Works of Love*[26] (1847), which also emphasizes

[9] Ibid., pp. 184–85 (267). [10] Ibid., p. 196 (277–78).
[11] Ibid., p. 244 (320). [12] Ibid., pp. 275–76 (348).
[13] Ibid., p. 293 (362–63). [14] Ibid., p. 301 (370).
[15] *Repetition*, pp. 160–64, *KW* VI (SV III 200–03).
[16] Ibid., p. 207 (241). [17] Ibid., p. 229 (263).
[18] *Concluding Unscientific Postscript to* Philosophical Fragments, pp. 23–57, *KW* XII.1 (*SV* VII 12–43).
[19] Ibid., p. 64 (48). [20] Ibid., p. 441 (383).
[21] Ibid., p. 481 (418). [22] Ibid., pp. 74, 388 (57, 337).
[23] *Two Ages: The Age of Revolution and the Present Age, A Literary Review*, pp. 106–07, *KW* XIV (*SV* VIII 99).
[24] *Upbuilding Discourses in Various Spirits*, pp. 293–94, *KW* XV (*SV* VIII 374–75).
[25] Ibid., p. 302 (381).
[26] *Works of Love*, p. 97, *KW* XVI (*SV* IX 95).

the authority of the Gospel as speaking *to*, not *about*,[27] and of the royal command, "You *shall* love."[28] The divine authority of the Christian proclamation is reiterated in *Christian Discourses*[29] (1848), and the vitiating consequences of trying to give reasons for ultimate authority[30] are discussed.[31]

In his continued occupation with the concept of authority, Kierkegaard regarded himself as not having authority, a view that he stated as early as the preface to the first[32] of the six volumes of discourses in 1843–44. This understanding of his role as that of a special kind of poet was expressed in numerous works[33] in various ways, particularly in the phrase "without authority,"[34] which became a motto for the entire authorship.

Having been occupied for a long time with the question of authority in many areas, especially in religion and also in logic

[27] Ibid., p. 14 (18).   [28] Ibid., p. 24 (28).

[29] *Christian Discourses*, p. 189, *KW* XVII (*SV* X 191).

[30] Related issues are the presumption of so-called presuppositionless philosophy and science and the status of the principle of contradiction. See Supplement, p. 212 (*Pap.* III A 11). See also, e.g., *Irony*, pp. 274, 311, *KW* II (*SV* XIII 346, 379); *Either/Or II*, pp. 170–71, 223, *KW* IV (*SV* II 154–55, 200); *The Concept of Anxiety*, p. 81, *KW* VIII (*SV* IV 350); *Philosophical Fragments, or a Fragment of Philosophy*, pp. 108–09, *KW* VII (*SV* IV 270); *Postscript*, pp. 110–13, 203, 304–05, 308, 315, 318, 347, 421–22, *KW* XII.1 (*SV* VII 90–92, 170, 261–62, 264, 271, 273, 301, 365–66); *Two Ages*, pp. 66, 97, *KW* XIV (*SV* VIII 63, 90). See also *JP* I 654, 699, 703, 705, 768; II 1240, 1610; III 3306 (*Pap.* VIII[2] B 86; I A 324; IV A 57; V A 68, 70; III A 48; VI B 98:45; VI A 145).

[31] *Christian Discourses*, p. 206, KW XVII (*SV* X 207).

[32] *Two Upbuilding Discourses* (1843), p. 5, *KW* V (*SV* III 11).

[33] See, for example, *Eighteen Upbuilding Discourses*, pp. 53, 107, 179, 231, 295, *KW* V (*SV* III 271; IV 7, 73, 121; V 79); *Three Discourses on Imagined Occasions*, pp. 14–15, 26–27, *KW* X (*SV* V 182, 192); *Upbuilding Discourses in Various Spirits*, pp. 122–23, 157, *KW* XV (*SV* VIII 216, 247; *On My Work as an Author*, in *The Point of View*, *KW* XXII (*SV* XIII 501); *The Point of View for My Work as an Author*, ibid. (505, 563, 571, 604). See also *JP* III 2653; V 5646, 5686, 5903; VI 6220, 6256, 6257, 6271, 6317, 6325, 6338, 6367, 6526, 6533, 6577, 6587, 6616, 6655, 6665, 6746, 6936, 6947 (*Pap.* X[1] A 333; IV A 87, B 159:6; VII[1] A 116; IX A 189; X[6] B 40, 41; IX A 390; X[1] A 56, 74, 100, 162; X[2] A 177, 196, 375, 475; X[3] A 77, 261, 389; X[5] A 166; XI[2] A 250; XI[3] B 57).

[34] The phrase is appropriately used as the title of the composite volume *Without Authority*, *KW* XVIII.

and philosophy, Kierkegaard found in the "phenomenon"[35] of Adolph Peter Adler a specific occasion[36] for a discursive treatment of the issue. From references in the journals,[37] it is apparent that Kierkegaard had known the writings of the Hegelian pastor on Bornholm. In his letter to the king requesting permission to write his dissertation in Danish rather than in Latin, Kierkegaard referred to the earlier permission granted to Adler.[38] In a letter of June 29, 1843, to his brother Peter Christian Kierkegaard, he expressed an interest in Adler as a "phenomenon worth paying attention to."[39] After the publication of his *Nogle Prædikener* in July 1843, Adler sent Kierkegaard a copy. It was in the preface to this volume of sermons that Adler asserted that he had had a divine revelation.[40] Six months later, in January 1844, he was suspended by his ecclesiastical superiors and in August 1845 was pensioned and removed from office.[41] About a year later, on June 12, 1846, four volumes[42] by Adler were published simultaneously. A few months earlier, Kierkegaard had published his *Postscript* (February 27, 1846) and *Two Ages* (March 30, 1846) and, having decided to conclude his career as a writer, had taken a vacation in Berlin (May 2–16, 1846). An observation in an entry[43] written during the Berlin sojourn indicates that he had not forgotten Adler, and then the appearance of the four latest Adler books[44] sharpened his attention and constituted the immediate occasion for Kierkegaard's main task during the summer of 1846.

After the last of the Berlin journal entries (*Pap.* VII[1] A 146,

---

[35] See title page, p. 1.

[36] See pp. 4, 25–26; Supplement, pp. 334–35 (*Pap.* X[6] B 62).

[37] See Supplement, pp. 212–15 (*Pap.* III A 11, B 130; V B 49:5; VII[1] A 143).

[38] *Kierkegaard: Letters and Documents*, p. 23, *KW* XXV.

[39] See Supplement, p. 213 (Letter 83).

[40] See Supplement, p. 339 (*Prædikener*, p. 3).

[41] For details as seen by Kierkegaard, see Supplement, pp. 215–19 (*Pap.* VII[2] B 241:1–9).

[42] See Supplement, p. 269 (*Pap.* VII[2] B 235, p. 127).

[43] See Supplement, p. 215 (*Pap.* VII[1] A 143).

[44] Kierkegaard purchased three of Adler's books on June 6, 1846, the day of publication: *Studier og Exempler, Forsøg til en kort systematisk Fremstilling af Christendommen i dens Logik*, and *Theologiske Studier* (*ASKB U* 11, 13, 12).

May 13, 1846), the next entry in Kierkegaard's journal is dated September 7, 1846. Just as the *Corsair* affair stopped Kierkegaard from walking the streets of Copenhagen as its preeminent peripatetic, for which he substituted carriage trips to outlying areas of the beautiful island,[45] so, too, his usual copious journal writing must have stopped because he was concentrating on what he called "The Book on Adler." The ostensibly final copy (*Pap.* VII² B 235) was written during the autumn of 1846 and January of 1847. The first preface is dated January 1847.[46]

"The Book on Adler" again posed for Kierkegaard the persistent question: should it be a signed work or under a pseudonym? His first idea was to call it a literary review under his own name, in accord with the intention to write no more after the conclusion denoted by *Concluding Unscientific Postscript*—with the possible exception of writing only reviews.[47] Another idea was to publish the literary review in a volume titled "Minor Works," which would also include what became *Upbuilding Discourses in Various Spirits* (March 13, 1847) under his own name.[48] Then he thought that "The Book on Adler" could be published as a work by Johannes Climacus,[49] the author of *Philosophical Fragments* and *Postscript*, but better yet, under a new pseudonym with Kierkegaard as the editor.[50] The one chosen was Petrus Minor, and the title would be "The Religious Confusion of the Present Age Illustrated by Magister Adler as a Phenomenon."[51]

Although the writing had been completed,[52] publication of the book was delayed[53]—indeed, Kierkegaard never published it, although he considered that "the book does deserve to be read."[54] He had scarcely finished the final copy (*Pap.* VII² B 235) before he wrote a report on the book.[55] Something should be

---

[45] See *The* Corsair *Affair*, pp. xxix–xxxi.
[46] See Supplement, pp. 226–27 (*Pap.* VII² B 270).
[47] See *JP* V 5877 (*Pap.* VII¹ A 9).
[48] See Supplement, p. 221 (*Pap.* VII¹ B 214, 218).
[49] See Supplement, p. 223 (*Pap.* VIII² B 22).
[50] See Supplement, p. 224 (*Pap.* VIII² B 24).
[51] See Supplement, p. 223 (*Pap.* VIII² B 21, 26).
[52] See Supplement, p. 221 (*Pap.* VIII² B 1); *JP* V 5997 (*Pap.* VIII¹ A 84).
[53] See *JP* V 6014 (*Pap.* VIII¹ A 164).
[54] See Supplement, p. 224 (*Pap.* VIII¹ A 252).
[55] See Supplement, pp. 221–23 (*Pap.* VIII² B 1–4).

done, he thought, to help a slow reader[56] and to make it more clear that Adler had only a vague idea of what a revelation is.[57] The book should include an appendix, an esthetic review of Adler's four latest books, and the illusion should be maintained that Adler had written only his dissertation and the four latest books.[58]

More important, however, than concern about titles and authorship was Kierkegaard's continuing concern about the contents of the book. This concern had two aspects, one of which was the effect that publication of the book might have on Adler. It was "not without distress, not without sadness"[59] that Kierkegaard wrote the so-called literary review. "He has a good head on him and has considerable experience in many *casibus* of life, but at the moment he is a little overwrought."[60] As Kierkegaard pondered publication and repeatedly reworked the manuscript, he continued to bear in mind the possible effect on Adler. "I do not at all like this whole business with Adler. I am in truth all too inclined to keep Adler afloat. . . . But the trouble is that I am sorry for A., and I am almost afraid that it [the book] will have too strong an effect on him."[61] With changes, "the book will be read in an entirely different way and I will be spared mentioning Adler, for it is cruel to slay a man that way."[62]

Kierkegaard was also concerned lest the central issue be submerged in the particulars of Adler's personal history. Ten months after completion of the manuscript, he wrote (December 1, 1847):

> I have now organized and laid out the book on Adler again. The arrangement now makes everything as luminous and clear as possible.
>
> The book has great merit. The trouble is that there really are

---

[56] See Supplement, p. 221 (*Pap.* VIII^2 B 2).

[57] Ibid.

[58] See Supplement, p. 222 (*Pap.* VIII^2 B 3).

[59] See Supplement, p. 237 (*Pap.* VIII^2 B 9:1b-c).

[60] See *Letters*, p. 156 (Letter 83).

[61] See Supplement, p. 224 (*Pap.* VIII^1 A 252).

[62] See Supplement, p. 225 (*Pap.* VIII^1 A 264). Cf., for example, pp. 132–33 and Supplement pp. 305–07 (*Pap.* VII^2 B 235, pp. 218–19). See also Supplement, p. 307 (*Pap.* X^6 B 56).

very few in our age who have enough religiousness to be able to benefit from it. In the long run, Adler with all his confusion still has more religiousness than most. The other trouble is that one gets involved with this confused person who has nothing to do and presumably therefore will write and write. But then the whole thing gets a wrong slant. In the book Adler is still a *Nebensach* [side-issue], but how easy it is for the matter to turn for a curious public into a cockfight between Adler and me.

No, rather let Adler go his way. Then the book will become a book of essays.[63]

The result of Kierkegaard's double concern about the contents of the book was that he made repeated revisions, deletions, additions, and reorderings. There are in all three integral versions of "The Book on Adler." Version III is the text of the present volume. But the reworking of the manuscript did not stop with that. Two years after completion of the first version and after having been reshaped in two subsequent versions, "The Book on Alder" had in reduced, altered form become part of a contemplated composite volume of essays, of which Kierkegaard wrote: "As for 'A Cycle of Ethical-Religious Essays,' it dates from an earlier period. Its composition is also more unusual, because it is the original larger work that is chopped into pieces, and the occasion for the whole work (Adler) is omitted, and a separate essay, no. 3,[64] added. I cannot get myself into it in such a way that I really have a desire to publish it. Moreover, it has been laid aside or put away more than once."[65]

The abandonment of "A Cycle" and the publication of Addendum II (on the genius and the apostle) of "The Book on Adler" as part of *Two Essays* in 1849 did not, however, end Kierkegaard's consideration of the remainder of version III. He pondered the possibility of publishing "Three Ethical-Religious Es-

---

[63] "A Cycle of Ethical-Religious Essays," with six essays. See Supplement, p. 225 (*Pap.* VIII[1] A 440).

[64] Essay no. 3 of "A Cycle" became essay no. 1 of *Two Essays* by H. H., "Does a Human Being Have the Right to Let Himself Be Put to Death for the Truth?"

[65] See Supplement, p. 325 (*Pap.* X[1] A 117).

says,"[66] by F. F. or M. M.[67] Or perhaps the third essay, involving Adler, "A Revelation in the Situation in the Present Age," could be published separately[68] and the first two, "Something about What Could Be Called 'Premise Authors'" and "The Dialectical Relations: the Universal, the Single Individual, the Special Individual" (the Introduction and Addendum I of version III of "The Book on Adler") could be published, without the ones touching personally on Adler, as "Two Ethical-Religious Essays" by P. P., with Kierkegaard as the editor.[69] But Adler as the specific occasion for the writing still remained the hindering consideration of yet another possible form of publication:

> The trouble with the "Three Ethical-Religious Essays" is: I do not name Adler, and the whole thing will be understood to be about me, as if I would half insinuate that I myself was the extraordinary; and the confusion will become as disastrous as possible just at that moment. If I name Adler, then I will have the desperate man to deal with, which I by no means want; that is why I altogether gave up publishing the essay about him.
>
> The best thing to do is not to publish them at all.
>
> The third essay perhaps could be published separately.[70]

But the remaining possibilities under consideration were not actualized, and for the same reasons that kept "The Book on Adler" from being published, with the exception of Addendum II, the essay on authority in *Two Essays* by H. H. Nevertheless, there was a lingering remnant of possibility, and four years after the publication of *Two Essays* Kierkegaard wrote a journal entry about "Three Ethical-Religious Essays" under a new pseudonym, which perhaps appealed to him more than the publication of the three essays: "N.B. If, instead of bearing the author-signature M. M., the three ethical-religious essays[71] should have

---

[66] See Supplement, pp. 333–34 (*Pap.* X⁶ B 57:3).
[67] See Supplement, pp. 329, 333–34 (*Pap.* X¹ A 534; X⁶ B 57:1, 2).
[68] See Supplement, p. 321 (*Pap.* X⁶ B 53).
[69] See Supplement, p. 335 (*Pap.* X⁶ B 63).
[70] *Pap.* X¹ A 544.
[71] See Supplement, pp. 333–34 (*Pap.* X⁶ B 57:3).

a proper pseudonym, I would call the author Emanuel Leisetritt, a pseudonym I perhaps could use, if not here, if I should ever again have need for a pseudonym."[72]

The impetus behind the repeated reworking of the original and the subsequently revised, reduced, and reordered manuscripts was stated in version I: "I have chosen my task in such a way that the treatment, because of its more universal and more ideal character, will be able to be read in every age."[73] The subsequent versions constitute a progressive elimination of the particular, the personal, and the historical. Finally only one part (Addendum II) of "The Book on Adler" was published as part of a work in which no mention is made of Adler, and his name is not in the title: *Two Ethical-Religious Essays*[74] (May 19, 1849). In this essay the issue, the concept of authority, remained, stripped of the elements clustered around the original occasion of the writing: Magister Adler.

Although the detailed complexity of the continual reordering, eliminating, adding, and revising of the manuscript of "The Book on Adler" was much greater than the short history above might suggest, the brief account may give the impression that it all was quite enough to occupy Kierkegaard from June 6, 1846, to May 19, 1849, when a small part of the Adler manuscript was published in *Two Essays* by H. H. On the contrary, during that time Kierkegaard began what has been called his second authorship, following the ending of the first with *Concluding Unscientific Postscript*. The review of Thomasine Gyllembourg's *Two Ages* and "The Book on Adler" as a contemplated literary review would have kept Kierkegaard within his definition of having finished writing in the strict sense. During that three-year period, "The Book on Adler" with all its prolixity was nevertheless a *Nebensach* to Kierkegaard, just as Adler was a side issue to the main question of authority in that book. During those three years he worked not only on versions of the Adler manuscript but also on "Herr Phister as Captain Scipio," *The Point of View for My*

---

[72] *Pap.* X⁵ A 93. The pseudonym was never used.
[73] See p. 27.
[74] In *Without Authority*, pp. 47–108, *KW* XVIII (*SV* XI 49–109).

Work as an Author, and *Practice in Christianity.* In addition he completed the writing and arranged the publication of *Upbuilding Discourses in Various Spirits* (March 13, 1847), *Works of Love* (September 29, 1847), *Christian Discourses* (April 26, 1848), *The Crisis and a Crisis in the Life of an Actress* (July 24–27, 1848), *The Lily in the Field and the Bird of the Air* (May 14, 1849)—and two months after the publication of *Two Ethical-Religious Essays* by H. H. (May 19, 1849) came *The Sickness unto Death* (July 30, 1849) and a little later *Three Discourses at the Communion on Fridays* (November 14, 1849).

The shock of the *Corsair* affair impelled Kierkegaard to start writing again despite his earlier resolve to stop, and the rich treasure of a second authorship was the yield. One can only wonder how much was contributed to the impetus in that new prodigious writing endeavor by the stimulus of work on the issue of authority in relation to Adler. Many would judge that the published result of that effort, "The Difference between a Genius and an Apostle," is a very valuable yield justifying three years of work—and then, in addition, the very substantial beginning of a second authorship!

The *Book on Adler* is significant also in another way. The numerous revisions of what appears to be a fair copy (*Pap.* VII² B 235) make the Adler manuscript unique in the authorship because the long process of writing and revising is manifest in great detail. The Danish scholar Johannes Hohlenberg concludes his discussion of the work with an emphasis on this aspect: "Hence the book is extraordinarily revealing, because it shows the working of Kierkegaard's mind better than any of the other books. If we want to get an idea of what qualitative dialectic has to say when turned upon a very definite question, we ought to study the book about Adler."[75]

The present volume is a translation of the third and last integral, complete version of *Bogen om Adler,* modified in some parts according to changes in versions IV and V after the original larger

---

[75] Johannes Hohlenberg, *Sören Kierkegaard,* tr. T. H. Croxall (London: Routledge, 1954), p. 196. Cornelio Fabro agrees with Hohlenberg and uses the quoted lines as the epigraph in his translation, *Dell'autorita e della rivelazione* (Padua: Gregoriana Editrice, 1976).

work was "chopped into pieces." The sources, together with the
pertinent manuscripts in the Kierkegaard Archives of the Royal
Library, Copenhagen, are various volumes of *Søren Kierkegaards
Papirer*, I-XI³, edited by P. A. Heiberg, V. Kuhr, and E. Torsting
(1 ed., Copenhagen: Gyldendal, 1909–48, and 2 ed., photo-
offset with two supplemental volumes, XII-XIII, edited by Niels
Thulstrup [Copenhagen: Gyldendal 1968–70], and with index,
XIV-XVI [1975–78], edited by N. J. Cappelørn). Changes in the
partial versions IV and V are indicated in the text.

Integral version I	(*Pap.* VII² B 235).
Integral version II	(*Pap.* VIII² B 7, 8:1).
Integral version III	(*Pap.* VIII² B 8:2, 9–27).
Partial version IV	(in the manuscript of "A Cycle of Ethi-cal-Religious Essays," *Pap.* IX B 1–8, X⁶ B 36–56).
Partial version V	(in the manuscript of "Three Ethical-Religious Essays," *Pap.* X⁶ B 57–63; *Pap.* XI³ B 1–6.

Integral version III with incorporation of changes in later versions IV and V:

Table of Contents (Pap. VIII² B 8:2)

Title and Pseudonym (*Pap.* VIII² B 26).

Editor's Preface (*Pap.* VIII² B 27).

Introduction	(*Pap.* VIII² B 7:1 = *Pap.* VII² B 235, pp. 5–29 with changes; *Pap.* VIII² B 9:1 = *Pap.* VIII² B 7:1 with additional changes; *Pap.* IX B 1 with new heading, extensive deletions, and additional changes in version IV).
Chapter I.	The Historical Situation (*Pap.* VIII² B 13–15 = *Pap.* VII² B 235, pp. 30-33:16 with extensive changes, deletions, shifts, and additions).
Chapter II.	A Revelation in the Situation of the Present Age (*Pap.* VIII² B 9:5 = *Pap.* VII² B 235, pp. 74–

93:12 with changes and deletions; *Pap.* IX B 4 = *Pap.* VIII^2 B 9:5 with additional changes; *Pap.* X^6 B 57:3 with new title).

Chapter III. Adler's Own Shifting . . . His Four Latest Books
(*Pap.* VIII^2 B 7:4–11 = *Pap.* VII^2 B 235, pp. 93:14–176:22 with extensive changes, shifts, deletions, and additions; *Pap.* VIII^2 B 9:6–11 = *Pap.* VIII^2 B 7:4–11 with additional changes, shifts, and deletions).

Chapter IV. A Psychological View of Adler as a Phenomenon and as a Satire . . .
(*Pap.* VIII^2 B 9:12 = *Pap.* VII^2 B 235, pp. 176:23–230 with changes; *Pap.* IX B 5 = *Pap.* VIII^2 B 9:12 with extensive changes, shifts, and deletions; *Pap.* X^6 B 55–6 = *Pap.* VII^2 B 235, pp. 218:21–219:33 with new title and additional changes).

Addendum I. The Dialectical Relations: the Universal, the Single Individual, the Special Individual
(*Pap.* VIII^2 B 9:13–14 = *Pap.* VII^2 B 235, pp. 33:19–53:34 with changes; *Pap.* VIII^2 B 9:15 = *Pap.* VII^2 B 235, pp. 66:9–67:19 and 66:26–34 fn. with changes; *Pap.* VIII^2 B 12; *Pap.* IX B 7, X^6 B 58, XI^3 B 2:3 = *Pap.* VII^2 B 235, pp. 43:8–45:10 with changes in versions IV and V; *Pap.* IX B 2, 3b).

Addendum II. The Difference between a Genius and an Apostle
(*Pap.* VIII^2 B 9:16–17 = *Pap.* VIII^2 B 7:8 = *SV* XI, pp. 95–98:35, and *Pap.* VII^2 B 235, pp. 141:8–150:31 with changes = *SV* XI, pp. 98:35–107:6; *Pap.* VIII^2 B 9:18 = *SV* XI, pp. 107:7–109).

THE RELIGIOUS CONFUSION OF THE PRESENT AGE ILLUSTRATED BY MAGISTER ADLER AS A PHENOMENON

A MIMICAL MONOGRAPH

by Petrus Minor

Edited by S. Kierkegaard

EDITOR'S PREFACE[1]

I myself perceive only all too well how close the objection lies
and how much is implied in the objection: to write such a large
book that in a certain sense is about Magister[2] Adler. But it really
is also only in a certain sense. I will not, however, hesitate to ask
the reader outright not to let himself be disturbed by the appearance of the first impression. If he, as I have done, will read, and
if in addition he is a theologian, I dare to guarantee him that from
this book he will acquire a clarity about and a deft drilling in
individual dogmatic concepts that usually are perhaps not so easily obtained. On the other hand, I also trust that the reader who
has the willingness and the attentiveness to want to read, if he also
has the theological qualifications to be able to judge, will agree
with me that what the author wanted to do, and what perhaps
was important to accomplish even for the times, could be done
only in that way. That is, however much I may deplore Mag.
Adler's confusion and what certainly, at least for the time being,
is lost in him, and however earnestly and slowly I have deliber-
ated publishing the book, [*deleted:* which with all good will and
devoid of any inimical disposition prompted by Mag. Adler himself nonetheless utilizes him as this book does] which therefore
has been lying here finished for over a year,[3] the author must be
jealous of his good fortune, because Mag. Adler was just what he
needed. Without him he could neither give life and ironical tension to the presentation of the concepts nor give the satirical
background that now is to be had entirely gratis. No physician
can be happier over a normal case of an illness than he must be
over Mag. Adler, and perhaps seldom has a person by going
wrong come as opportunely as Mag. Adler has for Petrus Minor.

   The whole book is basically an ethical inquiry into the concept of a revelation, into what it means to be called by a revelation, into how the one who has had a revelation relates himself
to the human race, to the universal, and the rest of us to him, into
the confusion the concept of a revelation suffers in our confused

age. Or, what amounts to the same thing, the whole book is basically an inquiry into the concept of authority, what it means to have divine authority, into the confusion, so that the concept of authority has been completely forgotten in our confused age. Now, the author could have proceeded in this way: he could have shown how this concept (a revelation) could become confused (the possibilities), in part also how it had become confused; he could seek to describe the whole age and its confusion. But then it perhaps would easily give the reader the impression that the confusion described was nevertheless a possibility that was not actually present, something he himself hit upon in order to have something to refute, so that consequently he in a way was shadowboxing.[4] How very different it is now, if not with Mag. Adler's help yet with the help of Mag. Adler, who demonstrates as completely as possible almost all possible confusions in connection with this concept, and who himself also claims to have had a revelation.

VIII²
B 27
77   By careful reading, I have understood the author in this way, and I wish that the reader will also understand the same. But it can scarcely be assumed that the author has had some intrinsically strange satisfaction in reading through Mag. Adler's many books. Yet he has done it, presumably because he was convinced of how it could serve his purpose, and no doubt during the work he became increasingly conscious of his purpose and thus of the appropriateness of his plan. He has utilized Mag. Adler as the base or made him a transparency for the confusion of the age. Even where the essay seems, as a literary review, to be occupied only with his writings, he has perhaps had the good fortune to bring into prominence a little feature that characterizes the age, or a little turn of the confusion that by the variation serves to elucidate the concept more clearly. By means of this plan, he has made it possible for the entire monograph to gain in vividness through continually having the tinge of being a clinical treatment, further, to gain an ironic redoubling—that the one who so splendidly satirizes the whole age (Mag. Adler) is the very one who probably most decisively has broken with modernity by having a revelation, so as a consequence he satirizes without knowing it—and finally to gain the closeness of present time.

And just as a good meal can be completely ruined by being served cold when it should be served hot, so it is also in the world of the spirit. A confusion always has the most interest *in praesenti* [in present time]—and here everything is *in flagranti* [caught in the act].

If anyone were to suggest that insofar as Mag. Adler has appealed to a revelation he stands completely outside or completely isolated in the age, I would answer to that: Not at all, this very confusion lies far closer to the age than one thinks, and understood in this way Mag. Adler is just as much in rapport with the age as, I could almost say, Strauss, Feuerbach,[5] et al. were with theirs. No generation can endure without religion. But then when the front rank, the militia of attackers who want to do away with Christianity (which enemies are by no means the most dangerous), has finished, then comes the second rank of the missionaries of confusion, those who either want to concoct a new religion or even want to be apostles. These are by far the more dangerous, simply because they are religiously influenced and religiously confused but to that extent are also in connection with what is deeper in human beings, whereas those others are irreligiously obsessed. The calamity of our age in politics, as in religion and as in everything, is disobedience, not being willing to obey. One only deceives oneself and others by wanting to make us think that it is doubt that is to blame for the calamity and the cause of the calamity—no, it is insubordination—it is not doubt about the truth of the religious but insubordination to the authority of the religious. But dialectically self-willfulness has two forms: either to want to overthrow the ruler or to want to be oneself the ruler; therefore, religiously: either to want to be a Feuerbach and self-willfully to do away with all religion, or self-willfully to want to be the apostle. Disobedience is the secret in the religious confusion of our age. This same disobedience also lies as the πρῶτον ψεῦδος [first falsehood], but more hidden and unconscious, at the base of what is the fundamental harm in modern speculation, that there has been a confusion of the spheres: profundity has been mistaken—for authority; the intellectual—for the ethical; being a genius—for being an apostle. —The book is (something that will seem strange to many)

VIII²
B 27
78

actually an upbuilding book—for the person who has the qualifications for allowing himself to be built up by reading what in another respect is strenuous.

And with this I will then recommend the book, asking the reader to read slowly, since the author frequently has had to search somewhat further back in order to get the perspective, wishing that I might once experience the good fortune of having a larger book read well. It would have been easy enough for me as the editor to break up the whole into smaller parts, into pamphlets at four pence; but the author objected to that as if his life were at stake—which is also the case. I for my part have also thought that people will themselves certainly perceive both that an orderly plan becomes impossible with such breaking up, and that our little country is not served by the complete disappearance of the species "literature," so that Denmark has only pamphlets and newspapers. [*Deleted:* —The book is (*same as 5:38–6:3*) strenuous. The book is (something that will appear even stranger to many) everything the author wishes to have written for the sake of his little bit of fame. In other words, there is in connection with this book an element of good fortune that is rarely offered, since perhaps rarely has a person by going wrong come so opportunely as Mag. Adler has for Vincentius Minor.[6]]

I must directly ask "my reader" to read this book; since it is of importance for my effort, therefore I intend to refer to it. This I have made sure of in a singular way. For various reasons I have let the manuscript lie in abeyance. I wanted, after having written discourses, simply to pattern a book more along the lines of dogmatics.[7] But precisely then I perceived that I incessantly had to presuppose this book. Therefore I decided to publish it.

VIII[2]
B 27
79

INTRODUCTION[8]

1846

Since our age, according to what the barber says (and the person who does not have the opportunity of keeping up with the times by means of the newspapers can very well be satisfied with the barber, who formerly, when people as yet did not have newspapers, was also what newspapers are now), is supposed to be an age of movement,[9] it then is not unlikely that many people's lives go on in such a way that they have premises for living but do not arrive at any conclusion—just like the age, which is an age of movement that has set the premises in motion but is also an age of movement that has not come to the conclusion. The lives of such people go on until death comes and puts an end to life, yet without, in the sense of a conclusion, bringing the end with it. That a life is over is one thing; it is something else that a life is finished by gaining its conclusion. Such a person can, in proportion to his gifts, also in his own immature life go on and become an author, according to his opinion of it. But this opinion is an illusion. For that matter, he may (since here we of course are able hypothetically to grant everything possible if only we insist upon what is decisive) possess extraordinary talents, exceptional knowledge, but he is not an author, even though he produces. His writing will be just like his life, material; perhaps this material will be worth its weight in gold, but it is only material. Here is not a poet, who poetically rounds out the whole; not a psychologist, who orders the particular and the individual in a total view; not a dialectician, who points out the place within the life-view at his disposal. No, although he writes, he is not essentially an author; he can write the first part, but he cannot write the second part; or, lest there be misunderstanding, he can indeed write the first and second parts, but then he cannot write the third part— the last part he cannot write. Therefore if he, naïvely misled by the idea that according to custom every book must have a last part, goes ahead and writes [*skrive*] a last part also, he will really make it obvious that by the last part he renounced [*fraskrev*] being an author. To be an author is certainly something one makes oneself by writing, but for that very reason it is also something one, strangely enough, can renounce simply by writing. If he had been really aware of the dubiousness of the third part— well, *si tacuisset, philosophus mansisset* [if he had kept silent, he would have remained a philosopher].[10]

In order to find the conclusion, it is first and foremost necessary to perceive very vividly that it is lacking and thereby in turn very vividly to miss it. Thus it is conceivable that an essential author, precisely in order to make obvious the dubiousness that so many people live without a conclusion, would produce a fragment, even though by calling it that he would cause no dubiousness and in another sense would supply the conclusion by supplying the corresponding life-view. A world-view, a life-view, is the only true conclusion to every production;[11] every poet-conclusion is an illusion. If the life-view is developed, if this stands complete and clear in its consistent coherence, one need not take the life of the hero, one may very well let him live—the premise is nevertheless fulfilled and set at rest in the conclusion, the development is nevertheless finished. But if the life-view (which of course must already be in the first part and be everywhere, although its lack really becomes obvious in the second, in the third, that is, the last part) is lacking, it helps but little that one has the hero die; indeed, it is of no help whatever if, in order that it be quite certain that he is dead, one even has him buried in the story—the development is by no means finished. If death had this power, then nothing would be easier than to be a poet, then poetry would not be needed at all. In actuality it is certainly true that every human being dies, his life has an end; but from that it does not follow that it has, that it had an end in the sense of a conclusion. "That it *had* an end," precisely this tense of the verb indicates that death is not what is decisive, that the conclusion can be reached while the man is living. To use death as a conclusion is a paralogism, a μετάβασις εἰς ἄλλο γένος [shifting from one genus to another]. Certainly death is a conclusion, but it follows from completely different premises; and certainly death is the final period, but in its abstract indifference it has nothing to do with whether the meaning is at an end, whether there was meaning in the dead person's life or not. Thus death neither adds nor subtracts; it does not change a person's life *in concreto*; on the contrary, it removes *in abstracto* the condition of life and thereby prevents any further change.

But the more the age of movement and the many individuals lack a conclusion, the more actively people seem to multiply the premises. This in turn has the effect that the conclusion becomes more and more difficult, because instead of the decisiveness of the conclusion there is a stoppage that, spiritually understood, is what constipation is in the animal organism; meanwhile an increase of the premises is just as dangerous as it is to overload oneself with food when one suffers from constipation, even if for a moment it brings relief. Then the movement of the age gradually changes into an unhealthful fermentation, just as when the sick person does not digest and assimilate the food but merely brings it into fermentation. The individuals whose lives likewise have only premises now also utilize this sickliness of the age to become authors, and their productions will be just what the times demand. Under such circumstances an essential author naturally would in every way recommend dieting, but the premise-authors are at your service in every way with ever new tasks, proposals, hints, suggestions, indications, projects—in short, with everything that by merely being a beginning stimulates impatience because it does not seem to contain any demand for perseverance, which is always necessary if there is to be any question of arriving at a conclusion. What nourishes a sickness always seems in the first moment to be a relief; and when, spiritually understood, the ethical is left out, the momentary is the sophistical, likewise also the perpetually repeated beginning. But the premise-authors (sophists) flourish; they gain both money (Aristotle mentions wanting to gain money as a mark of the Sophist[12]) and prestige by satisfying the demand of the times. Under such circumstances, an essential author is bound to fail completely. It would no doubt go with him as Socrates so ingeniously has described his life. It would no doubt go with him "as it would if a physician was accused by a cook or a confectioner, and an

VII²
B 235
8

Introduction

assembly of children judged the case; the cook and the confectioner childishly know about sweetness, flattery, and cleverly
know how to make what is unhealthful taste good. The physician knows only about what is healthful and does not even know
how to make it taste good."[13]

Just as opportunity makes thieves, so such an unhealthful fermentation makes bad authors in the same sense as one speaks of
bad money,[14] because the age's lack of a conclusion conceals the
fact that the authors lack it. With regard to being gifted and the
like, the degree of difference among premise-authors can be very
great, but they all have in common the essential feature of not
really being authors. In such a fermentation, outstanding people
go by the board, but even the most trivial pate can also manage
to become an author, at least of a little premise-contribution in
a newspaper. In this way there is advancement for the most trivial
pates, and from that it naturally follows that there is a great number, a multitude of authors, and therefore, also because of their
multiplicity, they can best be compared to sulphur matches,
which are sold by the bunch. One takes an author like that, on
whose head, just as on matches, a phosphorescent substance has
been placed: a proposal for a project, a suggestion; one takes him
by the legs and strikes him on a newspaper, and then there are
three or four columns. And premises without conclusions actually have a striking resemblance to phosphorescence—both go
off in a puff.

But despite the puffing, or perhaps just because of the puffing,
all premise-authors, whatever their degrees of difference, have
VII²
B 235
9 one thing in common: they all have a *propensity*, they all want to
produce an effect, they all want their writings to win an extraordinary distribution and to be read, if possible, by all humankind.
This peculiarity is reserved for people in such a time of ferment:
to have a propensity, to be on the move in the sweat of their
brows for the sake of the propensity and not really know themselves where they are tending, for if they know this *in concreto*,
then they also have the conclusion. This is as the saying goes: He
has a vague idea of something, but he doesn't know what it is.
Instead of making up their minds as individuals, each person for
himself, about what they want *in concreto* before they begin to

express themselves, they have a superstitious idea of the benefit of prompting a discussion. They have a superstitious idea with which they distort what of course ought to be reasonably understood through united efforts, that the efforts are the presupposition, and that it is the association that unites them, whereas it would be superstitious to assume, if one imagined an association of drunken men, that the association would make them sober. They have a superstitious idea that the spirit of the age, although individuals separately do not know what they want, would be able by its dialectic to make clear what it is they actually want, and thus by it Messrs. Propensity-Possessors could find out where they actually are tending. But this superstitiousness, which develops because the individual reflects himself fantastically into the infinity of the generation or because the individuals, each of whom lacks footing, imagine themselves to have a *common* footing in the generation, demands too much; like Nebuchadnezzar, it not only demands to have the dream interpreted, but to get to know the dream.[15] And yet the fermentation increases. All, each in his own way, are busily active in order, if I dare say so, to stoke the fire under the boiler with the flammability of the premises, but no one seems to think of the danger without the presence of an engineer.

The premise-author is easy to recognize, easy to describe, if only one remembers that he is the opposite of the essential author, that he has as extroversion what the latter has as introversion. Now it is a social issue. The premise-author has no concrete and more definite idea at all of what ought to be done, how the possible pressure can be remedied. He thinks something like this: "If only the alarm is sounded, it will surely be all right." Now it is a political, a religious issue. The premise-author has neither time nor patience to think it through more definitely. He thinks something like this: If only the alarm is sounded loudly, so it is heard over the whole country, so it is read by everyone, so it is the only topic of conversation in all societies, "then it will surely be all right." The premise-author thinks that the alarm is like a divining rod [*Ønske-Qvist,* wishing twig]—and he has not noticed that soon all have become alarmists who scream "with united effort"; indeed, he himself contributes his own bit to it by

VII²
B 235
10

wishing for what he has to offer: the alarm sounded as widely as possible. It completely escapes the premise-author that it would be far more reasonable if a man, especially in our age, the age of alarm, thought something like this: The alarm will surely be sounded; therefore it is better for me to refrain from it and to concentrate on a more concrete deliberation. People smile when they read all the romanticism from a bygone time, about how the knight rode out into the forest and slayed dragons, freed the en-chanted princes, etc., that is, the romanticism that there were such monsters in the forests and also enchanted princes. And yet it is just as fantastic when in a whole generation each one individ-ually believes in the power of the alarm to call forth enormous efforts. The alarmist must really believe that there is a marvelous reserve battalion nearby, since the actual people among whom he lives join in the screaming; consequently he cannot expect to find help from them. In the moment of danger, an ingenious person may have the bright idea of scaring the thief away by calling out a lot of names, as if all these devilishly stout fellows were nearby. It is ingenious, but the ingenious person does not himself believe that these many devilishly stout fellows are nearby; his ingenuity succeeds only in getting the thief to be-lieve it. But the alarmist is more obtuse; he believes very posi-tively in what ingenuity only fools another into believing. The seemingly modest thing, wanting only to sound the alarm, want-ing only to prompt a discussion, is not very praiseworthy if the experience repeated again and again must impress upon every-one the earnestness in his either considering some actual help or at least refraining from adding further to the confusion. If the firemen were to run around and sound the fire alarm, who then will put out the fire? If we all were to sound the alarm, who is it then who at the alarm will come hurrying to help? Perhaps at other times there have lived fantastic blusterers who would be made blissful in the fancy that if only they would, they could take all humanity on their conscience; but the so-called modesty's venture in the fantastic (by merely wanting to prompt a discus-sion) is no less ludicrous. And even if there were a sensible per-son, or a few sensible persons, who could help—is the alarm itself then a good? Indeed, the more the alarm propagates itself and

VII²
B 235
11

the noise increases, the more difficult it becomes just to hear the commander's voice.

The premise-author is the opposite of the essential author. The latter has his perspective. The most woeful confusion inevitably appears when people become momentary and then in turn superstitiously put all their trust in the moment[16]—what indeed is the moment in the next moment! In his particular production the essential author is continually behind himself; he is certainly striving, but within a totality, not toward the totality. He never raises more doubt than he can explain. His A never has a greater scope than his B. He never draws upon the uncertain.[17] In other words he has a definite life- and world-view that he follows, and in it he is ahead of the particular production, just as the whole is always ahead of the parts. With regard to the scope, whether it is much or little that he with his view has understood until now, he explains only what he himself has understood. He does not superstitiously expect that something from outside would suddenly bring him to an understanding, suddenly inform him about what it is that he actually wanted. In life a comic effect can result when a person passes himself off for another whose name he does not know, and consequently he does not learn until afterward what his name is. Scribe has wittily used this in a little play.[18] A young man shows up in a family, passes himself off as a cousin who has been away for many years. He himself does not know what the cousin is called until a bill received for the cousin is presented to him and helps him out of the predicament. He takes the bill and in a not unwitty aside says: It can always be good to find out what my name is. Similarly, the premise-author also produces a comic effect when he passes himself off as something other than he is by passing himself off as an author, and he finally must wait for something from the outside that will inform him about who he really is, that is, spiritually understood, what he really wants. The essential author, on the other hand, definitely knows who he is, what he wants; from first to last he takes care to understand himself in his life-view. It does not escape him that the expectation of an extraordinary result from a prompted discussion is a skepticism, that the apparent trustworthiness simply nourishes doubt.

VII²
B 235
12

Insofar as the essential author can be said to have a need to communicate himself, this need is entirely immanental, an enjoyment of the understanding to the second power, or it becomes for him a consciously undertaken ethical task. The premise-author has no need to *communicate himself*, because essentially he has nothing to communicate; indeed, he lacks precisely the essential, the conclusion, the meaning in relation to the presuppositions. He has no *need to communicate* himself; he is *one who is in need*.* And just as other needy persons fall as a burden on the state and the welfare department, so all premise-authors are basically needy persons who fall as a burden on the generation, since they want to be supported by it rather than that they themselves work and support themselves with the understanding that they themselves earn. There can be no meaning in existence unless every human being is granted as much understanding as he

VII²
B 235
13

**Note.* This circumstance has an exceedingly harmful influence on all literature and produces an immoral reversal in the relation between author and reader. Because those improperly called authors, who are the majority and so numerous that the whole class is named after them, are ones who are in need, who not only need the public's money and honors but even need the public in order, if possible, to arrive at understanding and meaning—then this is transferred as a matter of course to every author. But the very one who needs the public or discussion in order to find understanding is not an author. If in the true relation between author and reader there is to be any question of need, then it is the reader who needs the author. An author should never need; he must ethically discipline himself to be able to do without the public's money and honors. Yet someone can actually be an author although he is weak in this regard. But if he needs the public in order to find clarity and meaning in the matter, then of course the public knows more than he does, then of course he is a learner. But God knows why he then writes, and God does know—so it is a sad confusion to call him author. But the appearance flatters the vanity of the public, which with difficulty can tolerate an essential author who in himself knows that he is an author and ethically knows his responsibility before God. The public prefers to have its own henchmen, an ethically impaired talent, a bungler, [*deleted in version IV*: a Jewish peddler of hair ribbons,[19]] a shop assistant, as author—since he *needs* in every way, and in every way he needs the public for its instruction and information, for its forbearing indulgence, for its most gracious applause with the air of connoisseurs, for its money, for its honors. Naturally it is particularly the daily papers, journalistic writing, that contribute to turning everything upside down. Just as in the history of Greece there is a period called the period of the Sophists, so in modern times the sophistical by way of the daily press has become stock fare, a daily necessity.

VII²
B 235
13

needs, if he will honestly work. If he has great gifts and therefore can raise many doubts, then he must also have the powers
to achieve in himself the understanding if he wants it in earnest.
But everyone must be silent insofar as he does not have an understanding to communicate. Wanting only to sound an alarm is a
kind of splendid idleness and treason that merely saddles the generation with vagrants. It is easy enough to do that, easy enough
in this way to become self-important; it is also easy enough to
become a welfare case, and then it is easy enough to cry out to
the state: Support me. And every premise-author cries out to the
generation, "Support me." But Governance replies, "You shall
support yourself, and every person shall do that [*deleted in version
IV*: both civically and spiritually]." Thus the modesty of wanting
only to prompt a discussion is concealed arrogance, because if the
person concerned is not fit to be an essential author, then it is
arrogance to want to give the appearance of being an author.
The essential author is essentially a teacher, and the person who
is not or could not essentially be a real author is essentially a
learner. —Rather than *nourishing* (which every essential author
is; the difference is only in relation to gifts and scope), every
premise-author *consumes*.

VII²
B 235
14

He consumes, because he communicates doubt. This, of
course, is a *contradictio in adjecto* [contradiction in terms]; it is like
giving the hungry person, not food, but something that stimulates the appetite and then thinking that one is feeding him. He
consumes, [*deleted in version IV*: because he] communicates doubt
instead of being silent, only sounds the alarm, dashes off the con-
ditional clause [*Forsætning*] without having the main clause [*Efter-
sætning*]. Even if the propounding of a premise demonstrates a
talent, the consuming nevertheless consists in such an author's
intruding upon actuality in the unsettling sense of actuality.

The art in all communication is to come as close as possible to
actuality, to contemporaries in the role of readers, and yet at the
same time to have the distance of a point of view, the reassuring,
infinite distance of ideality from them.[20] Permit me to illustrate
this by an example from a recent work. In the imaginary psychological construction [*psychologiske Experiment*] "'Guilty?'/
'Not Guilty?'" (in *Stages on Life's Way*[21]), there is depicted a

distressed character in the most extreme mortal danger of the
spirit to the point of despair, and the whole thing is kept as if it
could have happened yesterday. To such a degree the production
is placed as close as possible to actuality that the person struggling religiously in despair hovers, so to speak, right over the
head of the contemporary age. If the imaginary construction has
made any impression, it must be like that which happens when
the wing strokes of the wild bird, in being heard overhead by
the tame birds of the same kind who live securely in the certainty
of actuality, cause these to beat their wings instinctively, because
those wing strokes are simultaneously unsettling and yet also
have something fascinating.[22] But now comes what is reassuring,
that the whole thing is an imaginary construction, and that an
imaginary constructor stands by. Spiritually understood, the
imaginatively constructed character is what one in a civic sense
calls a very dangerous character, and such people are customar-
ily not allowed to walk alone; a couple of officers are usually
present—for the sake of public security. Thus, for the reassurance
of public security, in that work there is also present an imaginary
constructor (he calls himself a street inspector[23]), who very
calmly shows how the whole thing hangs together, who theoretically educes a life-view that he completes by rounding out,
while he points elucidatingly to the imaginatively constructed
character in order to indicate how he makes the movements
according to the pulling of the strings. If this were not an imaginary construction, if no imaginary constructor were present, if
no life-view were represented—then such a work, regardless of
the talent it might display, would be only consuming. It would
be unsettling to come in contact with it, because it would only
convey the impression of an actual person who probably in the
next moment would go insane. It is one thing to portray a passionate person when there are both the accompaniment of
someone more powerful and a view of life that can control him
[*deleted in version IV*: (and I would still like to see how many
contemporary critics would be capable of handling the imaginatively constructed character so powerfully, of tossing him about
as the imaginary constructor does)]; it is something else that a
passionate person, in his very own personal actuality through the

VII²
B 235
15

means of a book, by becoming an author breaks loose and, as it were, assaults the rest of us with his unclarified doubt and his torments.

If one were to portray a person who believed that he had had a revelation but later himself went astray in it, and one did it as an imaginary construction, and for the sake of security there was an imaginary constructor along who thoroughly understood his job (and a whole view of life was presented), who used the imaginatively constructed character the way a physicist makes a demonstration—then everything would be in order and there would perhaps be much to learn from such a presentation. Perhaps the imaginary constructor had been convinced by observation that something like that could happen in his day and therefore set the time as close as possible, but, note well, was himself in possession of the explanation that was communicated. If, however, an actual person in the bewildered condition of the imaginatively constructed character rushes at the public by becoming an author, then he is exceedingly consuming. The abnormal, which by being controlled and forced into the total meaning of a life-view can be instructive, directly sets itself up as a teacher, but without being able to teach anything other than the abnormality and its pain. One is painfully moved by the obtrusive actuality of such a frustrated author, who in a purely personal way is in mortal danger and in a purely personal way wants to awaken our interest in him—or in his knowing no solution—wants to make us others anxious and afraid, to suffer as he does. [*Revised in version IV*: It is one thing when a physician, who is informed about treatment and healing, which he discusses in his medical practice, relates a case history. A physician at a sickbed is one thing, and a sick person, one who has leaped out of bed and by becoming an author, immediately describing his symptoms, obviously confuses being sick with being a physician,[24] is something else. Perhaps he can give utterance to his condition in the illness and in glowing colors present himself in a way altogether different from the way the physician does in his description, since to know no solution and deliverance provides a distinctive passionate elasticity in comparison with the composed language of the person who knows the solution. But nevertheless there is a decisive

VII²
B 235
16

qualitative difference between being sick and being a physician, and this difference is exactly the same as the decisive qualitative difference between being a *premise-author* and an *essential author*.]

[*Deleted, pp. 18–27, with reference to Adler, in version IV (Pap. IX B 1), No. I of "A Cycle of Ethical-Religious Essays"*: What has been said here about premise-authors so generally that it can apply to quite trivial minds and to the eminently gifted if they lack a definite life-view, lack the conclusion, also has its application to Magister Adler if it is admitted, however, that the application can be justified only when many a concession has first been made to his abilities and other qualifications. On the whole, *he has one premise*; it is distinguished absolutely from everything else, and it distinguishes him absolutely from all other premise-authors: *he has a revelation-fact to appeal to*[25]—or, more correctly, he himself seems to have become somewhat doubtful about what this revelation-fact really means—that is, he himself seems to make it manifest that he does not understand himself in his being exceptionally favored in this way. Otherwise a man who appeals to a revelation-fact would certainly not be called a premise-author. He becomes that only when he, by not understanding himself in it, changes that fact into a premise, into a miscellaneous announcement, into an inexplicable something about which one futilely seeks the explanation from him.

VII²
B 235
17

A critic is, ought to be, a ministering spirit; he is and ought to be, in the sense of ideality, the author's best friend, because he loves the author in his idea. As soon as the author gives a hint from the region in which he is or wants to be, the critic immediately makes a survey, then changes his clothes according to the region and the sphere, serving *e concessis* [on the basis of the other's premises], and from now on is the author's trusty friend— in the sense of ideality, because the critic is no family friend; he does not love the author's flesh and blood; he is no *Busenfreund* [bosom friend] who is satisfied with everything just because it is by the author. Magister Adler shouted from the clouds: I have a revelation-fact to appeal to—the undersigned is the lowly ministering critic, who in the faithfulness of ideality must go to all lengths to hold firmly to this. But not so that my critical, truly faithful friendship becomes a nuisance to my friend! It sometimes happens in the world that one becomes a nuisance precisely by being unswervingly faithful; of course, one's conscience is free in every way. I think of a young girl; at the moment of parting, when she will be separated from her beloved for a longer time, she says to him, "Promise me by all that is holy that you will remain faithful to me." He replies, "I promise; I will remain as faithful to you as a true critic is who loves his author in the idea." So they are parted; time goes on, and the young girl also goes on—and forgets her imploring request—she acquires a new lover. The beloved no. 1, the faithful one of first quality, the one eternally bound by the promise, returns. Unchanged, he has kept his promise of faithfulness—but see, the girl's change changes his unchanged faithfulness to an unchanged, constant satire on her. Basically it was also deucedly unfortunate that he should be so faithful. The girl would have been much better served by a similarly disposed person, who in the great moment of parting could swear and vow quite differently from the way the faithful man could, but at a distance could quite differently also easily forget both the girl and the oath and the faithfulness—in that case they would have been quits. Ironically enough, in the great moment of crisis it would again have become evident how these two still suited each other and completely understood each other.

Magister Adler stands and falls on the fact of his revelation, on how he understands himself in this extraordinary thing that is supposed to have happened to him, whether *he unshakably stands by it* (yet without his being insane) *or repenting he revokes it.* If there is dialectical ambivalence in him, then the true critic's unswerving faithfulness is indeed a satire; then, just like the young girl, he would indeed be better served by a critical lover who in the great moment of announcement could quite differently admire and sweat, in the great moment when we received the news, but also quite differently could easily forget the revelation and the fact and meaning of it.

As for an authorship that has a revelation-fact, to write an ordinary esthetic-critical review of the books and leave the revelation in abeyance is in my opinion to prostitute oneself as a critic. That is, it shows that one is neither an esthetician nor a

VII²
B 235
19

dialectician nor a theologian, but a rattle-brain in all three faculties. For an essential critic, the point is to remember in every line
he reads in such books that the author has a revelation-fact. Yes,
even if the author became seventy years old and wrote huge
folios, critically the point is to remember the revelation-fact,
whether he stands by it (yet without being insane) or repenting
he revokes it. A revelation-fact is, in qualitative dialectic, essentially different from everything else and in a qualitative dialectical
sense essentially belongs in the essentially religious sphere, the
paradoxical-religious. Only a dabbler could hit upon the idea of
insulting such an author by involving himself esthetically with
him or with his books. Whether the author himself was delighted
with this makes no difference, because if he is delighted with it,
this only demonstrates that he has lost his ideality. Yet the ministering critic, the faithful lover, must not relinquish that fact, not
even if the author becomes unfaithful to himself.

  I am well aware that the majority will not agree with me in
what has been said here; the majority will no doubt say, "*Posito*
[Suppose] that in other respects there is brilliance and originality
in Adler's books; then what difference does it make if he perhaps
has used too strong an expression; possibly he himself has thought
that it was a revelation." But I am completely devoid of sympathy with this opinion. My thought is this: A brilliant author is not
something unheard of in Denmark, and it is not of much concern
to me if in Magister Adler we had one more in the Danish language; yes, if I considered him only in this way, it could not
occur to me to write a review. No, but a man with a revelation-
fact, that is something that attracts my entire attention, not my
curious but my serious attention, whether I from him or through
him could learn something or become aware of something in
relation to an understanding of the sphere, to the elaboration of
which I am conscious of having dedicated my best powers. —I
am well aware that I do not agree with Magister Adler in what
has been said; I actually have no doubt that in all honesty, completely *bona fide* [in good faith], he would say, "If in other respects you cannot deny that what I write is sound and that I

VII²
B 235
20

actually am stirred by something higher—why then in a petty
little dispute about words carp on a perhaps exaggerated expres-

sion, something I have written in the heat of the moment, something I perhaps would not have written at all if I had allowed a fortnight to pass." And as willing as one can be, if the matter is to be understood purely esthetically, to make every concession to the undeniably overstrained person in mortal danger, as willing as I most of all could be to concede to him that he unquestionably is stirred by something higher, something that proclaims itself in a few felicitous thoughts, in a particular profound remark, in an occasional upbuilding and moving expression, in many a gripping impression, consequently as willing as I can be to concede this, I would still reply, "Your very answer contains the chief objection against you, because ethically it is lamentable frivolousness to jest in this way about a revelation-fact." Truly, far be it from me to write this in order to win the cheap victory of ridiculing what every fool is only all too inclined to ridicule. No, explanation and understanding are what I covet; consistency is the only thing I require; the matter in no way occupies me as amusement.

The religious sphere includes or ought to include the ethical;[26] therefore no esthetic critic dares to involve himself with it, and, above all, no critic dares to involve himself esthetically with the religious if the ethical makes an objection. And a revelation-fact is the tonic dominant that must be accentuated unconditionally. If the greatest poet who has ever lived, whose works the esthetician must admire unconditionally, had stated in a preface that he had had a revelation, that Christ had appeared to him and the poems had been directly communicated to him by the Spirit, then at that very moment (if all the spheres are not to be confused in dreadful nonsense) esthetics is forbidden to involve itself with the poems. The revelation-fact itself is in a qualitative dialectic, something infinitely higher than the esthetic worth of all the poems. Magister Adler cannot ask for more; but even if he were the most brilliant author who has ever lived, it would be an inexcusable obtuseness on my part if I did not, in comparison with all this brilliance, infinitely accentuate the revelation-fact, whether it now *convenere* [suits] Magister Adler or not. A critic must understand himself, understand how to use his powers, but for that very reason also understand where these cannot be used

VII²
B 235
21

at all. The most eminent critic who has ever lived is inactivated in relation to a man who holds firm in appealing to a revelation-fact. That one fact changes everything because there is no relation between human criticism and a revelation-fact. Even if what the remarkably favored one said seemed very strange to the critic, he will still have enough clarity to perceive that truth itself has its traditional side, that what once appeared very strange to an outstanding contemporary critic nevertheless in the course of time emerged as established truth. Faced with a revelation-fact, the competent critic must realize, precisely by reason of his competence, that he must either relearn, learn the new criticism from that remarkably favored person, or be completely silent—unless by means of some Socratic questions he would be able to come to grips with that remarkably favored person and make it obvious that the man himself was not informed about himself. A critic can also be ingenious, and he is allowed to be that; he is allowed to ask and ask and tempt with entrapping questions. Of course the man with the revelation-fact is allowed to refrain from answering, is allowed to be taciturn. But if he is not, if he perhaps is even uncircumspect enough to become loquacious, if he, instead of being taciturn and trying in loquacity to hold firmly to his fact, turns out to be, as one says, rather loose, then it is certainly possible that the presumably remarkably favored person would entangle himself in a calamitous situation. The same thing can also happen in another way. A critic has perhaps been silently attentive, and then the presumably remarkably favored person himself uncircumspectly becomes prolix and traps himself in prolixities.

VII²
B 235
22

If then there are irregularities not pertaining to what we would understand by Magister Adler's revelation-fact but pertaining to what he himself understands by it, to how he himself understands himself in it—then he is a premise-author, then he is consuming, then, unfortunately, the critic can get hold of him. All the brilliance, provided he really is an essentially brilliant author, that can possibly be in his books is of no value as nourishing in comparison with the consuming, the deficiency in which he as author entangles the public by his lack of clarity about what is qualitatively decisive. To foist on the public a revelation-fact and then himself not know finally what is what, what he himself means by it, is to characterize himself as a premise-author, because it is thundering in the most terribly loud tones and then basically expecting that the surrounding world will come to his aid with the explanation as to whether he has actually had a revelation or not. Such a phenomenon can then have profound significance as a bitter epigram on the age. In a tottering, irresolute, unsteady age, where in so many ways the individual is in the habit of seeking outside himself (in the sentiment of the surrounding world, in public opinion, in town gossip) what is essentially to be found only in the individual himself: the decision—in such an age a man steps forth and appeals to a revelation, or, more correctly, he rushes out like one who is terrified, with frightful horror in his countenance, still shuddering from that moment of contact, and proclaims that a revelation has fallen to his lot. *Pro dii imortales* [Ye gods], there must certainly be help here, there must certainly be steadfastness here! Alas, he only resembles the age all too much. In the next moment he himself does not definitely know what is what; he leaves it as such in abeyance—and meanwhile writes big, (perhaps) brilliant books. See, in those distant times when a man was vouchsafed lofty revelations, he used a long time to understand himself in this marvel before he began to want to guide others. That is, it can by no means be required of such a person that he must understand what surpasses human understanding, consequently understand the revelation, but he must understand himself in this, that it has happened to him, that it is the most certain of all that it has happened to him, and that, without any subsequent chatter, without any turning and twisting, it was and is and remains a revelation. Now, however, immediately the next morning one puts in the newspaper that one had a revelation last night. Perhaps one fears that the quiet solitary reflection (on what in the most extreme sense might very well alter a person's whole existence even if he never mentioned it to anyone) would lead one to the humbling but rescuing insight that it was an illusion, so one would drop the whole matter and would seek to become reconciled with God with respect to it, so one on lesser terms would truly become a teacher who knew how to teach others and to hold the highest infinitely in honor. Perhaps one fears this;

VII²
B 235
23

on the other hand, perhaps one hopes that the announcement could prompt a discussion, the result of which could become that it now was certain that one had had a revelation, and that it was what the times demanded. In that case one could indeed maintain that one actually had had a revelation, relying upon the enormous sensation the announcement awakened, relying upon the acclamation with which one was hailed, not to mention how reassuring it was that several of the "really excellent journals we have" had expressed themselves in approval of it, and as a consequence public opinion sanctioned to the nth degree* what, otherwise in the strictest, in the most isolating sense pertains to a particular individual, who with regard to this must unconditionally and exclusively seek certitude within himself.

How epigrammatic the situation would become when it is carried out purely esthetically without regard to whether any specific person actually has conducted himself this way! A man

VII²
B 235
24

shockingly steps forward and says, "I am called by God." Thereupon he says softly in an aside, "Basically, I am not entirely sure; I will now see what impression this makes on the age; if it declares for it, then it is certain, then I am called by God, and then I let matters take their course."** He perhaps hopes that if he has merely said these words the circumstances will seize him and, as it were, force him into the character, force him to become and be what he certainly has said he is but which he does not himself know for sure whether he is or not. Alas, to be called by God is surely the highest that can happen to any human being; such a called person stands, humble before God, higher than all others, higher than kings and emperors, public opinion and the troop of

---

*Note. That is, since every newspaper writes in the name of the whole nation, a country acquires a fantastic population, which is just as many times greater than the actual population as there are mutually disagreeing papers.

**Note. There is a story about a peasant who went around begging as a victim of a fire. One of the men he approached asked him sympathetically, "When was it, old man, that the misfortune occurred and your house burned down?" The peasant replied, "Well, you see it hasn't burned yet, but it will soon." See, the peasant was not entirely sure that it is the best world[27] in which we live; he was suspicious of human charitableness toward fire victims—therefore he presumably wanted first to find out how much could come in before he burned the place down.

journalists. It is to him that all the rest of us must look up, and he must with divine authority demand it of us, that is, he must be recognizable precisely by his appealing to his authority.[28] But the vacillating person wants to serve two masters; he wants to be called by God in a special sense, and then he also wants to be called by the age, be what the times demand. He uses the cry "I am called by God" as an interjection in order to get a hearing in the noisy crowd, and then he wants to convert his call from God into a call from public opinion.

VII²
B 235
25

That such a thing could happen at a time when all the decisive religious categories have really been abolished and everything has been pushed down into the category of the generation—is quite in order. But if it happens, then it would always be good if there is a contemporary ministering critic, an insignificant person who does not dare to appeal to any revelation but who on the other hand can hold the called one to the word and thereby contribute to making manifest what earnestness truly is: that *earnestness is the quiet composure of responsibility*, which understands itself in assuming the extraordinary, that it is not earnestness, however, as it is sometimes taken to be, to make a noise, to become red in the face, to look strained, to use the almost terrify-ing, extreme expressions and yet inwardly to be uncertain about what one is and what one is not. In our age, just as in every previous one, there can indeed be true extraordinaries appointed by God. But the world's change will still have a great influence on the outer appearance, even though the essence remains the same. Accordingly, for example, it would be suspicious if in our time a prophet appeared who resembled one of the ancient ones right down to the beard.

As a phenomenon *in our age* (thus just as much attention is paid to the age as to Adler), Magister Adler will become the subject for discussion in this little work. His books should not be evalu-ated esthetically and critically as if they were by an ordinary au-thor. No, he is to be respected by the insignificant ministering critic according to his unusualness; and his writings are to be used only in order to see whether he understands himself in being what he has passed himself off to be. Nor is there to be mention of what he teaches, whether it is heretical or not; all such things

must be regarded as unimportant compared with what is qualitatively decisive. On the other hand, the ethical accent of earnestness is to be placed, if possible, on what either must give him
divine authority or must repentantly be revoked—that he *has*
appealed to a revelation-fact.

VII²
B 235
26

If someone would ask who then am I, the one who is doing
this, my answer is: I am a ministering critic, an insignificant person who has only ethical justification, which every person has in
relation to an author. I am fully convinced that the apostle Paul,
as is readily seen in his writings, would by no means have re-
sented it if someone in an earnest discussion had asked him
whether he actually had had a revelation; and I know that with
the brevity of earnestness Paul would have cut it short and answered: Yes. But if Paul (may he forgive me for what I now say;
it must be done this way in order to illustrate something), instead
of briefly answering with earnestness, whether yes or no, had
launched into a long prolix speech somewhat like this: "Yes, well
now, I myself have indeed said it, but revelation is perhaps too
strong an expression, but it was something, there was something
of genius . . . . . "—well, then it would have been a different
matter. I can deal with geniuses all right. Good heavens, if it is
truly the great genius, then with esthetic propriety I gladly express my respect for the superior intellect from whom I learn. But
that I should show him religious submission, that I should imprison my judgment in obedience under his divine authority—
no, that I do not do, and neither does any genius require it of me.
But when a man unabashedly wants to reinterpret an intended
apostolic life as being genius without revoking the first—then he
confuses dreadfully.

Such things a critic must hold firm, as I shall now do in this
little book, not for the sake of confusion, but in order, if possible,
to throw light on some religious categories and to give a little
orientation in the age. Without recommending my own wares,
I dare also to promise that the person who will read attentively
will surely find enlightenment in the book, because I am not
unacquainted with my age and what is fermenting in it. I am
keeping abreast, even though I am like someone sailing in the
same ship who still has a separate cabin, not in the capacity of

VII²
B 235
27

some extraordinary as if I had authority, no, in the capacity of an eccentric who has anything but authority.[29]

In other respects, I am well aware how odd [*underligt*] the whole thing looks. About an author who so far has not been read very much [*synderlig*], I write a book that very likely will not be read either. Just as it is told of those two princely personages who were so very obese that they exercised by walking around each other,[30] so in a little country the exercise of author-activity becomes the private enjoyment, in which almost no reader participates, of one author's taking a stroll around the other's writings. Yet I have chosen my task in such a way that the treatment, because of its more universal and more ideal character, will be able to be read in every age. On the whole, I do not have the ability to write for the moment.]

VII²
B 235
29

¹Chapter I

The Historical Situation

THE COLLISION OF MAGISTER ADLER, AS A TEACHER IN THE STATE CHURCH, WITH THE ESTABLISHED ORDER; THE SPECIAL INDIVIDUAL WHO HAS A REVELATION-FACT

It was in 1843 that Magister Adler published his *Sermons*, in the preface to which he in the most solemn manner announced that a revelation had been bestowed upon him, that by this a new doctrine² had been communicated to him, and in the sermons themselves he made a distinction, whereby everything became decisively clear, between the sermons that were by himself and those that were dependent on the immediate assistance of the Spirit.* In the preface he informed us that the Spirit had ordered him to burn everything else that he had written.³ So he stood or in the preface he dramatically presented himself as an image of a new point of departure in the most decisive sense—behind him a conflagration and he, with the new, rescued like a refugee.

At the time he was a teacher in the state Church.⁴ However agreeable it may be for the state or the state Church to see, if is so, a new generation of prospective public officials growing up who are all equipped with abilities and competence entirely different from what the former ones had, however agreeable it may be to see the most remarkable and excellent abilities dedicated to the service of the state and, in the area of religion, of the state Church—it is self-evident that this joy has one condition—namely, that they actually do serve the state, that they want to use

---

*Note. In a certain sense this is nevertheless confusing, inasmuch as the qualitatively dissimilar sermons should not be published together; in any case, there is missing here a dialectical middle term about how he understands himself in the qualitative, decisive difference: to be dependent on the immediate assistance of the Spirit and to be without it.

their glorious abilities within its principles and acknowledge these *ex animi sententia* [with a sincere heart]. If that is not the case, the joy must change to concern and, if there is danger brewing, to concern and uneasiness about its own survival, but in any case to concerned sympathy for the individual or the individuals who thus fall short in their lives. The state and the state Church are not selfish, not tyrannical (something only the malicious and discontented want to make themselves and others believe). They are, in their own view, benevolent; when they accept the individual's service, they also intend to do him a service by assigning him the desirable, the suitable place for the appropriate and beneficial use of his powers.

Magister Adler's collision is easy to see: the collision of *the special individual with the universal*, increased by his also being an officeholder in the service of the universal. But since this collision occurs more frequently, I have treated it in more detail in Addendum I, to which referral is made.

But Magister Adler's collision has something even more crucial. He is the special individual who has a revelation-fact. By his revelation-fact, by the new doctrine,* by being under the direct impulsion of the Spirit, Magister Adler must himself readily become conscious of being placed completely outside the universal, completely *extra ordinem* [outside the order] as an *extraordinarius* in the most decisive sense, qualitatively different from every other special individual (the genius—the immediate genius or the genius of reflection), be he ever so great or ever so much a genius, when he nevertheless cannot appeal to having had a revelation. To want to be in the service of the established order under such conditions is a self-contradiction, and to demand of the established order that it should keep him in service is actually to want to make a fool of it, as if it were something so abstract that it could not concentrate with energetic consciousness on what it is and what it wants. To want to be in the service of the established order and then to want to serve that which aims, even if not in reality yet

VIII²
B 13
61

---

*Note. That Magister Adler has said something later about there being nothing new in his doctrine makes no difference. By his conduct he declared it in the most extreme and strongest expressions and was prepared in every way for the sensation on the occasion of the wonderful newness.

all the more formally, at the very life of the established order, is just as unreasonable as if someone wanted to be in a man's service and yet openly acknowledged that his work and diligence and mind belonged to another man. Nobody would tolerate that, and the reason one wishes that the universal, the established order, should tolerate it is that one has a fantastic-abstract idea of the impersonality of the universal, and a fantastic conception of livelihood, according to which the state must support every graduate. When the army is drawn up facing the established order, then wanting to be in the ranks and a *stipendiarius* [receiver of a stipend] but wanting to stand turned the opposite way cannot be done; the moment they are to march (as soon as life stirs), it will be apparent that he is walking the opposite way. An extraordinary with a revelation-fact must step out of the ranks. His importance demands it as does also the earnestness of the universal, because such a one is too important to *be together* in the ranks, and the earnestness of the universal demands unity and uniformity in the ranks, demands to see the *extraordinary* or to see that *he* is the extraordinary. In this *discrimen* [distinction] such an extraordinary has his place. This is his situation: on the one side to be pointed out as a special individual in comparison with the universal, so that no sagacious person could be his friend or even walk with him on the street, so that his friend, if he was sagacious, would swear that he did not know him,[5] at whom "those who passed by shook their heads"[6]—and then nevertheless to be the one who by a revelation and in virtue of it is to bring the new, to be the one from whom the new reckoning of time is to begin.

Magister Adler's collision with the universal is, therefore, that of the special individual who has a revelation. To want summarily to deny the possibility that this extraordinary experience could happen to a person also in our age would certainly be a very dubious sign. But if there is nothing new under the sun, neither is there any direct, uniform repetition—there are continually ever new modifications. Our age is an age of reflection and common sense. It might be assumed, then, that the person who in our age is thus called by God would be related to his age. He presumably would have superior reflective powers at his disposal

as a ministering factor. This, then, would be the apparent difference between such a called person in our age and one in an
earlier age (since the essential likeness is and remains the call)—
namely, that the called person in our age would as a ministering
agent have a ministering reflection, before which I, a lowly critic,
bow seven times, and seventy times before his call by a revelation. The called person in our age will not be merely an instrument (immediate) but will consciously undertake his call in quite
another sense than what always has been the case in a divine
call—will make up his mind that this extraordinary thing has
happened to him and understand himself in that.

Thus whether it is possible to think a divine call into human
reflection, to think a coordination of them, is a question that I, a
lowly ministering critic, would not dare presume to answer.
Only the life of the extraordinary person, if such a one did appear, would contain the answer. But I can, up to a certain point,
dialectically work through the idea until reflection runs aground.

If, then, everything is in proper order in this matter of a person's having been called by a revelation, but he had a superior
reflection as a ministering factor, he would then understand that
the ethical accompaniment to this call and having a revelation
corresponds ethically to an enormous responsibility in all direc-
tions, not only inwardly (that he himself was sure, understood
himself in the fact that this extraordinary thing had happened to
him, this we take for granted) but outwardly in relation to the
established order, because in reflection the extraordinary has the
dialectic of being the supreme salvation but also of being able to
be the worst corruption. His responsibility in reflection would
then be that he not become the worst misfortune for the established order and that with fear and trembling he see to it, as far as
he is able, that no one is harmed by a direct relationship to his
extraordinariness. If we now let the ministering reflection alone
give counsel, then the final consequence would be that, humanly
understood, he would completely destroy himself, the impression of himself, make himself as lowly and insignificant as possible, almost repugnant, because in reflection (where every qualification is indeed dialectical) he would properly understand that
the extraordinary, beyond the point where it is in truth and is the

VIII²
B 13
63

extraordinary, is and can occasion the most frightful corruption. In the final consequence of reflection, he would then transform the revelation-fact itself into his life's deepest secret, which in the silence of the grave would become the law of his existence, but which he would never communicate directly. —But see, precisely this would be to fail completely in his task, in fact, would be like disobedience to God. The person who is called by a revelation is specifically called to appeal to his revelation; he must indeed use *authority* by virtue of being called by a revelation. In a religious revival it is not up to the person who has been awakened in an extraordinary way to go out and preach this to people; on the contrary, it can be completely right and pleasing to God and obedience to God for this to remain the awakened person's secret with God. But if the person who by a revelation is called to communicate a revelation wants to be silent about the revelation-fact, then he offends against God and reduces God's will to nothing. It is the very revelation-fact that is decisive; it is this that gives him *divine authority*. It does not depend, as is taught in the confused philosophy of our age, upon the content of the teaching, but the revelation-fact and the divine authority that follows from it are what is decisive. If I imagined a letter from heaven, then it is not the content of the letter, no matter from whom it came, that is the main point. The main point is that it is a letter from heaven.

So it is seen that when a person places his reception of a revelation entirely into reflection, this in one way or another becomes something impenetrable or works itself into a self-contradiction. If the ministering reflection's idea is to conquer, then he will keep the revelation-fact itself hidden as a something isolated, in fear and trembling will keep watch on the terrible consequences that direct communication could have and will quake before the responsibility. But he thereby also gives up *the authority*; he presumptuously makes himself into a genius as a substitute for his having been called by God to be an apostle. That is, in reflection's idea a genius is the highest, an apostle an impossibility, since the category of apostle is precisely the divine authority.

Thus reflection comes to a halt at the question: whether it is possible that human reflection is able to undertake a call by a revelation, whether a revelation does not presuppose a contin-

VIII²
B 13
64

ued revelation. But on the other hand, since our age is an age of reflection and the human race may be assumed to be continually developing more and more in reflection, it seems, humanly speaking, obvious that if a person in such an age is called by a revelation he must have an element of reflection more than the person called in an earlier age. In the earlier age the reflection of the called person signified only a reflection within himself, that he understood himself in having been granted the extraordinary; now it must signify a reflection over his entire relation to the surrounding world. Thus, in the moment of the undertaking, the person called must consciously be able in one way or another to explain to himself both his responsibility *in concreto* and that the same thing *would* happen to him as happened to the person called in an earlier age. The person called by a revelation in our age must be the synthesis of his age's greatest maieutic and the one called, the synthesis of being the one called and the one devoting oneself. In addition to the divine authority (which is qualitatively decisive) granted to him, he must have an eminent wisdom for surveying the circumstances.[7]

The human dialectic cannot proceed further than to this admission, that it cannot think this, but also to the admission that this does not imply anything more than that it cannot think this. But the human dialectic, if it wants to understand itself, consequently to be humble, never forgets that God's thoughts are not human thoughts, that all this about genius and culture and reflection makes no difference, but that divine authority is what is decisive, that the person whom God calls in this way, whether he is a fisherman or a shoemaker (nowadays it is perhaps all too easy to understand that Peter became an apostle, but at the time it was much easier to understand that he was a fisherman!)—he is the apostle.

The divine authority is the category, and here also, altogether appropriately, is the mark: *the possibility of offense*. It is true that a genius can be an offense, *esthetically*, for a moment or fifty years or a hundred, but he can never be an offense *ethically*; what offends is that a human being has divine authority.

But with regard to the qualification of being called by a revelation, just as with everything Christian, in the course of time indolence and habit, lack of spirit or absence of spirit, and

VIII²
B 15
65

VIII²
B 15
66

thoughtlessness have been allowed to dampen the coiled spring. At one moment it was a hysterical woman who had a revelation, then a sedentary artisan, then a professor who became so *profound* that he could almost be said to have a revelation, then a peering genius who peered so deeply that he almost, nearly, as good as— had revelations. This gradually came to be what people understood to be called by a revelation, and in this sense Paul also had a revelation, except that he also had an uncommonly good head on his shoulders.

No, the divine authority is the category. Here there is very little or nothing at all for assistant professors and licentiates and paragraph swallowers to do. The assistance of these gentlemen is needed here no more than a maiden needs a barber to shave her beard and no more than a bald man needs a hairdresser to "style" his hair. The matter is very simple: will you obey or will you not obey; will you in faith submit to his divine authority or will you take offense—or will you perhaps not take sides—be careful, that also is offense.

VIII²
B 15
67

But, as mentioned, the coiled spring has been dampened or slackened in the parenthetical. Exegesis was the first parenthesis. Exegesis got busy: how was this revelation to be comprehended, whether there was an inner fact, perhaps a kind of *Dichtung und Wahrheit*[8] etc. etc. Strangely enough, Paul, to whom this pertains most, does not seem to have spent one single second on *wanting to comprehend in this sense*—but the rest of us, well, we are not Paul, and so we have to do something—since to obey him is not anything to do. Now, of course, from generation to generation at every university, in every semester one course on how etc. etc., from generation to generation every other year a new book about how etc. etc.—yes, it is an excellent diversionary means; in this way the prospect of reaching the point of obeying Paul is put more and more at a distance.

Philosophy, and along with it dogmatics, which mimics philosophy, was the second parenthesis. As befits a noble, highborn, human science, it said, "By no means am I going to get pettily involved in or let myself be disturbed by the question of who is the author of the book, whether he is only a fisherman and a lowly person. No, away with all pettiness! The main thing is the content of the teaching; I ask only about that. Just as esthetics does not ask who wrote a play but only what it is like, I am likewise indifferent to who the author is"—also indifferent to the fact that he is *the apostle*. Indeed, it is easy to speculate this way. *The apostle*, a human being with divine authority—that is precisely the hitch. It is easy to be finished with Paul in that manner—after all, one never reaches the point of beginning with him, or of beginning with his having divine authority. Scripture is treated so scientifically that it could just as well be by anonymities.

See, from the moment the parenthetical got underway there was, of course, plenty for assistant professors and licentiates and paragraph swallowers and peerers to do. As things went more and more in this direction, the category of being called by a revelation receded more and more; it became a triviality, a matter of indifference, which eventually almost everybody could run with; and then it went so completely out of fashion that finally it became a rarity to see anyone in this "equipage."

VIII²
B 15
68

———————

Then Magister Adler announced that he had had a revelation.

CHAPTER II

A Revelation in the Situation of the Present Age[1]

What seems to give Christianity and its learned or eloquent defenders such unusual success is the same thing that in so many ways exercises a restraining force and hinders individuals from personally coming to a qualitative-essential decision; it is the same thing that must finally play the victory into the hands of the atheists. This same thing is the much discussed eighteen centuries, whether the matter is thereby placed at such an enormous distance that the impression of what is decisive or the decisive impression vanishes in fantasy-twilight, or the argument is made paralogistically from the eighteen centuries to the truth of Christianity,[2] by which brilliant and triumphant demonstration the truth of Christianity is unfortunately only undermined, since in that case it becomes true only as a hypothesis, is transformed by this triumphant argument from an eternal truth into a hypothesis. Indeed, how would it occur to an eternal truth to stoop to demonstrate its truth by its having survived for so and so many years, stoop to wretched companionship with lies and deceit, which have also survived many years and still do—an eternal truth that from first to last is equally true, no more true in its latest moment than in its first; thus it did not come into the world bashful and awkward because it still did not yet have centuries to which to appeal, and thus it did not become foolishly conceited by having survived such a long time. Yes, a hypothesis is shy at the beginning; then it flaunts the years, but in return it is also liable to annihilation at any moment. Qualitatively understood, an eternal truth has only with itself to do; it has no relation to survival as evidence of its truth; the thousand years are no argument *pro* any more than newness in year one was an argument *contra*. The eternal truth is just as true in its first moment as it is in its latest.

Just as for God a thousand years is like one day,[3] so also with an eternal truth, and it is impudence on the part of the thousand years to want to fancy itself to be something. The eternal truth does not become more true with the help of the thousand years, and neither does it become more obvious by their help that it is true. To say something like that is, as they say, to speak in spoonerisms or to speak backward.[4]

Let us illustrate this with another situation. When an eminent thinker with the idea of consistency tightens the reins of thought to the utmost, there will be only few who understand him, the majority are put off. If, however, he relaxes the dialectical, talks nonsense from time to time, there will be many who understand him. When there are many who understand him, the person who speaks in spoonerisms says: Now he has come closer to the truth than previously; then no one understood him. Alas, alas, that is a mistake; the reverse is the case—because the thinker has abandoned the truth, there are many who understand him, that is, understand the untruth. So it is also when an eternal truth has survived a long time. In that case it most likely has become botched, and thereby many have joined in the game; then when someone speaks in spoonerisms, he thinks that the eternal truth has now become more obvious, more trustworthy. In other words, the eternal is not trustworthy enough; no, one thousand years and then a crowd! What a preposterous inversion! They want to demonstrate the truth and the trustworthiness of the eternal by means of what is infinitely deceitful: the years and the human crowd.

To be sure, Christianity is not an eternal truth in the sense of a mathematical or ontological theorem, but nevertheless Christianity has just as little to do with the category *surviving* if something *pro* or *contra* is supposed to be demonstrated by it. Christianity is the paradoxical truth; it is the paradox that the eternal once came into existence in time.[5] This paradoxical fact (an offense to reason, the object of faith) does not, because it is eighteen hundred years later, become more true than it was the day it occurred. That the eternal once came into existence in time is not a truth that must stand up to the test of time, is not something that *must be tested by human beings* but is the paradox *by which human beings must be tested,* and therefore it stands completely unaltered, and the eternal proudly disdains every impudent, importunate argument on the basis of the many years. Nor has the paradox itself survived for many years; it existed when Christ lived, and since that time it exists only every time someone is offended or truly believes. Whether the paradox had existed for one thousand years or for only a half-hour makes no difference; it does not become more probable because it existed for one thousand years and not less improbable[6] because it lasted for only a half-hour.

If being and becoming a Christian is to have its decisive qualitative reality, it is of primary importance that the whole illusion of subsequent history be eradicated, so that the person who becomes a Christian in 1846 becomes that by being contemporary with Christianity's entry into the world in the same sense as the contemporaries* were eighteen hundred years ago. For that purpose it is of primary importance that an unshakable qualitative difference be fixed between *the historical in Christianity* (the paradox that the eternal once came into existence in time, this paradoxical fact) and the *history of Christianity,* the history of its followers, etc. That God came into existence in human form under Emperor Augustus, that is the historical in Christianity, the historical in the paradoxical compound. It is with this paradox that everyone, in whatever century he lives, must become contemporary if as a believer he is to become a Christian. In this regard he has nothing at all to do with the history of Christianity. But one of the woeful aspects of our age is that it will soon become an impossibility to find a person who has the time and patience

VII²
B 235
77

*Note. With regard to all the dialectical issues pertaining to this (*the paradox, the moment, the dialectic of contemporaneity,* etc.), I must refer to a pseudonymous author, Johannes Climacus, to his two books, *Philosophical Fragments* and *Concluding Postscript to* Philosophical Fragments. For something so dialectically composed, it is impossible to give a résumé in a few lines; the report, if it is to be reliable, will end up being just as complicated and just as difficult as the original exposition, because if just one least little middle term is left out, the whole dialectic suffers. Whether what is said with regard to living organisms is entirely true—that when one limb suffers, the whole body suffers—I do not know, but with regard to the dialectical this is entirely true.

and earnestness and the passion of thought to respect the qualitative dialectic in a well-disciplined way.

When this requirement, to become contemporary with Christianity's entry into the world in the same sense as the contemporaries were, is understood properly, then it is *a true religious
requirement and specifically in the interest of Christianity.* The same
requirement, however, can be made by the *enemies,* by the *offended,* in order *to do harm.* As far as I know, this has not happened, which is very strange, because in our day attacks upon
Christianity have with renewed power and considerable talent
made the most extreme attempt.

But instead of insisting on this concept of contemporaneity,
orthodoxy has taken another road—with the help of the eighteen hundred years. If one were to describe this entire orthodox
apologetic endeavor in a single sentence, yet also categorically,
one would have to say: Its aim is to make *Christianity probable.*
Then one must add: If this succeeds, then this endeavor would
have the ironical fate that on the very day of victory it would
have forfeited everything and completely cashiered Christianity.
Therefore it is good that in their busy trifling these concerned
apologists, who do not know what they are doing, have not yet
succeeded completely;[7] it is good that a book is still anticipated
that will etc. To make Christianity probable is the same as to
falsify it. Indeed, what is it atheists want? Oh, they want to make
Christianity probable. That is, they are well aware that if they
can only get Christianity's qualitative extravagance tricked into
the fussy officiousness of probability—then it is all over with
Christianity. But the orthodox apologetic endeavor also wants
to make Christianity probable; thus it is working hand in glove
with heterodoxy. Yet apologetics has worked this way in all
naïveté, and this whole tactic, together with the relation here
between orthodoxy and heterodoxy, must be regarded as an
amazing example of what lack of character and lack of qualitative dialectic can lead to: that one attacks what one defends, that
orthodoxy and heterodoxy continue to be enemies who want to
exterminate each other, although they are allies who want one
and the same thing—to make Christianity probable.

VII²
B 235
78

Every defense of Christianity that understands what it wants must do the very opposite and with all its might and with a qualitative dialectic assert the *improbability* of Christianity. Such an introductory scholarship, which would develop the dialectic of the improbable and its scope, together with the existence-category (faith) that corresponds to it, would—especially if a Greek substructure is laid down in order to illuminate by contrast[8]—such an introductory scholarship would in our age be a festival of renewal[9] from which something still could be hoped. So far this seems to be hidden from the eyes of the theologians,[10] for I would still ask where it would be that one could find any trace of the qualitatively altered method. Under various names and right up to the latest speculative thought, the effort has been to make Christianity probable, comprehensible, to take it out of the God-language of the paradox and get it translated into the Low-German of speculative thought or the Enlightenment. Yet in order to despair of something, one has despaired of its succeeding (what irony!); or one has rejoiced that it succeeded, has on that occasion let Christianity receive congratulations (what irony!). The man who traveled from Jericho and fell among robbers[11] was not as badly situated as Christianity, because the orthodox apologetics that mercifully attended to it has done it just as much wrong as the robbers.

The essentially Christian *has* no history, because the essentially Christian is this paradox, that God once came into existence in time. This is the offense, but also the point of departure; whether it is eighteen hundred years ago or yesterday, one can equally well be contemporary with it. Just as the North Star never changes its position and therefore has no history, so this paradox stands unmoved and unaltered; and if Christianity existed for ten thousand years, one would not in the decisive sense get any further away from it than the contemporaries were. The distance is not to be measured with the quantifying of time and space, since the qualitatively decisive distance is that it is a paradox. Neither is the history of Christianity related directly to the essentially Christian in the way the survival of a tree in its growing is related to the sprout. The essentially Christian is something eternally concluded to which nothing is to be added or subtracted, and in

VII[2]
B 235
79

every generation and in every individual, if he is truly a Christian, the beginning is from the beginning, from that paradox.
The beginning is not there where the previous generation left
off, but from the beginning.[12]

As soon, however, as one confuses Christianity and the essentially Christian, as soon as one begins to count the years, one
begins to want to change the improbable into the probable. One
says: Now Christianity has survived (the essentially Christian, of
course, is a fact since eighteen hundred years *ago*) for three hundred years, now for seven hundred, now for eighteen hundred—
well, then it certainly must be true. By this procedure one manages to confuse everything. The decision (to become a Christian)
easily becomes a sheer triviality for the individual. It is already
easy enough for him to accept the customs in the city where he
lives, because the great majority do that; so would it not be altogether natural that he would become a Christian *along with*
them—when Christianity has survived for eighteen hundred
years! On the other hand, Christianity is weakened, made into a
triviality with the aid of the distance, with the aid of the eighteen hundred years. Something, if it happened contemporaneously, that would horrify people, would radically disturb their
lives, something, if it happened contemporaneously, that they
would either find offensive, would hate and persecute, if possible eradicate, or believing accept—that seems to be something
one can believe and accept as a matter of course (that is, leave it
undecided) since it was eighteen hundred years ago. Contemporaneity is the tension that does not permit a person to leave it
undecided but compels one either to be offended or to believe.
The distance, on the other hand, is the indulgence that encourages lethargy to the degree that the believing acceptance of
something as a matter of course becomes identical with leaving
it undecided. Why is it that no contemporary age can get along
with witnesses to the truth, and the man is scarcely dead before
all can get along with him splendidly? This happens because his
contemporaries, as long as he is living and they are living with
him in the situation of contemporaneity, feel the sting of his
existence; he forces them to a more strenuous decision. But
when he is dead, then they can very well be good friends with

VII²
B 235
80

him and admire him—that is, thoughtlessly and comfortably just leave the whole thing undecided. I wonder why Socrates compared himself to a gadfly[13] if it was not because he understood that his life among his contemporaries was a sting. When he was dead, they idolized him. When a person experiences a little event in his life, he learns something from it, and why? Because the event really comes to grips with him. The same person, however, can sit in the theater and see great scenes of tragedy, he can read about the extraordinary in the newspaper, he can listen to the pastor, and it all really makes no impression, and why? Because he does not become contemporary with it, because in the first two instances he lacks imagination; in the last he lacks the inner experience for really becoming contemporary with what is depicted, because he thinks like this: It is, of course, many years since it happened.

So now when for many years a disoriented orthodoxy, which does not know what it is doing, and a rebellious heterodoxy, which daimonically knows what it is doing and only to that extent does not know what it is doing, with the aid of the eighteen hundred years have joined forces to confuse everything, to give rise to one illusion more lunatic than the other, the one paralogism worse than the other, the one μετάβασις εἰς ἄλλο γένος [shifting from one genus to another] more confusing than the other—then the main task now is to be able to get the terrain cleared, to eliminate the eighteen hundred years, so that the essentially Christian occurs for us as if it occurred today. It is the eighteen hundred years that have inflated the objections to Christianity and the defense of it into volumes. It is the sixteen hundred, the seventeen hundred, the eighteen hundred years that have anesthetized the defenders and helped the attackers. It is the eighteen hundred years that have kept the lives of countless people in a delusion. With the aid of the eighteen hundred years, the defenders have invertedly made Christianity into a hypothesis, and the attackers have made it into nothing.

What the nothing but busy Johannes Climacus has done in this regard to ferret out every illusion, trap every paralogism, catch every deceitful locution cannot be repeated here.[14] He has done it in such a way that every more scholarly, cultured person, if he will earnestly spend a little time in the daily practice of the dialectical, will readily understand it. It certainly is not done in any other way, and it cannot be done in any other way either. Such things cannot be presented in a newspaper and be read "while one shaves."[15] It must be left up to the newspapers to write for busy people like that. Climacus's exposition is rigorous, as the matter entails. His merit is this: with the help of dialectic, to have imaginatively drawn (as one says of a telescope) that which is unshakably the essentially Christian so close to the eye that the reader is prevented from looking mistakenly at the eighteen hundred years. His merit is with the help of dialectic to have procured the view, the perspective. To direct one's eyes toward a star is not very difficult, because the air is like an empty space and thus there is as good as nothing in the way that stops or distracts the gaze. But it is otherwise when the direction the eye is to take is straight ahead, as down a road, and there are also throngs and crowds and disturbance and noise and busyness that the eye must penetrate in order to get the view, while every side glance, indeed, every blinking of the eyes, completely disturbs qualitatively; and it becomes even more difficult when one must also stand in an environment that *pro virili* [with all its might] works to keep one from getting the view. —And yet contemporaneity with what is unshakably the essentially Christian is decisive. But this contemporaneity is to be understood to mean the same as it did for those who were living when Christ lived.[16]

What is needed above all is to get the huge libraries and scribblings and the eighteen hundred years out of the way in order to gain the view. This is by no means a rash requirement by a high-flying dialectician; it is an altogether modest and genuine religious requirement that everyone must make—not for the sake of scholarship and the public, but for one's own sake, purely personally for one's own sake, if one is earnest about becoming a Christian; and it is what Christianity itself must require. The essentially Christian wants to stand unshaken like the North Star and therefore wants to stay out of the nonsense that only deprives it of life.

Yet the contemporaneity discussed here is not *the contemporaneity of an apostle*, inasmuch as he was called by a revelation *but is*

VII²
B 235
83

VII²
B 235
84

VII²
B 235
85

*only the contemporaneity that every contemporary had: the possibility in
the tension of contemporaneity of having to be offended or to lay hold of
faith.* To that end it is particularly necessary that there be an airing
out in such a way that it, as at one time, becomes possible for a
person to be offended in earnest or, believing, to appropriate the
essentially Christian, lest it turn out with the essentially Christian
as with a court case when it has been left undecided from time
immemorial, so that one is all at sea because of the abundance of
knowledge. The situation of contemporaneity is the creating of
tension that gives the categories qualitative elasticity, and what a
big dunce he must be who does not know what an infinite difference it makes when one for one's own sake considers something
in the situation of contemporaneity and when one casually thinks
about something in the delusion that it was eighteen hundred
years ago—in the delusion, yes, in the delusion, inasmuch as,
precisely because the essentially Christian is the qualitative paradox, it is a delusion that eighteen hundred years are longer ago
than yesterday.

If the situation in Christendom at present is such that it is particularly to the point to put an end to this tenacious apathy connected with the eighteen hundred years, then one cannot deny
that the sudden appearance of a man who appealed to a revelation could provide a desirable stimulus, because then an analogous situation of contemporaneity is formed. No thanks, all the
profound and speculative and learned and perspiring prattlers,
who can very well understand that eighteen hundred years ago
one had a revelation—they would be in a predicament. The one
who can at all understand that a person has a revelation must
understand it equally well if it happened six thousand years ago
or it will happen six thousand years hence or it happens today.
But perhaps the prattler has Christianly made a living on the
eighteen hundred years, has prattled himself into thinking that he
could understand it—because it was eighteen hundred years ago.
If the matter were not so serious, I cannot deny that I would
regard it as altogether the most exquisite comedy that could ever
be written in the world: to have all the modern exegesis and
dogmatics go through their courses—in the situation of contemporaneity. All those deceptive psychological devices, all that "to

VII²
B 235
86

a certain degree" and then again to a certain degree, all that bravura of profundity, and then above all the showy mediation[17] that explains—all that, since what is explained occurred eighteen hundred years ago, would make a splendid showing in contemporaneity with what was reinterpreted. It is altogether certain that one single Aristophanean comedy in that style would clear up the confusion of modern Christian scholarship much better than all scholarly combat.

Therefore when I, without as yet having seen his sermons and the preface to them, heard that Magister Adler had come forward and had appealed to a revelation, I cannot deny that I was astounded; I thought: either this is the man we need, the chosen one, who in divine originality has the new spring to refresh the lifeless soil of Christendom, or it is an offended person, but a crafty knave, who, in order to demolish everything, also an apostle's dignity, in order to collapse everything, brings a Christendom like the present one to the strenuous decision of having to go through its dogmatics in the situation of contemporaneity.

Given the latter assumption, I certainly would have been surprised if an offended person actually had been so sagacious. Although one cannot deny offended people talent and daimonic inspiration, they ordinarily nevertheless tend to be somewhat obtuse on the whole—that is, they really do not know quite how one is to go about the matter in order to do harm. They attack Christianity, but they place themselves outside it, and for that very reason they do no harm. No, the offended person must try to come to grips with Christianity in a completely different way, try to push up like a mole in the middle of Christendom. Suppose that Feuerbach,[18] instead of attacking Christianity, had gone about it more craftily. Suppose that he had laid out his plan in daimonic silence and then stepped forward and announced that he had had a revelation, and now suppose that he, like a criminal who is able to stick to a lie, had stuck unshakably to this story while he also sagaciously had found out all the weak sides of orthodoxy, which he nevertheless by no means attacked but only, with a certain innocent naïveté, knew how to hold up to the light. Suppose that he had done it so well that no one could get wise to his slyness—he would have brought orthodoxy into

VII²
B 235
87

the worst predicament. In the interest of the established order, orthodoxy fights to maintain the appearance that in a way we all are Christians, that the country is Christian and the congregations are Christians. When someone places himself on the outside and attacks Christianity, then, if he is victorious, the congregation is supposed to be troubled out of its cozy routine of being Christians in a way like most people; it is supposed to come to the decision to give up Christianity. What an inconvenience; no, then it is better to stick with the old. See, this is why the offended person achieves nothing.

Furthermore, when someone attacks Christianity and places himself on the outside, orthodoxy defends it by means of the eighteen hundred years; it speaks in lofty tones about the extraordinary acts of God in the past, that is, eighteen hundred years ago. As for the extraordinary and the extraordinary acts of God, it must be said that people lap it up the more easily the longer ago it was. So the offended person attacks Christianity; orthodoxy defends it with the help of the distance, and the congregation thinks as follows: If it was eighteen hundred years ago, then one can surely understand that something extraordinary happened. The offended one again achieves nothing. It would, however, have been different if he himself had ingeniously stepped forward with a revelation, if he, confoundedly well schooled in orthodoxy, knew how to conceal his daimonic sagacity in a singularly innocent naïveté, by means of which he would continually get orthodoxy into hot water, while like a burr he stuck firmly to orthodoxy. On the one hand, orthodoxy could not very well bring itself to deny that it was orthodoxy that he presented; on the other hand, it would be very damaging to have it said in such a direct way, which would force orthodoxy to make a clean breast of it in a situation of contemporaneity.

It is frequently said that if Christ appeared today—in Christendom—if he in an even stricter sense than formerly "came to his own,"[19] he would again be crucified. If it should be that the death penalty had been abolished, he would suffer the punishment that has replaced the death penalty, and orthodoxy in particular would be zealous to have him arrested and convicted. And why would it presumably happen this way again? Because contemporaneity provides the appropriate qualitative pressure;

VII²
B 235
88

distance, however, helps both to make something into nothing and to make something into the extraordinary almost in the sense of nothing. Why, indeed, were almost all offended by Christ when he lived if it was not because the extraordinary happened right before their eyes; therefore the one who wanted to talk about it had to say: It happened yesterday evening, yesterday morning, yesterday afternoon.* But when the miracle happened eighteen hundred years ago—well, then one can easily understand that it happened and that it was a miracle. Among the many precious and priceless syllogisms of [*added in version IV:* injudicious] clergy-discourse, this must be regarded as one of the most precious: that what cannot be understood if it happens today can be understood and believed if it happened eighteen hundred years ago if, note well, it is the marvelous, which at any time of the day, both four o'clock and five o'clock, surpasses human understanding. That is, if one only says that one can understand that those men eighteen hundred years ago believed that it was a miracle, then one can just as well say straight out that one does not believe it oneself. Yet people prefer to avail themselves of deceptive locutions such as this one, which appears to be so believing and yet precisely denies the miracle, since it says of those men that they believed it, namely, that they were serious about it, namely, that one does not believe it oneself.

To believe in the eminent sense corresponds quite rightly to the marvelous, the absurd, the improbable, that which is foolishness to the understanding,[20] and for that very reason it is altogether unimportant how long ago it was or if it is today. Anyone who has the remotest idea of dialectics in his head must perceive that the person who believes it if it happened eighteen hundred years ago can just as well believe it if it happens today— unless he believes it *because* it was eighteen hundred years ago, which is *not* to believe *at all*. If he believes this and that occurred

VII²
B 235
89

*****Note*. The pastor who, when he is talking about that essentially one and only subject for a sermon, the paradox, is unable to produce this effect and keep his listeners in the tension of contemporaneity, is essentially not a pastor. Viewed essentially, all his proficiencies etc. mean nothing at all; but this lack of present time adequately shows that he himself is not a believer, because in faith the believer, as much as any contemporary could be contemporary, is completely contemporary—with a paradox.

eighteen hundred years ago, then precisely in faith he is paradoxically contemporary with it as if it occurred today. Incidentally,
what nonsense the preacher-discourse furnishes on this point—
well, let us not talk about it, nor about how ordinary Christians
are reassured by this preacher-discourse in regard to their salvation. They are reassured, and against that there is nothing to say,
except that in our day it would certainly be both more important but also more difficult to make the congregation a little un-
easy and concerned in regard to their salvation. If only dialectics
did not exist; it only makes trouble. What more beautiful eulogy
on a country's clergy could be imagined than that they reassure
the congregation in regard to their salvation. And the clergy do
that in our day. At times there is nevertheless the complaint in
one or another of our excellent newspapers that a night watchman shouts too loudly and disturbs the inhabitants' quiet and
sleep. But there is no complaint about the clergy; they reassure
the congregation in regard to their salvation! If Christ were to
come to his own today, he would probably find the parishioners
sleeping, reassured with the clergy's assistance in regard to their
salvation.

    As was said, I had imagined a dilemma in connection with the
conception of the extraordinary,* that a man appeals to a revelation-fact: that he was either the chosen one or a daimonically

---

*Note. Generally every human being is inclined to imagine a dilemma in
relation to the extraordinary if he receives the proper tension-filled impression, has the elasticity to receive the pressure and to react to the pressure. The
principle of contradiction has its life and its power in passion. Therefore, as soon
as a person is really deeply moved by something, when he is in mortal danger,
when the extraordinary appears before him, when he stands impassioned with
his future fate in his hands, there is immediately an either/or. But since people
nowadays are devoid of passion, flabby as a wet bowstring, since in a spiritual
sense their priming powder is damp, then there soon remains only a tradition of
the time when human life was tightened by the principle of contradiction. Just
as one skeptically reads stories about the times when people became nine hundred years old and were gigantic in stature,[21] so also a slack and dissolute generation will soon hear skeptically and suspect sagaciously the story that people
have lived for whom an either/or was actually manifest, people who had their
lives in this tension, while the pace of their own lives was like that of an arrow
from a tightened bowstring, but this does not mean that for them there was an
either/or only once.

sagacious offended person. [*Added in version IV:* And this in turn, according to my concepts, was what the situation of contemporaneity, today's situation, might help us to: an either/or. And even if it does not happen in this way, what Christianity needs unconditionally, lest it suffocate and perish in indifference, is an either/or in relation to becoming and being a Christian. *End of text in version IV.*] Adler's conduct has in the meantime convinced me that there must be a third, since he is neither of the two. That he is not the chosen one, that this whole thing about his revelation is a misunderstanding, I shall show and substantiate later, yet not directly—far be it from me.*[23]

He is if possible even less a daimonically sagacious offended person—of that he has not the slightest trace or symptom. Therefore he is by no means without significance, and among my contemporaries I know no one other than Adler who in a stricter sense may be called a phenomenon. The powers of existence have taken hold of him, and as a phenomenon he is an anticipation of the dialectic that is fermenting at present. But the phenomenon itself does not know how to explain anything—

It would not surprise me if the slowness and tightfisted carefulness with which I go at this before I come to any conclusion on this matter will appear almost ludicrous to some people. By merely glancing at one of Adler's books or by merely hearing that he is supposed to have had a revelation, the majority will no doubt have enough to be finished with their judgment. When a bustler of that sort finds out that I have written a whole book and yet have arrived at the same result, he will laugh at me, he who promptly said the same thing. If a person who had especially exact, learned familiarity with Plato collected everything available about Socrates' daimon, compared it with whatever has been preserved from antiquity, and then arrived at the modest result that he could not determine anything, and if another person, who learned from Kofod's world history[24] that Socrates is supposed to have had a daimon, promptly arrived at the decisive result that one cannot know anything definite about it, then in a way the two certainly do have a result in common. And in our day if one has a result, well, then everything is fine. Yet would there not be a difference between the two, and would it not be really advantageous if our age, which is so busy with results, would consider how the matter stands with regard to negative results. Something that is non liquet *[not clear] can be the fruit of a year's labor, of great scholarship, of profound effort, and it can be the spit and image, can be obtained for four shillings in every grocery store. If there is a difference, if there is a glaring difference, this still may not be due to the results, which are almost identical. And yet everywhere there is a clamor only for results.*

VII²
B 235
91

VII²
B 235
92

that is, one must oneself be a teacher in order to learn anything from Adler.[25] Thus Adler is really a sign; he is a very earnest demonstration that the essentially Christian is a power that is not to be trifled with. But on the other hand, he is, rather than a chosen one, a person whirled around and slung out like a warning terror. Instead of being able to help the rest of us, he is more like the frightened [*deleted:* bewildered] bird that with wing strokes of anxiety rushes ahead of the storm that is coming [*deleted:* , while as yet people hear only a whistling; and his many thoughts are like the confused flock of birds that flee in disorder before the storm]. That one would therefore be justified in abandoning him or thinking poorly of his possibility is not my opinion at all.[26]

CHAPTER III

Adler's Own Shifting of His Essential Point of View, or That He Does Not Understand Himself, Does Not Himself Believe That a Revelation Has Been Given to Him.

LIGHT IS THROWN UPON THIS DIRECTLY-INDIRECTLY BY A BOOKLET THAT CONTAINS DOCUMENTS ON HIS DISMISSAL CASE, AND INDIRECTLY BY HIS FOUR LATEST BOOKS.

THE PROCEDURE IN THE INQUIRY

We have before us a man who has claimed to have had a revelation by which he has received a doctrine from the Savior. Another person can be justified in *flatly* denying the reality of this statement only if it can be clearly demonstrated that the person concerned is, in an altogether literal sense, insane. This is not the case with Adler. By his statement about himself, he is for the time being placed higher than every other human being, who, if he is to relate himself to him, *either* must submit, believing, to his divine authority, *or* must with skeptical reserve refrain from every affirmation and every negation. The present inquiry takes the latter, the skeptical position, but while it itself argues only *e concessis* [on the basis of the other's premises], neither flatly affirms nor denies, it pays close attention to whether it can hear from Adler's own utterances that he does not understand himself, is not in agreement with himself (*sibi constans*) and with his statement about himself.

To that end (1) Adler's replies and (2) his four latest books are utilized.

VII²
B 235
93

§1[1]

Papers Pertaining to My Suspension and Dismissal,
edited by A. P. Adler, M.A. Copenhagen.
Available at Reitzel's. 1845.[2]

In addition to some papers regarding a squabble about the chaplain's salary,[3] this piece contains mainly the questions put by the
ecclesiastical superior to Adler for an explanation of himself and
his teaching, together with Adler's replies and additional replies.

VII²
B 235
94

　　In order that everything may be accurate and be kept in mind
by the reader, it is perhaps best to recall that preface to his *Ser-*
mons.[4] Here Magister Adler tells how he was starting a work that
he wanted to have called "Popular Lectures on Subjective
Logic,"[5] a work in which he "with a superficial knowledge of
the Bible had undertaken to explain creation and Christianity."
He then continues, "One evening I had just given an account of
the origin of evil; then I perceived as if in a flash that everything
depended not upon thought but upon spirit, and that there existed an evil spirit. The same night a hideous sound descended
into our room. Then the *Savior** commanded me to get up and
go in and write down these words." Thereupon follow the
words,** which later stereotypically return again and again in his
prose and poetry.

　　We shall not go directly into the actual words at all, neither *pro*
nor *contra*, not even into the curious point that Christ speaks
almost like an assistant professor, since the words cited are exactly

---

**Note.* Adler himself italicizes this word.

***Note.* The words are as follows: "The first human beings could have had an
eternal life, because when thought joins God's spirit with the body, then life is
eternal; when the human being joins God's spirit with the body, then the
human being is God's child; so Adam would have been God's son. But they
sinned. Thought immersed itself in itself without the world, without the body.
It separated the spirit from the body, the spirit from the world. And when the
human being himself, when thought itself separates the spirit from the body and
the spirit from the world, the human being must die and the world and the body
become evil. And what becomes of the spirit? The spirit leaves the body. But
God does not take it back. And it becomes his enemy. And where does it go?
Back into the world. Why? It is angry with the world, which abandoned it. It
is the evil spirit. And the world itself created the evil spirit."[6]

like a section heading; we are still arguing only *e concessis* [on the basis of the other's premises]. But it is certainly clear that in that preface he most solemnly announces that he has had a revelation in which a doctrine has been communicated to him by the Savior. Indeed, it may be noteworthy that Adler, already before the revelation, was basically in the process of discovering the same thought that was communicated to him by the revelation, since it was in the evening "that he perceived as if in a flash that everything depended not upon thought but upon spirit, and that there existed an evil spirit." But again we will not become involved with this directly, only bearing in mind that the expression "as if in a flash" probably is not to be regarded as anything more or less than a metaphor for the speed of the perception or for the speed of the transition from not having perceived to having perceived. Moreover, the content of the doctrine communicated by the revelation is concentrated in the sentence, "that the human being's thought immersed itself in itself." But Adler seems to have fathomed this also before the revelation came to him, because in the preface he distinctly says of his work ("Popular Lectures on Subjective Logic"), "It was my own thought that had immersed itself in itself." Accordingly, there was not much left that was communicated to him by a revelation, but all the more definitely the accent falls on its having been communicated to him *by a revelation*, on this, that "the *Savior* at night commanded him to get up and go in and write down the following words." As soon as Adler holds to this with unshakable firmness, I do not have a yes or a no; my only concern is to argue *e concessis*. If, however, he does not hold fast to this, then he must reconcile himself to having it established by his own words that he himself does not believe that he has had a revelation, or that in any case he is so confused about the categories that he does not know what he is saying, because he does not connect any well-defined thought with the words.

The preface continues: "Then Jesus commanded me to burn my own works and in the future to keep to the Bible. As for the sermons and discourses from no. VI to the end, I know that they were written with Jesus' collaborating grace, so that I have been only an instrument." If Adler does not know this about the

VII²
B 235
95

others, or if he knows about the others that they are not, it is
really noteworthy that he publishes them, particularly in one volume, which like Noah's Ark comes to contain things that are
qualitatively very different. But this is Adler's affair. For me the
main point is that he has most solemnly said that he knows that
the discourses from no. VI to the end were written with Jesus'
collaborating grace, so that he has been only an instrument.*

Thus we have in Adler's call by a revelation an analogy to an
apostle's call, in his writing with the collaboration of Jesus' grace
and in his being only an instrument an analogy to the situation of
one who is inspired. Adler has both a doctrine that is communicated to him by a revelation and a development of this doctrine
that is inspired. The reader must continually hold fast to this in
the following, where it will be shown that Adler does not hold
fast to it, although he still does not feel called upon to revoke it
decisively. He confuses in a double way by *qualitatively changing*
and yet not *revoking.*[7] Everyone who is not completely confused
by the application of Hegelian dialectic in the existential spheres,
everyone who is not completely dulled by journalistic sophistry
will, without being exactly a dialectician, easily comprehend the
following. If someone, when he says he is going to explain something, makes a change in the essence of this something (the subject), he does not *explain* it, he *changes* it. By means of an *explanation the change takes place in the predicate* in such a way that what is

*Note. The solemnity of the statement is somewhat flawed, however, by a
few notes in the book itself, and about them, if the matter were not so serious,
I could be tempted to say that they probably were written with the collaborating
assistance of absentmindedness. One did indeed learn from the preface that the
sermons and discourses from no. VI to the end were written with Jesus' collaborating grace, but on page 20 one reads in a note (to Sermon IV, Maundy
Thursday, April 13, 1843): "This prayer was given to me by Jesus' collaborating
grace"; and on p. 26 (in Sermon V, Good Friday, April 14, 1843) one reads in
a note: "Here for the first time Jesus' collaborating grace came to my aid." Good
Friday, as is well known, comes after Maundy Thursday, Sermon V after no. IV,
and yet one learns in a note to no. V that the collaborating grace came here for
the *first* time to Adler's aid, after one has read the note to no. IV and after one
has read in the preface that he *knows* that the sermons from no. VI to the end
were written with Jesus' collaborating grace, which seems to suggest that he is
doubtful with regard to the notes in no. IV and V, if he did not absentmindedly
write the notes and again absentmindedly forgot that he had written them.

being asked about remains what it is but now by means of the explanation obviously becomes this. The explanation is the explicating predicate. If, however, the so-called explanation makes a change in the subject asked about, then of course it does not explain the subject asked about but introduces a new subject. If an explanation is such that it is a change, then, if confusion is not to be produced, this must definitely and decisively be expressed by acknowledging that instead of *explaining* the thing asked about one is *speaking about something else.* If what is asked about is something one has said oneself, if someone officially demands an explanation and yet the explanation is a change, then this, unless one wants to deceive or is oneself confused, must be expressed by solemnly revoking the first. If this does not happen, then, as was said, the confusion becomes a double confusion: (a) the first is allowed to stand in abeyance; (b) the second (the explanation, however, is a change of the first) has the appearance of being an explanation of the first.

The inquiry now turns to the questions the ecclesiastical superior found himself called upon to submit to Adler and also to Adler's reply.*

THE ECCLESIASTICAL SUPERIOR'S QUESTIONS

1. *Do you* (Magister Adler) *acknowledge having been in an excited and confused state of mind when you wrote and published your* Sermons *and so-called* Studies?**

The ecclesiastical superior's official letter is dated April 29, 1845; Magister Adler's reply, May 10, 1845, follows and reads: "Since I can show meaning and coherence in what I have written in my

---

*In margin: Note. The theological reader will be reminded by all of Magister Adler's quibbling, especially from question no. 2 to the end, of some modern exegete's maundering about what is to be understood by a revelation.[8] Now, of course, the exegete always has as his excuse that he himself has not been given a revelation. This is Magister Adler's merit, and in my opinion he for that very reason has far greater merit than the exegete in really making the modern manifest.

**Note. The question itself has in other respects a curious difficulty with regard to the answer. When one asks a man for a statement about whether at one time he was in a confused state of mind, there seems to be the implication

Sermons and *Studies*, I do not acknowledge having been in an excited and confused state of mind when I wrote and published them."[9] Strictly understood, this reply is not actually an answer to the question. By "meaning and coherence" one may, if anything, think only of the satisfying of the grammatical requirements that must be made of a lecture. But granted that there was more or less meaning and coherence in what was written, the author could nevertheless have been in an excited and confused state of mind. Moreover, to publish what is written is something separate, and one could, for example, calmly write something but betray an excited state by publishing it. Thus far Adler's reply is an answer to the question in neither the one sense nor the other; nor is it truthful, since not only one but many passages in *Sermons* clearly lack meaning and coherence. At best the answer can be regarded as an evasion, and therefore one still cannot say that by this answer Adler has changed the slightest in what he originally said about himself; here he is still consistent. This I count in his favor, since I continually argue only *e concessis*.

But then a little later there comes an additional answer. We shall suppress nothing that could seem to speak in Adler's favor and therefore bear in mind that when speaking of his last submission he himself declares: "In order if possible to arrive at an agreement with the authorities, I made, after a conversation with Bishop Mynster, as great an overture as possible when on July 5, I sent him the following letter."[10] In this letter, under no. 2, there is the following statement:*

---

that if he is willing to make a statement about this, willing to answer in the affirmative, then everything is all right again and the man is no longer in a confused state of mind. It is, however, conceivable that by his very willingness to go on answering in the affirmative the man perhaps would demonstrate even more obviously that he was in a confused state of mind. Suppose he answered: Oh, if nothing else is asked for, I certainly will not keep them waiting for me but with the greatest pleasure will state etc. In that case, the questioner is once again placed in the same awkward position. Generally it is very difficult to halt the dialectic that develops when one starts by assuming that a person has been in a confused state of mind; it is especially difficult to halt it by a statement from the person himself.

    In margin: Note. To be sure, it does not refer directly to the ecclesiastical superior's no. 1 but, so it seems, to no. 4, "whether Adler will admit that in his

"I acknowledge that the unusual, strange, objectionable, aphoristic, and abrupt form in which the ideas appear in many places in my *Sermons* and *Studies* may reasonably have awakened the misgivings of the high authorities."[12]

Now it comes; to be sure, Adler does not say that the authorities are right in concluding that he has been in an excited and confused state of mind, but he says that they are right in this, that in many places in his *Sermons* and *Studies* the ideas appear in an unusual, strange, objectionable, aphoristic, and abrupt form. He says further that the authorities have had reason to become dubious. Therefore Adler admits the premises, but he leaves the conclusion undecided. In the first reply he had denied the premise; in the last letter he admits the premise and he does not oppose the conclusion.* Precisely because Adler admits the premise, he must (if he does not want to support the ecclesiastical superior's assumption directly, and in that case he could of course say it directly) protect himself with all his might against the conclusion; in very definite words he must say: But nevertheless (and precisely because I have admitted the premise I must all the more firmly resist), nevertheless, I can by no means admit that I have been in an excited and confused state of mind.** It is a well-known practice of lawyers to admit the premises in this way and then by not drawing any conclusion to make it appear that the conclusion is something completely different, something that comes from an utterly different part of the world, something the

---

oft-mentioned writings there are many passages that are offensive, objectionable, or very inappropriate."[11] But if his no. 2 in the last letter is assumed to refer to the ecclesiastical superior's no. 4, then in the last letter there is no further response to the ecclesiastical superior's no. 1. But in turn this assumption is upset by the use of predicates in Adler's no. 2 that do not refer to the ecclesiastical superior's no. 4 but surely to his no. 1 (for example, "the unusual, strange, aphoristic, abrupt form"). One may therefore justly say that in Adler's no. 2 there is another reply to the ecclesiastical superior's no. 1. And perhaps all my scrupulous carefulness is wasted pains in connection with Adler's carelessness.

*Note. The conclusion is of course the content of the ecclesiastical superior's first question—ergo, have you been in an excited and confused state of mind.

**Note. That is, if Adler quite candidly admits this, then it follows *eo ipso* that he must in *optima forma* [the best form] revoke "what he in an excited and confused state of mind has written and published."

VII²
B 235
101

person concerned has at his arbitrary disposal, whether he wants
it or not, something that was separated from the premise by a
qualitative determinant. But when a premise, pregnant with the
conclusion, stoops menacingly over a person, when by his own
admission of the correctness of the premise he himself makes
the angle of inclination even greater, then he must very definitely protect himself against the conclusion, or it stands over
him and he himself has admitted it. Of course, even if he in a
definite statement defended himself against the conclusion, it
would not thereby follow that he has warded it off, since the
conclusion can sometimes be a pure formality that essentially
makes no difference. But if in this regard he does nothing at all,
he must be regarded as having lost on this point. The deceitful-
ness or thoughtlessness, that which further demonstrates his confusion, is that he allows such a reply to stand as an explanation,
that he does not comprehend the simple consequence: that he
must officially revoke his beginning—the first reply and then
Sermons and also *Studies* as written in an excited and confused
state of mind.

In the last letter there is added yet a third point, which, regarded as answer, presumably must be grouped under the ecclesiastical superior's question no. 1, which we keep in mind here.
No. 3 in the last letter reads as follows:

"that in the future, by working out and calmly developing the
ideas over a longer time,* I will see my way to have the Christian

---

Note. This hope has not been fulfilled exactly but is restated in the preface
to one of Adler's four latest books; and an alert reviewer (in *Kirketidenden*), who
is knowledgeable about what the public wants to know, has promptly pointed
out "that the author himself hopes at some time etc."[13] Since those hopeful
words in the letter of July 5, 1845, Magister Adler has written four new books,[14]
but the hope still finds its place only in the preface as a repeated hope. In this
way Adler will be able to continue to be a hopeful and promising author for a
long time. Yes, in all likelihood this hope will eventually become a standing
item in his prefaces—a kind of fixed idea that is sometimes found in authors, and
which never abandons them, not even in death. There is supposed to have been
an example of this in an author who continually wrote in the preface to each
little book he published that he hoped in the future to concentrate on a big
book, which he intended to publish soon—even in the last preface to the fragment of a little book this hope found its usual place.[15]

VII²
B 235
102

content unfold in a form more appropriate and more in accord with the specific words of Holy Scripture."[16]

With reference to Adler's hope for the future, one is involuntarily tempted to ask: But why such a hurry to get said in an inappropriate and less biblical manner that which in the future, by working out and calmly developing the ideas over a longer time, one will be able to unfold in a form more appropriate and more in accordance with the specific words of Holy Scripture? Is there any, or can there have been any reasonable basis for hurrying to do—in an inappropriate way—what one by the use of a longer time will be able to do in an appropriate way? And when, I wonder, does Magister Adler intend to begin the longer time that is needed for the calm working out? He has already written four books since then, but does he appear to have come any closer to what is appropriate?

And if it is so (as will be shown later, where Adler's reply to the ecclesiastical superior's question no. 2 is dealt with) that Adler himself authentically explains (N. B. that is, changes his first statement) that he has not had anything new to bring*—if this is so, then of course it is indeed a matter of seeing to it that the form becomes as appropriate as possible, that one uses time and patience in the working out, since there is no reason at all to hurry. Even if a person brings something new, it is still inexcusable to do it in a noisy way, but when he himself authentically acknowledges that he has nothing new to bring, then it is doubly inexcusable.

That Adler himself now authentically acknowledges (as an *explanation* of having had a revelation by which a new doctrine has been communicated to him by the Savior) that he has had nothing new to bring, we shall proceed to show by elucidating

---

*Note. That in the preface to one of the four latest books[17] he again fantasizes on the theme that "the person who has something new to bring must not allow any amalgamation with the old" must then be regarded as the new confusion Adler again has to bring. One is justified in assuming that in this preface Adler refers to himself, and one must further conclude that he nevertheless regards that first statement (which in the most solemn way passed itself off as being a revelation and thereupon was authentically explained by him as not being anything new) as something new.

VII²
B 235
102

VII²
B 235
103

VII²
B 235
104
Adler's reply to the ecclesiastical superior's question no. 2. This
no. 2 contains the main point, since here the question is raised
whether he actually has had a revelation, whether he himself
believes it, etc. Question no. 1 is of much less significance, and
actually I have dwelt on no. 1 only in order to give a foretaste of
his confusions.

> 2. *Do you perceive that it is fanatical and wrong to expect and
> to follow such presumably external revelations as, for example,
> those you described in the preface to your* Sermons?[18]

Adler's two replies, although they purport to be only explanations, are not explanations but changes that change his first statement without his feeling called upon to revoke decisively the
first. Yet there is a difference between his two replies. In the first
reply, having had a revelation by which a new doctrine is communicated to him is changed into an awakening by which he is
saved. In the second reply, having had a revelation by which a
new doctrine is communicated to him is changed into the beginning of an enthusiasm, into an expression for something as
vague and indefinite as enthusiasm. Instead of someone called by
a revelation and to whom a new doctrine is entrusted, we have
in the first case a religiously awakened person in the more ordinary sense, in the second an enthusiast of sorts. Educated as Adler
is by some Hegelian dialectic, it is not strange that he himself is
living in the delusion that these three designations (an apostle, a
religiously awakened person, an enthusiast) are more or less one
and the same, or that in explanation the one can be exchanged
for the other. But if there is something that is called qualitative
dialectic, then these designations annul each other, and the dilemma must continually be posed: if Adler wants to *acquiescere*
[hold to] the explanation, then he must revoke his first statement,
since the explanation is not an extended predicate about the first
but is a new position. Thus one can be very willing to concede
VII²
B 235
105
to Adler that he is such as one calls an enthusiast and the like, but
one cannot truly be willing to regard this conception as an explanation of what he in the preface to *Sermons* purports to be.

His first reply of May 10, 1845, reads as follows: "By my having written in the preface to my *Sermons* 'that Jesus commanded me in the future to keep to the Bible'; by my having preached him, by my having quoted the words of Scripture as proof texts, it must be obvious to which Gospel and to which revelations* I keep and have taught others to keep. But that there was a rescue in marvelous ways—as I have described in the preface to *Sermons*—is for me a fact that I cannot deny. Even if my *Sermons* and *Studies* are regarded only as a child's first babbling, lisping, imperfect voice, I nevertheless believe that the words testify that an event through which I was deeply moved by faith did occur."[20]

Now the volatilization is in full swing, and I ask the reader for patience so that I may quite slowly go about showing the uncertainty and confusion in every line—it splendidly illustrates a part of modern philosophy and dogmatics. In my opinion, going about it so precisely is not uninteresting once in a while, and in our dialectically confused times there could very well be someone who could benefit from reading this even if he is not at all interested in the matter.

So, then: "By my having written in the preface to my *Sermons* 'that Jesus commanded me in the future to keep to the Bible'; by my having preached him, by my having quoted words of Scripture as proof texts, it must be obvious to which Gospel and to which revelations I keep and have taught others to keep." But this is not at all obvious; even if one makes the greatest possible concession to Adler, there still always remains what is decisive, the main point, which he leaves out, while by his reply he seeks to *identify himself with every ordinary Christian*. That is, even if Adler keeps to the Christian revelation and the Christian Gospel, there still remains the difficulty, which is really what is being asked about, that he *by a revelation* has been ordered to keep to the revelation. An ordinary believing Christian keeps to the Christian revelation, but Adler was ordered by a revelation to

VII²
B 235
106

In margin: *Note.* Incidentally, there is something confusing in the plural Adler uses here in a connection other than that in which the ecclesiastical superior uses it; the ecclesiastical superior speaks in the plural about the fanatical revelations, and Adler speaks in the plural about the Christian revelation.[19]

keep to it. As far as that goes, it is not at all evident to which revelation he keeps, since he of course keeps first and foremost to the revelation that was granted especially to him, by which he was ordered to keep to the Christian revelation. Moreover, he himself says that Jesus commanded him in the future, but the question is not about *what* Jesus has commanded him or commanded him in the future but about Jesus' *having appeared to him and given him a command.* Even if Adler in the future became just like every ordinary believing Christian, there still always remains the decisive qualitative distinction (that which is being asked about): that by a revelation from Jesus himself he has been ordered to become like the others.* In addition, and this is the main point, Adler in his reply has left out what is especially emphasized in the preface. According to this, Jesus did not call him in the night to command him to keep to the Bible in the future. No,

VII²
B 235
107

"the Savior commanded him to get up and go in and write down these words"—that is, the whole passage that contains the new doctrine. When that was done, "Then Jesus asked him to burn his own works and in the future to keep to the Bible."[21] The ecclesiastical superior has not posed the question to Adler whether he, like other Christians, keeps to the Christian revelation and demanded his "yes" or "no" to this question. No, the ecclesiastical superior has asked whether he acknowledges that it is fanatical to keep to such revelations as, for example, the one described by him in the preface to *Sermons.* Adler replies: I keep to the Christian revelation. Indeed, even *after he himself has had a* **special** *revelation,* he wants to make it obvious that he keeps to the Christian revelation. But then he does not answer the question, or if the reply is to be regarded as such, then it also implies that he does not want to stand by the revelation described in the

*Note. It ought not to be overlooked that Adler entangles himself in a new difficulty. That is, dialectically it contains a meaningless contradiction: that someone by the paradoxical-extraordinary provision (a special revelation) should be called to become just like all the others. By a paradoxical-extraordinary call a person can be called only to become the paradoxical-extraordinary. By a revelation that entrusts a doctrine to a person, one cannot be called to become what all the others are or could be, not even to become a faithful adherent of this doctrine, but one is called to the extraordinary, to become its apostle.

preface to *Sermons,* and accordingly it must be demanded that he officially revoke the whole thing.

When Adler in the first sentence of this reply also appeals to "having preached Jesus" in order thereby to make "it obvious to which Gospel and to which revelations he keeps and has taught others to keep"—this is again not obvious from his reply. He once again leaves out what is decisive (that which is being asked about) and in his reply seeks in a volatile way to *identify himself with every ordinary believing Christian pastor.* The believing Christian pastor proclaims Christ and shows thereby to which revelations he keeps—that is correct, but the ordinary believing Christian pastor is not *called by any revelation* to proclaim Jesus. Insofar, then, as Adler as pastor proclaims Jesus, it is by no means thereby evident to which revelations *he* keeps. It would be obvious only if that preface to his *Sermons* did not exist, but that preface and the revelation described in it are precisely what was asked about by the ecclesiastical superior. The ecclesiastical superior has not asked Adler whether he, like every believing pastor, proclaims Jesus; no, the ecclesiastical superior has asked whether he acknowledges that it is fanatical to keep to revelations such as the one described in the preface to his *Sermons.* Adler replies: I proclaim Jesus. But then he is of course not answering the question, or the reply also implies the admission: I have never had any special revelation—and in that case the whole preface to *Sermons* must be officially revoked. In addition, in his reply Adler again leaves out something, and something very important, that was in the preface. There it reads: "As for the sermons and discourses from no. VI to the end, I know that they were written with Jesus' collaborating grace, so that I have been only an instrument." But no ordinary believing Christian pastor preaches this way. Ordinarily it is altogether correct that from a pastor's preaching Jesus it is obvious to which revelation he keeps, but in the special case that a pastor himself proclaims about himself that he has had a revelation and that he preaches only as an instrument—from that nothing can be concluded directly, unless what is special is taken away. Thus if Adler wants the syllogism in his reply to have force, the preface to *Sermons* is *eo ipso* revoked. But in that case it must be demanded that he officially revoke it.

VII²
B 235
108

Finally Adler says that he has quoted words of Scripture as proof texts "and from that it must be obvious to which Gospel and to which revelations he keeps." It does indeed seem to be so, since the lay and learned Christian uses Scripture as evidence and appeals to the words of Scripture as proof texts. Here, however, the difficulty is of a different kind, and one must instead ask Adler how he comes to use words of Scripture as proof texts. It is easy enough to dress up an inconsistency into a defense, but surely we should put the matter to him correctly. What can Adler want to demonstrate from Scripture? Does he want to demonstrate that in the year 1842 Jesus commanded him (Adler) to write down the words written in the preface to *Sermons*? He will hardly want that. In case these words and the doctrine they contain do not agree with the Bible, will he then conclude: Yes, then was it not Jesus who one night in December 1842 commanded me to write them down? If Adler is not more certain of his cause, should he then not have actually sounded an alarm, or should he at least have acquired a little more knowledge of Scripture than he, ac-

VII²
B 235
109

cording to his own explanation in the preface, had at that time? If, however, Adler stands firm by the position that those words in the preface are, as he has solemnly said, Jesus' own words, dictated to him (Adler) in his pen, then Adler cannot consistently appeal to words of Scripture as proof texts. In order to drive the Christians from the field, he can accommodatingly appeal to words of Scripture against them, but for himself this evidence can have no meaning. The words of Scripture, even according to the concepts of the strictest orthodoxy, are at their maximum Jesus' own words, but Adler, according to the preface to *Sermons*, also has Jesus' own words. How would he, except in the most foolish inconsistency, get the notion of wanting to demonstrate the Christianity of the words from their agreement with words of Scripture, he who after all knows from Jesus himself that they are Jesus' words.

Here we have the old issue again: if from Adler's appealing to words of Scripture as proof texts it is supposed to be obvious to which revelation he keeps, then those words in the preface to *Sermons* must go, must be revoked in the most solemn expressions of repentance. But Adler is unembarrassed; he unceremoniously argues backward: I appeal to words of Scripture as proof texts (which, note well, he can do consistently only if those words in the preface to *Sermons* do not exist)—ergo, which revelation I hold to is obvious. The ecclesiastical superior has not asked him whether he, like other Christians, appeals to words of Scripture as proof texts; but he has asked him whether he acknowledges it as fanatical to hold to such revelations as, for example, the one described in the preface. Either Adler's reply is no reply to the question or it contains the revocation of those words and the whole preface. In that case, it must be demanded that the revocation be made officially.

Thus the first sentence in his first reply to the ecclesiastical superior's no. 2 shows itself to be sophistical or thoughtless. If this is really the explanation, then, repenting, he must revoke the preface to *Sermons*, because the reply is no enlightening explanation of the first but is a change. From the reply and the explanation one does not learn what Adler understands by what he in the preface has claimed himself to be, but one learns (strangely enough by way of an explanation that is supposed to explain what was asked about earlier) what he himself now thinks about himself, almost as if that first did not exist at all.

The next sentence in his first reply to the ecclesiastical superior's no. 2 reads as follows: "But that there was a rescue in marvelous ways—as I have described in the preface to *Sermons*—is for me a fact that I cannot deny." But it certainly is not demanded that he should deny a fact. I for my lowly part am as far as possible from demanding it; I demand only that he either stand firm by what he himself has claimed himself to be or solemnly revoke what he has solemnly claimed. He does neither. He does not decisively hold fast to his first statement; he changes it, and yet he wants to give this change the appearance of being an explanation. That he does not stand firm by what he has said about himself in the preface to *Sermons* (that which was asked about by the ecclesiastical superior) is not difficult to see, because there certainly is a qualitative, decisive difference between: *having through a revelation received from the Savior an entrusted doctrine* and *being rescued in a marvelous way.* If Adler, when he wrote the preface and later the reply, had possessed the necessary Christian

VII²
B 235
110

knowledge, he naturally would have known this; but one who in
the meantime does not have any presuppositions to make firm
the essentially Christian, except for some Hegelian dialectic, can
easily make a mistake.

Let us determine a little more exactly the difference between
the two statements. When a person is said to be rescued in a
marvelous way, it is assumed that what he is saved into does exist,
indeed, has perhaps existed for a long time; but he, alas, has been
led astray, perhaps has trifled away his years in frivolity and dissi-
pations, or wasted them in confusing studies, or defiantly turned
his back upon the well-known, or harvested the sad results of a
vacillating and vapid upbringing etc. Now he is rescued in a
marvelous way; it may be in this way or that, which one can
work out more extensively or briefly in proportion to the psychological knowledge one has of such histories of religious
awakening. It is assumed to be Christianity that he has been saved
into, but he is rescued in a marvelous way. Suppose, for example,
that it happened this year; then accordingly Christianity has
lasted for eighteen hundred years. Certainly no change occurs in
it for the sake of the one saved; alas, no, but the person who has
gone astray is saved in a marvelous way into what has lasted unchanged for eighteen hundred years and in which all others are
assumed to have their lives.

It is, however, something else entirely and something qualitatively different when someone is entrusted with a doctrine by a
revelation. This doctrine certainly did not exist previously; consequently a change has taken place in that in which the salvation
is to be found. Perhaps the person called has not been, humanly
speaking, on the path of perdition at all. No, a change takes place
in the objective, and it is this that the person called is supposed to
communicate as it has been communicated to him by a revelation. The one who is called by a revelation and entrusted with a
doctrine is called to be teacher. He certainly is called for his own
sake, but principally and essentially for the sake of others (the
teleological); he is to proclaim this new doctrine. But the person
who is *rescued* in a marvelous way is not entrusted with any new
doctrine; he is not appointed to be a teacher in an extraordinary
sense or to communicate something new; he must be quiet and

VII²
B 235
111

humbly adapt himself in the old. The consciousness of being *rescued* in a marvelous way cannot tempt him to regard himself as something extraordinary, since this consciousness, continually humbling, rather reminds him that he was so far along on the path of perdition that a marvelous way was necessary in order that he could be rescued.

In this way I think I have defined the difference. Let us now look at Adler. In the preface to *Sermons*, there is no hint that Adler had been saved, that he had been *rescued*; no, in the preface Adler was the one called by a revelation, to whom a new doctrine was entrusted. Not until the reply (note well, to the question about the meaning of the preface to *Sermons*) does this explanation appear. It is, of course, no explanation of the preface; it is a totally new view, a new character in which Adler appears, as if he were beginning it just now, as if he had no precedent, he who indeed has such a precedent, about which a question is asked. If someone had passed himself off as king and now the ecclesiastical superior submitted to him the question about what he meant by VII²
B 235
112 saying something like that about himself, and he then "explained" that by it he had meant that he was counselor of chancery, then this reply is no explanation, it is a new statement—first he passes himself off as king and then as counselor of chancery. The dialectical deceit or thoughtlessness consists in not revoking the first statement but pretending that the latter is an explanation of the first.

The last sentence in Adler's first reply to the ecclesiastical superior's no. 2 reads as follows: "Even if my *Sermons* and *Studies* are regarded only as a child's first babbling, lisping, imperfect voice, I nevertheless believe that the words testify that an event through which I was deeply moved by faith did occur." Now, the *last* is a very nebulous statement: that an event occurred in which he was deeply moved by faith. The event is indeed also described precisely in the preface to *Sermons*, that there was a nasty sound that went through the room and that then the Savior commanded him to get up and write down the words. The ecclesiastical superior did not ask Adler whether an event had occurred but about the event described in detail in the preface to *Sermons*. This statement by Adler about himself, that an event

through which he was deeply moved by faith did occur, is something altogether different from what is told in the preface. There
have been many instances along this line, that a person through
coming into mortal danger, for example, has been deeply moved
by faith.[22] By any reading of tracts, one will be able to come up
with a considerable assortment of such personal records in which
it is told of a person's having been deeply moved by faith through
an event. So the explanation for having had a revelation by
which a new teaching was communicated to Adler is now supposed to be that an event occurred through which Adler was
deeply moved by faith. This can best be regarded as a reminiscence of Adler's exegetical studies, because this is the way Paul's
conversion, for example, is exegeted: something happened.
What it is one cannot say; it was an event etc.[23]

VII[2]
B 235
113

With regard to the *first* in that last sentence of the reply, it
might seem to be praiseworthy author-modesty, a compliment
to others, in connection with his first attempt to call to mind "a
child's babbling, lisping, imperfect voice"; and an esteemed, cultured public that in its lack of categories has a most cherished
preference for complimentary chatter would certainly like it if
there was nothing else in the way. But should one nevertheless
not also be able both to overdo modesty and to be modest in the
completely wrong place? When one has said of something that
it was written down according to the *Savior's* own dictation, it
really is not suitable to admit as an explanation for the same thing
that it is a child's lisping babbling. When it is said of the sermons
that they were written in such a way that the author has been
only an instrument, it is really not suitable to admit as an explanation for the same sermons that they are a child's lisping babbling.
Yes, if Adler began as a person ordinarily does, he of course must
be free in connection with his first attempt to call to mind a
child's lisping babbling; but when one begins with a revelation
and with the Savior's dictation, if one begins with being only an
instrument, then it really is not suitable. Adler seems to be so
absentminded that this author-custom of hoping sometime later
to be able to do it better comes much too *geläufig* [easily] for
him—in relation to what has been revealed to him. See, when a
person begins an undertaking in a confused and excited state, it
can be entirely in order that he hopes for a perfectibility, hopes

that he will succeed in doing it better later when he has gained calm and composure. But a man who begins with a revelation and the Savior's dictation must hope for perfectibility only in an *inessential* sense; he must rather fear that in the course of time that first will not stand before him as vividly as before; but if such a person dares to hope *essentially* for a perfectibility, then this is blasphemy. To be sure, Adler does not exactly say that he himself regards these words in the preface and sermons in this way, but how does he dare (if what is in the preface is in truth true for him) to involve himself in any such accommodation by saying, "Even if my *Sermons* and *Studies* are regarded only as a child's first babbling, lisping, imperfect voice," and to involve himself in such a way that "he nevertheless believes that the words testify that an event did occur." Consequently when his solemn statement that Jesus has commanded him to write down the words cannot gain a hearing for him, he wants to involve himself with one who does what in Adler's eyes (if what is in the preface is in truth true for him) must be the most dreadful presumptuousness—to regard it as a child's lisping babbling.

VII²
B 235
114

Or has the ecclesiastical superior given the matter this turn; has the ecclesiastical superior mistaken the point to such a degree that he has regarded the whole production as Adler's and now esthetically asked him whether he would admit that it was something imperfect? By no means, he has quite correctly argued *e concessis*. Indeed, it is on the whole inconceivable where Adler found this about "a child's lisping, babbling voice." In the preface to *Sermons* it is not at all Adler's voice that is heard; it is Jesus who is dictating something to Adler in his pen. Then Adler's reply has meaning only on the assumption that the whole preface is fiction and mental derangement; therefore Adler's first attempt, to compose a revelation, must be regarded as a child's lisping, babbling voice. And what then does one dare to hope for the future through Adler's continued effort; may one then dare to hope that the next time he composes a revelation it will be a better piece of work? But in any case the preface to the sermons must be revoked as solemnly as possible.

Adler's *hope concerning his perfectibility essentially contains the revocation of the preface and of the sermons inasmuch as it identifies both parts as his own production*. But then one must demand that he

officially revoke the first statement if in other respects he hopes
for his perfectibility, and he does hope for that. He himself declares in the second letter (of July 5) under no. 3: "that in the
future, by working out and calmly developing the ideas over
a longer time, he will see his way to have the Christian content unfold in a form more appropriate and a form more in
accord with the specific words of Holy Scripture."[24] Consequently the words, which according to Adler's own solemn
statement were written down by him according to the Savior's
dictation, have not had an entirely appropriate form. The sermons, which according to Adler's own solemn statement, were
worked out through Jesus' collaborating grace, so Adler has been
only an instrument, have not had an entirely appropriate form—
Magister Adler, however, hopes that in the future (when he perhaps is released from the revelation and Jesus' collaborating assistance) he, the Magister, will certainly be able to find a more
appropriate form. It is inconceivable that Adler has been able to
write the first and second replies to the ecclesiastical superior's
no. 2 unless he first must somehow have forgotten what was in
the preface to *Sermons*. His beautiful hope of a perfectibility is
basically the death sentence upon the preface, is basically an
affirmative answer to what the ecclesiastical superior asked him
under no. 1, whether he was not in an excited and confused state
of mind when he wrote and published his sermons.[25] Adler must
be assumed to have absentmindedly forgotten what was in the
preface to his *Sermons*; subsequently he wanted to please the authorities with the help of an amiable author-modesty that hopes
for a significant perfectibility. Perhaps one or another reminiscence of his theological studies entered in. There certainly has
been much talk about Christianity's perfectibility.[26] And Christianity is indeed also a revelation. Yet in the New Testament
there is hardly anything about its perfectibility. But sixteen or
seventeen hundred years after Christianity's entering into the
world, this perfectibility theory originated. Well, there is still
always a little excuse in the great distance and the world's considerable change since that time. But to go through a world-
historical course like this in his own lifetime: to begin with having a revelation and then two years later already to be in full

VII²
B 235
115

VII²
B 235
116

swing with perfectibility—yes, that certainly is an originality never heard of before.[27] Adler is indeed the one who has had a revelation; consequently it is he who must stand firm, even if others denied it—and then he is the one who exegetes his own revelation in the same way as a rationalistic exegesis and dogmatics have exegeted Christianity's revelation.

So it appears that Adler's first reply to the ecclesiastical superior's no. 2 question sophistically or thoughtlessly contains a shifting of his entire first standpoint; in place of his being called by a revelation and having a teaching entrusted to him, he substitutes being rescued in a marvelous way. According to his own authentic view (on the basis of which we are clearly justified to argue, although we object to it only when it is supposed to be an explanation of his first statement, since it is no explanation but an essential change, and an essential change calls for its recognizable expression in a decisive form, which is solely the revocation of the first statement): he keeps to the Bible, he preaches Jesus Christ, he appeals to words of Scripture as proof texts; in short, he is just like every other ordinary Christian, except that he is rescued in a marvelous way. *But ergo:* **he has, according to his own authentic view of himself, nothing new, no new doctrine to bring, nor has he had it**. The confusion is due only to his allowing the first statement to stand. If there is to be the least ethical meaning or earnestness in Adler's whole endeavor, he must revoke his first statement[28] and be satisfied with his last, to be like all other ordinary Christians, except that he is *rescued* in a marvelous way.

This was the first change, but that is not the end of it. With the first change, we still remain within the sphere of the religious, even though there is a qualitative, decisive difference between being rescued in a marvelous way and being entrusted with a new doctrine by a revelation.

We now go on to Adler's last letter and the reply contained in it to the ecclesiastical superior's no. 2 question. In order to do everything that can be done in favor of Adler, we shall again bear in mind that he himself regards this letter "as great an overture as was possible for him."[29]

VII²
B 235
117

His second reply reads as follows:

"I do not insist upon regarding my *Sermons* (or *Studies*) as revelations alongside or opposite to Christianity, but I regard the words written down in the preface to *Sermons* and my frequently recurring dogmatic categories as reference points that have been necessary for me in order in the beginning of the enthusiasm to set the Christian substance securely in a form."[30]

See, that did it! Alas, what good is it to burn those Hegelian manuscripts when one continues to be such a Hegelian who is so good at mediation? First Adler says that he does not insist* that they are revelations. He does not insist on it; that is, he says both yes and no;[31] that is, he brushes up the well-known line: A is certainly B, but on the other hand it nevertheless is not B. They are revelations, but he does not insist upon that, because to a certain degree they nevertheless are not revelations. They are revelations of sorts to a certain degree;[32] perhaps they are related to an actual revelation as the magistrate's moonlight is to actual moonlight.[33]

Further. He says: I do not insist upon regarding my *Sermons* (or my *Studies*) as revelations. Here in his reply Adler carries the ecclesiastical superior's question too far, inasmuch as the ecclesiastical superior had asked him only about that revelation in the preface to *Sermons*. Indeed, how would it occur to the ecclesiastical superior to ask Adler whether he regarded all of *Sermons* and *Studies* as revelations, since he himself has not said that they were.

Now comes the main point: "He regards the words written down in the preface to *Sermons* and his frequently recurring dogmatic categories as reference points that have been necessary for him in order in the beginning of the enthusiasm to be able to set the Christian substance securely in a form." Consequently he regards those words as reference points. But the ecclesiastical superior has not asked him *how* he regards those words, but how he regards Jesus' commanding him to *write down the words*. Adler

---

*The reader perhaps notices the oddity that even in his first reply he had said less, because he had changed having had a revelation, by which a doctrine was entrusted to him, to being rescued in a marvelous way. But in the last reply, in which he makes the greatest possible overture, he begins again to declare that nevertheless he has to a certain degree had a revelation.

gives it the appearance of being a learned or scholarly confer-
ence, where these words are stated, and now the discussion is
about how they are to be regarded. The ecclesiastical superior
actually asks where Adler obtained those words, what it means   VII²
B 235
119
that Jesus has dictated them to him. When one wishes only to
give an exegesis of the contents of a document, it can to that
extent be altogether unimportant whether the document is on
plain or stamped paper; but legally this distinction is sometimes
decisive. Similarly here, Adler wants to explain something about
the words—almost as if he would say: It makes no difference
whether the words are by Jesus or by me—but the ecclesiastical
superior asks specifically about this: that the words, according to
Adler's solemn statement, are Jesus' words. Therefore the reply
is not a reply to the question; what is decisive has been left out
completely, unless it is included in the reply that those words
are not revealed to him (Adler) but are his own; and in that case
it must be demanded that he officially revoke the preface to
Sermons.

Adler considers "those words *written down* in the preface"; by
this careless form he misleads everyone to believe that the discussion is about words that he (Adler) himself has written down in
the same sense as I am now writing down these words. But according to the preface it was indeed when the *Savior* at night had
commanded him to get up that he (Adler) wrote down the words
as dictated. This, of course, is certainly the qualitative difference.

Adler "regards those words written down in the preface **and**
his frequently recurring dogmatic categories as reference points."
Thus for Adler himself there is no essential difference between
those words in the preface and his dogmatic categories; for him
both are on the same level of authority—and yet those words in
the preface are the Savior's dictation, whereas the dogmatic categories are Adler's invention, which is why he quite correctly uses
the possessive pronoun in saying: *my* dogmatic categories. If in
Adler's own view the dogmatic categories and the words in the
preface are qualitatively *au niveau* [on the same level] with each
other, then it follows quite simply that he must also say: *my* words
written down in the preface. And yet these words were indeed
dictated to Adler by the Savior himself.

Adler regards the words in the preface and his dogmatic categories (thus both parts equally) "as reference points." According
to language usage, a reference point is a temporary stipulation. It
may very well happen that later the reference point [*Holdning-
spunkt*] does not prove to be altogether true, but in danger one
seizes it in a moment of impulse in order to have something to
hold on to [*holde sig til*]. When two people dispute between
themselves and confusion begins to set in, one seizes something
as a reference point, one lays this down temporarily in order to
have something to hold on to. When a person has not had time
to clarify his thoughts properly and yet wants to communicate,
he seizes a single stipulation and provisionally establishes this
firmly as the reference point. Later, when he has more time, he
examines whether the particular stipulation that must serve as a
reference point is indeed entirely true or not. With regard to
Adler's categories, it may be permissible and legitimate now to
name as reference points what later will undergo penetrating
examination, since nothing is deemed to be a hindrance to being
able to hope for their perfectibility—at least their perfection is
not a hindrance. But with regard to those words in the preface
that were written down by Adler according to the Savior's dictation, it is blasphemous of Adler to call them reference points
"that were necessary for him (Adler) in the beginning of the
enthusiasm." We should then dare to hope that Adler, when he
has calmed down after the first impulse of enthusiasm, will produce something clearer and more complete, according to his
own conception, than what was dictated by the Savior to him in
his pen. It is inconceivable that Adler has been able to write this
reply without first in a kind of absentmindedness having forgotten what was in the preface, forgotten that he has had a revelation, and regarded the words as his own.

For Adler those reference points were necessary "in the beginning of the enthusiasm." Consequently, Adler was enthusiastic
that night in December 1842 when he wrote down the words—
they were perhaps written in enthusiasm. Ordinarily one would
only with difficulty find two more different categories than
writing in a state of enthusiasm and writing according to dictation. Or (this abomination is unavoidable, because Adler has

VII²
B 235
120

worked himself into a blasphemy) was it perhaps Jesus who was in the beginning of enthusiasm that night? It is his condition, then, that actually must be asked about, since he indeed was the one who dictated.

So Adler was in a state of enthusiasm. Well, that is something quite different. If in the preface to his *Sermons*, instead of what is there, Adler had written: In an enthusiastic moment at night a light dawned on me, whereupon I got up and lit the lamp and wrote down the following words—then it would scarcely have occurred to the ecclesiastical superior to call him to account with questions. Then Adler's hope for his perfectibility would have been all right, since those words are certainly not to be considered (on the assumption that they are Adler's own words—I usually argue only *e concessis*) so perfect that they *could not* become more perfect. It seems, however, either inconceivably thoughtless and confused or brazen to offer the ecclesiastical superior such a reply, as if the discussion were about this infinitely nebulous category, enthusiasm, and about to what extent Adler has been enthusiastic, since the question is still about his having said that he had a revelation and has a doctrine according to the Savior's dictation.

The reference points were necessary for Adler in the beginning of the enthusiasm in order "to be able to set the Christian substance securely." The *Christian substance*, but there is no question at all about that, but certainly about the *new doctrine* he has received from the Savior.

Adler himself regards those words in the preface as something imperfect that is to be supplanted by something more perfect. Indeed, he says: The reference points were necessary *for him* (the purely subjective category) *in the beginning of the enthusiasm* (therefore when he was still a little confused) in order to be able to set the Christian substance securely *in a form* (the careless expression "in a form" clearly refers to the hoped-for more perfect and more suitable form, therefore in comparison with which the Savior's form was the unsuitable one). Who in all the world who reads only Adler's reply would ever think that he was speaking about the words that pursuant to his own statement were written down according to the Savior's own dictation? If the words in

VII²
B 235
121

the preface are, as Adler has said, the Savior's, then his reply is
nonsense; but if they are Adler's own words, then the preface
must most solemnly be revoked. That Adler himself has been
unable to see that this is the best evidence of his being confused.

Now, if those words in the preface, according to Adler's own
authentic view (which we protest only when it is supposed to be
the explanation of his first statement), are for him only what his
dogmatic categories are for him, if the words are reference points
for him, moreover, if these reference points were necessary for

VII²
B 235
122

him, Adler (the subjective category), only in the beginning of the
enthusiasm, if they were necessary for him only in order to set
something else securely and this something else was and is the
Christian substance—*then in this is contained Adler's own authentic
explanation that he has had nothing new, no new doctrine* to bring that
he has received through a revelation.* Any reasonable person must of
course believe that the new, the new doctrine, was contained in
the words in the preface, which are the Savior's dictation—but
see, for Adler the words in the preface are merely reference
points that were necessary in the beginning of the enthusiasm.**
The other points in the ecclesiastical authority's letter are less

*Note. I have already pointed out in a note[34]—and here in the right place will
do it again in order to give the reader the impression of contemporaneity—that
Adler, as was to be expected, again begins anew. In the preface to one of his four
latest books, he discusses particularly how "the person who has something new
to bring must prevent any amalgamation with the old." So Adler has indeed had
something new to bring. In this latest book, however, he has, so it seems,
chosen the least troublesome of all the categories, that is, he is something of a
genius and the like.[35]

***In margin: Note. The one who has done some reading in certain modern theology
and exegesis and therefore knows something about how Holy Scripture has been treated
as the immediate,[36] the first expression of enthusiasm, the perfectibility of which is to be*

VII²
B 235
123

*hoped for, etc., and yet it is called a revelation, will continually be reminded of this in
Adler's whole argumentation.* But what is unparalleled in Magister Adler is that he
is also the one who himself has had the revelation that he explains in this way!
One does not detect such a striking contradiction in modern exegesis and dogmatics, since only the one party always appears, and one never has the opportunity to hear Paul protest, he who certainly had had a revelation. But Magister
Adler appears one for both and both for one: he is himself the one who has had
the revelation and is also the exegete! But for that very reason Magister Adler
so splendidly manifests what the modern is.[37]

important; but now to the end of the story. Then on September 13, 1845, followed Adler's dismissal. It might seem to come strangely, almost somewhat unmotivated, by coming right after such compliant and important concessions on Adler's part. It might seem so, but if one takes adequate time one will surely say more correctly that it comes motivated precisely by the concessions, because the importance of the concessions, if they do not contain a formal and solemn revocation of the first statement, makes his dismissal unavoidable. That he, despite such concessions, still labors under the delusion that he is standing firm by his first statement makes it very evident that he is confused, that he has no idea at all of what he is saying about himself.[38] If Adler taciturnly and without dialectically yielding a hair's breadth had stood rigidly by his revelation-fact, the matter would have been much more difficult for the state Church, which would almost have to pass judgment in the case—whether a man in our day can be justified when he passes himself off as having had a revelation. But precisely here is the profundity in Bishop Mynster's attitude in this matter, that he has helped Adler by means of some concessions to establish further that he is confused, and thereby in turn to necessitate his dismissal, inasmuch as the concept flips over,[39] as Hegel says, and the concession demonstrates precisely the confusion.

VII²
B 235
124

Thus from the entire affair with Adler, from his dismissal, there is no result for the state Church or for anyone, layman or teacher, in the state Church. Never in all eternity can Adler's dismissal become a precedent, inasmuch as Adler was not dismissed because he has claimed to have had a revelation but because by means of his concessions he has further substantiated that he is confused. In the way he at the beginning announced that he had had a revelation, in all of his initial conduct, there was something that was bound to prompt a supposition that he was excited and in a confused state of mind. Yet he was not dismissed; no, he was suspended,[40] which was natural so that more detailed information could be obtained from him. Now Adler comes out with concessions and details, and precisely these make it evident that he is confused—with the aid of the concessions he convicts himself, and the state Church does not get a chance

VII²
B 235
125 either to act or to judge in the case that a teacher in the state Church has claimed to have had a revelation.

No Christian, and thus no Christian ecclesiastical superior either, can be willing to allow the syllogism: a man has claimed to have had a revelation in which the Savior has communicated this and that to him—ergo, the man is mentally deranged. If the state Church ever allows this conclusion, it has destroyed itself. That is, if one must conclude that the man is in a confused state of mind, then one must demonstrate it by something else, or by the way he himself speaks of having had a revelation. But this procedure is exactly what is used in the Adler affair.[41] No believer will then be brought into tense uneasiness by the thought of a teacher's being declared to be in a confused state of mind and dismissed because he claimed to have had a revelation, [42]inasmuch as Adler was not dismissed *for that reason*, and neither has a conclusion to his confused state of mind been drawn directly from that statement. No enemy of the state Church will have this charge to throw in its face, that the Church, which itself is built upon a revelation, has dismissed a teacher as being in a confused state of mind because he claimed to have had a revelation; since Adler was not dismissed *for that reason*, neither has a conclusion to the confused state of mind been drawn *directly* from that statement. Adler's case has been handled as correctly as possible. It was above all important that the accent of the dismissal fell at the right place—right after the concessions—and next, that the affair had no tail, and therefore its decision could not become a precedent. This cannot possibly happen, because in the premise for the conclusion there is not a more universal definition. At the basis of the verdict, there is a conception of what it means to be in an

VII²
B 235
126 excited and confused state of mind; by finding this conception applicable to Adler, it has been concluded that he was in this state, but nothing more universal was established from which any conclusion is to be drawn as a matter of course for the future.

Bearing in mind the content of Chapter I, let us think of the circumstances of the affair in a different way in order to elucidate it once more. Suppose a teacher in the state Church proclaimed that he had had a revelation through which the Savior had communicated something to him; suppose that even under the most penetrating scrutiny not the slightest indication could be discovered that he was in an excited and confused state of mind—what then? Well, then in all eternity it will not do as a matter of course to conclude from his statement: ergo, he is in a confused state of mind. I certainly think, however, that it is quite simple, that in the capacity of the established order and resting on an altogether definite historical past revelation, the state Church is justified in dismissing him. The special extraordinary with a revelation-fact must step out of the ranks. The state Church is justified in dismissing him without pension and without becoming involved in all the many ludicrous considerations that, together with the worthiness of an apostle, of a reformer, are reserved for the philistinism of our day in being able to think that such a person, in addition to being an apostle and a reformer, may also see to it that he gets a good appointment, and in any case a pension. The state Church is justified in dismissing him; yet I think that it will never be in the situation of really having to do that in earnest, because the true extraordinary will himself take the step, will himself, perceiving the necessity of being properly situated, resign. As stated, it is nonsense that an apostle wants to be a teacher in an established state Church; anyone who has a conception of qualitative dialectic will easily perceive this.

From this point of view, one will again see the incidental particularity of Adler's dismissal, on the sole basis of which Adler has been dismissed. He has not been dismissed because he has claimed to have had a revelation—no. Neither has he been declared to be in a confused state of mind because he has claimed to have had a revelation—no. But he was suspended because there were, from various indications, misgivings about his state of mind. From his replies and concessions it became additionally clear that he was in a confused state of mind; for that reason he was dismissed. Thus it was both perspicacious and entirely in order that the ecclesiastical superior arranged the questions to Adler in such a way that in no. 1 he is asked whether he acknowledges that he was in an excited and confused state of mind when he wrote and published his *Sermons* and *Studies*, and only after that asks in no. 2 whether he acknowledges that it is fanatical to hold to such revelations as, for example, the one described in the

VII²
B 235
127

preface to his *Sermons*. This shows, namely, that the ecclesiastical superior bases the circumstantial evidence for Adler's confused state of mind on something other than this statement about having had a revelation.

§2[43]

ADLER'S FOUR LATEST BOOKS*

The Procedure in the Inquiry

Let us make the task of the inquiry very clear. We have before us a man who has claimed to have had a revelation from the Savior, in which a doctrine was entrusted to him. It has now been shown in § 1 that he does not understand himself, is not in agreement with himself, that he neither has a firm and qualitatively unshaken concept of what a revelation is nor does he stand unshakably firm by his assertion.

Now, if in addition this man wants to be an author, what may one then expect and be justified to ask of him? Presumably, before he writes about anything else, one may ask that he will disclose whether in the meantime he has earnestly made clear to himself what Christianly must be understood by a revelation and then how he now understands himself in his first statement about himself, whether he will revoke it or solemnly stand by it again, and then step forth accordingly.

A. The Contents of the Books—That They Contain Nothing at All of the Matter in Question

The contents of the books are in other respects absolutely unimportant to this inquiry if it is so that they contain nothing for the elucidation of that revelation-fact or for the elucidation of the statement concerning it.

This is now precisely the case. *There is not the least thing about this in Adler's four latest books; his first statement is as if forgotten.* If

*Note. Studier og Exempler; Forsøg til en kort systematisk Fremstilling af Christendommen i dens Logik; Theologiske Studier; Nogle Digte [Studies and Examples; An Attempt at a Short Systematic Exposition of the Logic of Christianity; Theological Studies; Some Poems].

one were to characterize him as author, one must say *he is a private, confused lyrical genius* who casually exegetes incidental Bible verses "accordingly as these appeal to him."

He does indeed recur, both jargonizing and exegeting, frequently enough to that doctrine communicated to him by the revelation, but it is treated entirely as if it were his own doctrine; *it is never mentioned that it was communicated to him by a revelation; he does not deduce from that its divine truth, nor does he claim for himself the divine authority due him* (if we argue *e concessis*). Moreover, he has now acquired a new jargon, which he has never claimed was communicated to him by a revelation; and this jargon in every way enjoys the same honor, namely, to appear in demented repetition to the *n*th power.*

> B. *What Must Now Be Concluded Since the Four Books*   VIII²
> *Contain Nothing at All about That Revelation-Fact*   B 7:7
> *and Have No Relation to It.*   24

The Procedure in the Inquiry

The reader will easily see that the issue is about *Adler's self-identity*, whether he is in identity with himself, whether being an apostle (called by a revelation and entrusted with a doctrine) is thus identical with being a private, confused lyrical genius, whether the transition is so insignificant that the very same man can let the first statement stand as nothing and become the latest as a matter of course. Now if there had been no intrinsic irregularities in Adler's first statement, then the demand would certainly be that he revoke his latest, but since there is an intrinsic irregularity in his first statement, there is a greater probability that after all he has always been what he has now become, a private,

---

*Note. It may be observed as a curiosity that the new jargon has acquired dramatic form. It is a conversation between God and Christ before the foundation of the world was laid. Indeed, Adler is so accurately informed that he even mimically reinforces the dialogue by telling that when they had come to an agreement, God ("proud of his equal") said to Christ: Now you are my son; today I gave you birth.** When one consorts with God and Christ in this manner, it is not so strange that one can fancy having had a revelation.

**(See *Forsøg til en kort systematisk Fremstilling af Christendommen*, p. 3, note.)

VIII²
B 7:7
24

confused lyrical genius, and in that case needs only to revoke his first statement about having had a revelation. Since Adler's four latest books contain nothing at all about that revelation-fact of his or about the statement concerning it, since he on the contrary has summarily become a private lyrically confused genius, the conclusion is quite simply this: ergo Adler is confused. We will not, however, take the matter quite so simply but seek by way of a few more specific conclusions to clarify Adler's confusion in each instance and thereby elucidate some dogmatic concepts.

Conclusions

a. *That in absentmindedness Adler must have completely forgotten that he has had a revelation*—but then he is indeed confused.

Such absentmindedness is then practically identical with confusion; that a man can forget his cane somewhere in the city is an innocent matter; that a man forgets his name or perhaps even that he is married and goes ahead and becomes engaged is bad enough; but to forget that one has had a revelation—that is a kind of blasphemy. If a man is called by a revelation, then he is one who is called by a revelation as long as he lives, unless he revokes his first statement. If through a revelation a man has received a doctrine, then as long as he lives he is obligated to argue on the basis of it if he does not solemnly revoke his first statement. There is something shocking, at least to me, in just imagining that a person could be so absentminded or so light-minded that he could forget having had a revelation or, if he himself doubts the correctness of his statement, could forget to revoke it. And yet in the four latest books Adler has inverted the relation. As if that doctrine were his own discovery, he seeks to recommend and interpret it instead of arguing inversely: it has been revealed to me; it has been written down by me according to the Savior's own dictation—ergo.

b. *Or that Adler must be assumed to be of the opinion that the absolute qualitative transition into the world of spirit can be made as a matter of course*—but if that is his opinion, then he is indeed confused.

VIII²
B 7:7
25

In civil matters, on the whole in the world of the finite, it can very well happen that a man begins all over again even more than once and without any fuss lets the past be forgotten, that a man can change his profession, tries his luck in a new career, and without any fuss lets the past be bygone and forgotten. But if a man thinks that this can be done in the world of spirit, this opinion is enough to demonstrate that he is confused. In the world of the finite, the randomness of the changes may be all right; it may be true as the proverb says: *variatio delectat* [change delights], but in the world of spirit continuity is not only a joy but is spirit itself—that is, continuity is spirit, and not to respect continuity qualitatively is to have one's life outside the sphere of spirit, either in the sphere of worldliness or in the sphere of confusion. Continuity is not sameness, in continuity there is also change, but the continuity is that every change is made dialectically in relation to the preceding. When the change is qualitative (as the change from apostle to genius, from the paradoxical-religious sphere to that of immanence, from existing paradoxically on divine responsibility to privatizing as a genius), continuity's final expression, since the change is consciously reflected in the continuity, is the revocation of the first, which in turn, insofar as one has communicated the first, is required to be communicated officially. In the world of spirit, fabulousness is confusion, and equally so the absentmindedness that does not notice that the change is qualitative. To the same degree to which one has ventured further, even to claiming to have had a revelation, to the same degree the fabulousness and absentmindedness are more dubious. But the metamorphosis from apostle to becoming a genius is so decisive, so qualitative, and in addition so reversed that least of all in the world can it be ignored or treated as if it were nothing.

c. *Or that Adler must be assumed to be of the opinion that to be a genius of sorts is a further development, in a forward direction, of being an apostle.* —But if he is of that opinion, then he is indeed confused.

Now, if Adler's opinion is in truth as it is assumed to be, then he certainly should not only not be censured because he has not revoked his first statement but should be praised because he has

VIII²
B 7:7
26

not stopped with being an apostle but has gone further—and has become a private genius.

Presumably Adler (the Hegelian, later the apostle) perhaps finds himself, together with his revealed doctrine, in a new stage, and now he has stepped out of the immediate (as a *revelation* is termed in the Hegelian *veiled* language) into reflection and now understands the revelation, and does not stop with—the revelation he himself has had. See, when Christianity entered into the world, it proclaimed itself to be a revelation and has steadily maintained this. But then time passed, and gradually all became Christians of sorts, and many centuries later there lives a generation in geographical Christendom that, with the aid of some geniuses who went further than the apostles, thinks it is going further by understanding and comprehending the revelation. Consequently the same revealed doctrine comes to be treated by entirely different people, by a generation that is many centuries removed from that first one. The distance encourages confusion. One cannot get hold of the apostles and place them personally in confrontation with scholarship that goes further and comprehends the revelation, or rather in all cunning comprehends that it really was not a revelation. Scholarship, encouraged by the distance, has taken on a double role; it psychologically weakens the impression of the apostles' statement and then comprehends the revelation; and then when scholarship has finished, it is not so easy to comprehend what it actually has done: has it cunningly tricked the apostles' statement about its being a revelation out of its trustworthiness, and then comprehended the revelation, or has it first believingly accepted the apostles' statement—and then comprehended the revelation?

But here we fortunately have before us a man who has announced that he has had a revelation; here there can be confrontation at any moment. Should it then also be all right to go further by becoming a genius? The man who himself has had a revelation must certainly know what is what with regard to the revelation that was granted him: he must *either* stand firm by it, that it was and is and remains a revelation, and in that case speak and act and write in conformity with it, *or* he must say

VIII²
B 7:7
27

that he has now understood and comprehended it. But a little caution! What, indeed, can he have understood? Has he understood that it was no revelation? Then of course he must revoke his first statement. After all, he certainly is not a third party in relation to himself, as scholarship is in relation to the apostles, who, if scholarship should succeed in demonstrating that they had had no revelation, would be the ones from whom a revocation would have to be required. Or if he has better understood that it was a revelation, then he must indeed stand by it, argue on the basis of it, act in accordance with it, transform his whole existence in relation to it. On the other hand, he may not, by going further, cast away a revelation as a thief casts away stolen goods when the police are after him—because in that case he is a deliberate deceiver, which Adler certainly is not. But neither may he let this matter of the revelation lie in abeyance unexplained, while he, acting as if nothing had happened, goes further—along an entirely different road—because in that case he is confused.

d. *Or that Adler must be assumed to be of the opinion that being a kind of apostle is almost identical with being a kind of genius.*—But if he is of that opinion, then he is indeed confused.

Now, if the opinion is the truth, then that which otherwise is confusion would be quite all right, that a man begins with being an apostle and then summarily supplies a sequel in which he becomes a kind of genius, inasmuch as when the definitions are identical, there is of course a connection between the first statement and the latest and there is good sense in the connection. But suppose the relation is different! Honor be to the genius; if Adler actually is such a one, well, I certainly will not begrudge him that or enviously disparage this merit. But to begin with having had a revelation, if then the *summarum* is that this is to be understood as meaning that he is a kind of genius, then perhaps the first statement must be somewhat like what is called an audacious expression for being a genius—indeed, it certainly is a hitherto unheard-of confusedness and confusion. The qualification "genius" is certainly completely other than and qualitatively dif-

VIII²
B 7:7
28

ferent from being called by the Savior through a revelation and
having received a doctrine from him. To have, if you please,
something new to bring by virtue of being a genius certainly is
(as lying within the sphere of immanence the newness consequently can indicate only the primitivity of the reproduction)
something other than and qualitatively different from having received a doctrine from the Savior through a revelation. We speak
of the primitivity of genius, of its originality, but surely these
qualifications are still not identical with having had a revelation!

Yet nowadays such confusion prevails in the conception of the
different spheres that there undoubtedly are many who basically
posit such an identity between an apostle and a genius, even if
they shudder to say it directly. Therefore it will not be out of the
way accurately and categorically to define these concepts in relation to each other, and it will be in line with this inquiry to do
that, because if Adler had a moral respect for qualitative definitions of concepts, if he was not as a Hegelian lacking in ethics
and ethical education, it would never occur to him to let stand in
abeyance his first statement about himself and then to be a kind
of lyrical genius. Yet with regard to this inquiry reference is
made to Addendum II; here just what pertains to Magister Adler
is sufficient.

Authority is the qualitative difference between a genius and an
apostle. Let us now consider Magister Adler. According to his
own solemn statement, through a revelation he has received a
doctrine from the Savior and is himself called through a revelation. Thus as a consequence it must be required of him that he
use authority, speak, act, write with authority. Let us consider
the situation. A man has heard Magister Adler's statement; so this
one sits and waits for Magister Adler to step forward now with
authority, since whether we others are willing to bow under it is
of course our own affair. But what does Magister Adler do instead of this? Indeed, instead of what he is doing he could almost
just as well take off to Deer Park. He forgets the whole story and
settles down in idyllic coziness out in the country and exegetes
some Bible verses "accordingly as these appeal to him"; just like
an *Otiosus* [idler], he makes ever new attempts at being brilliant;

VIII²
B 9:8
49

VIII²
B 9:9
49

just like a loafer he sits and keeps a literary pub for brilliant remarks. What the person called by a revelation usually impresses
repeatedly upon others, that the doctrine has been revealed to
him, Magister Adler has completely forgotten in absentmindedness, and a critic must remind him of it. But here, if ever at all,
the point certainly is either/or, either he must step forward in the
character of the first statement, or he must revoke it; *tertium non
datur* [there is no third]. But no, this *tertium* is already given: the
man is confused.

*The genius has only an immanent teleology; the apostle is absolutely
paradoxically positioned teleologically.* Let us now consider Adler.
He begins with being called by a revelation (therefore positioned   VIII²
absolutely teleologically) and as a sequel summarily proceeds to   B 7:10
produce four books, in which he attempts to define himself hu-   29
moristically, completely without a teleological relation to anyone, as a lyrical poet, who has no more to do with the reader than
the nightingale with the listener;[44] in short, he defines himself   VIII²
entirely *à la* one or another of the pseudonymous authors.[45] As   B 7:10
well as he has been able to do it, his four latest books are kept in   30
the mode of silence. Silence here means the humorous revocation of the teleological relation. It is this silence that essentially
characterizes several of the pseudonymous writers, and accordingly they are named: Johannes de Silentio, Frater Taciturnus.
From Adler one even learns "that silence is genius." Silence is a
qualification in form; for that matter, mathematics can be written
in the mode of silence. As soon as the production is made into a
Selbstzweck [an end in itself], the production is in the mode of
silence. Thus if Archimedes sat and drew his circles[46] in order to   VIII²
help the besieged city, he was not a humorist, but if he drew   B 7:10
circles for the sake of the production itself, then his production   31
was in the mode of silence.

Consequently: Adler's sequel to being an apostle is to be a
private lyrical genius. Should this also be legitimate? Here if ever
the point is: either/or, *either* he has, himself called by a revelation,
received a doctrine and then must conform the character of his
existence to it, or . . . . . *tertium non datur* [there is no third]; but
no, it is perhaps already given: the man is confused.

Appendix to Chapter III[47]

The reader will recall that continually throughout this whole book the argumentation is only *e concessis*. It is nowhere directly denied that Adler has had a revelation; on the contrary, it is assumed, since he himself says it, and likewise everything that he says is assumed; but the self-contradiction is thereby again made apparent.

§ 1. In order to illustrate the presence of confusion, Adler's replies to the ecclesiastical superior's questions are utilized. The dilemma may be stated here as follows: *either* all his separate replies are nonsense, *or* in themselves they tacitly contain essentially the revocation of his first statement. If the latter is assumed, then the confusion is this, that he is not in earnest about the revocation but acts as if nothing had happened, or he himself notices nothing, lets the replies have meaning and reality, which they have only insofar as they are the revocation of the first statement.

The argumentation within the dilemma was this. In the replies Adler identifies himself in such a way with what was printed first (the preface to *Sermons, Sermons, Studies*) that in the common and ordinary sense he must be regarded as the author of them—but if he is the author, then the doctrine is indeed not revealed, then he indeed has not written it down according to Christ's dictation, then he has not been only an instrument. —Adler authentically acknowledges that he does not have anything new; on the contrary, like every other ordinary Christian he keeps to Scripture, proclaims Jesus, appeals to the words of Scripture as proof texts for what he says—but in that case all the first statement about the revelation is essentially revoked. —Adler hopes that later he will be able to present the doctrine (*what was revealed* and *dictated to him by the Savior*) better; consequently he hopes for the perfectibility of the doctrine. But this hope is altogether meaningless, yes, blasphemous, if that doctrine is not Adler's own; and if it is his own, then of course he has had no revelation through which the doctrine was communicated to him by the Savior.

§ 2. Next, in order to illustrate that the confusion is present, consideration is given to Adler's four latest books. Instead of what one would be justified in expecting if Adler did not continue to be in a confused state, instead of the fruit of composure—*either* information about how he understood himself in the extraordinary that had happened to him *or* revocation—one finds that he, literally occupied with all kinds of things, has settled down and has established himself as a private lyrical genius. That he is a genius can readily be granted to him, especially here, where we have nothing whatever to do with such things. But as soon as his four latest books are compared, in the sense of earnestness and with regard to identity, with his first statement, the dilemma appears: *either* the four latest books, even if their incidental content were most excellent, *considered as books by Adler*, that is, *considered totally*, are to be regarded as nonsense, *or* there is also tacitly contained in them essentially the revocation of his entire first statement. If the latter is assumed, then the confusion consists in this, that Adler acts as if nothing has happened or notices nothing and is not in earnest about the revocation.

VIII²
B 7:11
32

If, then, in the future there is to be earnestness and meaning in Adler's life, he must *either* revoke his first statement and be content with what he actually is in his four latest books if these are considered without relation to his first statement, *or* he must cancel his latest statements as a defection from his idea and his call, and then solemnly acknowledge, something he by the bungling of his replies has confused, that he has had a revelation and has received from the Savior a new doctrine, and then act, speak, and write in the capacity of being such a person. His first statement is indeed such that if all sophists joined together they would not be able to find an escape, unless the Hegelians would be the judges. If, however, he continues, if he leaves both parts in abeyance, he demonstrates thereby that he is in a confused state of mind.

By this it is in no way to be understood that he is what in daily talk is called insane; no, by this it is to be understood that he, lacking education in Christian concepts, lacking moral respect for qualitative definitions of concepts, is to such a degree not master of himself and his thoughts that he can even bona fide be blasphemous. This is certainly something different from what A. himself speaks about, that as an author he has suffered damage in the form, which he, instead of changing, *theoretically* finds quite in order, just as when he, instead of ceasing to pilfer, theoretically makes out that thievery in the world of spirit is entirely permissible.

A Psychological View of Adler as a Phenomenon and as a Satire on Hegelian Philosophy and the Present Age

§ 1

PSYCHOLOGICAL EXPOSITION

The purpose of this section is to prepare for the crisis, to provide some presuppositions by which the crisis in Adler's life *could* be made psychologically understandable. It would undeniably be both a more interesting and a more gratifying work to dare to operate purely poetically with only the assistance of possibility, because even the most copious actuality never has the pure ideality of possibility but always has something accidental in it. But to poetize in this way is, of course, not suitable here, since it is a contemporary whose life is being discussed here, and therefore poetic license here would become something else, would become an attributing of something to a man. Yet what it loses in poetical ideality, because Magister Adler is not a poetical character and cannot have the pure transparency of a poetical character, is regained in another way; because by his being an actual person the satire becomes more emphatic than if a poet had created such a character.

The psychological exposition is then limited by the actuality, which always contains an element of the accidental. Even the understanding and explanation of his life that Adler can have in his innermost being will contain something accidental, because no actual human being is pure ideality; thus a particular episode in his life will always have an accidental *lack* or an accidental *superfluity*. And out of deference to actuality the psychological exposition that can be given here is in yet another sense limited by actuality. Thus it is conceivable that someone who knew

Adler's life intimately, someone who had his confidence, could
know about something (a life impression, an event, an experience, etc.) that, considered as presupposition, would merit attention to the highest degree, but which the person who knew
about it could in no way be justified in sharing with others, not
to mention making it public in print. Therefore the inquiry must
stay within more general qualifications, have a more universal
character, at most utilize the particular clues Adler himself may
have provided. The art is to join these universal qualifications in
such a way that psychologically something still results from it. In
this way the inquiry can in no way infringe upon Magister Adler,
since essentially it utilizes only the wholly universal, which is
contained more universally in the presuppositions of the entire
age, while on the other hand it completely renounces any private
view of Magister Adler, for which I have no data at all. As a
consequence of this, Magister Adler, without being guilty of an
untruth, will be perfectly justified to say that this view is not true,
inasmuch as he then especially emphasizes what *he* alone can
know. On the other hand, a reader may even find the view very
true, because he can understand Adler only more universally.

On the whole, one person can never understand another person altogether privately. Every third party (and that, after all, is
what one person always is in relation to another) always understands the communication somewhat more universally. Nor may
one person require more of another, and every mature individuality will be in possession of the necessary resignation in this regard in order to be able to live in association with others. Ostensibly it is an imperfection in earthly life that basically a person
cannot entirely, cannot thoroughly make himself understandable
to others; on closer inspection one will surely be convinced that
it is a perfection, since it suggests that every individual is religiously structured and is to strive to understand himself in confi-
dentiality with God. Most people probably do not notice either
this imperfection or that it is a perfection. The multitude, the
crowd, all agree, so they think, in thousands; they understand
one another entirely in thousands. The better philosophers,
however, know that there have never lived two persons who
have completely understood each other. But of course the less

VII²
B 235
178

time and self-mastery and perseverance a person has for wanting to understand himself, the more bustling loquacity he has or, more correctly, the more he is in possession of bustling loquacity or, more correctly, is in the service of bustling loquacity—the more easily it goes with understanding all the others and with being understood by all the others.

We imagine, then, a theological graduate who has successfully passed his final university examination with the best grade. He is more than ordinarily gifted, not without talents; he may be assumed, in the esthetic sense, to have lived so much that existence will sometime be able to take notice of him in a decisive way. It must, however, be said that right up to this moment he has not come, either as a child or as a youth or as a theological student, in any decisive contact with Christianity, even less with the earnest question of whether he himself is a Christian. In this regard he must be assumed to have continued to live, as so many do, in the commercial language's current definitions of being a Christian: to be baptized, confirmed, to have identified himself as a Christian when he matriculated at the university etc., to have gained a *quantum satis* [sufficient amount] of theological information, to have become a graduate.

So he is a theological graduate, but being superbly gifted he of course cannot terminate his studies with a final examination. On the contrary, he only now really begins to study, and of course the study of Hegelian philosophy, a philosophy that, supported by omnipotent opinion, presumably stands at the peak of all scholarliness, outside of which there is no salvation, nothing but darkness and obtusity. With enthusiasm for philosophy's hero, gladly following the motto: "You lack everything; study Hegel and you have everything," enchanted by the hope of gaining everything, in all likelihood thanking the gods in Greek style[2] for being contemporary with the highest development of the human race—he begins his study. He does not possess one single qualification that could make him inwardly aware that this philosophy completely confuses Christianity; there is no deeper religious life in him that might hold him back from entering into this philosophy. In a religious sense, he lacks the full marching equipment of orthodoxy and of a deeper religious impression; he is

VII[2]
B 235
179

lightly armed, and thus it is all too natural and easy for him to
understand carelessly what Hegel has carelessly taught, that his
philosophy was the highest development of Christianity.[3] Indeed, religiously he is even so lightly armed that this question
does not occur to him at all.

So, then, he studies, and, although carried away by the age, he
does with zeal and interest what many a conceited person does
carelessly and only in order to be in fashion; he even delivers
lectures at the university on this philosophy[4] and publishes a
popular account of Hegel's objective logic.[5] To be *au fait* [at
home] with the world-view that one's contemporaries admire is
always pleasant. When in addition one in a purely personal way
finds rest in and has recourse to it, then one's existence, spiritually understood, is secure. A person becomes conscious that
he completely belongs in the age in which he lives, and he dares
to claim to have his place among the more prominent. Here
there is no delay before the individual understands himself within
the thought-world of the age, no despondency, no hazardous
and painful oral examination of subjectivity; one swiftly goes
along and is thereupon carried by the age in order, in the age and
with the age, to strive further, everything *uno tenore* [without
interruption].

Magister Adler is now at the age when one usually feels a need
to finish one's apprenticeship in order then to teach others. Usually at this age, which is the crucial age of maturity, there comes
a need to make up one's mind about one's own life. Before making the transition and going further in life, a person once again
turns back to his earliest recollections, to the unforgettable impressions of his upbringing. He examines how he now relates
himself to what he at that time understood and appropriated in
a childlike way. He examines whether he is in harmony with
himself, whether and to what extent he understands himself in
understanding what he learned first, and his concern is that his
life in a deeper sense might be a personal life in essential coherence with itself. Someone or other stands here at the cross-
roads: whether he will let go of what he learned first, chop down
the bridge, and hold to what he learned later, or whether he will
go back to his childhood and learn in reverse, because as a child

he learned from adults, and now he himself as an adult is to learn
from a child, learn from his childhood. If it had been the case
with Adler that he, in turning back to himself in this way, en-
countered some essential Christian recollection, some decisive
impression of the essentially Christian, then the matter would
have become different and in time something more earnest. But
his life-development was such that it was quite natural that he
reached his high point in becoming a Hegelian, in exactly the
same sense as Hegelian philosophy was humankind's highest
development. Magister Adler could have no misgiving in assuming that Hegelian philosophy thereby in turn was the culmination of Christianity; it was indeed self-evident, and also in turn
that he as a Hegelian was an extraordinarily developed and cultured Christian, superbly suited to teach the Hegelian philosophy, and therefore also Christianity, since these categories were
identical.

Magister Adler then seeks an appointment, not as professor of
philosophy or of Hegelian philosophy, for which he *also* had
qualified himself, but as a pastor, as a teacher of the Christian
religion, for which he *also* had qualified himself—through the
study of Hegelian philosophy. And he receives a call. On the
strength of having passed the final university examination with
the highest grade, on the strength of his more general education,
on the strength of his capacities, he hopes to be equal to the task.
On the strength of his rather exceptional acquaintance with Hegelian philosophy, he presumably even hopes to become an unusually competent pastor. This is not at all immodest, by no
means. If it is true that Hegelian philosophy is the highest development of Christianity, then it is *eo ipso* an advantage for a pastor
to know this philosophy intimately. —Not, then, in the way a
man ordinarily, at least sometimes, begins his activity as a pastor,
after rejuvenating himself, in the earnestness of making up his
mind, through his childhood's impression of the essentially
Christian, in harmony with a strict Christian upbringing, with
the Bible in hand; no, on the strength of a graduate degree, with
Hegel's eighteen elegantly bound volumes,[6] and hoping that
there will be abundant leisure for further studies of and for new
books about Hegel— Magister Adler becomes a pastor.

He does not become a pastor in the capital city—it is not inconceivable that someone could succeed in slipping through, indeed, in going proudly through life as a pastor, as a Christian pastor—in Hegelian categories. Magister Adler becomes a rural pastor and thus is brought essentially into contact and into a responsible relation with simple, ordinary people who, lacking acquaintance with Hegel, as the case may still be out in the country, have an earnest even though meager Christian education, so that they, ignorant of every volatilization, believe simply in the essentially Christian and have it with them as something present. Simple, believing people do not associate with the essentially Christian in such a way that they have it historically at a distance of eighteen hundred years, and even less do they have it imaginatively at a mythical distance.

Magister Adler becomes a rural pastor and comes to live in rural remoteness. The conception he himself has of Hegelian philosophy, perhaps also the conception of himself that this philosophy can give him, makes it probable that Magister Adler will scarcely find anyone among his colleagues or his other acquaintances with whom he really is able or wants to associate intimately. Consequently Magister Adler comes to live completely isolated with his Hegelian philosophy, which is perhaps more suitable for the capital cities. So it must be; if the conditions are to be tightened for a crisis, the person involved must first of all be isolated and kept in isolation or keep himself in isolation.

On the other hand, it is altogether improbable that Magister Adler would rusticate; he is too gifted for that. And he is too much occupied intellectually to become a "L'Hombre[7] pastor" or to accomplish the anti-apostolic climax, as indeed sometimes happens—that is, the apostles are called from fishing to catch human beings;[8] a man is appointed as a pastor to catch human beings and ends up fishing, hunting, etc.

The situation is now established: a man who is entirely occupied with Hegelian philosophy becomes a rural pastor, lives in rural remoteness and in the intellectual sense in perfect isolation. If one considers the situation purely esthetically, it is so humorous that it could be used splendidly in a sequel to *Gulliver's Travels*,[9] because in the intellectual sense the misrelation of the situa-

tion is exactly as painfully wrong as the more physical one that
Swift describes. A *purus putus* [dyed-in-the-wool] Hegelian essentially has nothing in common with simple people; in the intellectual sense he must logically say of them what a nobleman by
birth once said of the middle class: They are not born—that is,
they do not exist, they are another animal class. A pastor, on the
other hand, should have precisely the essentials in common with
the simple people, in the most profound sense should be vividly
penetrated by the consciousness that the differences of intellect
and culture are really only a jest.

It undeniably takes a good head and above all a copious religious idea to be able to associate with other people in such a way
that there is not a single person with whom one can exchange a
single word about what occupies oneself most deeply. I do not
believe that Hegelian philosophy has sufficient inwardness to be
able to support a person in such circumstances. I believe that it
will end badly for every Hegelian who in this way never gets a
chance to play his philosophical trump cards.

The simple congregation quite simply represents the essentially Christian, and as a pastor and spiritual adviser Magister
Adler *is pledged* to be involved with it. In the capital cities, where
a Hegelian has recourse in the exclusive, cultured circles, it perhaps is possible proudly and with proud disregard to guard oneself aristocratically against "simplicities." But Magister Adler as a
Hegelian is a wild, alien bird in the country, utterly without
recourse, and yet is just as disproportioned in the intellectual
sense in relation to his surrounding world as Gulliver was among
the very tiny, little people or among the giants. Whereas Gulliver
still had the advantage and the alleviation that he was only a
visitor, Magister Adler, on the other hand, despite his dispropor-
tion, is essentially in the relationship by being appointed pastor,
and he is also too intelligent not to perceive that in relation to
simple peasants it is foolish to be proud of his philosophy.

It cannot be denied that it is a desperate situation; and yet
inwardly, with regard to responsibility, it is even more desperate.
To stand in the pulpit (thus before God) and proclaim what one
in accordance with one's education is presumably far beyond; to
sit at a deathbed and comfort a dying person with what one is

VII²
B 235
184

oneself far beyond; to sit at a deathbed and perhaps witness that the dying person, who gratefully presses the pastor's hand, blessedly dies in the faith in what the pastor at the deathbed is far beyond! To know how a poor but pious family prepares for Holy Communion, with what solemnity they go up to the holy place—and then the pastor, who is way beyond this, and then the pastor, the teacher, if only he gets into the mood, actually steals this from these simple people, that is, by perceiving their fervor and emotion! To be developed in such a way that one, if one was really earnest about Hegelian philosophy, would instead feel obliged to tear the simple people out of their mistaken beliefs— and then to be appointed as pastor to teach them what is simple. And then the responsibility—that one is a pastor! And then to be without any diversion, without recourse and alliance—since in the capital city Hegelian philosophy perhaps consoles with a proud consciousness, but with difficulty out in the country, and not at all when one is a pastor.

It is well known that loneliness can drive a person to extremes, but Magister Adler's situation is worse than one of loneliness, since it is also one of contradiction and self-contradiction, and hovering above are the terrors of responsibility. Then when some time has passed in this way, when the contradiction and terror encircle him more and more closely, then the situation finally comes to this: a Hegelian who had gone further has now almost arrived at the turning point of decision, whether he will *become a Christian*—and this moment enters his life *one year after* he, happy and fortunate, *has been appointed as a Christian pastor.*

VII²
B 235
185

§ 2

THE CRISIS IN MAGISTER ADLER'S LIFE
[*ADDITION IN VERSION IV:* AND THE SYMBOLIC ACTION
ACCOMPANYING IT]

Then an event occurred, and Magister Adler's life was changed. I cannot, of course, give specific information about what this event was. The only thing I could do would be poetically to feel my way in possibilities, but no factual information is to be gained in that manner. The one who might reasonably be assumed to be able to provide exact and definite information would be Magister Adler himself. [*Deleted in version IV:* But the foregoing (Chapter III) has specifically shown his confusion to be that he himself did not know what is what; after first having provided a very detailed description of an event that is supposed to have taken place at night (when a nasty sound went through the room and then the Savior commanded him to get up[10] etc.), then, prompted by the ecclesiastical superior's inquiry, he substituted for this concrete version the general and indefinite version that it was an event.[11]] [*In margin of version IV:* But with him one seeks in vain. After first having provided a detailed description of an event that is supposed to have taken place at night ("when a nasty sound went through the room and then the Savior commanded him to get up and write down" and write down the words that are communicated in the preface to his *Sermons*), he then, prompted by the ecclesiastical superior's inquiry, substituted for this concrete version the general and indefinite version that it was an event.*]

If the desire for more explicit information stops at the confusion of Magister Adler (the person concerned), every third party, and thus I also and this inquiry, can be very satisfied with the stipulation: there occurred an event and Magister Adler's life was changed, yes, even with the stipulation that the event was—that Magister Adler's life was changed. *The main point is* (and if Magister Adler had not originally taken it upon himself to say more, everything would so far have been in order) that Magister Adler *by a qualitative leap was transported from the medium of philosophy, and specifically the fantastic medium of Hegelian philosophy* (pure thought and pure being), *into the sphere of religious inwardness. The main point is that by a qualitative leap from the objectivity of abstract thinking Magister Adler came to himself, because all religiousness lies in subjectivity, in inwardness, in coming to oneself.* It is another matter that Magister Adler, within the religious qualification of coming to oneself, may be said to have not yet come to himself, insofar as he, although religiously defined, nevertheless as an excited

*Note. See *Skrivelser min Suspension og Entledigelse Vedkommende*, edited by A. P. Adler, M.A., Reitzel, 1845, p. 18.

person is still outside himself. But in contrast to the objectivity and disinterestedness of abstract thinking, he may be said to have come to himself insofar as he has come to be concerned about himself. This is what is new, what his whole life development has been ignorant of, this religious impression of himself in self-concern. —It dawned upon him, as Magister Adler himself says in the preface to *Sermons*, before he begins the story about the revelation, that it depended not upon thought but upon spirit.[12]

The crisis was accompanied by a symbolic act, the facticity of which there is no reason to doubt: "Magister Adler burned his Hegelian manuscripts."[13] When one has broken with Hegelian philosophy in such a decisive way, there is then assurance that one will never again indulge in it prolixly; then by a single step one is safe from temptations to it and a relapse into it. Alas, this urge to give an inner decision a striking expression externally is often deceptive. Perhaps it has not very infrequently happened that a young girl, who before the eyes of the assembled family has solemnly destroyed every reminder of the faithless lover, burned all his fulsome letters, then the next day contrived, almost without being conscious of it, to see—the faithless one. Not infrequently there is an alarming misrelation between the inner decision (the strength of the resolution, deliverance, healing) and its outer manifestations. If one desires to draw correct conclusions, one can hardly conclude directly from the latter to the former; one can rather conclude inversely that the greater the need for a striking outer manifestation of the decision, the less the inner certitude. That the outer is not always the inner[14] holds not only for ironists, who consciously deceive others by a false exterior, but frequently also holds for immediate natures, who unconsciously deceive themselves, indeed, sometimes seem to have, as it were, a need for self-deception. If, for example, a man scarcely takes time to sleep and eat, just to be able unceasingly to proclaim and propagate a view beatific to humankind and also to demonstrate its correctness early and late—one would surely believe that the man must have a firm and strong conviction. Alas, it is, however, not always the case; at times he has no firm conviction at all but needs to have many people agree with him—so that his conviction can become convincing to himself. Strangely

enough, he does have a view; he does have something to communicate, and it looks as if people need him and his firm conviction—alas, it is he who needs people, he who wants to convince
himself by convincing others. If in the intellectual sense one
were to place him in a vacuum, he will have no conviction; on
the other hand, to the degree to which many people listen to
him, to the same degree he perceives that he has a conviction,
and to the same degree to which many people agree with him,
to the same degree—he himself becomes convinced.

Every more earnest person who is accustomed to deal circumspectly with himself prefers to avoid the striking outer decision,
or at least takes care lest it come prematurely. A more earnest
person prefers to conceal the decision and to test himself in silent
inwardness in order to see if it might not deceptively be the case
that he, because he is *weak*, needs the *strong* outer manifestation
of the decision. If a person can persevere in silent inwardness, can
endure being totally changed without changing the slightest outwardly, he then can easily take the striking step; not so with the
opposite. If I were to imagine two drunkards, both of whom
have resolved to drink no more: the one has solemnly thrown the
bottle and the glass out the window and has commenced total
abstinence; the other one continues to have the bottle and full
glass before him as previously, but he does not drink—which of
these two may be considered to be the more surely rescued? The
physical is so easily confused with the moral; the rescue consists
not in smashing the bottle and the glass but in ceasing to drink.
No, to be able to be entirely as one ordinarily is, to live among
the daily and continual recollections of the old and yet to be
changed in the deepest ground of one's being—yes, that is the
art. But if the change is there, then it is also reliable, and then
one can always gradually change the outer, if one has first very
earnestly seen to it that the change was not *before others in the outer,
but before God in the inner.*

I will imagine two individuals. At a decisive moment an essential change takes place in both of them, but the one immediately
expresses the change in the outer decision; only over the course
of seven years does the other attain the outer change that corresponds to the inner change that took place in him at that

VII²
B 235
188

moment, and therefore his change has nothing striking for others because it is apportioned over seven years—which of the two person's changes may be regarded to be more secure?

Therefore, instead of burning the manuscripts, Magister Adler perhaps would have been wiser and more circumspect to continue for a period to devote a specific hour or two every day to being occupied with Hegel in order to satisfy himself that he actually was changed, inasmuch as the physical and the moral can so easily be confused: abandoning Hegel with the burning of his Hegelian manuscripts. If my memory does not fail me, it happened that the celebrated Kanne,[15] whose life had known considerable spiritual upheavals, at one time, deeply moved by the essentially Christian, burned all his mythology manuscripts—and yet he relapsed again. In fact, Goethe also burned his manuscripts that contained poetic works,[16] and when he had done that he did indeed become a poet.

What happened with Goethe certainly did not happen with Magister Adler, namely, that only after having burned his Hegelian manuscripts did he really become an out-and-out Hegelian. But on the other hand, deceived by this striking outer decision, he has achieved the result that in self-deception it is concealed from him that he continues to be a Hegelian. Lyrically, subjectively, Magister Adler is fully and firmly convinced that he once and for all has eternally broken with Hegelian philosophy—by burning the manuscripts—that by a revelation he is eternally rescued from the prolixities of Hegelian philosophy. But see, when he is then induced to explain what he understands by this revelation and how he understands himself in its having happened to him, he regresses to the old Hegelian volatilizations. If someone were to point that out to him, it would not be inconceivable that he would reply, "How can you come now with such an unreasonable objection, that basically I am a Hegelian? By all that is holy, I assure you I burned my Hegelian manuscripts that night. Now believe me!" In this way Magister Adler places Hegelian philosophy in an extremely comic situation, inasmuch as it is utilized by a religious revivalist, who fully and firmly lyrically maintains that he has had a revelation, to volatilize the concept itself. [*Deleted in version IV:* Hegelian philosophy actually

VII²
B 235
189

explains away the revelation. Adler solemnly maintains that he has had a revelation and then, *à la* Hegel, instructively explains that a revelation actually is unthinkable, but does not notice the discrepancy himself—since, after all, he has burned his Hegelian manuscripts. The further one has the revelation at a distance from oneself (for example, at a distance of eighteen hundred years), the better it apparently goes with the volatilization, but one can scarcely get a revelation closer to life than by having had it one-self, and the volatilization cannot become more comic than when both parts are supposed to stand firm: that the same man has had a revelation, and that the explanation is that a revelation is not objectively thinkable but is a kind of mental illusion.] But by this Adler has the merit that he indirectly-satirically makes manifest the contradiction in Hegelian philosophy. When we take away the eighteen hundred years, the hiding place,[17] and place Hegelian philosophy in the situation of contemporaneity, its operation clearly shows that it deceitfully *explains away* a reve-lation instead of openly *denying* it. Only the extraordinary merit of the comic is reserved for Magister Adler: to be in every way the man for everything, the man with the revelation and the man with the explanation.

§ 3

MAGISTER ADLER'S EXCELLENCE

VII²
B 235
190

The good, the excellence in Magister Adler is that he was shaken, was deeply moved, that his life has thereby acquired a rhythm very different from the cab-horse trot [*Drosketrav*] in which most people, in the religious sense, dawdle [*dorske*] through life. Whether it is now breathless busyness or worldly desire or abstract thinking or whatever the distraction may be, it is certain that most people, in the religious sense, go through life in a kind of absentmindedness and preoccupation; they never in self-concern sense each his own *I* and the pulse beat and heart beat of his own self. They live too objectively[18] to be aware of something like that, and if they hear mention of it they tranquil-ize themselves with the explanation that such things are hysteria, hypochondria, etc. With regard to each his own self, most people live as if they were continually out, never at home. The events and enterprises of their lives flutter vaguely about this self. Perhaps they at times shut their door—in order to be at home—but they do not shut out the distracting thoughts, and thus they are still out. Magister Adler's excellence is that in the earnest and strict sense he must be said to have been fetched home by a higher power, because prior to this he certainly in the wide sense was out or abroad, the time when he was a Hegelian and objective. In the worldly sense, the prodigal son's trouble was not due only to his traveling abroad but to his wasting his resources in the foreign land. In the spiritual and religious sense, perdition is to travel abroad, to be out, to become objective, so that one receives no decisive impression of oneself by remaining at home with the inward self-concern of conscience.

All religiousness lies in subjectivity, in inwardness, in being deeply moved, in being jolted, in the qualitative pressure on the spring of subjectivity. When one considers people as most of them are, it cannot be denied that they do have some religiousness, some concern to be enlightened and instructed in religious matters, yet without having these matters come close enough to them. That is, if one looks more closely, one easily discovers that in their religiousness they still relate themselves *to themselves* at a certain distance; they form good resolutions *for the future*, but not *in the moment*, not for this instant, in order to begin at once. They do not begin the execution simultaneously with the resolution; simultaneously with forming the resolution, they have instead the idea that there is still some time, even if it is only a half-hour, before they are to begin. They make sacred pledges, they resolve: tomorrow etc.; but they are unacquainted with what is actually decisive: *to become totally present to oneself* in self-concern. Therefore they do indeed have religious conceptions, at times also find upbuilding, but nevertheless I know of nothing better with which to compare their religiousness than a drill session out on the commons. Just as this stands in relation to a battle and to being in battle (where there is danger, which is lacking out on the commons), so this religiousness-at-a-distance stands in relation to inward religiousness. And just as when an officer who as an observer has been along in a campaign in foreign service and

VII^2
B 235
191

upon his return home arranges, by orders from above, a maneuver on the commons that resembles the battle, so pastors likewise arrange at times some religious scenes instead of preaching—that is, they esthetically place the religious at a distance again. All esthetics, as Aristotle has rightly said, is *imitation*[19] and thereby at a distance, not in the medium of actuality, but a sermon should be precisely in the actual moment of the present. In a certain sense a preacher should be such that the listeners have to say: How can I get away from this man? His sermon catches up with me in every hiding place, and how can I get rid of him, since he is over me at every moment?[20]

In their religiousness the majority of people at most become present to themselves in a *past* or in a *future*, but not in a *present*. They think about the religious, hear it talked about, consider it in fantasy-impressions, have it with them in the form of a wish, of a longing, of a presentiment, of an illusory resolution and intention; but the impression of the religious, that it is to be used now, right now, now in this moment, they do not receive. They think about the immortality of the soul; at a distance they rest in this consciousness, but they do not at the same moment have concern's and self-concern's use for what is thought. Instead they think like this: It is always good to know that you are immortal in order to be on the safe side when at some time you die, which most likely will not be for some years. Thus they do not at the same moment think the thought of death together with the consciousness of immortality; they do not bear in mind that every moment one does not have the consciousness of immortality within oneself one is actually not immortal. They are like the well-fed person who works for the next day's food, but not like the hungry person who must use immediately what he can get. Basically they have their lives in other categories, which gives them a deceptive security while they busy themselves with and concern themselves about the religious. They do not grasp that the religious is the *one thing needful*;[21] they consider it *also to be needful*, especially for difficult times. They understand very well that a person can die of hunger when he does not have anything to live on, but they do not grasp that a human being lives on the Word that proceeds from the mouth of God.[22] When such

VII²
B 235
192

at-a-distance religious persons speak about the religious (and pastors of that kind are of course not altogether rare; indeed, they are even of a better sort in comparison with pastors who play L'Hombre, breed cattle, and raise calves), one immediately perceives in their discourse that they themselves are not present in it, just as they also do not exist in it. Therefore, even if during the preaching the listeners do not sleep, which nowadays is less frequent, yet they are absentminded, because in the discourse itself there is an in-between, a space (between the need and the satisfaction of the need, between the means of salvation and the immediate use of it), which is the space of illusion, of time-wasting, of procrastination. One perceives in the discourse that there is not this fresh influx from the richness of what has been experienced, which now in the moment of the discourse arises to a present life; one perceives that it is not as if the speaker must almost defend himself against this richness, defend himself against the superior power of the present. One perceives instead that every time he wipes the sweat from his brow it is as if he went home and fetched a new item, as if he had to go and fetch what he is to say. On the other hand, the person who is present to himself in the religious has available, in his mouth and in his heart,[23] what he is going to say—indeed, just as nowadays in well-equipped houses one has running water on each floor and does not need to walk down and fetch it at the pump but merely needs to turn on the tap, in the same way such a religious person has the essentials within himself at the present moment.

VII²
B 235
193

To be totally present to oneself is the highest and is the highest task for personal life; it is the power in virtue of which the Romans called the gods *praesentes.*[24] But to be totally present to oneself in self-concern is the highest religiousness, since only in this way is it absolutely comprehended that a human being absolutely needs God at every moment; then everything that belongs to past or future time, to indefinite time on the whole, to equivocations, excuses, subterfuges, etc., pales and disappears like other phantasms that also belong to indefinite time, to dawn and dusk, and retreat before the light of day.

When one is not present to oneself, one is absent in the past or in the future; then a person's religiousness is perhaps a recollection or an abstract intention; then one perhaps dwells piously in the piety of a vanished antiquity, or one in the spiritual sense builds the "bigger barns" of objective religiousness, but this night shall your soul be required of you.[25]

To be sure, most people do have religiousness; they have it in the form of an idea, but they have not made up their minds about when it actually is to be used. Is it to be used on the day of need? No, then it is natural to become impatient and to despair halfway. Is it to be used on the day of joy? No, then it is not needed. Is it then for everyday use? No, then there is no proper occasion for it. Then when is it to be used!

To be sure, most people do have religiousness, have it in the form of an idea, hold it in their hands, as it were, but *what* it actually is, on that they have not really made up their minds— whether it is a burden, an obligation, an additional imposition, or is an abundance of all blessings; whether it is a comfort in an emergency or is the highest of all true joy.

VII²
B 235
194

To be sure, most people do have religiousness; they have it in the form of an idea, have it with them as one can have a medicine on hand, but they have not really made up their minds about *how* it is to be used: whether it is to be used totally so that it totally penetrates the soul, or partially, like a soothing palliative; whether it is to be used as a medicine in an acute illness, or as it is used in a chronic illness; whether one should be afraid of becoming so addicted to it that one cannot do without it, or it is the highest not to be able to do without it.

So, to be sure, they do have religiousness, but inwardly they have not made up their minds about when it is to be used, what it is, how it is to be used. They *have* religiousness, but they are not *had* by it. Yet it holds true only in a worldly way, in connection with egotistic self-assertion, that it is correct to say: I have a beloved, but I am not had by her, that it is correct to say: *res sibi non se subjicere rebus* [subordinate things to oneself not oneself to things].[26] In the godly sense, in the relation of the religious person to God, the opposite holds true, if religiousness is to be the one thing true, the one thing needful,[27] the one thing blessed.

So it is with most people, but not so with Magister Adler. He is truly shaken; he is in mortal danger. To use one of my favorite expressions, which is attributed to another author: he is out on 70,000 fathoms of water.[28] What he finds out must be used immediately, the help he calls out for must be used immediately—or he sinks in that very second; he is absolutely subjective, inwardly wounded, and therefore must be present to himself in the need. Yes, Magister Adler is so far removed from the secure ground of apathy and illusion that instead he is tossed out into extreme mortal danger in such a way that this is about to annihilate him "this very day," "tonight," "at this moment."[29] Thus in the momentary situation of mortal danger he is struggling excessively between the self-defense of overexertion and the surrender of inwardness.

VII²
B 235
195

But it is an excellence in Magister Adler to be shaken this way, a qualitative excellence, and I certainly will not begrudgingly disparage the worth of this excellence. Just as it is an excellence to be truly in love, truly enthusiastic, so it is also an excellence, in the religious sense, to be shaken and thereby to have found the place of which it is said: *Hic Rhodus hic salta* [Here is Rhodes; leap here].[30] Religiously understood, where is this place? It is neither on Gerizim nor in Jerusalem,[31] neither in thinking nor in scholarship, but at the most tender and most subjective point of inwardness. When one is deeply moved there, one is properly positioned and in place. And this emotion is in turn the true working capital and the true wealth. I certainly will not speak begrudgingly about this excellence in Magister Adler, but neither will I speak inquisitively. There is a cowardly, soft religiousness that does not itself want to be out upon the deep in decisions but inquisitively wants to feel the shudder with which one, presumably safe oneself, sees another struggling out upon the deep, a cowardly and soft religiousness that itself shrinks from going through these dreadful experiences that demonstrate what an enormous power the religious is, but prefers to see the demonstration conducted on someone else. Just as the phantoms of the netherworld sucked the blood of a living person in order to live for a while,[32] so cowardly and soft religious people are basically aware that their religiousness is a hypocritical and prinked-up thing; therefore they would like on occasion to manage to cope with some strong impressions—at second hand. Religious peo-

ple of that kind are not a bit better than the idlers who long for
an execution, a big fire, etc. in order, themselves in no danger,
to shudder voluptuously at seeing a person's death agonies. But
just because there are religious people like that, and all too many
of them, it is important, especially in our sensible and soft sagaciously refined Christendom, that the one who has been deeply
moved should not in his inwardness give up, that in holy anger
he should know how to get behind these cowardly soft ones in
order to force them out in the current, instead of abandoning
himself to them for entertainment and drama. But for that Magister Adler lacks reflection and composure and schooling and
holy discipline, and therefore it cannot be denied that even if
everything else about him were in order, he nevertheless does
harm because instead of helping others out into decisions he
provides diversion to the cowards and soft ones, who love vo-
luptuous shudders.

VII²
B 235
196

But his excellence surpassing that of most people nevertheless is and remains qualitative and, especially in our age, is to be
valued highly. The more that culture, education, and understanding get the upper hand, the more that people begin to live
by way of comparison—the more common becomes a certain
proficiency in treating spiritual qualifications in lawyer fashion.
People everywhere know equivocations and exceptions and lim-
itations and excuses. Now brazenly, now timidly, one appeals to
the example of others; thus one continually avoids a decisive
impression of spirit. Culture and education and sensibleness and
social life work toward making people, in the religious sense,
absentminded, spiritually abstracted.

This excellence in Magister Adler is also perceptible in his
writings, and the good in them must be traced to this excellence
of his. The good (however much it is a defect in another way) is
that Magister Adler does not get time to shift his thoughts, feel-
ings, moods, his states of mind into another medium, into a more
ideal medium of communication, but that he himself is totally in
the present moment and in turn produces on the reader the impression of the present. [*Deleted in version IV:* What I have shown
in the introduction[33] to this book to be Adler's flaw as author so
that he is not an essential author, *changed to:* What in one way is

a defect in him, for which reason one may not call him an essential author,] that he comes too close to actuality, is in another way the good in him, because even though he himself, by being altogether in the moment, totally confuses, he is nevertheless quite able to have an effect, to stimulate, to grip the reader. And this he actually does. What he has to say is not said by an indifferent man and is not fetched from far away; no, he *is in* the haste, *in* the danger, *in* the struggle or *in* the rest of consolation, *in* the hope, and what he says he has right at hand; it is an outburst, a veritable outburst of feeling, of deep emotion, and not infrequently one must say that he assaults the reader, so to speak, with his outbursts.

Thus in Adler's style there is at times an almost audible lyrical seething, which, although esthetically evaluated faulty in form, still may have its inciting significance for the reader. One does not fall asleep over him or become absentminded; instead one becomes impatient at a person's moving the whole machinery of one's actual personality so close in to life. Esthetically evaluated his style has no merit, and I cannot find a single example in all his books that I dare to commend as correct in form; there is always something incidental (but this is due to his being himself only in the moment of actuality and to his coming too close to actuality in the alarming sense), either too much or too little, either an abundance, whereby he becomes prostrate, so to speak, in the attack, or a scarcity, which indicates that the imagination is inadequate, and which causes one to see that he is gasping for breath. [34]But this incidentality, the imperfection, this unruliness in turn contributes to giving the impression of actuality and to that extent can also produce an effect, at least a disquieting and alarming effect. In a certain sense the impressions of actuality are always the most instructive, note well, when a person himself understands how to be the teacher. The impressions of actuality are the tasks, but of course an author is not (by analogy to an alarming natural phenomenon) to induce the reader to help him; on the contrary, even though he maieutically conceals the result, he is to be the teacher who knows the answer. But in the deeper sense of totality and continuity, Magister Adler is not informed; he is not an author, but he is himself a task. If Magister Adler ever

really masters himself and his thinking, then the question of com-
mending him can arise if he masters coming as close to actuality
as possible; now, however, one must say that it is his qualitative
excellence that he is deeply moved and shaken, but he is not an
essential author.

§ 4

THE FUNDAMENTAL DEFECT IN ADLER THAT
CONDITIONS THE MISRELATION

*The fundamental defect is that Magister Adler's theological, Christian-
theological education and schooling are deficient and confused and have
no relation to his lyrical emotion, while he nevertheless, presumably misled by the idea of being a theological graduate, pastor, philosopher, believes himself able to explain something and is carried away in productivity instead of seeking quiet and education and discipline in the language
of Christian concepts.* That he has burned his Hegelian manuscripts
makes no difference whatever, because, since he has not taken
the time to acquire proficiency in the language of Christian concepts, the consequence is quite simple, that he has nothing at all
to hold on to if burning the manuscripts was really identical with
renouncing this philosophy; but then in turn there is a very simple consequence, that if he nevertheless becomes productive his
productivity will either come to be based on confusing Hegelian
reminiscences or independently become conceptually confusing,
or a mixture of both.

Now, if it is so that even just being beautiful is an excuse for
much, being in love a defense for much thoughtlessness, being
enthusiastic a defense for much precipitousness, having made a
great discovery a defense for running naked through the streets of
Syracuse[35]—well, then being deeply moved and shaken in the
religious sense ought to be a defense for much imperfection, and
in connection with Magister Adler a critic certainly ought to
beware of being querulous and narrow-minded. But thoughtlessness, precipitousness, offense, in short, that which should be
excused, or that there is something that must be excused, does
not mean that there is dubiousness with regard to the good, with
regard to the excellence that should contain the excuse. No, the

VII²
B 235
199

offense must consist in something else that is incidental. Running naked through the streets of Syracuse, for example, has nothing at all to do with the discovery, which therefore remains absolutely just as good. Accordingly it is entirely in order that the great discovery contain the excuse for the offense, that because of the discovery one completely forgets that he is naked, just as Archimedes himself did. Only prudery could dwell long on the offensive aspect, and only a dementedly elated philistinism in a market town could reverse everything and arrive at the opposite opinion: It is certain that yesterday Archimedes ran naked through the streets—ergo he has made no great discovery [*deleted in version IV:* , *ad modum* (according to the pattern): philosopher John Doe is thin-legged—ergo he is no great philosopher³⁶]. It would be different, however, if Archimedes' great discovery had been doubtful, because a misunderstanding, a mistake (instead of a great discovery) provides no excuse for an offense. This actually is also philistinism's way of thinking, because philistinism has no conception of the great and the lofty and therefore has no intimation either of the excuse contained in the great. It is the same with the philistine in interpreting the exceptional as with commission agent Bæhrend in connection with the bird that, as is well known, dropped something down on the table—the agent said, "If I had done that, there would have been an uproar."³⁷ In the same way the philistine leaves out the point; he says: If I had done that—yes, indeed, but the philistine is no Archimedes either. But as was stated, if there are irregularities with regard to the discovery, then Archimedes has no excuse.

But Adler's excellence was that he was deeply moved, shaken in his inmost being, that accordingly his inwardness came into existence, or he came into existence in accordance with his inwardness. But to be deeply moved in this way is a very vague expression for something as concrete as a Christian awakening, and yet more may not be said about Magister Adler. To be shaken (somewhat in the sense in which one speaks of shaking someone in order to awaken him) is the more universal basis of all religiousness; being shaken, being deeply moved, and subjectivity's coming into existence in the inwardness of emotion are shared by the pious pagan and the pious Jew in common with a

VII²
B 235
200

Christian. On the common ground of the more universal deep emotion, the qualitative difference must be erected and must manifest itself, because the more universal deep emotion refers only to something abstract: to be deeply moved by something higher, something eternal, an idea. One does not become a Christian by being religiously moved by something higher; and not every outpouring of religious emotion is a Christian outpouring. In other words, emotion that is Christian is controlled by conceptual definitions, and when deep emotion is transformed into or expressed in words in order to be communicated, this transformation must continually take place within the conceptual definitions.

In connection with all the inwardness that reflects on the purely human, the merely human (*thus in connection with all inwardness in the sphere of immanence*), to be deeply moved, to be shaken, is to be taken in the sense in which one speaks of shaking a man until he wakes up. The historical is only that he has been shaken;* he is not to become something else through the shaking but is to wake up and become himself. If this deep emotion expresses itself, bursts out in words, the transformation in feeling and imagination takes place within such concepts and definitions of which it can be said that every human being discovers them in using them. The transformation is not limited by specific qualitative concepts that have a historical validity outside the individual and higher than every human individual, and paradoxically higher than every human individual, a paradoxical historical validity.

Let us take being in love in the purely erotic sense. With regard to being in love purely erotically, there is no specific qualitative difference between a Greek, a Jew, and a Christian. The lyrical outbursts of being in love are solely within the qualifications of the purely human and not within specific qualitative definitions. The lyric is evaluated according to the expression of the purely human, even though nuanced in the individuation of

VII²
B 235
201

*Note. On this matter, I refer the reader to Johannes Climacus, *Concluding Postscript,* to the distinction between religiousness *A* and *B,* or that which has the dialectical in first place and that which also has the dialectical in second place.[38]

national character and of personality, which *qua* difference is still a vanishing aspect in the immanent human equality, eternally viewed.

It is different with the qualification: a Christian religious awakening, *which lies in the sphere of transcendence.* The individual's being deeply moved by something higher is far from being an adequate qualification, because completely pagan views, pagan conceptions of God, can be expressed in deep emotion. In order to be able to express oneself Christianly, proficiency and schooling in the Christian conceptual definitions are also required in addition to the more universal heart language of deep emotion, just as it is of course assumed that the deep emotion is of a specific qualitative kind, is Christian emotion.

But now since Christianity over the centuries has gradually penetrated the whole development of the world in a more universal way so that its conceptual language has passed into a volatilizing, traditional usage (which is right in line with being a Christian of sorts by virtue of living in geographical Christendom), it can easily happen that someone who only in the more universal sense is deeply moved by something higher summarily expresses himself in Christian conceptual language; of course, it certainly was to be expected. The defect and irregularity are then twofold: the person deeply moved happens to speak a language that is unrelated to his emotion, since the language is specific, qualitatively concrete, and his emotion more universal; and he, as is natural, speaks this language in a confusing way. That is, if one is not in the stricter sense deeply moved by the essentially Christian, and on the other hand is not familiar with, accustomed to, and strictly disciplined in the conceptual language within which one is expressing one's emotion, then the same thing happens with a person as with someone who speaks too fast and does not articulate carefully—he babbles. In the Christian religious domain this is not only regrettable but terrible, because there is not only the danger of saying something unclear, something foolish, but there is also the danger of unconsciously becoming blasphemous.

[*Deleted in version IV:* What is required for a Christian awakening is on one hand the Christian emotion and on the other the

VII²
B 235
202

firmness and definiteness of conceptual language.] But in our age there is a shortage of both, both of being deeply moved and of education in concepts. Individuals start out in the lyrical, and the conceptual language is confused in thoughtless or volatilizing brilliant associations, while speculative thought is busy with comprehending Christianity, which happens all too easily because those who have a strict Christian schooling are more and more rare. But if one starts with the premise that the essentially Christian is something vague and indefinite, well, then one can easily mediate.

To see a riding master ride an unbroken horse is a proud sight (so it was when Christianity at its beginning forced human nature into its conceptual language); to see a less practiced rider ride a well-trained horse is acceptable (so it was in the times of strict orthodoxy, when respect for the strict system that had been handed down helped individuals); but when an untrained rider rides an unbroken horse, then all is lost; the rider does not help the horse nor the horse the rider.

Now, if Magister Adler is regarded as a Christian religiously awakened person, his trouble is simply this: that he is not adequately familiar with basic Christian conceptual language. Therefore he has no qualitative, unshakable criterion by which he himself can test whether his being deeply moved is a Christian religious awakening, and when he wants to express his emotion he has no qualitative recourse to the qualitatively distinct conceptual language. The clearest evidence of this is that what should contain the greatest certainty that his awakening was a Christian awakening (that he has been called through a revelation from the Savior) specifically betrays his uncertainty, [*deleted in version IV:* which is shown in this, that he does not understand himself in what has happened to him,] because he has not even made up his mind about what is to be understood by a revelation.

Therefore if Magister Adler had been a layman (lawyer, physician, military officer, for example), it perhaps would have gone somewhat better with him. After being deeply moved by a powerful religious impression, he would then, in view of not being a theologian, have sought quiet in order to become fully conscious of himself, sought schooling with teachers of Christian

VII²
B 235
203

orthodoxy, and in this way he perhaps would have succeeded in attaining the necessary proportionality before he began to express himself. But Magister Adler was a theological graduate, he was even a pastor, he was a philosopher—then should he not long ago have superbly possessed the schooling in concepts requisite for being able with certainty to express his emotion [*deleted in version IV:* within the Christian qualitative definitions]? So it seems perhaps, but, alas, the knowledge acquired for the theological degree—unless one brings along to the university from one's childhood and upbringing that which purely religiously is of infinite value: a profound veneration for Christianity so that someday in the later moment of decision one resolutely and with bold confidence stands by the choice, would rather give up everything else than change the least jot in the essentially Christian—alas, the knowledge acquired for the theological degree, even if it could have ever so much worth considered as knowledge, is of but little use in orderly resistance to [*deleted in version IV:* , is of but little use in connection with] an emotion that goes to extremes. As a pastor he presumably did not have opportunity to pursue a course of study, since he was, after all, fully occupied with Hegel—and as a Hegelian he was initiated, with full devotion and conviction initiated into the total confusion of the essentially Christian. But *ex animi sententia* [with a sincere heart] to be an adherent of a particular philosopher and his philosophic view, through it and in it to have experienced the culmination of his life and his life development—for a man that is about the same as what seriously falling in love is for a woman. If the falling in love has had reality, then it certainly is of little help to burn all the letters "he wrote to her"; here methodical and slow work is required. If being a Hegelian has had reality, then burning the Hegelian manuscripts is of no use. That it truly has had reality for Magister Adler, I do not doubt; indeed, it would have been most lamentable if even his study of Hegel had been only desultory.

VII²
B 235
204   I will now briefly show how the misrelation between Magister Adler's subjective emotion and his education in Christian concepts is manifest at decisive points in his performance as an author. The extent to which he can be called a Christian religiously awakened person is dialectical, and this is naturally also included

in the misrelations. That is, this can be judged only by paying attention to his statements, but these are confused simply by being in the language of Christian concepts, which he has not mastered.

a. [39]*Here, then, we stand* [*deleted in version IV:* again *at what* the whole present book is about,] at Magister Adler's *first* statement, [*deleted in version IV:* that much discussed preface,] *the preface to his* Sermons *or, more accurately, what is contained therein.*

Magister Adler was deeply moved by something higher, but now when he wants to express his state in words, wants to communicate, *he confuses the subjective with the objective, his altered subjective state with an external event,* the dawning of a light upon him with the coming into existence of something new outside him, *the falling of the veil from his eyes with his having had a revelation.* Subjectively his emotion is carried to the extreme; he wants to select the most powerful expression to describe it and by means of a mental deception grasps the objective qualification: having had a revelation.

In order to throw light upon the confusion in the use of the concept of revelation, I will first take an example of the kind of inwardness that pertains to the purely human, an example from the sphere of immanence. The person who truly falls in love is able to say that he also discovers erotic love [*Elskov*], and everyone from ancient times who has fallen in love has been able to say the same. Falling in love is a qualification of pure, immediate inwardness. It has no other dialectic than inwardness's own dialectic; it has no dialectical qualification outside itself; it is the immediate identity of the subjective and the objective. Erotic love is falling in love; the primitivity of falling in love is the coming into existence of erotic love itself. Erotic love does not exist as something objective but only comes into existence each time someone falls in love and exists only in the lover; not only does it exist only *for* the lover, but it exists only *in* the lover.

It is different with every relation in the sphere of transcendence, and in turn it is different with the Christian concept of a revelation. The essentially Christian exists before any Christian exists; it must exist in order for one to become a Christian. It contains the qualification by which a test is made of whether

VII[2]
B 235
205

someone has become a Christian; it maintains its objective continuance outside all believers, while it also is in the inwardness of
the believer. In short, here there is no identity between the subjective and the objective. If the essentially Christian enters into
the hearts of ever so many believers, every believer realizes that
it did not arise in his heart,[40] realizes that the objective qualification of the essentially Christian is not a reminiscence as erotic
love is of falling in love. It is therefore a volatilization of the
concept, a dislocation of all the essentially Christian, when one
admits the wordplay that a revelation is a qualification belonging
to subjectivity, or is the direct identity of subject-object, is an
apparently objective something that nevertheless is subjective in
the same way as erotic love *qua* an objective something is an
illusion and falling in love is the reality. No, even if no one had
become aware that God had revealed himself in human form in
Christ, he still had revealed himself; indeed, this is also why every
contemporary (in the immediate sense) retains a responsibility if
he did not become aware.

So Magister Adler was deeply moved. That in the first moment of being deeply moved one easily runs the risk of a mistake,
that of mistaking one's own change for a change outside oneself,
that of mistaking the perception of everything as changed for the
coming into existence of something new—that is familiar
enough. I do not need to dwell on such things. If Magister Adler
for some time has continued to be ensnared in this mistake, it
would be foolish to censure him, partly because it is nobody's
business, and partly because it is human. The question is only
about expressing oneself in this state. Once one is ensnared in the
mistake, it is all too easy to support the mistake with a composed
fiction and dramatically to obtain an event, an episode, an account of how it occurred. Not only every religiously awakened
person but everyone who to a significant degree has inwardness
also has a propensity and a proficiency for making his monologue
into dialogue—that is, to speak with oneself in such a manner
that this self becomes a second being who has a consistency outside oneself—that is, to redouble oneself. One can fictively go
further along this path and have a fictive second person with
whom one speaks and invent a whole episode. Precisely because

VII²
B 235
206

the person who has predominant inwardness seldom finds anyone with whom he can really speak, there develops within him this need, this wealth of privation, to redouble himself. When one understands how to use it properly, it is actually a wealth. The question is only about expressing oneself if one is ensnared in this self-redoubling. The more fantasy one has in this case, the more easily it goes with continuously having revelations. It is reflection that makes manifest the redoubling, and fantasy then fantastically steps over to the side of the apparent self and dramatically gives support.

Now, if from an earlier time and from a rigorous and earnest schooling in concepts Adler had had an unconditional veneration for the Christian qualitative dogmatic concept "a revelation," he would have had something with which to resist, something to hold on to, something that might prevent the rash expression. But Magister Adler, unfortunately enough, is a Hegelian. There can now be no hope that something would rescue him from the mistake, since all his scholarliness must confirm him precisely in the idea that he altogether correctly, philosophically accurately, characterizes his subjective change with: having had a revelation. By a confusion of the subjective and the objective, Magister Adler is ensnared in the opinion that he has had a revelation; by having had a revelation, he presumably thinks that he has broken entirely with Hegelian philosophy, which cannot accommodate the qualitative concept of a revelation and therefore has volatilized it to signify a change of the subjectivity. But this concept of a revelation fits Magister Adler's mistake exactly, and specifically by this he is confirmed in calling his subjective change a revelation. It is easy to see how the basis of the confusion consists in this, that the concept of revelation does not stand firm, that at one moment it is to designate a break with the Hegelian philosophy of identity and the immanent process, but on closer inspection it is to designate only a change of the subjectivity, a qualification that is precisely the Hegelian concept of: a revelation.[41]

Hegelian philosophy is actually the historicizing philosophy of identity,[42] which follows a world-historical process in such a way that it certainly is not the single individual who by himself

develops everything, but humanity as subjectivity that accom-
modates within itself all the elements of the development in the
immediate identity of subject-object. At no point is there a transcendent point of departure that qualitatively stands unshakably
firm in such a way that the inverse view and conception do not
see it in that range of subjectivity (of humanity). The next moment every new point of departure is an element in the process
and in this way manifests itself to be only a determinant of the
übergreifende [overlapping] subjectivity, which is humanity, the
human race. Christianity proclaims itself to be a transcendent
point of departure, to be a revelation in such a way that in all
eternity immanence cannot assimilate this point of departure
and make it an element. Now, if this qualitative paradox is qualitatively to stand unshakably firm, the world-historical process
cannot come off at all. This qualitative paradox is for the world-
historical process what a cross, according to popular belief, is
for the devil; the devil must step aside for it, this cannot be mediated. Since Hegelian philosophy stands here at the crossroad, it
must either break outright with Christianity or give up the
predicate "Christian philosophy." Hegelian philosophy, however, does neither of the two; it invents mediation and volatilizes
the concept of a revelation. It does not deny a revelation but
explains it away; it explains the concept of a revelation to such an
extent that it becomes the expression for the immediacy of the
subjectivity, certainly not the individual subjectivity, but the
subjectivity that is the human race, humanity. Now the method
is afloat, and the historicizing philosophy of identity is completely victorious.

VII²
B 235
208

So it is with the concept of revelation in the world-historical
development. Christianly understood, it is an objective determinant, a qualitative paradox that must stand unshaken as such. Let
us now take a single subject, a single individual. The individual
subject's life also has a development; it also has new points of
departure. Thus, for example, falling in love is a new point of
departure, but also only in such a way that in the next moment
it is an element in the subject's development—that is, the subjectivity is *übergreifend* [overlapping]. But now—to have had a revelation! If the concept is held firm qualitatively in the Christian

sense, the individual has gained a transcendent point of departure that cannot be mediated. But then the individual must indeed also hold this firm qualitatively and not first say that he has had a revelation and then afterward say that by a revelation is to be understood deep emotion, an awakening, etc. That is what Magister Adler does, [*added in margin of version IV: Note.* See the book quoted] except that the confusion is even to the second power. He first bogs down in a mental deception and fancies that he has had a revelation; then he solemnly announces that he has had a revelation; and then, when [*addition in version IV:* on the occasion of the ecclesiastical superior's inquiry,] he is to explain in more detail, his explanation is essentially that of the philosophy of identity. He breaks with Hegel, he burns the manuscripts, and *summa summarum*, when everything has been heard, it is still Hegelian philosophy that has been victorious.

[*Deleted in version IV:* The dialectically practiced reader will easily perceive not only that here the argumentation is *e concessis* (on the basis of the other's premises) and dilemmatic but also that a conclusion has been drawn backward. The dialectical movements are approximately these: either Adler has had a revelation, and then he must stand firm by it, act according to it, by virtue of it, with consistency; or he has had no revelation. He himself says that he has had a revelation, but it is easy to show by his later statements that he does not stand firm by it. Indeed, it is easy to show that he does not even hold firmly to the Christian concept of a revelation—ergo, we conclude that he has had no revelation. He is first deceived by himself, and then is deceived by Hegelian philosophy, with which he thinks he has broken.] ^{not-applicable}

VII²
B 235
209

But this whole confusion has its basis in his having no education in Christian concepts, no schooling that stands in a relation to his subjective state of being deeply moved, while on the other hand he quite seriously has found repose and satisfaction in the Hegelian volatilization of concepts. *Naturam furca expellas tamen usque recurret* [You may drive out Nature with a pitchfork, yet she will ever hurry back]![43] Even his break with Hegel is by no means Christianly qualitative, to say nothing of being held firm qualitatively in the Christian sense, and the break itself is a kind of Hegelianism—which is why we also later quite correctly find him understanding his first statement as an element in his life development. But if a revelation as a point of departure, in the human race or in the individual's life, is to be regarded as an element, then of course the process itself is higher than the individual element, and the whole concept of revelation is volatilized.

Yet Adler used this word; he solemnly announced that he had had a revelation, that the *Savior* at night had commanded him to get up, etc.—*et semel emissum volat irrevocabile verbum* [and the word once let slip is beyond recall][44]—at least a greater self-conquest is called in order to revoke what was said than to keep oneself from saying it.

b. *Magister Adler's replies* [*addition in version IV: Note.* These are contained in the quoted little book.] *to the ecclesiastical superior's question.* —What was said, however, meets with serious opposition from the ecclesiastical superior. Magister Adler is induced to explain himself further, and now Hegelian philosophy, perhaps unconsciously to him, is at hand to help him out of the predicament.

Magister Adler's "reply" essentially contains, in various forms and locutions, a Hegelian volatilization of the concept of revelation. [*Deleted in version IV:* This, however, has been so adequately pointed out in Chapter III, section 1, that I need merely refer to it and at most recall] [*addition in version IV:* This can be shown here merely by pointing to] the main features. (1) He interprets having had a revelation and having received a teaching from the Savior as identical with being rescued in a marvelous way (a religious awakening in the more ordinary sense); (2) he explains having had a revelation, the factual details of which he himself so painstakingly gave in his first statement, as identical with its being such an event; (3) he says that he does not insist that his revelation is on the same level as that of Scripture and of an apostle, that is, he has only had what one in a nebulous sense could call a revelation, a casual revelation *ad modum* a casual promise of marriage; (4) he hopes for the perfectibility of the communicated doctrine, that is, he understands his first statement as an element in an endeavor—that is, he revokes the frequently mentioned revelation.

VII²
B 235
210

The confusion is continually due to Magister Adler's not having respect for or mastery of Christian conceptual language,
while the impetus of his deep emotion misleads him to express
himself. [*Addition on a loose sheet in version IV:* But in comparison
with a modern theological confusion and *in specie* (in particular)
the Hegelian confusion of concepts, this Adlerian confusion has
also a purely comic value. It is now about 1800 years since Christianity came into the world—as a revelation, and about as long
since Paul declared himself called by a revelation to spread Christianity. But then 1600 or 1700 years later there arose an exegetical and dogmatic wisdom that understood all this differently.
It knew how to explain a revelation as an inner fact, as incanta-
tion, enthusiasm, deep emotion—as the immediate. The next
discovery was the theory of perfectibility, that a revealed doctrine is perfectible. Well, now, there is always a little excuse in
the great distance and the significant change in the world since
that time. It is no longer possible to get hold of Paul and confront
him with the interpretation of his own words by such an exegesis
and dogmatics, and on the other hand the exegetes and dogmaticians do not themselves maintain that they have had a revelation.
It is different with Magister A.! In his own life to have gone
through a world-historical cycle—to receive a revelation to
begin with, then for two years to explain exegetically what a
revelation is (something no one could understand better than
he), and then two years later to have a full-blown theory of the
perfectibility of the doctrine (i.e., dictated to him, according to
his own declaration, by Christ or written down by him at
Christ's command), revealed to him (*deleted:* because that which
Christ had dictated to him was still imperfect)—such originality
certainly has never been heard of before!]

 c. *Magister Adler's four latest books** [*addition in version IV:* N.B.,
and in margin: *Note. They all came out at one time in 1846.]
—Time, quiet were what Magister Adler needed now, a rigorous, fundamental, Christian schooling in concepts in order to
acquire the desirable proportionality [*deleted in version IV:* between subjectivity's deep emotion and the qualitative unshak-
ability of the categories of thought]. Magister Adler himself says
that "in the future, by calmly working out the ideas over a longer

time, he will see his way to give these a more appropriate form"
[*marginal addition in version IV: Note.* See that quoted little book,[45]
p. 23, in reply (from July 5, 1845) to the ecclesiastical superior's
inquiry under no. 1.

Consideration is given and can be given here to this whole
productivity only insofar as it serves to shed light on Mag. Adler.
The remarkable thing is that these four later books have no relation at all to what is qualitatively decisive, to have had a revelation and to have had a doctrine communicated by the Savior; the
author, however, treats that doctrine, insofar as it is occasionally
touched on, as if it were his own. Furthermore, that these four
later books contain nothing at all to shed light on that extraordinary event; instead it seems as if the whole story of the revelation
is forgotten. Finally, that these four later books contain nothing
to shed light on how the author understands *himself* in the fact (it
is not asked, after all, that he *comprehend* the extraordinary) that
the extraordinary has happened to him. And since this is the case,
this remarkable situation means that the whole productivity in
the four books is out of character, that the author is different from
the one he was. This is the main point of my inquiry, to show the
lack of identity between Mag. Adler's first and later statements.
In order to show this, the argument proceeds dilemmatically in
this way. *Either* that statement contained in the preface to the
sermons (about having had a revelation and having received
from the Savior a doctrine) is in his character as an apostle, and
in that case the whole productivity in the four later books is out
of character. *Or* the character in the four later books (that of
being a sort of lyrical genius) is his character; and then his first
statement (the preface) must be revoked, yes, in repentance be
revoked. Either/Or, *tertium non datur* (there is no third). That is,
the *tertium* is confusion, or there is a lack of identity between the
first statement and the later, although Mag. A. considers them to
be one and the same.]—and then he commences (1846) a new,
voluminous productivity, in which with regard to qualitative
education he still is found to have come no further [*deleted in
version IV:* indeed, rather to have become even more careless,
since he no longer seems to feel any need to understand himself
qualitatively in his having had a revelation]. That he himself

seems to realize that he needs a pause, that instead of acting on the basis of this view he continues his productivity, is psychologically very characteristic and, worse yet, an indication that it will be difficult for him to take time really to collect himself in earnest. That a man, who in busy activity accomplishes the opposite, uses the cliché that he hopes to change in the future— usually means that there probably will not be any change. The need that he might have for change acquires no power over him simply because it is continually stated, so that it finally becomes for him only a need to say it now and then, or to say it frequently, while he does the opposite. Strangely enough, Holberg has not used this trait in the representation of the busy trifler;[46] it would have been altogether characteristic of the busy trifler if he had used the cliché, "The mass of business transactions is unbearable, but after New Year I will completely retire from business life." It is quite certain that this line, when the spectator, aided also by a dramatic situation, is bound to realize that it was a cliché, would exactly characterize the ceaseless pace of his busy trifling, that he was incurable. When a student has been preparing a long time for his final university examination, so that with every year it becomes less likely that he will ever actually take it, until it becomes a cliché: I will take it next time—then it is clear enough that he will not take any examination. For this very reason Trop[47] is to be hopelessly given up, because he has his hope in the form of a cliché.

To be sure, Magister Adler hopes [*addition in version IV:* (July 5, 1846)] for the future, but if one asks about the position of his four latest books (1846) in a literary effort or in a personal life-development, about where Adler, in the intellectual sense, is at present (which is different from asking about a particular statement, a particular explanation of a Bible passage, a particular study, etc.), then one must say that he has become productive in the wrong place, that his productivity sails before a spurious wind. [*Deleted in version IV:* In other words, if one is to determine ethically and ethically-religiously the place where Adler ought to be at present, whether he has either kept silence or expressed himself, one must say: A man who begins by announcing that he has had a revelation from the Savior and has received a doctrine, and who then later in his reply makes it clear that he has only a very careless idea of what is to be Christianly understood by a revelation, such a man for the time being has nothing to do either with exegeting separate passages in Scripture or with being brilliant in big books; no, he is simply and solely to regain his composure in order either to sanction his first statement about himself or officially to revoke it—all other productivity is only diversion and a continuation of confusion. But Adler does not do this.] *In other words, instead of giving himself time, becoming quiet, regaining his composure,* pursuing a course of study, instead of acquiring a qualitative respect for what it means to have had a revelation and coming to an understanding with himself and to a qualitative decision, *in short, instead of being silent and acting and working—he actually becomes productive with regard to this**—*that he has not yet become quiet,* that "he is overstrained, that he is shaken, pale, that he is ready to jump, that in the future, by calmly working out the ideas over a longer time, he hopes etc."[49] The first and last task is to get out of the tension, [*deleted in version IV:* but instead of that he becomes productive about his state in tension, and moreover he devotes himself to a distracting productivity with regard to detached details, particular Bible verses, and other such things. *Changed to:* to understand himself in the revelation-fact, but instead of that he becomes productive about his state and *otherwise deceives himself with a terribly grand means of diversion*: a voluminous productivity about detached details, particular Bible verses, particular thoughts, a prolix productivity on loose sheets.]

[*Deleted in version IV:* Here it is again apparent that Adler lacks education in Christian concepts, that his lyrical state of being deeply moved has no relation to it; this is apparent in his having]

---

*Evaluated esthetically, this productivity falls short by coming too close to actuality, by very directly *giving* [*give*] *himself* instead of hiding himself and poetically rendering [*gjengive*] the lyrical [*deleted in version IV:* . Who has not experienced crises and tensions in his life, and the more inwardness the more the productivity hides itself in it, but one does not produce in tension, whereby one only offensively, as one in another sense says it, produces oneself; and even if one has not gained repose completely]; all true esthetic production nevertheless is and should be a forgery in relation to one's purely personal life.[48]

[*changed to:* Here it comes again—Magister Adler has] so little respect for the concept of a revelation that he can leave open and vague his statement about having had a revelation himself, yes, can almost entirely forget the whole *Geschichte* [story] and become productive about everything else possible [*deleted in version IV:* but not strive to understand himself]. And then the misrelation is something else, that he lacks the ethical firmness to gain quiet in order "in the future, by calmly working out the ideas, etc."[50]

VII²
B 235
213

Everyone who knows something about the dangers of reflection and the dangerous walk along the road of reflection also knows that it is dubious when a person, instead of getting out of the tension through resolution and action, becomes productive about his state in tension. Then there is no effort to get out of the state, but reflection fixes the situation for reflection and thereby fixes (the word taken in a somewhat different sense) the man. The more richly thoughts and expressions offer themselves, the more briskly the productivity advances—in the wrong direction—the more dangerous it becomes and the more it hides from the person concerned that his work, his extremely strenuous work, his very interesting (perhaps also for a third party who has a total view) work, is a work of bogging himself down deeper and deeper. That is, he does not work himself loose but works himself fast and becomes interesting to himself by reflecting on the tension [*deleted in version IV:* and diverts himself with an utterly piecemeal productivity about detached details, with isolated short articles]. One observes clearly enough that Magister Adler is unfamiliar with, and with the use of, the countless safety measures that the able seaman on the ocean of reflection knows and continually uses in order to test the direction of the productivity, to log the speed, to determine where one is, by halting for a moment, by quite arbitrarily choosing trivial and mechanical work in order to probe the intellectual powers, by stretching reflection in a totally opposite direction in order to see if there is any illusion involved etc. No, Magister Adler advances productively at an *unbroken* pace, which seems quite consistently to increase with every step forward. And so in production he is as if out on the sea of reflection, where no one can directly shout to him, where all navigation markers are dialectical, and he is steering at a considerable speed—in the wrong direction.

If from an earlier period Magister Adler had now had the impression of a rigorous ethical view, if ethically he had had an earnest schooling, this certainly would have been of benefit to him now. But Magister Adler's life-development was such that [*deleted in version IV:* without any challenge of a more profound life-impression] it quite naturally was bound to culminate in Hegel's philosophy, which, as is known, has no ethics.[51] Even to the most earnest ethicist who is out upon the waters of reflection, it can happen that he at some time makes a mistake for a moment, but he will quickly discover it, because he tests his life in order to see where he is. Even to the most earnest ethicist it can happen that he is at some time ensnared in a self-deception for a moment, but he will soon discover it. When a more earnest person says to himself, "You must take your time, collect yourself in composure, so that in the future you can present the ideas in an appropriate form" and he then notices that he still remains in the old ways, he then discovers that it is shadowboxing with regard to his composure, and he becomes earnest about it. He immediately defines the terms so that the indefiniteness of time will not deceive him; he starves himself out through common work lest he deceive himself and waste his time on a productivity that actually interests him because he has a dim idea that there is something else he should be doing. What Poul Møller says somewhere* is so true and so mature: "During fairly complete idleness, one can still avoid boredom as long as an obligatory task is being neglected through the idleness, because one is then somewhat occupied by the continual struggle one is in with oneself. But as soon as the duty ceases, or one no longer feels any reminder of it at all, boredom sets in. The private tutor who from moment to moment postpones a working hour enjoys himself as long as he is on the point of going to his pupil, but when he has decided to skip the hour his enjoyment ceases. The reminder by conscience in that example was something unpleasant that served as a stimulation for something pleasant. A poet who is writing a

*Note. See *Samtl. Skr.*,[52] III, p. 217 middle.

VII²
B 235
214

VII²
B 235
215

tragedy, although it was part of his plan of life to study for a degree, will do it with greater enthusiasm than he will do it later if he gives up that plan." In the same way it may also be the dim consciousness that instead of being productive he ought to be doing something else that makes Magister Adler so productive and makes his productivity so interesting to him, since he, rather than becoming clear to himself through his productivity, instead defends himself against what ethical simplicity would bid him to do.

Magister Adler, then, has no decisive ethical presuppositions; Hegelian philosophy has taught him to do without an ethics. Thus there is nothing to halt him and make him see his latest productivity, even if it was the most brilliant ever written, as a mistake that does not lead him closer to understanding himself in what is decisive for his life: to have had a revelation—but leads him away from it. Hegelian philosophy would be so far from being able to explain this to him that it must rather encourage him in the idea that the direction of his productivity is the right one.

Hegelian philosophy has no ethics; therefore it has never occupied itself with the future, which is essentially the element or medium of ethics. Hegelian philosophy looks at the past, at the six thousand years of world history, and now is busy with showing each individual development to be an element in the world-historical process. Charming! But when he was living, the late Prof. Hegel had, and every living person has or at least ought to have, an ethical relation to the future. Hegelian philosophy knows nothing about this. From this it follows quite simply that every living person who with the help of Hegelian philosophy wants to understand himself in his own personal life falls into the most foolish confusion.[53] In Hegelian fashion, he will be able to understand it only when it is past, when it has been traversed, when he is dead—but now, unfortunately, he is living.[54] With what, then, is he actually to fill his life while he is living? With nothing, since he actually is only waiting continually for the moment of death in order in the backward turning of that moment to be able to understand the traversed life. But if the life traversed was filled with nothing, what then is there really to understand?

VII²
B 235
216

Or if a person is still living, is living forward in the direction of life's momentum toward the future, and in this way is still filling part of his life with something, then in Hegelian fashion he must as quickly as possible view what has been traversed as an element in the development of his life. But each time he is to view something traversed as an element in his life, he must turn around during that time, must halt being an existing person in the ethical direction of the future. Thus the more he as an enthusiastic Hegelian hurries to view as an element what has been traversed, the shorter the traversed becomes, so that he at last comes very close to himself in a strange situation: he cannot find time to live out something because he must immediately view it as an element. In ethical simplicity, in religious simplicity, one is of the opinion that life here on earth is a time of work, in which at every moment there is to be a striving forward—then in eternity there certainly will be time to contemplate. But Hegelian philosophy teaches a person the trick: to anticipate one's own pastness, as Johannes Climacus says.[55] Hegelian philosophy redoubles the individual and thus brings about within one and the same personality a strange encounter between a living person and a contemplating person on life's way. Insofar as he is a living person, he is to go forward; insofar as he is a contemplative person, he is to go backward. When these two come very close to each other, then life quite correctly comes to a halt, that is, the living person cannot move ahead of the contemplating person who must inspect, since, after all, the living person and the contemplating person are one and the same individual.

Let us now consider Magister Adler. He has gone astray in reflection; he is absorbed in reflection on his state in a tension instead of working himself out of it. Yes, this is how an ethicist will view him and his productivity. But a Hegelian [*deleted in* version IV: (to be sure, Adler has burned his Hegelian manuscripts, but for all that the Hegelian philosophy can still haunt him)] must encourage him in his idea that his procedure is the right one, since he is now in the process of viewing this condition as an element in his life-development. Magister Adler has had a revelation; his reply has shown that he does not have within him the Christian qualitative concept of a revelation but only volatil-

VII²
B 235
217

ized definitions in which to wrap himself. Instead of now collecting himself, he takes over, so it seems, lock, stock, and barrel, "all the *Wirtschaft* [works] on his own account" and makes all this, along with his four latest books, into the lyrical element in his life-development. He himself is aware that "he has been harmed in the form of the four latest books,"[56] he who the year before had hoped in the future to find the appropriate form. Adler himself certainly must find it dubious that he, after having hoped in the future etc., in the year 1845 has come no further in 1846 than to be harmed in the form, thus to the awareness that the form is not yet the appropriate one. The relation between the two statements shows quite correctly his wrong direction. When he the first time said that he hoped in the future etc., there was still a kind of hope, but now he has even become calmed down and finds it quite in order that he has been harmed in the form—in the books that came after the stated hope. And why does he find it in order? Well, quite naturally, because he, instead of getting out of what was wrong, takes time to view it as an element—in his life-development. But Magister Adler's life-development does not as yet exist (in the sense of pastness); only that exists which has been experienced up to now, but this is what he wants to understand as an element—in what? Yes, here comes the difficulty. Once Magister Adler's life is over and it lies completely finished before the observer, then there can perhaps be a question of understanding the particular section as an element, but simultaneously, when one is in something, to be able to become conscious that it is an element in a totality that is yet to come—that just will not do. That a man anticipates his future—well, yes, there is some sense in that—but to anticipate his past!

VII²
B 235
218

Only ethics can place a living person in the proper position; it says: the main thing is to strive, to work, to act, and if one has taken a wrong direction of reflection, then above all to come back from it. Therefore ethics would refer Adler to his first statement, that he has had a revelation, and require him to give himself time to understand himself in it, in order then either to stand by his first statement or solemnly to revoke it.

As he does everywhere, so also here Magister Adler has an indirect merit by unconsciously satirizing Hegel. A quiet still-life

professor is better able to skulk through life in an illusion of retro-
spection; he himself is number 0 and therefore presumably is
busy only with the past and with understanding it as an element.
But when an awakened person, who has even burned his Hegelian manuscripts, nevertheless tries to view his lyrical muddled
state as an element in his life-development, he certainly gets Hegelian philosophy into hot water, by which it is not served at all.

VII²
B 235
218

§5.⁵⁷

[*VERSION IV:* VI.

AN INOFFENSIVE SATIRE ON ESTABLISHED CHRISTENDOM

X⁶
B 55
58

As an introduction to this little satire, I will imagine an event, a
fact. A theological graduate, cum laude or, for that matter,
summa cum laude, is personally living in essentially pagan categories, personally has no impression of Christianity, but this does
not strike him as strange, for he does have theological knowledge
and a scholarly education to a high degree. Then the time comes
for him when he can be considered in a search for an official
appointment; he seeks—and becomes a *Christian* pastor in Christendom. After having been a pastor for some time, he is suddenly
so very powerfully moved by the religious—something that psychologically is quite in order simply because as a pagan or although a pagan he has become a Christian pastor, that is, because
earlier he was unaware that he was not a Christian and in that
condition had undertaken to be a pastor—that he is carried away
into religious eccentricity, mistakes himself for an apostle—and
he must be removed from office. In this event that I have here
imagined, there is a double satire: that he, essentially as a pagan,
becomes—a Christian pastor—and that he, brought considerably
closer to the essentially Christian, is dismissed. In none of these
events does the Church administration actually have anything to
reproach itself for. He was, after all, a theological graduate, therefore qualified for an official appointment; he was, after all, a
Christian in such a way as all are Christians and *de occultis non
judicat ecclesia* (concerning hidden things the Church does not
judge).⁵⁸ As for the latter, his removal from office, that of course
was unavoidable.

X⁶
B 55
59

I should think that such an event, if I imagine its taking place in actuality, would in the first satire contain something very awakening; it would provide an opportunity to give a glimpse into what it perhaps means that all are Christians of sorts. One might have misgivings about whether there is nevertheless something illusory about the many Christians in geographical Christendom. Here there can be no question of judging and condemning. It is, after all, a fictive event; moreover, all such external busyness is quite alien to me and my nature. But especially for each individual such an event could be an awakening for thinking about this matter, that all as such are Christians, whatever result he may arrive at with regard to the rest.[59]

Perhaps this is not the case (I know nothing and want to know nothing), but let us imagine that many go on living as Christians and actually are pagans, inasmuch as existence, the surrounding world, has transformed itself into a huge illusion that again and again in every way strengthens them in the notion that they are Christians. Let us imagine these many people later in life, each one][60] as the founder of a family. Then these simulated Christians in turn *bring up* their children—in Christianity—what then will that generation of Christians become?

On the whole it is certainly characteristic of our age that the concept of *upbringing*, at least in the understanding of antiquity, is disappearing more and more from the speech and lives of people. In antiquity the importance of a person's upbringing was valued very highly, and it was understood as a harmonious development of that which will carry the various gifts and talents and the disposition of the personality ethically in the direction of character. In our day there seems to be an impatient desire to do away with this upbringing and on the other hand to emphasize *instruction*. There is a desire to have the young learn quickly, and as early as possible, a great deal and all sorts of things, learn what can almost tangibly be guaranteed to be knowledge and to amount to something. Formative education, the ethical education of character, is not anything like that and requires much time and diligence. In our day people seem to think that if one merely sees to it in every way that the child learns something, learns a language, mathematics, religion, etc., then in other

VII²
B 235
219

VII²
B 235
220

respects the child can more or less bring up himself. In every age and in every country this certainly is a great mistake, but it becomes especially corrupting in Christendom. Therefore, if an individual is not to be outright defrauded of Christianity, one of two things must be done: *either* he must, from his early childhood and as long as he is entrusted to one's care, be kept away from any relation to Christianity, be allowed to grow up without any Christian knowledge whatever, in order that as an adult he can get a decisive impression of Christianity and choose for himself; *or* from his earliest childhood the parents must take the responsibility of conveying to him by means of a rigorous Christian upbringing a decisive impression of the essentially Christian. But if he is allowed to grow up from infancy in the common notion that he is a Christian as a matter of course, everything humanly possible is done to deceive him with regard to human life's absolute qualitative decision. He is then a Christian in about the same sense as he is a human being, and as little as it occurs to him later to reflect earnestly on whether he really is a human being, so little will it ordinarily occur to him to make an accounting to himself with regard to whether he actually is a Christian.

VII²
B 235
221 I will now imagine—since it is against my nature to meddle in any other person's relationship with God, even merely in such a way that I would be aware that there is a man like that—I will imagine a father of a family. He is competent in his occupation, socially engaging, not lacking in wit, well liked by all, hospitable and sociable at home; he does not scoff at religion (even if this is dangerous, it is perhaps better for children because it provides elasticity); neither is he in the strictest sense indifferent. But he is a Christian of sorts; he would find it strange, affected, and conspicuous to make more fuss outwardly or inwardly about this matter. He is a Christian of sorts, and through the reading of several modern books he agrees with the view that Christianity is the highest culture of the mind and that every cultured person is a Christian. In his domestic life, whether or not there are guests, he never finds any occasion to express himself religiously about religious matters. If on a rare occasion it happens that some eccentric religious person attracts some attention and becomes the subject of the day and thereby also a subject for discussion in that father's house, the judgment upon such a person and upon

his conduct is not a religious but an esthetic judgment, which brands such a tone and such a manner as objectionable, as something that cannot be tolerated in the circle of the cultured.

This man's wife is a lovable woman, free of all modern unfeminine caprices, tenderhearted as mother and wife. At a particular moment in her life, she has also felt a need for deeper religious consciousness. But since such matters and such concerns have never been brought up between her and her husband, and since she perhaps has an exaggerated respect for the demands in regard to culture by her superior-to-her husband, she fears that it would betray a lack of culture or would offend if she wanted to speak about religious subjects. Therefore she is silent and with feminine devotedness completely adjusts herself to her husband, becomingly dedicates herself, which he masculinely finds so very suitable; and these two harmonize as a married couple rarely does in Christendom.

The children grow up under the eyes of these parents. Nothing is spared to develop their minds and to enrich them with knowledge, and while the children are growing this way in knowledge and insight, they are unconsciously appropriating the parents' cultured manner; therefore this family is truly a very pleasant home to visit. It follows, of course, that the children are Christians; after all, they were born of Christian parents, and thus it is just as natural as that someone is a Jew who is born of Jewish parents*—how in all the world would anything else occur to the

VII^2
B 235
222

---

*To be Christian because one is born of Christian parents is the fundamental illusion from which a host of others is derived.[61] One is a Jew by being born of Jewish parents; quite so, since Judaism is essentially connected to and bound in natural qualifications. But Christianity is a qualification of spirit, so that in it there is neither Jew nor pagan nor *born* Christians. It is fitting that from being a pagan, from being a Jew, from being born of Christian parents, one *becomes* a Christian, since the qualification of spirit is higher than the qualification of nature. On the other hand one cannot very well *become* a Jew, since one must be born a Jew. One cannot be a Christian and yet not be a Christian, but one can be a Jew and yet not be a Jew, because the qualification of nature predominates. That is, if a Jew is not a believing Jew, he is just as fully a Jew, but a Christian who is not a believing Christian is not a Christian at all. The qualification *Christian* is one of which it must be said absolutely: one is not *born* with the qualification; it is exactly the opposite; it is precisely what one is to *become*, what one is to *come to be.*

children? That there are Jews, pagans, Mohammedans, fetish worshipers, they of course know from history and the scholarly instruction in religion, but they also know it as something that does not in any way pertain to them [*deleted in version IV:* , and on the other hand they know nothing at all about the possibility that one can be a Christian and yet not be a Christian].

Let us then take the oldest of the children; he is now at the age when he is to be confirmed. It follows, of course, that the youth answers yes to the questions the pastor puts to him; how in all the world would anything else occur to the youth? Has one ever heard that anyone has answered no, or has a single word ever been hinted to the youth that he, too, can answer no? On the other hand, it perhaps may have been pointed out to him that he should not answer too loudly and not too softly either, but should do it in a becoming and courteous manner. He perhaps remembers having heard his father say that there was something affected about this whispering yes at confirmation. It is to such a degree obvious that he is to answer yes, indeed, to such a degree that his attention, instead of being directed to the answer, is directed to the purely esthetic side of the formality. So he answers yes—neither too loudly nor too softly, but with the cheerful boldness and yet modest propriety that is becoming in a young person. On the day of confirmation, the father is somewhat more earnest than usual; yet his earnestness has more of a festive than a religious character, and thus it completely harmonizes with the high spirits that take over after they have come home from church, when the father is not only pleasant as usual but applies his talents to really making this day a festival day. The mother is moved; she has even cried in church. But motherly tenderness and worldly concern for the child's future destiny are certainly not reserved to Christianity. Thus the youth on his confirmation day will probably have a more solemn impression of the father, a moving impression of the mother; he will gratefully and joyfully remember this day as a beautiful recollection, but he does not receive any decisive Christian impression. The youth gets the impression that this day may be a more significant moment in his life—if not as significant as, for example, becoming a student and being admitted to the university.

VII²
B 235
223

The youth is confirmed, and now little by little the busy time
for him begins when he must prepare for his officer's examination—we may assume that he will take that path. He passes his
examination with honors, goes to college, distinguishes himself
further; the parents have real joy in the son, whom they nevertheless seldom see, now that he has moved out of the house and
is always busy. He is successful, at the age of twenty-six he is
already a captain.

Our young captain falls in love. She is an attractive, lovable
girl, completely according to the parents' wish, and the already
pleasant family gains a new charm by taking her into its circle
and by all the cozy atmosphere that pervades the home life when
it is indicated that the older generation will now be rejuvenated
in a new one. The captain is really in love. But to be really in
love is certainly no specific qualification of the essentially Christian; there have certainly been lovers in Greece just as much as
in Christianity—indeed, the erotic qualification is really not
Christian. The wedding date is set; a church wedding is considered to be the most ceremonious. The captain's father is of the
opinion that a church wedding, with the impression of the
church's lofty arches, with the organ tones, with the entire sur-
roundings, and through bringing the pastor into his proper sur-
roundings, puts the soul in a ceremonious mood quite different
from that when one sneaks off in a carriage to a pastor to be
married in a small reception room. Add to that what the captain's
father has also said, "that a nemesis rests upon all secrecy, that any
unforeseen fatality acquires an almost ridiculous power over a
person. If, for example, the carriage took a wrong direction, or
it tipped over and a crowd gathered—if it was a generally known
and official matter that the unfortunates were on their way to a
church wedding, well, it would of course always be an unpleasant interruption; but what if it was a secret, was supposed to be
a secret, what if it was a quiet wedding they were going to in
complete privacy!"

So the captain stands before the altar with his young bride—a
lovely couple! And the pastor asks: Have you counseled with
God and with your conscience etc.? What is the captain to answer? Well, obviously the captain, who in the erotic sense is

VII²
B 235
224

really in love, does not have to be asked twice if he will have the girl. So he answers yes, not too loudly and not too softly, but with precisely the noble, self-conscious, and yet modest bearing that is so becoming in a young man. Whether this yes is quite exactly a reply to the pastor's question does not occur to the captain at all; he is happily in love, happily and confidently and honestly convinced that he will make the girl as happy as he can.

So the husband and wife are united. The organ tones peal a mundane farewell; the wedding party walks in procession; the crowd gazes in wonder, almost in envy, at the charming pair, and everyone who has a chance to look more closely sees the love shining out of the captain's eyes. Yes, there is reason to be envious of him, reason for the family to be proud of him: he is young, talented, well-developed, masculinely handsome, honest enough truly to be in love, happy in his love, faithful in sincere resolve.

Now suppose this to have taken place in geographical Christendom. Who has then been more deceived with regard to Christianity than our captain himself! The person who has never heard anything about Christianity is not deceived in this way; but the person who, without having received the slightest decisive impression of the essentially Christian, who from the very beginning is strengthened in the notion that he is a Christian—he is deceived. How in all the world will it occur to him to be concerned about whether he is, or about becoming, what he in his earliest recollection has been convinced that he is as a matter of course? Everything has strengthened him in this conviction. Nothing has brought him to a halt. The parents have never spoken about the essentially Christian; they have thought: The pastor must do that. And the pastor has thought: Instruct the lad in religion, that I can surely do, but actually convey to him the decisive impression, that must be the parents' affair. This is the way he grew up, was confirmed, became a lieutenant, captain— now a Christian married man.

If someone, unless he was a pastor,* would in all earnestness

VII²
B 235
225

---

*Note. It is quite right that by virtue of his position a pastor produces a different effect than someone who, having no office but only a religious interest, speaks to a person. It is, however, perhaps not infrequent that the person spoken

ask our captain if he is a Christian, the captain would no doubt
smile. There would be nothing coarse and insulting in this smile,
as if he wanted the smile to let the asker understand that he surely
was an obtuse person—no, the captain is too cultured for that,
since he really is a cultured young man. But he would involuntarily smile, because the question would seem to him just as
strange as if someone asked him if he actually is a human being.
If at the tea table that evening in our captain's house someone
told the story about Socrates, that he is supposed to have said that
he did not know for certain whether he was a human being,[63] the
captain would perhaps say, "It is undeniably ironic enough, and
one cannot help but smile at it; yet on the other hand there is also
something odd about introducing that kind of doubt, which
touches life's foremost, simplest, and most rudimentary presuppositions. For example, today a man in all earnestness asked me
if I am a Christian. Moreover, remarks such as that may give a
person a distaste for life if instead of becoming something in the
world one is supposed to lose time by thinking about whether
one is a human being, or about what amounts to the same in
a Christian country, whether one is a Christian. It is another

VII²
B 235
226

VII²
B 235
227

---

to secretly weakens the impression because by a *reservatio mentalis* [mental reser-
vation] he inserts the middle term: It is the pastor's livelihood. One finds it quite
in order for the pastor to speak this way, and why? Because it is the pastor's
livelihood. One does not receive the pure impression of the intrinsic value of
the religious and its claim on a human being. If a private person were to spend
all his time and energy on the religious, many people would perhaps regard the
expression in his mouth as lunacy but all right in the pastor's mouth, not because
of the expression itself but in view of its being the pastor's livelihood. One
would be unable to understand that the religious should have such a reality that
it could occupy a person solely for its own sake but find it all right that someone
occupies himself with the religious when it is his livelihood. It is the same in
other situations. Without a doubt there are in every generation many who, like
North Americans, regard speculating and philosophizing as a kind of loafing
and lunacy.[62] If they find out that someone spends his whole day thinking, they
regard him as a loafer and an eccentric. It is another matter, however, if someone is appointed and paid as an official teacher of philosophy; then they find it
quite in order for him to speculate—since, after all, it is his livelihood. One
person earns his living by cleaning chimneys, another by philosophizing; but
cleaning chimneys and philosophizing are six of one and a half dozen of the
other; the one has no more worth than the other if it is not a person's livelihood.

VII²
B 235
226

matter if one wants to make a career of theology. But an officer
surely can be satisfied with taking for granted that he is a human
being and a Christian, if with propriety he then does not en-
croach on the religious, does not indulge in any uncultured
mockery of it." And the captain's young wife will not be surprised by this talk; in every way she is convinced that he is a
human being, and she wishes that nothing may delay him in
becoming a general.

Let us now imagine the opposite, that someone by a rigorous
Christian upbringing has already as a child received a decisive
impression of the essentially Christian. If this is to happen, the
parents themselves must essentially be Christians so that the child
receives the continual impression of how the parents in everyday use lead a religious life, occupy themselves with the essentially Christian both for their upbuilding and in order to express
it in their conduct. So the child grows up, and at the age that is
most receptive and the memory of which is most reliable, the
decisively Christian will imprint itself unforgettably on his soul
and κατὰ δύναμιν [potentially] modify his character. Might there
be, as stated, some connection between the fact that one seldom
meets a person of character these days and that people have no
proper idea of what upbringing is, that one confuses learning
(*discere*) with being brought up, learning with learning to obey,
to bow under the powerful and daily impression of the ethical
and the religious?

That such a child would now be a Christian in the stricter
sense because it has had an earnest Christian upbringing would
again be an illusion. Next to being Christian because one is born
of Christians comes the fallacy: his parents were devout Christians, ergo he is a Christian. No, the unforgettable and deep impression of the essentially Christian in one's upbringing is only a
presupposition.

VII²
B 235
228

So, then, this child also goes out into the world. He undeniably has the presuppositions pertaining to becoming a Christian;
humanly speaking, everything humanly possible has been done
for him. But as yet there is no decision, because, even if his yes
on confirmation day is the result of the upbringing, it is still not
the decisive yes.

With the years, totally different aspects of life, totally different factors in the soul will probably come to assert themselves; the young person will sense impressions that are completely unfamiliar to him. The rigorous Christian upbringing is a presupposition and of such a nature that he must grow up to it in order really to take possession of it. Just as parents at the age when children grow most rapidly have the clothes made somewhat larger, made to grow into, likewise it can in all earnestness be said of someone who has had a rigorous Christian upbringing that his parents have given him clothing that is made to grow into, but also clothing no one can grow out of.

The young person will now become acquainted with the world and the worldly, and there will perhaps come a time when it naïvely seems strange to him that his parents have kept from him the glad gospel that is proclaimed on the dance floor of youth. If the worldly acquires any power to sweep him off his feet, there may come a time when he impatiently thinks that his parents have deceived him. The captain probably never discovers that he is deceived; he has indeed been initiated into and formed by that in which his life has its continuance. But the other one, as a child he has heard nothing at all about the glory the world has to offer, or he has heard only a strict warning against it. With the presupposition of his earnest Christian upbringing, he stands like an alien, yes, like one deceived, in all this worldliness that now, when he himself sees it, seems altogether different from what was described to him as a child.

Yet, humanly speaking, what can be done has been done for this young person. His life must lie before him in such a way that he cannot avoid a crisis; he must come to a decision whether he wants to become a Christian or actually will give up Christianity. If what Socrates says is true, that the most frightful thing of all is to have one's life in an error,[64] then this young person must be considered fortunate, [65]because even if he makes a mistake and doubts, he must do it so decisively that for that very reason there remains hope for his rescue. It truly is the case that the most desperate decision is infinitely preferable to this furtive life that slinks along year after year in illusory security.

In a Christian country (and it is still a question whether there

VII²
B 235
229

is not something sophistical in directly joining the modifier
"Christian" with such abstract categories as country, state, nation, kingdom[66]—categories that are above the category of personal individuality and subjectivity and particularity) there is for
everyone a dangerous possibility of missing out on the highest
decision: to become a Christian. Whether it is sheer illusion that
a person imagines himself to be a Christian or whether a person
has received a decisive impression of the essentially Christian
through a rigorous Christian upbringing, it applies just as fully to
him: to become a Christian. In a Christian country, reminders
and admonitions may well be necessary in regard to this. But
Magister Adler's life contains precisely such a reminder. The difficulties in regard to becoming a Christian that can appear for
the one who is strictly brought up in Christianity, the sense in
which the upbringing is nevertheless only a presupposition, the
precariousness that such an upbringing may have, the responsibility parents thereby take upon themselves, but also inversely,
by not doing it—Magister Adler's life or its crisis of course does
not shed any light on all such things. He gives entirely the impression of a pagan who has suddenly come in contact with the
essentially Christian. But for that very reason his life is a reminder, or can be that for many, because he was indeed a Chris-

VII²
B 235
230

tian of sorts just as all are Christians; he was confirmed, was a
theological graduate, a Christian pastor in geographical Christendom—and yet the crisis discloses what must be understood by
his being a Christian. It is an event that is the reminder here, and
therefore the reminder is indirect; it is up to the single individual
whether he on his own will allow himself to be reminded. It is
not the same as when a revivalist thunders and judges, which can
so easily embitter people instead of benefiting them. No, Magister Adler influences by his life and thus influences indirectly. His
significance for contemporaries will presumably not be due as
much to what he became through the crisis or to the productivity
that derives from it as to what the crisis indirectly discloses and
denounces, how in geographical Christendom one can be a
Christian of sorts and even become a Christian pastor without
having the slightest impression of Christianity in the direction of:
becoming a Christian.[67]

ADDENDUM I[1]

The Dialectical Relations: the Universal, the Single Individual, the Special Individual

[*ADDED IN VERSION IV:* ETHICAL-RELIGIOUS DIALECTIC
AND POETICAL COMPOSITION]

Since our age is an "age of movement" that wants to bring forth something new, it must more frequently experience this collision between the universal and the single individual, a collision that in itself can always have difficulty enough, but sometimes also a difficulty that does not lie in the collision itself but in the one who collides. That is, if the special individual loves the universal, thinks humbly of himself as an individual in relation to the universal, with fear and trembling shrinks from being in error, he will make everything as easy and good as possible for the universal. And this conduct is a sign that it nevertheless was possible that he was an actual extraordinary. But if the individual does not love the universal, does not honor the established order, something one can very well do although one has something new to bring, if in his innermost being he perhaps has not made up his mind about what he is but merely dabbles at wanting to be an extraordinary, only investigates whether it pays well to be that—then with his knowledge (of chicanery) he will in part make everything as difficult as possible for the established order, and in part do it without becoming really aware of it himself, because basically he cannot do without the established order and therefore hangs on to it, attempts to shove the responsibility away from himself and onto the universal in order pettifoggingly to get the universal to do what he himself should do. When a person gets the idea that he must be separated from another person with whom he lives in the closest relationship, if he himself is certain

VIII²
B 9:14a
50

VII²
B 235
33

VII²
B 235
34

and decisively resolved, the painful process of separation becomes easier. But if he is uncertain, irresolute, then he very likely wants to do it but yet does not really have the courage to venture, if he is a deceitful fellow who wants to shove the responsibility from himself but steal the wages of the extraordinary—then the separation becomes a protracted story and for a long time remains a painful, aching, tiresome alliance.

Let us assume that a theological graduate in our age has come to hold the view that the oath of office is unwarranted. Well, then he can express that freely and unreservedly if he considers it advantageous. "But then he will disqualify himself for promotion and perhaps will achieve nothing at all, create no sensation, because a graduate is too small a magnitude, and in addition he does not really have any control over the state Church since he is a private individual." Consequently (now I am thinking of a selfish person who not only does not love the established order but is basically an enemy), what can he do then? For the time being he is silent. Then he seeks an appointment as a teacher in the Church; he receives it; he takes the oath of office. So now he is an official in the state Church. Then he publishes a book in which he propounds his revolutionary view. The circumstances of the whole matter are now changed. It would have been easy for the state to reject a theological graduate, easy to say to him: Well, if you have these views, you cannot become an officeholder. And the state Church would not have come to deal with this case at all; at most it would have needed to take a preventive measure against him in particular—not to appoint him. But the theological graduate was ingenious and ingeniously understood how to make himself important in a totally different way. The responsibility that the graduate should have taken upon himself for his singular view and would have dearly purchased by sacrificing his future in the service of a higher call, while he sought to make the affair as easy as possible for the established order— the responsibility is now shifted over onto the state Church, which becomes the agent that must *dismiss* him, who by having become an officeholder has also made an attempt to interest the whole profession in his fate. As a theological graduate, he is looked upon only as one, but as an officeholder he attempts to be

VII²
B 235
35

looked upon as thousands, counting also on the advantage that now it is the state that must take the step. Thus there is now abundant opportunity to vex the established order, since there perhaps must also be a diocesan court, and it still is not inconceivable to have at least a dissenting minority on his side, and then in turn, with the help of the newspapers, this minority could be made into the intelligent party, also into a demonstration that in the whole profession there is dissension and a dislike of the oath of office etc. In this way such a revolutionary tries cowardly and underhandedly to make as much trouble as he can for the universal.

However much the state or the state Church may be conscious of being in the truth [*Sandhed*], of having right on its side, and also of having sufficient soundness [*Sundhed*] to isolate such a person without fearing that many would be harmed by it, it nevertheless cannot ever be serviceable to the state or the state Church to have its first principles subjected to discussion very frequently. Every life, every existence has its hidden life, its root life, in its basic presupposition, in its basic principle, from which the vital energy proceeds to give growth. From physiology it is well known that there is nothing more injurious to digestion than continual reflection on digestion; similarly, also in the realm of the spirit, it is most injurious when reflection too often makes a mistake and, instead of serving in the transaction that discloses the hidden work of the secret life, it falls upon the basic principles themselves. If a marriage were to reflect continually on the reality of the marriage, it would *eo ipso* become a mediocre marriage, since the energy that should be used for carrying out the tasks of the married life would be used by reflection to waste away the foundation. If a man who has chosen a specific occupation were to reflect continually on whether this occupation was the right one, he will *eo ipso* become a poor partner. Therefore, even if the state or the state Church has sufficient soundness to discharge the revolutionary, it is nevertheless harmful that reflection is occasioned. Of everything that should be secret and hidden it holds true, as the ballad says: If you speak only one word.[2] It is easy enough to say such a fateful word, but the harm it can cause is incalculable, and it perhaps takes a giant to stop the harmful effect

VII²
B 235
36

of a word that a Peer Ruus let slip out in his sleep.[3] If the state or
the state Church frequently has to suspend many such individuals, the appearance is finally conjured up that it is the state itself
that is *in suspenso*; suspending is always the result when one is not
resting upon the foundation but the foundation itself is made
dialectical.

Such a thing can easily become dangerous for the state, chiefly
because that kind of discussion is also most tempting—to all mediocre pates, all babblers, all stuffed shirts, and therefore especially the public. That is, the more concrete the subject is that
one is to ponder and on which one is to express oneself, the more
quickly and clearly will it be apparent whether or not the one
speaking has the qualifications for being able to join the discussion. But the huge tasks, they are really something—for the most
trivial gossipmongers. It is perhaps not out of the way to call this
to mind, since our age, an age of movement, in many ways aims
to bring the basic presuppositions under discussion in state and
Church; from this it readily follows that a fabulous human mass
bestirs itself and starts gabbling in the discussion-game, a public
that understands nothing at all, whereas the huge size of the task
advantageously conceals the respective ignorance of those discussing and of the discoursing.

If a teacher wants to do a favor for a good-for-nothing pupil,
he can do it in various ways, but among others he can also do it
by assigning him such a huge task that the examiners are unable
to conclude anything at all from the insignificance of his answers,
because the enormous size of the task deprives them of the criterion. Perhaps I can illustrate this with an example from the world
of scholarship. One rarely manages to get a scholarly blatherpate,
who basically knows nothing, to become involved in anything
concrete. He does not talk about a specific dialogue by Plato;
that is too insignificant for him—it perhaps would also disclose
that he had not read it. No, he talks about Plato in general, or
perhaps even about Greek philosophy in general, but then especially about the wisdom of the Indians and the Chinese. This,
Plato in general, Greek philosophy in general, Eastern profundity in general, is the enormously large, the limitless, which advantageously hides his ignorance. Similarly, it is also much easier

VII²
B 235
37

to talk about changing the form of government than to deal with a very small concrete task; and the injustice against the few competent people consists in their seemingly becoming, because of the enormous magnitude of the issue, equals with every Tom, Dick, and Harry who "also express themselves." In this way it is much easier for a chatterbox to criticize our Lord than to judge a grammar school pupil's Danish composition, indeed, than to judge even a matchstick; if only the task is concrete, he will, it is hoped, soon betray how obtuse he is. But our Lord and his governing of the world are something so enormously large that in a certain dizzily abstract sense the most foolish can join in the talk as well as the wisest.

Our age is perhaps only too close to sophistry; the greatest issues are subjected to discussion in order to encourage the most trivial and thoughtless people to join in the discussion. Let us not forget that that noble reformer, the simple wise man[4] in Greece, who had the Sophists to deal with, had his strength in driving the Sophists from behind the mask of the abstract and the all-encompassing, had his strength in making the conversation so concrete that everyone who conversed with him and intended to speak about some enormous subject or other (administration of the state on the whole, public education on the whole, etc.) was brought, before he was aware of it, to speaking about himself— whether he knew anything or did not know anything. One would almost think that our contemporary sophists, plus their addendum, the public, are conscious of how they use a mask, because it is indeed customary, it is popular opinion, to regard it as being in bad taste if anyone sets to work on such a sophist, relieves him of all his fantastic attire, and makes him what he is, a poor devil who in the name of the public, of criticism, and of the century has made so much noise. It is supposed to be in bad taste; however, it seems to me that it is in the worst taste for the poor devil when one has relieved him of those outer garments and he now stands before us in his natural size. But in our age one impresses—by means of outer garments. Similarly, it is impressive when someone receives an enormously big package in the mail, but when the package is found to be nothing but wrapping paper, it is no longer impressive.

VII²
B 235
38

But back to the theological graduate. Perhaps someone would say, "But it is indeed hard to demand of a man who has qualified himself for a position that he will obstruct his future so that he does not even have left the hope of receiving a pension that he could have if he, after having been appointed, was dismissed." Yes, of course it is hard, but it also must be hard—to be an extraordinary. Yes, it is so hard that no one, if he understands it, could wish to be a person like that, even though the one who in truth is such a one will assuredly find comfort and satisfaction and blessedness in his God-relationship. The true extraordinary will definitely not be comforted or seek relief or find relief in the universal but only in God; and therein lies the dialectical that is the torment and the crisis, and also the blessedness.

When, however, an age becomes devoid of character, it is certainly possible that one or another individual has a few symptoms of wanting to be an extraordinary, but he cannot manage it, and therefore he wants the universal to help him achieve it; he wants the universal, the established order, and himself to combine forces to let him become an extraordinary. How preposterous! The extraordinary is specifically to bring the new point of departure; in relation to the established order he is like the person whose feet are at the door and will carry the old away[5] —and then the established order itself is supposed to help him. No, the universal must just tighten its opposition, and if the established order does not do that, then here again something sophistical develops, just as in the discussion of the enormous tasks—so that to be the extraordinary becomes the easiest of all, something to which every bungler aspires, something for all those who otherwise are fit for nothing. In our day there are plenty of epigrams that the age itself produces without understanding them or paying attention to them. Let us not forget that nowadays a martyr, a reformer, is a man who smells of perfume, a man who sits with a wreath on his head and gorges at banquets, a man who is comfortably well-off, a man who actually ventures nothing at all and yet acquires everything, even the title of reformer. His title—the wittiness of our age still consists in grinding out hackneyed witticisms mocking governments for their titles and orders; it has not discovered that it is actually the public and public opinion that

VII²
B 235
39

play with titles when they, like children who play soldier, appoint to world-historical and absolute rank the most important person they have on their side. But if the established order does not tighten the reins, then everyone who will not obey finally becomes a reformer. When the father becomes weak, when domestic life is disturbed by mutinous reflection, the naughty child very easily mistakes himself for a kind of reformer. When the schoolmaster loses the reins, the impertinent pupil very easily mistakes himself for a kind of reformer. It has therefore gone so far in our day that it actually does not take courage to defy the king, to annoy and insult the administration, but certainly a little courage to say a word to the opposition right down to the jubilant rabble, courage—to speak *against the reformers.*[6]

What then are the dialectical relations between (a) the *universal* and (b) the *single individual* and (c) the *special individual*, that is, the extraordinary? When the single individual only reproduces the established order in his life (of course differently according to what powers and abilities, what competence he has), then he relates himself to the established order as the normal individual, the ordinary individual; he unfolds the life of the established order in his existence. For him the established order is the foundation that educatively penetrates and develops his abilities in likeness to itself; he relates himself as an individual whose life is inflected according to the paradigm of the established order. Let us not, however, forget (since the dissatisfied and malicious-minded are eager to spread false rumors) that his life is by no means devoid of spirit because of this. He is not merely one more who reels off words that go according to the paradigm. No, he is free and essentially independent, and to be such an ordinary individual is quite in order, usually the highest, but also qualitatively the most significant task that is assigned to any human being and that therefore is assigned to every human being.*

VII²
B 235
40

*Note. Everyone in the state and the state Church is to be and therefore also ought to be an individual, but not the extraordinary individual. In conscientiousness and responsibility before God, that is, through his eternal consciousness, everyone is an individual. He never becomes mass; he is never enrolled in the public. With responsibility before God and after having tested himself in his conscience, he attaches himself to the whole as a limb and takes it as his task to

As soon, however, as the single individual lets his reflection move him so deeply that he wants to reflect on the basic presupposition of the established order, he is at the point of being inclined to wanting to be a special individual, and as long as he reflects in this way he is rejecting the *impressa vestigia* [footprints] of the established order, is *extra ordinem* [outside the order] on his own responsibility. And when the single individual continues along this road and goes so far that he does not as the ordinary individual *reproductively renew the life of the established order* **within himself** by willing, under eternal responsibility, to order himself within it but wants to renew *the life of the established order by bringing a new point of departure* for it, *a new point of departure in relation to the basic presupposition of the established order*, when he by submitting directly to God must relate himself transformingly to the established order—then he is the extraordinary. That is, then this becomes the place allotted to him, whether he is justified or not; here he must be victorious and here find his judgment—the universal must exclude him.

As everywhere, so it holds true especially here that the qualitative dialectic is to be respected with ethical earnestness. That is, in an age devoid of character, the sophistic can emerge that someone who is inclined to be an extraordinary wants this intention to benefit him even in the service of the universal; then on that basis he even becomes someone out of the ordinary among the ordinary. A sad confusion that has its basis in a thoughtless, frivolous quantifying. Either a person should want to serve the universal, the established order, express this, and in that case his merit becomes proportional to the faithfulness and scrupulousness with which he knows how to conform himself to it, knows how to make his life into a beautiful and rich and true reproduction of the established order, to develop himself as a type for the established order—or he should be an extraordinary in earnest, and then he, *extra ordinem*, should step out of the line, out of the ranks where he does not belong. But in our times everything is

---

be faithful in the reproduction, while the responsibility of eternity saves him from the purely animal category: to be the crowd, the mass, the public or whatever other droves there are that give one occasion to have to speak of human beings as one speaks of a drove of cattle.

confused. A dissatisfied officeholder, for example, still wants to be something extraordinary, because he is an officeholder—and also dissatisfied. Sad, immoral confusion! If he is dissatisfied because he has something new from God to bring to us, then out of the ranks, "a rope around his neck,"* and then let him talk; then the situation is what a true extraordinary needs and must demand in order to be able to gesticulate and start the carillon ringing. But if he does not have something new from God to bring to us, then it must by no means be reckoned an advantage for him that he is dissatisfied—and also an officeholder. But the lack of character and the prying cowardice of the age finally make a kind of dishonorable narrow-mindedness out of being of some benefit: either wholeheartedly a faithful officeholder or a reformer with a sword over his head, in mortal danger, in self-denial. Εἷς κοίρανος ἔστω [Let there be one lord],⁸ and thus also let there be one who is the extraordinary. If a whole generation wants to be king and a whole generation wants to dabble in being extraordinary, then it becomes rubbish. And the result of that is only delay. If Governance had meant to give the generation an extraordinary, it must accordingly be expected that perhaps not even a forerunner will be sent, but we must be satisfied with something very simple, one who very simply can clear the way, very simply can throw out all these false prophets and has a little meaning and pith to bring into the enervated and meaningless situation again. When, namely, a whole generation has become reformist, the true reformer cannot at all begin to appear in his truth, that is, to call to mind an earlier locution: just as when at a fire everyone is giving orders, the fire chief cannot give the orders.⁹

It is the *point of departure* that makes the difference between the ordinary individual and the special individual; in other respects it may very well be that, humanly speaking, an ordinary individual

*Note. Caesar tells that it was a custom among the Gauls that everyone who made a new proposal had to stand with a rope around his neck—so that they could promptly get rid of him if it did not amount to anything.⁷ If this commendable custom were to be introduced in our day, God knows whether the country would have enough rope, since the whole population has become project planners, and yet perhaps in the first place rope would not even be needed—possibly there would be no one who would volunteer.

VII²
B 235
42

VII²
B 235
43

is greater than an actual extraordinary. The final criterion by which people take rank is the ethical, in relation to which the differences [*deleted in version V:* (even in the special sense of being called by God)] are negligible, but the worldly mind inversely determines the order of precedence according to the difference. [10]Let us take an example of such a *consummate individual,* and let us really rejoice that we have examples to point to; let us name *honoris causa,* but also in order to throw light on this relation, the admired Bishop of Sjælland [*changed in version V to:* the state Church's leading prelate, assuredly also its most faithful servant;] [*deleted in version V:* and everyone does well to admire here, because one must find joy in admiring the person who expresses the universal, since]—he also expresses the universal and one can learn from him. [*Deleted in version V:* Bishop Mynster does not have the least of what one in the strictest sense might call the description of the special individual. On the contrary, with sublime serenity, happily resting in his conviction as the rich content of an abundant life, with admonishing emphasis, with a sober composure of earnestness bordering on a magnanimous little ironic turn toward confused pates, this man has continually acknowledged that it was not something new that he had to bring, that on the contrary it was the old and familiar. He has never rocked the pillars of the established order; on the contrary, he himself has stood unshakable as a main pillar.[11] And when he revises the first edition of his earliest sermons, "he finds nothing to change in the essentials"[12] (as if since that time he perhaps had been so fortunate as to cope with one or another newly arrived systematic novelty); and if at some time on his deathbed he revises all the sermons, not for a new edition but to attest to the correctness of them, he will very likely again find "nothing to change in the essentials." No, it was all the old and familiar— which nevertheless found in him such a fresh and refreshing emanation, such a noble, beautiful, and rich expression, that in a long life he moves many people, how amazing, by the old* and familiar, and that after his death he will continue to move many people, who will long for *this* old and familiar as one longs for the

VII[2]
B 235
44

*and that after his death many, moved, will long for this old man and this old

charm of youth, as in the heat of summer one longs for the cool-
ness of the spring—how amazing, that it should be something old
and familiar! Truly, if at some time at the very beginning a doctrine must wish for an apostle who in the strictest (*deleted in version
V:* in the paradoxical) sense stands outside the ranks as an extraordinary, at a later time the same doctrine will wish for the kind of
stewards[13] who have nothing new to bring, who on the contrary
earnestly have their joy in expressing the universal themselves,
their joy in marching along in the ranks and teaching the rest of
us to keep time—if only we are careful to look alertly up to the
right.

When should a girl be married? Antiquity answers: "When she
is a girl in age but a woman in understanding."[14] When should a
man become a teacher?* When he has the vigor of youth and the
wisdom of an old man. And when does he reach his peak? When
he is an old man in[**] years and understanding, but as vigorous
in heart as a young man. What is it to preserve oneself, which,
essentially understood, is a man's highest task? It is, when the
blood is warm and the heart beats violently in the days of youth,
then to be able to cool down with almost an old man's composure; and it is, when the day declines, when it draws near to
taking its leave, then to be able to flame up with the fire of youth.
But is this not an insult to His Right Reverence to sit and write   VII²
something like this? If what has been stated is true, then Bishop   B 235
Mynster is indeed no great man, then he has indeed never fol-   45
lowed along with the times, then he does indeed not know what
the demand of the times is, to say nothing of his having himself
been able to invent it. No, he has not invented anything.
Whether he perhaps has not been able to (yet as a keen psychologist he very likely knows human follies from the ground up and
consequently possesses the key to the great storehouse where the
diverse demands of the times lie piled up), I shall not presume to
decide, but it is certain that he has not invented anything.]

The new point of departure is the difference between the true
ordinary and the true extraordinary; the essentially human crite-

---

*When he is a man in age but in wisdom an old man.
[**] age and wisdom

rion, the ethical, they both have in common. When the single individual actually is the true extraordinary and actually has a new point of departure, when he comprehends his life's distressing difficulty in that *discrimen* [distinction] between the universal and the singular *extra ordinem* [outside the order], he must be unconditionally recognizable by his being *willing to bring a sacrifice.** And this he must be willing to do *for his own sake* and *for the sake of the universal.*

Precisely because the extraordinary, if he is truly that, must through his God-relationship be conscious that he κατὰ δύναμιν [potentially] is stronger than the *summa summarum* [grand total] of all the established order, he has nothing at all to do with a concern about whether he will be victorious. No, he is completely free of this concern, but on the other hand he has the special singular's dreadful responsibility for every step he takes, whether he is now scrupulously following his orders down to the least detail, whether he is definitely and solely and obediently listening to God's voice—the dreadful responsibility if he heard or has heard wrong. For that very reason he must desire for himself all possible opposition from the outside, desire that the established order would have powers to be able to make his life a *tentamen rigorosum* [rigorous examination], since this testing and its pain still are nothing compared with the horror of the responsibility— if he was or had been in error! For example, if a son should feel called to introduce a new view of the home life (and just as a son is bound in piety, so every individual should and ought to be bound in piety in relation to the universal): would he not then, if it was truth in him, desire precisely that the father would be the strong one who could take a stand against him with the full power of fatherly authority? That is, the son would not so much fear to submit if he had been wrong, consequently to have to

VII²
B 235
46

In margin: *Note. That is, the established order as the established order is the legitimate and the strongest in the literal sense; it is not the single individual who is to be the superior in the literal sense, but the *special* individual, whose superiority is in the suffering of self-sacrifice. That he is sacrificed is the expression for the strength and legitimacy of the universal, and yet it is also the expression for his superiority, because his suffering and death are the victory of the new point of departure.

return, humbled but saved, to the old, as he would shudder before the horror of winning—if basically he had been wrong.

So it is with the true extraordinary; he is the most nonchalant person about that temporal concern of the worldly heroes, whether what he has to proclaim will be victorious in the world. On the other hand, as a poor sinner he is anxious, is overwhelmed every time he considers his responsibility and whether he in any way could have been mistaken; indeed, the weight of responsibility can rest on him so heavily that it seems as if he would stop breathing. For that very reason he desires opposition: he—the weak one, he—the strong one, who, although a solitary human being, κατὰ δύναμιν is stronger in his weakness than the united might of the established order, which naturally has the power both to flog him and to execute him as if it were nothing at all. When berserk fury came upon our northern fathers, they had themselves constrained between shields; in the same way the true extraordinary also desires that the power of the established order will form appropriate opposition.

Accordingly, Magister Adler, if he otherwise truly is the extraordinary, quite honestly would have to be happy that as the leading prelate in the Danish state Church there is a man like Bishop Mynster, a man who, without being cruel or narrowminded, by personally strictly obeying has disciplined himself to dare, with the heavy emphasis or gravity of earnestness, to require the universal of others, a man who surely can manage things if only the true extraordinary is there. Accordingly, Mag. Adler would then not need, as otherwise could be made necessary, to lend the established order a little of his power so that it could form appropriate opposition to him. But in any case Adler's cause owes much to Bishop Mynster's attitude. A weaker man in that position, a man who himself perhaps had a few symptoms of wanting to be somewhat extraordinary—in that case Adler probably would not have been dismissed, the situation would therefore not have been consistently and competently settled.* Then the whole thing would surely have become a

VII²
B 235
47

[*Deleted in version IV:* *Note. Then it is one of those obtuse opinions by which a weak age wrongs the competent ones, and with its own weakness as the criterion almost designates firmness of government as a craving for power, the meaningless "curious something." [*In version IV the preceding paragraph was changed to:* Accordingly, the extraordinary must quite honestly desire that there be, as the supreme ruler of the established order, a man who, without being cruel or narrow-minded, has the strength to dare to require the universal of others, a man who can surely manage things if only the true extraordinary is there. The extraordinary is then exempted from what otherwise could be made necessary, to lend the established order a little of his power so that it could form appropriate opposition to him. But in any case the cause of the extraordinary always owes much to such a man. A weaker man in such a position, a man who himself had a few symptoms of wanting to be somewhat extraordinary—in that case the whole thing is confused.]

A confused extraordinary to introduce the new and a weak-kneed government official to resist certainly do match each other, but only as being of the same poor kind. [*Addition in version IV:* And our age may very soon come to manifest such a condition.] If our age lacks true extraordinaries, then our age also lacks those earnest characters, those individuals disciplined in the highest sense (*ad majorum disciplinam non ad hujus seculi levitatem instituti* [reared in accordance with the customs of his parents, not in the frivolousness of the age]),[15] who by means of self-discipline know how to keep others under control—and to that extent also to bring up true extraordinaries. Lax concepts and indeterminately fluid relations do not shape a true extraordinary; they only pamper and corrupt him. Possibly our age does not need a true extraordinary at all but rather those basically honest men who with godly resignation understand it as a task not to invent anything new but with life and soul to be faithful in the established order.[16] But whether our age now needs extraordi-

opinion that a competent government official would have something against the individual in question—because he as a government official wants to have things in order and to do his duty and to discharge his responsibility, because he is at one's service with a helping hand when he sees that the person in question is not aware of what he must do, sets him straight by getting him dismissed and out of the ranks when the person in question is so absentminded as to act as if nothing had happened.]

naries or not, it stands firm that the true extraordinary is recognizable by his being willing to make a sacrifice.

The men of movement in our day (the inauthentic extraordinaries) understand and take up the matter in a different way. It is perhaps after a completely sensible, finite consideration of the circumstances, the motive, etc. that a man comes to the *conclusion* that he has a new proposal to make. From now on he is finished with inward self-deepening and responsibility before God—after all, he has come to a conclusion. He now confronts the established order, and the τέλος [goal] of his striving is that his proposal, his plan, must win. It is fixed and firm that his plan is the truth; the task and the work are only to carry it to victory.

It is easy to see that the relation is the opposite of the true extraordinary's. The latter is solely occupied with his instructions and his relation to God, solely occupied with the underground work in the mine, that of digging out the treasure or of perceiving the voice of divinity. He jests lightly about being victorious in the world, because he knows very well that if only everything is in order with his relation to God, his idea will surely succeed even if he falls. In his relation to God the true extraordinary becomes conscious of his heterogeneity with temporality, and therefore in the *spatium* [space] of this heterogeneity he has room in which he can move in venturing for his cause, in venturing life and blood. The man of movement has no eternal conviction; therefore, in the eternal sense, he cannot possibly be secure. Neither is he occupied solely with gaining this security—for that very reason he has no room and no time for venturing much of anything. His cause is totally *homogeneous* with temporality; thus the τέλος of his striving is not only that it will be victorious *but that its being victorious* will basically *convince* the man of movement that *he was right*, that his proposal was true. Therefore he will not only use again the same people who constitute the established order, but he *needs them*, if only they will wear a new uniform in keeping with his plan.* It is easy to see how the dialectic of

VII²
B 235
48

*****Note.** If it happens, then the man of movement believes that the world has been helped. Even essential reformers have become stuck in the illusion that a changed uniform (an external change) was a true reformation. This is why reforming takes place so fast and so easily—and the world continually remains,

VII²
B 235
49

striving must turn out for the one who wants to overthrow [*støde omkuld*] the established order and out of fear of falling himself does not dare to push [*støde*], since to fall would not only be an unfortunate circumstance but also, so he thinks, would demonstrate that he had been wrong. Everything revolves, as stated, around being victorious, not just because his plan as such must be true, but also in order that his plan, by being victorious—can become true. He does not have certainty but attains it only when he has been victorious. The true extraordinary, however, has the heterogeneous certainty, has eternity's certainty, whether or not he falls.

To want to move in that way is basically like wanting to volunteer to do a trick—"provided it succeeds"—and for the sake of completeness including that on the poster. The person who wants to move something must himself stand firm, but the man of movement has nothing firm; it is not firm—until it has become firm, that is, afterward. Therefore he could wish the established order to be weak and infirm in order to be victorious the

---

as Luther says, like a drunken peasant, who, if you help him up on one side of the horse, falls off on the other side.[17] People believe that it is a king, an emperor, the pope, a tyrant, or a national leader from whom all corruption comes; if only he can be overthrown, the world is saved. Now a reformer places himself at the head, points to the bearded man sitting on the throne—he is the one. If it were true and not a fantastic delusion, then the world would undeniably be an exceptional, splendid world where there would be only one corrupt person and all the rest of us would be splendid people. Let us recall a Socratic question that was raised in a similar dialectical situation: I wonder if it is also the case with horses, that there is only one person who corrupts them; all the others know how to ride.[18] Any reformation that is not aware that basically it is every individual who must be reformed is *eo ipso* an illusion. If one has a little ingenuity and wants to use it in such a wretched way, one can easily win people over to one's opinion—but the person who believes that the world has become better because it has accepted his opinion in this way must be very obtuse. Even the great reformer Luther cannot be entirely acquitted of a certain prejudice in this regard, because he, admittedly with noble and lofty enthusiasm, knew how to defend Christian freedom against the pope but was not sufficiently dialectically attentive to defending it and himself against obtuse copycats and adherents. Therefore his reformation ironically enough fostered the same evil it fought: an exegetical] slave spirit, a hyper-orthodox Lutheran coercion that was just as bad as the pope's.

more easily. If this is not the case, he must use every means to be victorious: cunning, ingenuity, handshakes, compliments, a trumping "Well, I'll be damned!" and a concessive "I beg your pardon." The reformer's conduct must be like that of the person who seeks a job of running errands in the city, or like that of an agile grocer on a busy market day. In regard to the plan itself, he must even bargain at the appropriate place, get it appropriately muddled with the help of committees, and above all a message must go to the public with an extremely cordial and ingratiating invitation: Will a most honored cultured public do the grocer, or what was it I wanted to say, the reformer the honor of being godfather to the child—and then finally this muddle is victorious.*

*Note. In these times people are simply and solely busy about being victorious.[19] They seem to live in the delusion that if only one is victorious, then never mind the method, just as if the method by which a person is victorious were unimportant, whereas when there is a question of the relation in the world of spirit it is the decisive element, or, to express it even more exactly, it is one and the same as the victory. Of course, in connection with money, titles, horses and carriages, torchlight processions and cheering, and other such crudities, the method is unimportant, the method of acquisition is not identical with the possession. Thus one can come into the *actual* possession of money—by many a shabby method. One can *actually* get a torchlight procession and have achieved it by many a shabby method. But in the things of the spirit there is no such external, palpable, crude actuality; the profundity and the elegance in the spirit are that *the method of acquisition* and *the possession* are *identical*. Therefore the person who in connection with the things of the spirit is unaware of this but is made happy in the delusion of having been victorious, although the method was certainly *schofel* [shabby]—he does not notice with what elegance the profundity of the spirit is pulling his leg—that is, he has not been victorious at all but has satirized himself.

Let us mention the terrible highest example. If Christ had not been victorious by being crucified, but in modern style had been victorious through officiousness and a frightful gift of gab so that none of the voters could refrain from voting for him, through a cunning that could make people believe whatever it might be, if Christianity had victoriously entered the world *in that way*, and Christ had been regarded as the Son of God—in that case it would not have entered the world at all and Christ would precisely not have been the Son of God. What would have been victorious would not have been Christianity but a parody of Christianity. To be sure, to sagacious people this may seem to be a cursed *Notabene* [note well], that spirit is not like money, that the mean person can brazenly boast that he nevertheless did *actually* come into possession of the

VII²
B 235
51

VII²
B 235
51

Such a man of movement cannot possibly stand and cannot possibly venture to stand alone as an individual and in that way find room for venturing life and everything. On the contrary he himself needs the majority in order to obtain certainty that it is true, that what he wants is worth anything. He wants to move others, and basically he wants the others to hold on to him so that he can stand firm. But then, of course, there is no movement because he does not stand firm until the matter is settled and the majority has won; as long as this is not decided (and this is indeed the space in which movement should take place), he does not stand firm.

VII²
B 235
52

It is easy to see that when one has the man of movement's view of existence the opinion must develop that considers *venturing* as lunacy or obtuseness. In all fairness it must be conceded that from this standpoint it does appear that way, but in return the man of movement also looks rather comical from another standpoint, the man of movement who does not stand firm the moment this is needed (as long as the cause is in the minority) but stands firm only when he is not needed, the man of movement who oddly enough thinks that it all is due to him. All movement presupposes a point, a fixed point outside (anyone will assure himself of that if he will consider its dialectic)—and in the same way the true extraordinary is the point outside—he stands on that Archimedean point outside the earth, that is, in his absolute relation to God he has a fixed point *extra ordinem*—*et terram movebit* [outside the order—and will move the earth].[21] But he also has room in which to move when it is a matter of life and death and floggings and the like, which surely cannot be of help if one wants to persuade the majority to join in, and which could not conceivably happen to the one who is in the majority. Whether the true extraordinary is victorious today, tomorrow, or in a thousand years makes no difference to him, because he *is victori-*

money ("the unrighteous mammon"[20]),did actually win; but for every noble person it is an indescribably happy comfort that there still is one place where there is eternal *justice*. In the realm of spirit a victory is not possible in any accidental and external way but is possible only in an *essential* way; but the essential way is neither more nor less than the reduplication of the victory, just as in the world of spirit the form is the reduplication of the content.

ous; his relationship to God is his victory; indeed, if what he has to proclaim is never victorious in the world, he might answer: So much the worse for the people themselves.

See, this attitude is that of movement, but the man of movement has nothing eternal and therefore nothing firm, and consequently he does not have the courage to become the *recognizable* individual who wills and wills to *venture* something. Essentially he does not act at all. In raising an outcry, he feigns a sally; his activity culminates in shouting something. Just as when children are playing and one of them suddenly shouts, "Let's play this," so the man of movement shouts, "Let's do this." Then when they have become numerous, when the majority is on their side and the cause has been pushed through—not until then does the man of movement actually come out in the open as really recognizable; that is, he goes around with New Year's greetings, saying, "It was really I who stood at the head of the movement and the new trend." At times there is even the bewildering situation that one sees with amazement that when everything is settled there are even several men of movement who go around and congratulate, and each one says: It was really I who stood at the head of the movement etc. So it is now apparent that there was not only one person but even several at the head. This droll bewildering situation contains a profound truth—namely, that there was no one at all who stood at the head, and in a way one person is just as justified as the other to go around and congratulate. A true extraordinary, who stood alone, abandoned, in the designated pillory of special singularity, a true extraordinary who became recognizable by being executed—well, of course he certainly cannot go around later to congratulate—but neither can he be confused with someone else.

The man of movement perhaps could instead be called a puddling stick. The essential difference between movement and puddling is that the direction of movement is forward; puddling is movement up and down and around, like the dasher in a butter churn, like the feet of a peat-treader, like rumor and gossip, like a ladle in the cook's hand when she stirs the batter. So it is only an illusion when these men of movement, thinking that they themselves are not standing still, mock the competent ones, the

VII[2]
B 235
53

unshakable ones, who are indeed standing still. Puddling, however, is not movement; there is no puddling in a river when it is
flowing but in still-standing water; nor is there puddling in it
when it lies still and deep. Neither does it amount to anything
through puddling. Here one can apply what the fisherman says,
that in certain months there are plenty of bites but only nibbles,
or that the fish bite falsely. The nibble is symptomatic and indicates that the fish are really not interested, and what happens by
way of puddling is also always merely something symptomatic.

What is set forth here is easy to understand; if anyone finds it
difficult, then I cannot help it that by becoming totally earthly
and worldly a modern age has succeeded in forgetting what even
paganism understood.

VIII²
B 9:15
50
Allow me then to explain once again the dialectic of the special individual and allow me to do it by referring to an authentic
Greek account by Aristotle. As is known, Aristotle affirms the
teleological view everywhere, in physics also.[22] He insists that
nature has a τέλος [end, goal]. Nature has a tendency to express
the rule, to produce the normal. But it does not always succeed
in this; sometimes nature is unlucky and produces something
deformed, mutilated, defective, etc. Aristotle groups all such
mishaps in one category and calls it: the prodigy (τὸ τέρας).[23]
VIII²
B 9:15
51
Thus in the Greek sense the prodigy is the abnormal, the stunted,
the imperfect. We, however, are Christianly accustomed to regard the prodigy as the extraordinary that is higher than the
norm, than the universal. Yet the true dialectic of the prodigy is
the unity of these two elements. Therefore Christianity has to
become foolishness to the Greeks,[24] because the fact that the god
[*Guden*][25] revealed himself in suffering was precisely the paradox.* Suffering is the abnormal, is weakness, and yet it is the
negative form of the highest—the immediate form is beauty,
power, glory, etc., but that the highest has its adequate form in

In margin: *Note. As a formula this relation is the prototype for being the
chosen one in the religious sense, since in the Greek sense the chosen one was
a Pamphilius of good fortune. Furthermore, it follows that there is an infinite
qualitative difference between Christ and every chosen one. Christ is himself
the sphere of the paradox, and the chosen one is the derivative who bears the
mark of belonging to this sphere.

the immediate form shows precisely that this highest is not the
extraordinary highest. In one sense (the Greek sense) the dialectic of the prodigy is to be lower than the universal, and then
only in the paradoxical sense to be higher than the universal.
The prodigy is not the universal plus a little; no, the prodigy is
lower than the universal and only then higher. The agreement
with the universal that the special individual must seek through
self-sacrifice consists in this, that by also wanting to be the universal he does not become too much; he does not have *immediate*
superiority over the universal, but *suffering* superiority. It is this
unity of humility and elevation that makes him bearable. The
universal is assigned to the one whom God has not favored in the
sense of special singularity, and he becomes great in proportion
to his expressing this; but the one whom God has especially favored is in a sense first pressed far below the universal. This is
divinity's jealousy for itself, but also the expression for divinity's
love of the universal, so that no one will have anything to com-
plain about.

In the terrible *responsibility* that the true extraordinary must
continually bear in mind (since he does not have a conclusion
once and for all), there is also the concern that when he assumes
the position *extra ordinem* his example can inveigle others, weak,
unstable, light-minded, inquisitive people, to want to attempt
something similar also, so that consequently his example can become a trap, a temptation. In other words, the concern that usually plagues busy, gadding people—to get some copycats, some
adherents who agree with him, to get a society established that
has its own seal—that concern he does not know. In this regard
he is quite frivolously facetious; he does not even have the sagacity that cows have; when a cow stampeding wants to make an
attempt in the extraordinary, it first looks to see whether it is
gaining sympathy among the public or among all the cows in the
field—if not, it cautiously sticks its tail between its legs. The true
extraordinary will know how to make sport of vanity and conceitedness, but the terrible thing, whether he has harmed any
other person, whether he occasioned any person light-mindedly
to want to try his hand at what involves the heaviest responsibility of the special singular—this terrible thing he understands in a

VIII²
B 12
54

radical way. In a time of movement such as ours, when symptoms of wanting to be a little extraordinary are epidemic, he must
with fear and trembling especially keep watch on his tremendous
responsibility. Therefore, precisely here he will in turn make his
position as forbidding as possible, as unappealing and untempting as possible. For that reason he also desires tough opposition.
If the light-minded merely see that enduring something is becoming a bit earnest, they soon fall away; yes, they even change
into an opposition against the extraordinary. Light-mindedness
would flippantly like to take the extraordinary as a playmate; if it
perceives that this cannot be done, it concentrates its childish
anger against him. But every extraordinary unconditionally owes
it to the established order first of all by some profound step to
transform, if possible, his extraordinariness into aversion, lest his
example do harm. And a true extraordinary in our day (after
reflection and sensibleness have developed so enormously) must
be informed about everything possible, know the dangers and
irregularities.

Thus what the true extraordinary finds necessary to do in honesty toward the established order must be profoundly carried
through. And what is profundity really? It is the deep existential
carrying out of an idea that through the relationship of conscience is related to God. Nowadays people think that it is very
glorious if someone is so fortunate as to be struck by a profound
thought, to make a profound remark, now and then *horis successivis*
[hour by hour] to compile something profound that in every
other hour one *existentially* denies. No, just as perseverance (in
contrast to the flaring illusion of the moment) is the true virtue,
so also profundity is not an utterance, a statement, but an existing. Profundity is the metaphorical, transferred expression that
indicates how many feet a person's existing draws in the same
sense as one says this of a ship. But the ship is not said to draw
[*stikke*] so and so many feet deep in the same sense as a probe that
one sticks into something momentarily, but it is the decisive
qualification in relation to the ship's entire and daily existence
that it draws so and so many feet. Or to illustrate the same thing
in another way: the more extensions a telescope has, the better it
is, and thus also the more extensions a person has before the

VIII²
B 12
55

secret of his innermost life is reached, the more deeply he draws. The profound mind is not an esthetic qualification with regard to genius but is essentially an ethical qualification. For that very reason, it must be for everyday use by the one who is really to be called profound, yet not so it becomes conspicuous, since the conspicuous is again an esthetic qualification. Let us think of ships: when two ships are sailing together, whatever difference there may be with regard to how many feet they draw is not seen—no, they both are sailing.

In order to elucidate this entire matter, let me purely poetically and with the freedom of poetry fashion an example. I select for this a genius at a climax of reflection. But I will also make the matter as difficult as possible. He is a genius. But he did not know that from the beginning. Such a thing is quite conceivable and in addition is the difference between the immediate genius and the genius of reflection; the latter needs a blow in order to become what he latently was. As such, he has therefore gone on living without understanding himself. He has educated himself for government service; he has even become an officeholder at a very young age; he is a pastor.

Only now does the event occur that gives him the blow. At the same moment he understands himself in his extraordinariness, which he also in another sense comprehends as his wretchedness, namely, that he cannot have his stronghold in the universal. But above all, with his eminent reflection he at the same moment surveys the whole responsibility of his position.

Here, then, his *discrimen* [crucial decision] is either to take his extraordinariness in vain as a brilliant difference and cause irreparable confusion or, first and foremost before he considers communicating the whole new view that has dawned on him,* to sacrifice himself and thereby reconcile himself with the universal.

That he himself is willing to resign his office is the least of it; an honesty such as that will not satisfy him or his ethical concern.

VIII²
B 12
56

In margin: *Note. The extraordinary (the genius) may very well have something new to bring, also from God, but he does not spontaneously conduct himself as God's instrument; he is a lowly human being. Least of all does he have what is qualitatively decisive, divine authority. This is the apostle's. The relation of the genius to God is dialectical.

Let us now begin. It is therefore assumed that this, the extraordinary or this by which he became the extraordinary, has happened to him. From this moment his life is taken over by a higher power. The question now is about the reflective inventiveness with which he takes on his task. Reflection is the mediator whose help he will use primarily in order to render himself harmless.

Dialectically he will now perceive immediately that the extraordinary has the *discrimen* [distinctive mark] of danger, that what in him is truth can become for others the greatest corruption. Therefore he will at the same moment inclose himself in impenetrable silence, close himself off from everyone else, so that no uncircumspect utterance, no undietetic uncircumspection would ruin the whole thing in loquacity, but the extraordinary would take time to settle in the pause of silence (*in pausa*[26]). One does not put a new patch on an old garment, or new wine into an old wineskin, lest the hole become larger and the wineskin burst[27]—and the very same thing will happen if by uncircumspect association in hasty busyness the new is bungled in with the old—then it only does harm. At the same moment reflection will immediately teach him silence, the silence in which he dedicates himself just as the mother devotes herself to existing only for the sake of the child, the silence that precludes every communication to any other person, lest something wrong be communicated or in a wrong way.

But this, the new, must be communicated. The silence must not abort it as a fetus is aborted. But no impatience! There is a nervous tremor that in trembling impatience can neither hold on to anything nor beneficially give up anything—let us not be deceived by it! Everyone who knows what it is truly to be resolved knows very well that one can persevere and hold firmly to a resolution. A man may be so situated in life that he calmly has said to himself before God: The way I am taking is bound to lead me to the stake—and nevertheless he calmly goes step by step. But impatience says: The sooner the better,* and the nervous

*Note. The necessary slowness is also a cross, which must be borne in faith and humility. Let me name the highest, from which we, believing, should learn. When the angel had announced to Mary that she would give birth to the child

impatience, bordering almost on insanity, says: If only it does not
cease, if only the pressure within me does not vanish, so the
dreadful thing would have to be said of me: The children are
near to the birth, and there is no strength to give birth (Isaiah
37:3). But it is certainly also terrible to give birth to wind because
of sheer busyness. Here it is not a matter of animal sluggishness,
whereby an utterly worldly, almost merely vegetating person,
can let time go by. The one who has ever served an idea and has
ever been deeply moved by the eternal knows very well that this
collision of the eternal and the temporal in the moment, in the
present, is a dreadful tension that can all too easily become sleeplessness, and all too easily insanity. He knows also that with regard to this moment it seemed as if all would be lost if this moment was not used. But he knows also that there is a remedy for
this symptom: faith. If someone in holy resolution has resolved to
sacrifice his life and then in nervous impatience goes ahead and
throws his life away and is executed, the sooner the better—has
he been of any benefit, and has he then actually kept his resolution? The point is simply that time and reflection not be allowed
to shake his resolution. But on the other hand, rather than foolishly having it happen right away today, there is another remedy;
this remedy is faith, is humility, is daily dedication. And it is then
also only in an overwrought or sensuously excited delusion that
the eternal takes on, not symptomatically for a single moment
but continually, a likeness to what is most opposed to the eternal:
the sensuous eternal moment. Here, as with the thirst of that rich
man burning in hell,[29] the point is: seize it, seize it, seize it while
it is foaming—oh, despair, in the next moment it is all over. Pick
the flower, pick the flower—in the next moment it is already
withered. How terrible if someone in that frame of mind makes
the mistake of wanting to treat the eternal in the same way!

VIII²
B 12
57

---

through the Spirit[28]—well, the whole thing was certainly a miracle—why,
then, should this child take nine months like other children? Oh, what a test for
faith and humility, that even that which is divine uses the slowness of time! See,
this was the cross. But Mary was the humble believer; through faith and humility she came to herself, although everything was miraculous. She remained the
same quiet, humble woman. She did not ask which day we would write down,
what time it would be—she believed!

VIII²
B 12
57

So, then, the new must be communicated, must be placed in the context of the established order, and the special individual, as is said, must take the blow by being the special individual and thereby give the blow. Dialectically there is a doubleness here: that the blow actually, in a qualitative sense, becomes the blow, and that the established order is brought every sacrifice. No more than God is a God of confusion[30] is the extraordinary one called to confuse—and then perhaps to run away from it. He is to love the established order and therefore be willing to sacrifice himself. Just as one handles strong medicine with extreme caution (not in order not to use it but in order to use it properly), guards against a direct contact, so the special individual guards against a direct relation. He is one who is dedicated.

When we now poetically* pursue this thought further, there must be the idea of making oneself repugnant. The extraordinary is not *directly* the extraordinary; he is not the extraordinary until the thought intervenes that he is lower than the universal. This dialectic can be rendered in such a way that the extraordinary first makes himself the repugnant one, so that no one could wish to resemble him or be like him. In this pain lie, among other things, his self-sacrifice and the reconciliation with the established order that he in his love for it has to bring.** That busybodies and fools and windbags desire something else in order to get something to spread and something to mimic, that desperate extraordinaries detest discipline and restraint and would rather let themselves and others have a fling as *fratres et sorores liberi spiritus* [brothers and sisters of the free spirit][31] does not matter.

VIII²
B 12
58

*Note. A freedom of self-determination such as has been poetically presented here will, however, probably never appear in actuality. In actuality God will certainly know how to keep the genius under control in an unfree, suffering way, in agony if it is made necessary, so that he really profoundly understands the pressure that presses him under the universal.

**In margin: Note. It happens to the extraordinary (in immediacy) that he is sacrificed, but in reflection he himself must know it and hasten the crisis. It happens and it must happen, inasmuch as it is grounded in existence's own dialectic between the universal and the special individual. So it must be, but because the immediate individual has not foreseen it, has not been conscious of it in advance (which is implicit in reflection), the conflict in existence that he brings about will also cause a great confusion in which many will be lost, and for which he still bears a kind of responsibility.

But how, then, does one make oneself repugnant? Let us first recapitulate. The extraordinary has come to himself in his extraordinariness. He has inclosed himself within himself. Not a word has betrayed anything, not a look; and neither is his silence conspicuous, since that of course betrays something. He is just like other people, talks like other people about what is happening—therefore no one can know that he is silent. A person can be silent in two ways: he can be absolutely mum, but then the silence is suspicious, or he can talk about everything else possible—to be silent is to keep silent in reflection. And yet it has happened to him, and there lives a person who with a life dedicated in holy resolution works in complete silence. Yes, it is exhausting, but the greater his superiority is above others, the more dreadful the battle of responsibility in himself. It is a great, great suffering to be infinitely superior. But no impatience.

So how is he to make himself repugnant when this, note well, must be done in such a way that he does not thereby cause harm, so that he does not go ahead and make the new repugnant but makes himself repugnant? The extraordinary must of course (since everything here is poetical) know in an eminent sense what even I, who am only a lowly ministering critic, the poet, am somewhat informed about: how undermined our age is in a religious sense—while busy people hold general assemblies about trivialities, and while the thunder of cannons summons to amusements.[32] When that is the case, it must not be difficult to find in the sphere of the daimonic the fool's costume and the blackened clothing that could make him repugnant, that could prevent the dreadful consequence for him that because he collided with the universal it therefore should be something great. Let us remember well what was said previously: in the whole world there is still no one aware of what has happened with him any more than this pen is that I am holding in my hand, or the inkwell into which I dip it, yet without obtaining the thoughts from it.

He would then *mir nichts und Dir nichts* [without further ado] resign, make the whole matter of his being a pastor into a passing notion, into a droll whim—and see to it that this would become the authentic interpretation. He thereby would at least have done everything he was capable of doing so that his example would not tempt others. To be out of the ordinary in that way, that is, by instability, carelessness, and lack of firmness—no one could want that. Dialectic teaches caution in the handling of strong medicine, teaches one first to make it possible that it can be used without doing harm, and only then does one use it. When extraordinariness is represented temptingly as a brilliant distinction, such an example can have a harmful influence on the perhaps usually faithful adherents of the established order, if nothing else then by making them a little impatient about their position. On the other hand, by temporarily weakening the impression in self-sacrifice, he would have made it possible that he could be singled out as a special individual without carrying anyone along with him.[*]

Along this road he could now go further. But such a thing

[*Addition in version IV:* [*]*Note.* If anyone says: But there the extraordinary indeed begins with an untruth, yes, makes God a confidant in the untruth with which he begins—then the answer must be: All *true* communication of truth must always begin with an untruth. This is partly because it is impossible to tell the whole truth in one minute or in an even shorter time. On the contrary, it takes perhaps a long, long time for that. This is also partly because the first untruth is only a reduplication—the true communication of truth is circumspectly aware of the contingency that it was indeed possible that the recipients were in untruth, in which contingency the direct communication of the true would become untruth. This is "reflexion"—the critical element in the communication of truth.[†] To name the highest, Christ's own life manifests this, because when one is God it is indeed an untruth (in the sense in which truth is only direct) to come in the form of a lowly servant; and seen from another angle it was also an untruth, since he had come to the world to suffer and die, an untruth to accept for one single moment public favor and permit this misunderstanding. I will, however, not develop this further. But in the extraordinary precisely this belongs to his dreadful responsibility, that strictly speaking he begins with an untruth. And in relation to the extraordinary, to begin with an untruth is unavoidable, it is dialectically intrinsic to the matter itself. If this untruth is not included, then the extraordinary does not remain the extraordinary; it is then taken in vain, becomes a direct superlative in relation to the universal. But this is an utterly undialectical definition of the extraordinary.

[†]In this way Socrates' ignorance was indeed an untruth; but it truly is only or it is precisely reduplication's expression for his truly wanting to communicate the truth that he was profoundly-ironically aware that those who should receive the communication were possibly in the untruth of all kinds of illusions; then it would not do to communicate the truth very directly, convivially pouring out his heart, or declaiming, or didacticizing.

cannot be carried through *in abstracto*. The art "to deceive people into the truth" is a quality of genius that in the one in whom it is eminent (and here, of course, everything is poetical) is altogether inexhaustible, and every second changeable into a thousand possibilities. The one who knows only one or two or six ways in which to deceive is not a genius; in eminent reflection there are infinite possibilities at every moment.

During all this, the compass by which the steering was done would of course have to remain unaltered, without deviating a point in inwardness. Obviously this method is slow; it is not something for hotheads. It is, however, terrible to work silently this way with all one's might—in a certain sense—against oneself.* What if one died beforehand and there was no one who knew any more about it than my pen or the inkwell into which I dip it, yet without obtaining the thoughts from it! It is very moving when Hamlet in the moment of death almost despairs over the thought that the enormously strenuous hidden life he has lived in the service of the idea would be understood by no one, indeed, that no one would get to know it.[34] But if Hamlet goes soft in death, he could indeed have spoken in life, that is, let the whole thing slip out. Yes, it must indeed be dreadful when such a person of inclosed reserve thinks of the busyness around him, which has scarcely five minutes to waste on understanding the richness of thought in a prodigious work. But if Hamlet shudders, and if this shuddering gains the upper hand, then it is vanity! There is a remedy for all nervous impatience: it is faith, humility. The God in whose service the extraordinary has dedicated himself, the God who has been called upon every day for witness and aid—he knows it, indeed everything; he surely is not a busy trifler. And what more is needed! Then if death comes and

---

*Note. To be sure, this is only in a certain sense. The method is neither more nor less than the consistent redoubling of truth in itself. But *Mundus vult decipi* [the world wants to be deceived].[33] Insofar as the method is slow, it is calculated precisely to hinder the deception; for this very reason it deceives people into the truth instead of the more usual method of helping people into the deception by way of assurances of the truth. That is why every juggler always and immediately makes a hit, because he simply wants to deceive; thus he wants what the times demand—*Mundus vult decipi*.

puts a period in a wrong place—no, death simply cannot put a period in a wrong place, because it certainly cannot come without God's will.

Then when the extraordinary has worked against himself in this way, has made himself repugnant so that no one would be tempted by his example, yes, then humble before God he could beat his breast and say, "Now the first thing has been done; the sacrifice to the universal has been made. Humanly speaking, I am diminished; no one will be led astray by my example, and I am not importunate toward God either and do not summarily make his cause mine. No, despite all my work I also annihilate myself—then the honor is God's."[35]

Addendum II[1]

The Difference between a Genius and an Apostle

What is it that the erroneous* exegesis and speculative thought have done to confuse the essentially Christian, or by what means have they confused the essentially Christian? Quite briefly and with categorical accuracy, it is the following: they have shifted the sphere of the paradoxical-religious back into the esthetic and thereby have achieved the result that every Christian term, which by remaining in its sphere is a qualitative category, can now, in a reduced state, serve as a brilliant expression that means all sorts of things.[2] [*Deleted in* Two Essays: But the mistaken exegete and dogmatician have not also claimed to have had a revelation themselves; this is reserved for Adler. He can—indeed, just as it says in the rhyme: "Who can do it best? Our pastor can." All of Adler's ample explanations of genius are quite right as esthetics, and some of it would be quite right if he did not have a first position: being called by a revelation. In his explanations of genius there is not a trace that he in any way, categorically understood, has an idea of the qualitative and specific distinctiveness of the essentially Christian, although he continually uses Christ's name, yes, although he claims to have had a revelation from the Savior.] When the sphere of the paradoxical-religious is now abolished or is explained back into the esthetic, an apostle becomes neither more nor less than a genius, and then good night to Christianity. Brilliance [*Aandrighed*] and spirit [*Aand*], revelation and originality, the call from God and genius, an apostle and a genius—all this ends up being just about one and the same.

---

*Furthermore, the error is not only that of heterodoxy but also of ultraorthodoxy and of thoughtlessness generally.

In this way an erroneous scholarship has confused Christianity, and from the scholarship the confusion has in turn sneaked into the religious address, so that one not infrequently hears pastors who in all scholarly naïveté *bona fide* prostitute Christianity. They speak in lofty tones about the Apostle Paul's brilliance, profundity, about his beautiful metaphors etc.—sheer esthetics. If Paul is to be regarded as a genius, then it looks bad for him; only pastoral ignorance can hit upon the idea of praising him esthetically, because pastoral ignorance has no criterion but thinks like this: If only one says something good about Paul, then it is all right. Such good-natured and well-meaning thoughtlessness is due to the person's not having been disciplined by the qualitative dialectic that would teach him that an apostle is simply not served by having something good said about him when it is wrong; then he becomes recognized and admired for being what is unimportant and for what he essentially is not, and then, because of that, it is forgotten what he is. Such thoughtless eloquence could equally well hit upon the idea of praising Paul as a stylist and an artist with words or, even better, since it is well known that Paul also carried on a trade, claim that his work as tent maker must have been such perfect masterwork that no tapestry maker, either before or later, has been able to make anything so perfect—since, if only one says something good about Paul, everything is all right. As a genius, Paul cannot stand comparison with either Plato or Shakespeare; as an author of beautiful metaphors, he ranks rather low; as a stylist, he is a totally unknown name—and as a tapestry maker, well, I must say that I do not know how high he can rank in this regard. See, it is always best to turn obtuse earnestness into a jest, and then comes the earnestness, the earnestness—that Paul is an apostle. And as an apostle he again has no affinity, none whatever, with either Plato or Shakespeare or stylists or tapestry makers; they all (Plato as well as Shakespeare and tapestry maker Hansen) are without any comparison to Paul.

A genius and an apostle are qualitatively different, are qualifications that belong each in its qualitative sphere: **of immanence and of transcendence**. [*Deleted in* Two Essays: *The qualification "genius" lies within the sphere of immanence.*] **(1) Therefore**

XI
96

the genius can very well have something new to bring, but this in turn vanishes in the human race's general assimilation, just as the difference "genius" vanishes as soon as one thinks of eternity. [*Deleted in* Two Essays: *The qualification "apostle" lies within the sphere of transcendence.*] The apostle has something paradoxically new to bring, the newness of which, just because it is essentially paradoxical and not an anticipation pertaining to the development of the human race, continually remains, just as an apostle remains for all eternity an apostle, and no immanence of eternity places him essentially on the same line with all human beings, since essentially he is paradoxically different. (2) The genius is what he is by himself, that is, by what he is in himself; an apostle is what he is by his divine authority. (3) The genius has only immanent teleology; the apostle is absolutely teleologically positioned paradoxically. [*Deleted in* Two Essays: —This last clarification is of importance especially in our age, and for that reason I shall dwell on it more fully.]

1. All thinking draws its breath in immanence, whereas the paradox and faith constitute a separate qualitative sphere. Immanently, in the relation between persons *qua* human beings, every difference is for essential and eternal thinking something vanishing, a factor that surely has its validity momentarily but essentially vanishes in the essential equality of eternity. Genius, as the word itself says (*ingenium*, the innate, primitivity (*primus*), originality (*origo*), pristineness, etc.), is immediacy, natural qualifications; the genius *is born*. Long before there can be any question of whether the genius will or will not assign his rare endowment to God, the genius already is and is a genius even if he does not do that. With the genius there can occur the change of developing into being what he κατὰ δύναμιν [potentially] is, of coming into conscious possession of himself. Insofar as the expression "paradox" is used to designate the new that a genius may have to bring, it is still used only in the inessential sense of the transitory paradox, of the anticipation that condenses into something paradoxical, which, however, in turn vanishes. A genius may be paradoxical in his first communication, but the more he comes to

XI
97

himself the more the paradoxical vanishes. Perhaps a genius can be a century ahead of his time and therefore stand as a paradox, but ultimately the human race will assimilate the one-time paradoxical in such a way that it is no longer paradoxical. [*Deleted in* Two Essays: The paradoxicality and paradoxes of the genius are not the essential paradoxicality.]

It is different with an apostle. The word[3] itself indicates the difference. An apostle is not born; an apostle is a man who is called and appointed by God and sent by him on a mission. An apostle does not develop in such a way that he gradually becomes what he is κατὰ δύναμιν. Prior to becoming an apostle, there is no potential possibility; every human being is essentially equally close to becoming that. An apostle can never come to himself in such a way that he becomes aware of his apostolic calling as an element in his own life-development. The apostolic calling is a paradoxical fact that in the first and the last moment of his life stands paradoxically outside his personal identity as the specific person he is. Perhaps a man has long since arrived at the age of discretion [*deleted in* Two Essays: , has consciously taken over his life in relation to its natural qualification, is a self-conscious and developed person]; then he is called as an apostle. By this call he does not become more intelligent, he does not acquire more imagination, greater discernment, etc.—not at all; he remains himself but by the paradoxical fact is sent by God on a specific mission. By this paradoxical fact the apostle is for all eternity made paradoxically different from all other human beings. The new that he can have to proclaim is the essentially paradoxical. However long it is proclaimed in the world, it remains essentially just as new, just as paradoxical; no immanence can assimilate it. The apostle did not act as the person distinguished by natural gifts who was ahead of his contemporaries. Perhaps he was what we call a simple person, but by a paradoxical fact he was called to proclaim this new thing. Even if thought considered itself capable of assimilating the doctrine, it cannot assimilate the way in which the doctrine came into the world, because the essential paradox is specifically the protest against immanence. But the way in which such a doctrine entered the world is specifically what is qualitatively decisive, something that can be disregarded only through deceit or through thoughtlessness.

2. A genius is evaluated purely esthetically according to what his content, his specific gravity, is found to be; an apostle is what he is by having divine authority. *The divine authority is what is qualitatively decisive.* It is not by evaluating the content of the doctrine esthetically or philosophically that I will or can arrive at the conclusion: ergo the one who has delivered this doctrine is called by a revelation, ergo he is an apostle. The relationship is just the reverse: the one called by a revelation, to whom a doctrine is entrusted, argues on the basis that it is a revelation, on the basis that he has authority. I am not to listen to Paul because he is brilliant or matchlessly brilliant, but I am to submit to Paul because he has divine authority; and in any case it must become Paul's responsibility to see to it that he produces this impression, whether anyone submits to his authority or not. Paul must not appeal to his brilliance, since in that case he is a fool; he must not become involved in a purely esthetic or philosophic discussion of the content of the doctrine, since in that case he is absentminded. No, he must appeal to his divine authority and precisely through it, while he willingly sacrifices life and everything, *prevent* all impertinent esthetic and philosophical superficial observations against the form and content of the doctrine. Paul must not commend himself and his doctrine with the aid of the beautiful metaphors; on the contrary, he would surely say to the individual, "Whether the image is beautiful or [4]it is threadbare and obsolete makes no difference; you must consider that what I say has been entrusted to me by a revelation; so it is God himself or the Lord Jesus Christ who is speaking, and you must not become involved presumptuously in criticizing the form. I cannot, I dare not compel you to obey, but through the relationship of your conscience to God, I make you eternally responsible for your relationship to this doctrine by my having proclaimed it as revealed to me and therefore by having proclaimed it with divine authority."

Authority is what is qualitatively decisive. Or is there not a difference, even within the relativity of human life, although it immanently disappears, between a royal command and the words of a poet or a thinker? And what is the difference but this, that the royal command has authority and therefore forbids all esthetic and critical impertinence with regard to form and content? The poet, the thinker, on the other hand, does not have any authority, not even within this relativity; his utterance is evaluated purely esthetically or philosophically by evaluating the content and form. But what is it that has radically confused the essentially Christian but this, that in doubt we have first become almost uncertain whether a God exists and then in rebelliousness against all authorities have forgotten what authority is and its dialectic. A king exists physically in such a way that one can physically assure oneself of it, and if it is necessary perhaps the king can very physically assure one that he exists. But God does not exist in that way. Doubt has made use of this to place God on the same level with all those who have no authority, on the same level with geniuses, poets, and thinkers, whose utterances are simply evaluated only esthetically or philosophically; and if it is said well, then the man is a genius—and if it is said exceptionally and extremely well, then it is God who has said it!!!

In this manner God is actually smuggled away. What is he to do? If God stops a person on his way, calls him by a revelation, and sends him out equipped with divine authority to the other people, they then say to him, "From whom do you come?" He answers, "From God." But see, God cannot help his emissary in such a physical way as a king can, who gives him an escort of soldiers or police, or his ring, or his signature that all recognize— in short, God cannot be of service to human beings by providing them with physical certainty that an apostle is an apostle[5]— indeed, that would be nonsense. Even the miracle, if the apostle has this gift,[6] provides no physical certainty, because the miracle is an object of faith. Moreover, it is nonsense to obtain *physical* certainty that an apostle is an apostle (the paradoxical qualification of a relation of spirit), just as it is nonsense to obtain *physical* certainty that God exists, since God is *spirit*. So the apostle says that he is from God. The others answer, "Well, then let us see if the content of what you teach is divine; then we will accept it, also that it has been revealed to you." In this way both God and the apostle are cheated. The divine authority of the one called should be specifically the sure defense that would safeguard the doctrine and keep it from impertinences at the majestic distance of the divine, but instead the content and form of the doctrine must let itself be criticized and sniffed at—so one can by that way come to a conclusion as to whether it was a revelation or not. In the meantime the apostle and God presumably must wait at the door or with the doorman until the matter has been decided by the wise ones on the second floor. According to God's stipulation, the one who is called should use his divine authority to drive away all the impertinent people who are unwilling to obey but want to be loquacious; and instead of getting people on the move, the apostle is changed into an examinee who as such comes to the market with a new doctrine.

[7]What, then, is authority? Is authority the profundity of the doctrine, its excellence, its brilliance? Not at all. If, for example, authority would only signify, to the second power or doubled, that the doctrine is profound—then there simply is no authority, because, if a learner completely and perfectly appropriated this doctrine by way of understanding, then of course there would be no difference anymore between the teacher and the learner. Authority, however, is something that remains unchanged, something that one cannot acquire by having perfectly understood the doctrine. *Authority is a specific quality that enters from somewhere else and qualitatively asserts itself precisely when the content of the statement or the act is made a matter of indifference esthetically.*

Let us take an example, as simple as possible, in which the relation is nevertheless manifest. When someone who has the authority to say it says to a person, "Go!" and when someone who does not have the authority says, "Go!" the utterance (Go!) and its content are indeed identical; evaluated esthetically, it is, if you like, equally well spoken, but the authority makes the difference. If the authority is not the other (τὸ ἕτερον[8]), if in any way it should indicate merely an intensification within the identity, then there simply is no authority. If, for example, a teacher is enthusiastically conscious that he himself, existing, expresses and has expressed, with the sacrifice of everything, the teaching he proclaims, this consciousness can indeed give him an assured and steadfast spirit,[9] but it does not give him authority. His life as evidence of the rightness of the teaching is not the other (τὸ ἕτερον) but is a simple redoubling. That he lives according to the teaching does not demonstrate that it is right, but because he is himself convinced of the rightness of the teaching, he lives according to it. On the other hand, whether a police officer, for example, is a scoundrel or an upright man, as soon as he is on duty, he has authority.

In order to elucidate more explicitly the concept of authority, so important to the paradoxical-religious sphere, I shall follow up the dialectic of authority. *In the sphere of immanence, authority is utterly unthinkable, or it can be thought only as transitory.** Insofar as it is a matter of authority in the political, civic, social, domestic, and disciplinary realms or of the exercise of authority, authority is still only a transitory factor, something vanishing that either disappears later even in temporality or disappears inasmuch as temporality and earthly life itself are a transitory factor that vanishes with all its differences. The only basis of any relation between persons *qua* human beings that can be *thought* is the dissimilarity within the identity of immanence, that is, the essential likeness. The single human being cannot be *thought* as being different from all others by a specific quality (then all thought ceases, as it quite consistently does in the sphere of the paradoxical-religious and faith). All human differences between persons *qua* human beings disappear for thought as factors within the totality and quality of identity. I shall certainly respect and obey the difference in the factor, but I am permitted to be built up religiously by the certainty that in eternity the differences vanish, the one that makes me distinguished and the one that subordinates me. As a subject I am to honor and obey the king with

---

*[10]Perhaps it happens here with some reader as it happens with me, that in connection with this discussion of "authority" I come to think of Magister Kierkegaard's *Upbuilding Discourses*, where it is so strongly accentuated and emphasized, by being repeated in the preface every time and word for word: "they are not *sermons*, because the author does not have *authority* to preach."[11] Authority is a specific quality either of an apostolic calling or of ordination. To preach is precisely to use authority, and that this is what it is to preach has simply been altogether forgotten in our day.

undivided soul, but I am permitted to be built up religiously by
the thought that essentially I am a citizen of heaven[12] and that if
I ever meet his departed majesty there, I shall not be bound in
subservient obedience to him.

This, then, is the relation between persons *qua* human beings.
But between God and a human being there is an eternal essential quali-
tative difference,[13] which only presumptuous thinking can make
disappear in the blasphemy that in the transitory moment of
finitude God and a human being are certainly differentiated,
so that here in this life a human being ought to obey and worship
God, but in eternity the difference will vanish in the essential
likeness, so that God and human beings become peers in eternity,
just as the king and the valet.

Between God and a human being, then, there is and remains
an eternal essential qualitative difference. *The paradoxical-religious*
relation (which, quite rightly, cannot be thought but only be believed) *appears when God appoints a specific human being to have*
divine authority—with regard, note well, to what God has entrusted to him. The person called in this way does not, in the
relation between persons, relate himself *qua* human being; he
does not relate himself to other people in a quantitative difference (as a genius, an exceptionally gifted person, etc.). No, he
relates himself paradoxically by having a specific quality that no
immanence can revoke in the likeness of eternity, because it is
essentially paradoxical and *after* thought (not prior to, before
thought), against thought. If such a called person has a doctrine
to bring according to divine order and, let us imagine, another
person has arrived at the same doctrine by himself and on his
own—these two will not become alike in all eternity, because
the former by his paradoxical specific quality (the divine authority) will be different from every other human being and
from the qualification of the essential likeness lying immanently
at the basis of all other human differences. The qualification "an
apostle" belongs in the sphere of the transcendent, the paradoxical-religious sphere, which, altogether consistently, also has a
qualitatively different expression for the relation of other people
to an apostle—in other words, they relate themselves to him in

XI
102

faith, whereas all thought lies and is and breathes in immanence. But faith is not a transitory qualification any more than the apostle's paradoxical qualification was transitory.

Thus in the relation between persons *qua* human beings, no *enduring* [*bestaaende*] or *constant* [*bestandig*] difference of authority was *thinkable*; it was something vanishing. Let us, however, for a moment dwell on some examples of such so-called relations of authority between persons *qua* human beings that are true under the conditions of temporality in order to become aware of the essential view of authority. A king, of course, is assumed to have authority. Why, then, do we find it offensive that a king is brilliant, is an artist etc.? It no doubt is because one essentially accentuates in him the royal authority and in comparison with this finds the more ordinary qualifications of human differences to be something vanishing, something inessential, a disturbing incidental. A government department is assumed to have authority in its stipulated domain. Why, then, would one find it offensive if in its decrees such a department was actually brilliant, witty, profound? Because one quite properly accentuates the authority qualitatively. To ask if a king is a genius, and in that case to be willing to obey him, is basically high treason, because the question contains a doubt about submission to authority. To be willing to obey a government department if it can come out with witticisms is basically making a fool of the department. To honor one's father because he is exceptionally intelligent is impiety.

Yet, as stated, in the relation between persons *qua* human beings, authority, even if it exists, is something vanishing, and eternity abolishes all earthly authority. But now in the sphere of transcendence. Let us take an example that is very simple, but for that very reason also as striking as possible. When Christ says, "There is an eternal life," and when theological graduate Petersen says, "There is an eternal life," both are saying the same thing; there is in the first statement no more deduction, development, profundity, richness of thought than in the second; evaluated esthetically, both statements are equally good. And yet there certainly is an eternal qualitative difference! As God-man, Christ possesses the specific quality of authority; no eternity can mediate this or place Christ on the same level with the essentially human likeness. Christ, therefore, taught with authority.[14] To ask whether Christ is profound is blasphemy and is an attempt (be it conscious or unconscious) to destroy him in a subtle way, since the question contains a doubt with regard to his authority and attempts in impertinent *straightforwardness* to evaluate and grade him, as if he were up for examination and should be catechized instead of being the one to whom all power is given in heaven and on earth.[15]

Yet rarely, very rarely, does one hear or read these days a religious address that is entirely correct. The better ones still usually dabble a bit in what could be called unconscious or well-intentioned rebellion as they defend and uphold Christianity with all their might—in the wrong categories. Let me take an example, the first that comes along. I prefer to take a German, so I then know that no one can hit upon the idea, not the most obtuse and not the most malicious, that I am writing this about a matter that in my opinion is immensely important—in order to point a finger at some clergyman. In a homily for the fifth Sunday in Lent, Bishop Sailer* preaches on the text John 8:47–51. He selects these two verses: "*Wer von Gott ist, der höret Gottes Wort* [Whoever is of God hears the word of God]" and "*Wer mein Wort hält, der siehet den Tod nicht* [Whoever keeps my word will not see death]" and thereupon comments, "*Es sind in diesen Worten des Herrn drei grosze Räthsel gelöset, mit denen sich die Menschen von jeher den Kopf so oder anders zerbrochen haben* [In these words by the Lord three great riddles are solved, over which people have racked their brains since time immemorial]."

There we have it. The word *Räthsel* [riddle], and especially *drei grosze Räthsel* [three great riddles] and then what follows, *mit denen die Menschen d e n K o p f sich z e r b r o c h e n haben* [over which people have *racked their brains*] promptly lead our thoughts to the profound in the intellectual sense, the cogitating, the ruminating, the speculating. But how can a simple apodictic statement be profound—an apodictic statement that is what it is only by having been said by such and such a person, a statement that

---

*See *Evangelisches aus Joh. Michael Sailers religiösen Schriften*, by August Gebauer (Stuttgart: 1846 [*ASKB* 270]), pp. 34, 35.

by no means is to be understood or fathomed but only believed? How can a person hit upon the idea that a riddle in the nature of cogitating and ruminating profundity should be solved by a direct statement, by an assertion? The question is: Is there an eternal life? The answer is: There is an eternal life. Now, where in the world is the profundity? If Christ is not the one who has said it, and if Christ is not the one he has said that he is, then the profundity, if the statement is in itself profound, must still be ascertainable.

Let us take theological graduate Mr. Petersen; he, too, says: There is an eternal life. Who in the world would hit on the idea of ascribing profundity to him on the basis of a direct statement? What is decisive consists not in the statement but in the fact that it is Christ who has said it; but what is confounding is that in order, as it were, to lure people into believing, one says something about profundity and the profound. A Christian pastor, if he is to speak properly, must quite simply say, "We have Christ's word that there is an eternal life, and with that the matter is decided. Here it is a matter neither of racking one's brains nor of speculating, but of its being Christ who, not in the capacity of profundity but with his divine authority, has said it."

Let us go further, let us assume that someone believes that there is an eternal life because Christ has said it; then in faith he avoids all the deep profundity and cogitating and ruminating "with which people rack their brains." On the other hand, let us take someone who wants to rack his brains profoundly on the question of immortality—will he not be justified in denying that the direct statement is a profound answer to the question? What Plato says about immortality[16] is actually profound, attained by profound cogitating; but then poor Plato does not have any authority.

The point, however, is this. Doubt and disbelief, which make faith worthless, have, among other things, also made people ashamed of obeying, of submitting to authority. This rebelliousness even sneaks into the thought process of the better ones, perhaps unconsciously, and so begins all this extravagance, which basically is treason, about the deep and the profound and the wondrously beautiful that one can glimpse etc. If one were to describe with a single specific adjective the Christian-religious address as it is now heard and read, one would have to say that it is *affected*. Ordinarily when mention is made of a pastor's affectation, one perhaps has in mind that he decks himself out and dolls himself up, or that he speaks in a sentimental tone, or that he rolls his *r*'s like a Norwegian and wrinkles his brow,[17] or that he strains himself in energetic postures and revivalist leaps etc. Yet all such things are of minor importance, even though it is always desirable that such things not occur. But it is corrupting when the thought process of the sermon address is affected, when its orthodoxy is achieved by placing the emphasis on an entirely wrong place, when basically it exhorts believing in Christ, preaches faith in him on the basis of what cannot at all be the object of faith. If a son were to say, "I obey my father not because he is my father but because he is a genius, or because his commands are always profound and brilliant," this filial obedience is affected. The son emphasizes something altogether wrong, emphasizes the brilliance, the profundity in a *command*, whereas a command is simply indifferent to this qualification. The son is willing to obey on the basis of the father's profundity and brilliance, and on that basis he simply cannot *obey* him, because his critical attitude with regard to whether the command is profound and brilliant undermines the obedience.

Similarly, it is also affectation when there is so much talk about appropriating Christianity and believing in Christ on account of the depth and profundity of the doctrine. One ascribes orthodoxy to oneself by emphasizing something altogether wrong. Thus all modern speculative thought is affected by having abolished *obedience* on the one hand and *authority* on the other, and by wanting despite that to be orthodox. A pastor who is entirely correct in his address must, when he quotes words of Christ, speak in this way: "These words are by the one to whom, according to his own statement, all power is given in heaven and on earth. You, my listener, must now in your own mind consider whether you will submit to this authority or not, accept and believe these words or not. But if you refuse, then for God's sake do not accept the words because they are brilliant or profound or wondrously beautiful—because this is blasphemy, this is wanting to criticize God." As soon, namely, as the dominance of authority, of the specifically paradoxical authority, is established, then

XI
106

all relations are qualitatively changed, then the kind of appropriation that is otherwise permissible and desirable is an offense and presumptuousness.

But how, then, can the apostle demonstrate that he has authority? If he could demonstrate it *physically*, he would simply be no apostle. He has no other evidence than his own statement. This is just the way it must be, since otherwise the believer would enter into a direct relation to him, not into a paradoxical relation. In the transitory relations of authority between persons *qua* human beings, authority will as a rule be physically recognizable by power. An apostle has no other evidence than his own statement, and at most his willingness to suffer everything joyfully for the sake of that statement. His speech in this regard will be brief: "I am called by God; do with me now what you will; flog me, persecute me, but my last words will be my first: I am called by God, and I make you eternally responsible for what you do to me." If in actuality it were so, let us imagine it, that an apostle had power in the worldly sense, had great influence and powerful connections, by which forces one is victorious over people's opinions and judgments—if he then used the power, he *eo ipso* [precisely thereby] would have forfeited his cause. That is, by using the power, he would define his endeavor in essential identity with the endeavor of other people, and yet an apostle is what he is only by his paradoxical heterogeneity, by having divine authority, which he is able to have absolutely unchanged, even if he, as Paul says, is regarded by people as being of no more worth than the dirt on which they walk.[18]

XI
107

3. *The genius has only an immanent teleology; the apostle is absolutely teleologically positioned paradoxically.*

If any human being can be said to be positioned absolutely teleologically, it is an apostle. The doctrine communicated to him is not a task given to him to cogitate about; it is not given to him for his own sake. On the contrary, he is on a mission and has to proclaim the doctrine and to use authority. Just as little as a person sent into the city with a letter has anything to do with the contents of the letter but only with delivering it, and just as little as the envoy sent to a foreign court has any responsibility for the contents of the message but only for conveying it properly, so an apostle primarily has only to be faithful in his duty, which is to carry out his mission. Even if an apostle is never persecuted, his sacrificial life consists essentially in this: "that he, himself poor, only makes others rich,"[19] that he never dares to take the time or the quiet or the freedom from care in pleasant days, in *otium* [leisure], to be enriched by that with which, through its proclamation, he enriches others. Spiritually understood, he is like the busy housewife who herself, in order to prepare food for the many mouths, scarcely has time to eat. And if he, when he began, dared to hope for a long life, his life will still remain unchanged until the end, because there will always be ever new ones to whom to proclaim the doctrine.

Although a revelation is the paradoxical fact that passes human understanding,[20] one can still understand this much, which also has manifested itself everywhere: that a person is called by a revelation to go out in the world, to proclaim the Word, to act and to suffer, is called to the unceasingly active life as the Lord's messenger. On the other hand, that a person would be called by a revelation to remain in undivided possession of the estate, in busy literary *far niente* [idleness], to be momentarily brilliant and subsequently a collector and publisher of the dubieties of his brilliance—this is almost a blasphemous thought. XI
108

It is different with a genius. He has only an immanent teleology, he develops himself, and as he develops himself he plans this, his self-development, as his activity. He surely acquires significance, perhaps even great significance, but he is not himself teleologically positioned in relation to the world and to others. A genius lives within himself, and he can humorously live in secluded self-satisfaction without therefore nullifying his talent if only, without regard for whether others benefit from it or not, he develops himself earnestly and diligently, following his own genius. The genius is by no means therefore inactive; within himself he perhaps works even more than ten businessmen; he perhaps accomplishes a great deal, but each of his accomplishments has no τέλος [end, goal] outside. This is simultaneously the humanity of the genius and his pride: the humanity consists in his not defining himself teleologically in relation to any other person, as if there were anyone who stood in need of him; the pride consists in his relating himself immanently to himself. It is modest of the nightingale not to demand that anyone must listen to it, but it is also proud of the nightingale that it does not care at all to know whether anyone listens to it or not.

The dialectic of the genius will be especially offensive in our day, when the crowd, the masses, the public, and other such abstractions seek to turn everything upside down. The honored public, the power-craving crowd, wants the genius to express that he exists for its or for their sake; the honored public, the power-craving crowd, sees only one side of the dialectic of the genius, is offended by the pride, and does not perceive that this is also humility and modesty. Therefore the honored public, the power-craving crowd, wants also to nullify an apostle's existence. It surely is true that he exists entirely for the sake of others, is sent out for the sake of others; but it is not the crowd and not humanity, not the honored public, not even the honored cultured public, that is his master or his masters—it is God—and the apostle is the one who has *divine authority* to *command* both the crowd and the public.

The humorous self-satisfaction of the genius is the unity of modest resignation in the world and proud elevation above the world, is the unity of being a useless superfluity and a costly ornament. If the genius is an artist, he produces his work of art, but neither he nor his work of art has any τέλος outside. Or he is an author who destroys every teleological relation to the surrounding world and defines himself humorously as a lyric poet. The lyrical quite rightly has no τέλος outside itself. Whether someone writes one page of lyrical poetry or folios of lyrical poetry makes no difference with regard to defining the direction of his work. The lyrical author cares only about the production, enjoys the joy of the production, perhaps often through pain and effort, but he has nothing to do with others. He does not write *in order to*, in order to enlighten people, in order to help them onto the right road, in order to accomplish something—in short, he does not write: *in order to*. And so it is with every genius. No genius has an "in order to"; the apostle *absolutely paradoxically* has an "in order to."[21]

XI
109

SUPPLEMENT

KEY TO REFERENCES

Marginal references alongside the main text and Supplement are to volume and page [VII^2 B 235 100] in *Søren Kierkegaards Papirer*, I-XI^3 (note the differentiating letter A, B, or C, used only in references to the *Papirer*), edited by P. A. Heiberg, V. Kuhr, and E. Torsting (1 ed., Copenhagen: Gyldendal, 1909–48), and 2 ed., photo-offset with two supplemental volumes, XII-XIII, edited by Niels Thulstrup (Copenhagen: Gyldendal, 1968–70), and with index, XIV-XVI (1975–78), edited by N. J. Cappelørn. References to the *Papirer* in English [*JP* II 1500], occasionally amended, are to volume and serial number in *Søren Kierkegaard's Journals and Papers*, I-VII, edited and translated by Howard V. Hong and Edna H. Hong, assisted by Gregor Malantschuk, and with index, VII, by Nathaniel Hong and Charles Barker (Bloomington: Indiana University Press, 1967–78).

Other marginal references alongside the text in Addendum II are to volume and page [XI 100] in *Søren Kierkegaards samlede Værker*, I-XIV, edited by A. B. Drachmann, J. L. Heiberg, and H. O. Lange (1 ed., Copenhagen: Gyldendal, 1901–06). The same marginal references are used in Sören Kierkegaard, *Gesammelte Werke*, Abt. 1–36 (Düsseldorf, Cologne: Diederichs Verlag, 1952–59).

References to Kierkegaard's works in English are to this edition, *Kierkegaard's Writings* [*KW*], I-XXVI (Princeton: Princeton University Press, 1978-). Specific references are given by English title and the standard Danish pagination referred to above [*Either/Or*, I, 100, *KW* III (*SV* I 80)].

References to correspondence are to the serial numbers in *Breve og Aktstykker vedrørende Søren Kierkegaard*, I-II, edited by Niels Thulstrup (Copenhagen: Munksgaard, 1953–54), and to the corresponding serial numbers in *Kierkegaard: Letters and Documents*, translated by Henrik Rosenmeier, *Kierkegaard's Writings*, XXV [*Letters*, Letter 100, *KW* XXV].

References to books in Kierkegaard's own library [*ASKB* 100] are based on the serial numbering system of *Auktionsprotokol over Søren Kierkegaards Bogsamling* [Auction-catalog of Søren Kierkegaard's Book-collection], edited by H. P. Rohde (Copenhagen: Royal Library, 1967).

In the Supplement, references to page and lines in the text are given as: 100:1–10.

In the notes, internal references to the present volume are given as: p. 100.

Three spaced periods indicate an omission by the editors; five spaced periods indicate a hiatus or fragmentariness in the text.

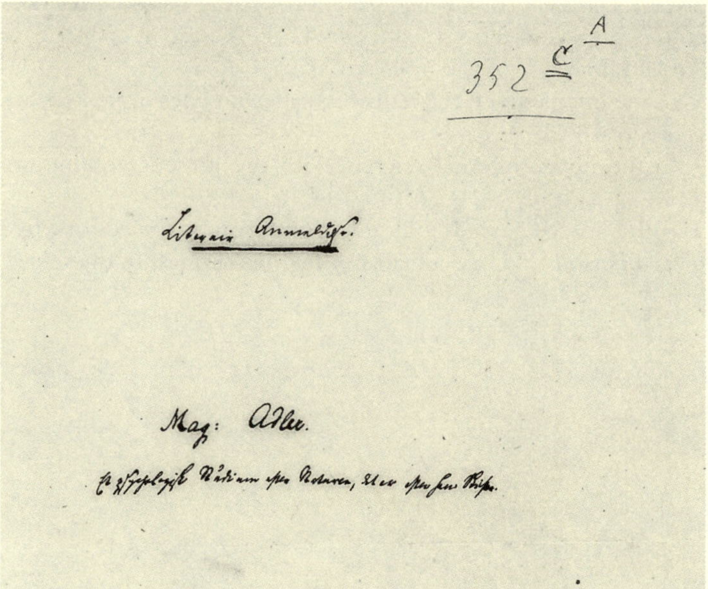
A
352 C
Literair Anmeldelse.
Mag: Adler.
af
S. Kierkegaard.
VII B 242

Literary Review.

Mag. Adler.

A Psychological Study from Nature, That Is,
Based on His Writings.

by
S. Kierkegaard.

No 299.

8 Marts 1847

Mindre Skrifter

✗

S. Kierkegaard

999.

VII B 217

[VII B 217-218]

8 March 1847

Minor Works

by

S. Kierkegaard.

352 C

Nr. 489.

Nutidens religieuse Forvirring
belyst ved Mag. Adler som Phænomen

en mulig Monographie

af

Johannes Climacus.

VIII B 21

udgivet
af
S. Kierkegaard.

NB. har Manuscriptet og ieg i gjennem før
at overgive til Climacus.

7 Forsaavidt bliver da den Udgang "Min Læser" at
henføre til mig selv som Udgiveren og Til-
freunde til Forordet.

VIII B 22

NB Alt bliver bedst at gjøre Forordet til Udgiveren, der bliver en bedre
som Experiment.

VIII B 23

The Religious Confusion of the Present Age
Illustrated by Mag. Adler as a Phenomenon

A Mimical Monograph

by

Johannes Climacus.

Edited
by
S. Kierkegaard.

Nutidens religieuse Forvirring
belyst ved Mag Adler som Phænomen.

En mindre Monographie

af

Petrus Minor

udgivet af
S Kierkegaard.

The Religious Confusion of the Present Age
Illustrated by Mag. Adler as a Phenomenon.

A Mimical Monograph

by

Petrus Minor

Edited
by
S. Kierkegaard.

[Editorial marking by editors of the *Papirer* is not reproduced.]

Nr. 29 c.

Tvende ethisk = religieuse.
Smaa = Afhandlinger.

af

H. H.

Oplg 525; trrrnet fra
"Hverdgs- Hjtorie" mia
runde Cyrer, tollon Cryst;
6 faanglen en velin.

[X⁵ B 9] 1a

Two Ethical-Religious

Essays.

by

H. H.

Edition 525; format like
"A Story of Everyday Life"
but smaller type and closer
print; 6 copies on vellum.

Tvende ethisk-religieuse

Smaa-Afhandlinger.

Af

H. H.

Kjøbenhavn.
Gyldendalske Boghandling.
Trykt hos Louis Klein.
1849.

Two Ethical-Religious

Essays.

By

H. H.

————————

Copenhagen.

Gyldendal's Bookstore.

Printed by Louis Klein.

1849.

Om Forskjellen mellem et Genie og en
Apostel.

1847.

The Difference between a Genius and an
Apostle.

1847.

Ene ... ...

... af.

m. m.

46-47

[X⁶ B 57]

Three Ethical or Ethical-Religious

Essays

by.

[*Deleted:* F. F.]
M. M.

[Editorial marking by editors of the *Papirer* is not reproduced.]

Contents.

SELECTED ENTRIES FROM
KIERKEGAARD'S JOURNALS AND PAPERS
PERTAINING TO
THE BOOK ON ADLER

To be sure, there ought to be a continued and intensified foreshortening and abbreviating of the abstract, the metaphysical
(both in the sense in which painters foreshorten the perspective
and in the stricter sense of foreshortening, since the doubt,
through which the system works itself forward more and more,
must be overcome and thereby become less and less talkative),
but if in so doing metaphysical thought also declares that it thinks
historical actuality,[1] it is on the wrong path. After the system has
completed itself and has reached the category of actuality, the
new doubt[2] appears, the new contradiction, the last and the most
profound, whereby the metaphysical reality is decisive for historical actuality (the Hegelians distinguish between existence
[*Tilværelse*] and reality: the external phenomenon exists, but insofar as it is taken up into the idea it is real. This is quite correct,
but the Hegelians do not define the boundary, to what extent
each phenomenon can become real in this way, and the reason
for this is that they see the phenomenon from the bird's-eye
perspective of the metaphysical and do not likewise see the
metaphysical in the phenomenon from the perspective of the
phenomenon)—namely, the historical as the unity of the metaphysical and the accidental.[3] It is the metaphysical insofar as this
is the eternal bond of existence, without which the phenomeno-
logical would disintegrate; it is the accidental insofar as with
every event there is the possibility that it could take place in
infinitely many other ways; the unity of these (divinely regarded)
is *providence*, and (humanly regarded), *the historical*. The meaning
of the historical is not that it is to be annulled but that the individual is to be free within it and also happy in it. This unity of
the metaphysical and the accidental is already implicit in self-

consciousness, which is the point of departure for personality. I become conscious simultaneously in my eternal validity, in, so to speak, my divine necessity, and in my accidental finitude (that I am this particular being, born in this country at this time, under all the various influences of changing conditions). This latter aspect must not be overlooked or rejected; on the contrary, the true life of the individual is its apotheosis, which does not mean that this empty, contentless *I* steals, as it were, out of this finitude, in order to become volatilized and diffused in its heavenward emigration, but rather that the divine inhabits and finds its task in the finite.—*JP* II 1587 (*Pap.* III A 1) July 4, 1840

III
A 11
10

If the presuppositionlessness[4] of the philosophers were the case, an account would still have to be made of language and its entire importance and relation to speculation, because in it speculation does indeed have a medium that it has not provided itself, and what the eternal secret of consciousness is for speculation as a union of a qualification of nature and a qualification of freedom, so also language is [for speculation] partly an original given and partly something freely developing. And just as the individual, no matter how freely he develops, can never reach the point of becoming absolutely independent, since true freedom consists, on the contrary, in appropriating the given and consequently in being absolutely dependent through freedom, so it is also with language, although we do find at times the ill-conceived tendency of not wanting to accept language as the freely appropriated given but rather to produce it for oneself, whether it appears in the highest regions where it usually ends in* silence or in the personal isolation of jargonizing nonsense. Perhaps the story of the Babylonian confusion of tongues may be explained in this way, that it was an attempt to construct an

III
A 11
11

arbitrarily formed common language, which, since it lacked fully integrative commonality, necessarily broke up into the most disparate differences, since here it holds true that the *totum est parte sua prius* [the whole is prior to its parts], which was not understood.

In margin: *the negation of language.
—*JP* III 3281 (*Pap.* III A 11) July 18, 1840

From sketch of Either/Or, *I:*

I must include hypochondria in "Either/Or" in order always to characterize the isolated elements in isolated subjectivity.[5] This I should like to do in "Either/Or"—and then mediate in B's papers in Part Two.—*JP* V 5549 (*Pap.* III B 130) *n.d.*, 1842

Interested Knowing and Its Forms.

What knowing is without interest.
   It has its interest in a third (for example, beauty, truth, etc.), which is not myself.
   therefore has no continuity.

Interested knowing entered with Christianity.
   The question of authority.
      of historical continuity
      of doubt
      of faith.

Is knowledge higher than faith? By no means.
         —*JP* II 2283 (*Pap.* IV C 99) *n.d.*, 1842–43

From letter to Peter Christian Kierkegaard:

. . . You know that there is in town a Magister Adler, who became a pastor on Bornholm, a zealous Hegelian. He has come over here to publish some sermons in which he will probably advocate a movement in the direction of orthodoxy. He has a good head on him and has considerable experience in many *casibus* of life, but at the moment he is a little overwrought. Nevertheless it is always possible that this is a phenomenon worth paying attention to. . . .—*Letters*, Letter 83, June 29, 1843, *KW* XXV

From draft of Anxiety:

. . . Even in our little Denmark men have come to the rescue of logical movement. In his "logical system,"[6] which, despite all

V
B 49:5
107

movement, does not come further than to ¶ 23 (the beginning of
the doctrine of quantity) and, despite its proud title, was not able
to emancipate itself from a very subordinate existence in a periodical, Professor Heiberg nevertheless succeeded in making
everything move—except the system, which comes to a halt at
¶ 23, although one might have believed that the system of itself
would have moved itself through an immanent movement, and
the more so because the author indicated in the "Preface" the
course of the development, namely, that the published essay was
"the first contribution to a long-cherished plan of setting forth
the logical system." This he wished to do, not merely for its own
sake, but as a means by which he also "intended to pave the way
for an esthetics, which for some time he had hoped to present."[7]
Just an example: the professor explains to us that in order to form
the transition from quality to quantity "it is not enough to define
quantity as unqualified being in general; it is the *annulled* quality;
that is to say: quantity is not the first presuppositionless being but
is the being that, after the quality has been presupposed and then
annulled, returns to the same indeterminateness."[8] Now this may
be quite correct, but the difficulty lies in the fact that both being
and quality are treated as identical. But being is no quality; logically speaking, it is rather the empty, the contentless, the indeterminate, whereas even according to Hegel's definition, quantity
is *einfache Bestimmtheit* [simple determinateness],[9] and therefore it
is not essentially being but essentially determinateness. Thus
when one proceeds from being and annuls this in order to return
to it again, one will never arrive at quality, and much less a new
quality. —Magister Adler (in his *Popular Lectures on Hegel's Objective Logic,*[10] Copenhagen 1842) makes the movement even better. He says (p. 48), "if the quality is indifferent, quantity appears
as the qualifying factor." One would be tempted to answer him
with an emphasis even greater than that of the Lacedemonians:
If?[11]—*Pap.* V B 49:5 *n.d.*, 1844

V
B 49:5
108

VII'
A 143
83

... In immediacy conscience is infinite, and it accentuates
infinitely the distinction between good and evil. One must then
assume (if the objection* is to mean anything) that by thinking

abstractly a person is capable of becoming so abstract that he no longer has any conscience or that the ethical has completely evaporated and he has become metaphysically volatilized. But this is impossible. Just as God has limited a human being physically, so he has also set bounds to him in a mental sense, if in no other way, simply by his being created, and a human being has not created himself. With his imagination a human being is able to see for millions of miles, but with his physical eyes he cannot see so far; and no matter how long he continues to indulge in this fantasy, his eyes still never see any further. . . .

*The objection, therefore, usually comes from those who have to be called unhinged individuals, who have grown dizzy out in the infinite (Adler, for example, who thought that one could not distinguish between the voice of God and the voice of the devil[12]).—*JP* II 1348 (*Pap.* VII[1] A 143) *n.d.*, 1846

Outline and sketch of version I:

1.

The externals of Adler's life.

That he was dismissed. —The state Church's complete justification; the normal and the relation of the universal to the extraordinary.[13] —Adler himself ought to have resigned; a person who at some point feels himself placed outside the universal should himself make the collision as difficult as possible for himself, but as easy as possible for the universal, because he ought to love the universal, and in no way want to slip out of it easily himself or want any excuse, fearing most of all to be in error. Only through a suffering may he gain the superiority of the extraordinary.—*Pap.* VII[2] B 241:1

The one who is extraordinarily positioned must also express it by not standing in rank with the universal—the extraordinary must be willing to make a sacrifice—it is foolishness to ask to be in the service of the established order and express something entirely different: the sophistry when one does not love the universal but only one's point of view, to want to sell one's life as dearly as possible, to want to embarrass the universal.—*Pap.* VII² B 241:2

Basically Mag. Adler ought to be happy to have a man like Bishop Mynster opposite him, a man who so normally, so paradigmatically, expresses the universal and who has strength.

—*Pap.* VII² B 241:3

2.

He has a revelation-fact.
Everything revolves around that—or he must
be held firmly to that.

That a phenomenon such as this was bound to occur in our day. The whole modern biblical criticism that demolishes the differences ultimately has the result that the apostles' position must in an assault be made the position of all Christians.
Fragments developed the concept "contemporaneity"[14]
in order to cut away the posthistorical.
This has now happened through A. but in a lamentable way.—*Pap.* VII² B 241:4

3.

In the later writings he no longer holds this revelation-fact fast in a qualitative dialectic.
The comic that a living man, in relation to a fact in his own life, runs through the whole rigmarole of modern exegesis that has insisted upon explaining and explaining the miraculous: that it is ecstasy, internal fact, genius.
In the latest books, he continually arrives at the category "genius" (this word appears on at least every third page). He now seems to want to be satisfied with being a genius.[*] By this everything is dreadfully confused. —The infinite qualitative difference between an apostle and a genius. —The apostle is what he is
only by authority; it does not belong to a genius to say: Re-

pent—but the authority with which it is said determines who it is who is speaking. —But in our day all the spheres are confused. (In the sermon address the numerous confusions by which the apostles are really made into geniuses, and doubt is thereby occasioned, since these by no means rank as high as geniuses.)

In the latest books he no longer talks about that fact, or about his definitely knowing that these words were written under the immediate inspiration of the Spirit (as it says in *Sermons*.[15]) Now he is merely a genius, yet without having revoked that fact, the words of which he uses verbatim. He fictionizes with rather great freedom and at times even confuses himself with Christ. He fictionizes and says: Christ said to our Lord, etc. This is still all right insofar as it is poetical. But later on he forgets that he himself has fictionized it and cites as follows: One must recall that Christ said to our Lord.

VII²
B 241
262

He now dabbles in everything possible, and he (the man of confession: Confess, confess) in many passages has appropriated from the pseudonymous writers the principle of silence. This principle is the exact opposite, is the expression for self-deepening, which certainly is not needed when one has a revelation-fact as a starting point.

Thus it is not strange that he so often reverts to the justifiableness of intellectual theft—which one would ordinarily least think could be the subject for consideration by someone who has over all people the advantage of having a revelation-fact, unless he then has been robbed, but that is simply not the case.

He who at first fancied that the world would be surprised and therefore allowed the type to stand so that a second edition could immediately come out was later of the opinion that he would be understood only after a hundred years. He has now, imitating the pseudonymous writers, wanted to be humorously indifferent to all people—he who calls out: Confess, confess, communicate, communicate.

He is an out-and-out hodgepodge.—*Pap.* VII² B 241:5

[*] Already in the little booklet containing the documents in his dismissal case,[16] Adler begins to haggle and return to the role of genius.—*Pap.* VII² B 241:6

3.

On the whole, everything is lost, and his promotion to genius is an enormous satire upon himself.

His entire wisdom is the tumultuous—today, the moment, without any ethical conception that ethically every moment is the moment—the nervous anxiety about letting the moment pass unused—the superstitious, the fantastic, the immorality in it.

Therefore by his existence he explains nothing at all in existence. His call, if it is anything at all, is a poet-call, not a call that at the same time explains the universally human existence.

He has leaped out of Hegel's metaphysics and flopped down into the religious, but he has never had any ethics or ethical education and discipline.

Dizziness is actually his genius; the genius of that frightful *confinium* [border territory] between good and evil that is the great.

Good and evil cannot be definitely separated
(Abraham)

therefore the recklessness of sensate genius; it does not care if a few suffer wrong, provided that the great advances (*à la* Napoleon), and one takes the direct analogy from nature (*à la* D. Juan [*deleted:* who says: See, does not the sun whore with every flower; round about it (ladyloves) are born[17]], who jumps at the chance).—*Pap.* VII² B 241:7

4.

He actually gives the impression of a pagan who has suddenly become a Christian or has come in contact with the essentially Christian.

For this very reason he explains nothing in relation to the issue of our age: how can the person who is brought up in Christianity become a Christian? One would not think that Adler had been brought up in Christianity; the sad insight such a person gives into what is ordinarily understood by a Christian upbringing.

VII²
B 241
264

The epigrammatic in: (1) that he became a pastor when he was an out-and-out pagan; (2) that he was dismissed when he had come somewhat closer to becoming a pastor.—*Pap.* VII² B 241:8

See what he himself with a certain frankness says in the preface to *Sermons.*[18]—*Pap.* VII² B 241:9

5.

A little about his writings.

Instead of thinking a thought, Adler at times merely keeps company with the enigmatic until by repeating it day in and day out he becomes beatified in a kind of fantastic clairvoyance—that it must be something. In the same way others have used numbers (one uses them just like liquor, stimulating, intoxicating). If a person were to pace back and forth and in a conjurer's solemn voice say 7, 14, 21—there must be something in it; 7, 14, 21—he will finally become dizzy and believe that he stands face to face with the enigmatic, with the great Pan etc. If someone were to write on small scraps of paper short sentences such as: The king went through the gate etc.—if after having affected a solemn voice he intones them like someone who is conjuring, it would finally seem to him as if the secret of the whole world were contained therein. The more incidental, the briefer the words are, the greater is the fantastic effect, because the imagination can create a whole world from such a sentence. If he were to rent the equipment of the lottery, if with the solemnity of the oracle he were to take these little tickets from the wheel of fortune while the guard presented arms; and His Excellency Ørsted took off his hat—then he certainly would also produce a fantastic effect upon a great many people.

    He is not an author, but he dashes off a quantity
    so it will take an author to write a book
    from his books.—*Pap.* VII² B 241:10

Just as a teacher gives the pupil disconnected words from which to write a composition, so A. dashes off disconnected sentences—perhaps to make an author of the reader. The only difference is that the teacher understands what he is doing, but A. seems not to understand himself.

> Adler is, as I am involuntarily reminded by so often abbreviating his name—he is A; he lacks B.—*Pap.* VII² B 241:11

He is not without lyricism, felicitous style, not without profundity.

> He is, however, particularly profound in one form: that truth indirectly makes untruth manifest. (This I long ago have already shown in all its subtlety in my dissertation on irony;[19] and later a pseudonymous writer, Quidam of the imaginary construction,[20] utilized it, so that when he firmly holds his idea, he changes all complaints against him into a confession.—*Pap.* VII² B 241:12

No reasonable ground for making 4 books out of the latest.
                                                    —*Pap.* VII² B 241:13

He is dangerously overstrained.—*Pap.* VII² B 241:14

He has not made any attempt to attach himself to the pseudonymous writers.[21]—*Pap.* VII² B 241:15

> the lyrical seething in the style has been taken from the pseudonymous writers. He did not have it before, not in *Sermons.* —What is in *Kirketidenden* is not true:[22] that the pseudonyms and he are almost simultaneous, since he is later, and this is very decisive.
> > constructing rhetorically upon the conditional clause, no main clause, etc.: something he has learned from Quidam of the imaginary construction.

N.B.

What is under 4 is to be used in the conclusion and be titled:
The Moral.

—*Pap*. VII² B 241:16
—*Pap*. VII² B 241: 1–16 *n.d.*, 1846–47

From draft of "minor works":

All the last four books²³ are to be published in one volume
under the title:

Minor Works by S. Kierkegaard.

—*JP* V 5954 (*Pap*. VII¹ B 214) *n.d.*, 1846–47

From draft of "Minor Works":

Contents
 I. Discourse on the Occasion of a Confession.
 II. Literary Review. Adler.
 III. What One Learns from the Lilies in the Field
    and from the Birds of the Air. 3 Discourses.
 IV. The Gospel of Sufferings.

—*JP* V 5956 (*Pap*. VII¹ B 218) *n.d.*, 1846–47

Report
 on "The Book on Adler."

—*Pap*. VIII² B 1 *n.d.*, 1847

Addition to Pap. VIII² B 1:

About Chapter III of the book

The book, as it is finished now, is rich in content and interesting.
If the reader will take time and read slowly, he will convince
himself of this. If, however, something should be done to help a
slow reader, it would be to rework Chapter III and give a somewhat more facilitating and perceptible summary.

It should be done in this way

Chapter III

Clarification of A.'s not understanding himself in having had
a revelation, since he has only a vague idea and anything but a
Christianly qualitative concept of what a revelation is. . . .

—*Pap.* VIII^2 B 2 *n.d.*, 1847

Addition to Pap. VIII^2 B 2:

VIII^2
B 3
7

Then in an appendix to the whole book on Adler, his latest four books should be esthetically reviewed.

For that everything of a more general nature now found in Chapter III, 2 is to be used.

The illusion should be maintained that A. had not written anything but his dissertation and then the four books.

The illusion should be strengthened in this way:

As author of these four books, A. characterizes himself as a person who is shaken—he converses with God and Christ in a manner so confused that now one must expect that he will have visions and revelations, and it is really strange that he has not already had them.

VIII^2
B 3
8

The illusion should be strengthened in this way: in the four books A. adheres to the Bible and then to a few theses, a kind of doctrine to which he continually returns; one would almost think that it had some special significance for him, that he had dreamed it, just as one dreams numbers. It is certain that it has become fixed in him, and perhaps one will learn that eventually he fancies that it has been revealed to him.—*Pap.* VIII^2 B 3 *n.d.*, 1847

Addition to Pap. VIII^2 B 3:

Contents of the Appendix

Introduction

1.

On the misrelation of the great range of the books in volume and the meager contents. —The mutual misrelation between the books.

2.

The characteristics of the contents of the books.

3.

The author is best characterized as a confused genius, whose essential genius is dizziness.

4.

The external beauty of the books.

—*Pap.* VIII² B 4 *n.d.*, 1847

From draft:

The Religious Confusion of the Present Age
Illustrated by Mag. Adler as a Phenomenon

A Mimical Monograph
by
Johannes Climacus

Edited
by
S. Kierkegaard

—*Pap.* VIII² B 21 *n. d.* 1847

Addition to Pap. VIII² B 21:

N.B.

The entire manuscript must be read through in order to be assigned to Climacus.

But in the preface the ending "My Reader" is to be transferred to me as the editor's addition to the preface.

—*Pap.* VIII² B 22 *n.d.*, 1847

Addition to Pap. VIII² B 22:

N.B.   It is best to make the whole preface the editor's, who speaks about the books as a third party.

—*Pap.* VIII² B 23 *n.d.*, 1847

It would perhaps be most correct to create a new pseudonym instead of Johannes Climacus, since he is already marked as the one who has said he is not a Christian.[24]

e.g.

Petrus Minor.
Thomas Minor
Vincentius Minor
Ataraxius Minor.
—*Pap.* VIII^2 B 24 *n.d.*, 1847

With regard to Adler, the only mitigating thing one could do for him would be to explain that in former times it frequently happened that a religious speaks of what Christ had said to him or to her, or that a religious speaks in the name of Christ and says *I*. There are examples of this on every page of Abraham à St. Clara.[25] But the point is that it has its place within the whole consciousness of the age. Furthermore, none of them thinks of referring to such words as a special commission (unlike Adler, whom Christ commanded to write it down). And then to do it in our day, when he is utterly bereft of any corresponding idea in the contemporary consciousness, and then to do it in such a way that he himself is no help at all in determining more precisely how he understands himself in it.

I do not at all like this whole business with Adler. I am in truth all too inclined to keep Adler afloat. We need dynamic personalities, unselfish persons who are not immersed and exhausted in endless consideration for job, wife, and children.

But perhaps for the present one could write to him and request him to revoke that preface and then drop publication of the book. And yet the book does deserve to be read. But the trouble is that I am sorry for A., and I am almost afraid that it will have too strong an effect on him. . . .—*JP* V 6044 (*Pap.* VIII^1 A 252) *n.d.*, 1847

N.B.

"The Book on Adler" lends itself best to division into many small separate parts. It will not be understood as a whole—and it will be fatiguing because it is continually about Adler, which, however, in my thinking is just the point. Then there will be, for example, a section about the concept "premise-authors," about the universal, the single individual, the special individual. A second section: a revelation in the situation of contemporaneity. A third: about the relation between a genius and an apostle etc. This can be done superbly, and then the book will be read in an entirely different way and I will be spared mentioning Adler, for it is cruel to slay a person that way.—*JP* V 6049 (*Pap.* VIII¹ A 264) *n.d.*, 1847

December 1, 1847.

VIII¹
A 440
194

I have now organized and laid out the book on Adler again. The arrangement now makes everything as luminous and clear as possible.

The book has great merit. But the trouble is that there really are very few in our age who have enough religiousness to be able to benefit from it. In the long run, Adler with all his confusion still has more religiousness than most. The other trouble is that one gets involved with this confused person who has nothing to do and presumably therefore will write and write. But then the whole thing gets a wrong slant. In the book Adler is still a *Nebensach* [side-issue], but how easy it is for the matter to turn for a curious public into a cockfight between Adler and me.

VIII¹
A 440
195

No, rather let Adler go his way. Then the book will become a book of essays. In that regard the book is all organized now by means of making adaptions for the addenda.

The contents will then be as follows:

1. Something on premise-authors (it is the introduction). It can end like this:

> Just as Lichtenberg, in my opinion felicitiously and in any case correctly, has pointed out that there is a kind of prose, a much-used kind, that may be called graduate student prose,[26] so I hereby introduce the expression: premise-authors.

2. A premise-author on the revelation-fact
   (conclusion of the introduction).

3. A revelation in the situation of contemporaneity.
   Hypothesis: it is assumed that a man has stepped forth suddenly and claimed a revelation—how would this be manifest?

4. Addendum I. The dialectical relations: the universal, the single individual, the special individual.

5. Addendum II. The difference between a genius and an apostle.

6. Magister Adler as a satire on Hegelian philosophy and the Christianity of our time.
   —*JP* 6079 (*Pap.* VIII[1] A 440) December 1, 1847

Preface to version I of "The Book on Adler":

VII[2]
B 270
309

Preface

Essentially this book can be read only by theologians, and among them in turn can essentially interest only the single individual insofar as he—instead of perhaps becoming self-important and my judge by the objection: how could I hit on the idea of writing such a big book about Adler—submits to the work of reading and then looks for the sense in which A. is the subject of the book and the sense in which he is utilized to illuminate the age and to uphold dogmatic concepts, in which sense just as much attention is paid to the age as to Adler.

What in other respects I could wish to say in a preface (since I do not write in some newspaper or in some periodical, I may use the preface for some more general comments) about the literary relations between author, reader, and critic, I have been fortunate enough to find expressed better and more pithily than I can say it by a man whom I have always venerated, old Fichte, a man in the great sense, a character in the elevated sense, a thinker in the noble Greek sense. What he has said in this regard VII[2]
B 270
310 may indeed also be necessary to be said in our age, while the circumstance that it was said almost fifty years ago can perhaps gain a hearing for what is said. There is something mitigating in the fact that it is a deceased person who is speaking, something

that may make the reader more receptive to the rigorous discourse, in the fact that, if the world generally is wrong now, it then also must have been wrong fifty years ago. When a living person speaks to his contemporaries, he may be tempted to present it as if the world had previously been good but in the last fourteen days it had become all wrong. The contemporaries are in turn embittered by it, and rightly so, since it undoubtedly is the case that the world at all times has been just about equally good or equally bad. Scrutiny of the age, portrayals of the contemporaries, our age's notions, and the like are so easily misused purely rhetorically; that is, the speaker or author arranges the presentation so it can make a brilliant showing and have an effect at the moment and is less concerned about having a firm, definite view of the age, or about considering that the task is perhaps too great. If a speaker wants to entice people, he says: It must be said to the honor of our age, and it must not be suppressed or misconstrued, that a new life is beginning to stir, that there are continually becoming more and more, etc. When he thunders the next Sunday, he says: Or has the corruption of our age not yet reached its peak, is there actually a degree that has not yet been reached when presumably a greater moral laxity is to be seen, etc. These various views are sometimes published in one volume, and the less attentive reader reads, then shuts the book in amazement and thinks: God knows in what age this man actually lived. No, then it is better to let a deceased person speak. If a pastor had reflected on his discourse and chosen for the theme: the luxuriousness of our age, and on Saturday afternoon he accidentally discovered a sermon from 1718 on the luxuriousness of our age—I believe he would benefit his listeners more by reading this aloud than by delivering his own. The main point is not that one person thunders and others must put up with it; the main point is that we all, individually, become wiser. And when a deceased person speaks, there is in a sense no one who speaks; then we all can listen.

VII²
B 270
311

The passage is found in an essay, *"Nicolais Leben und Meinungen." Sämtl. W.*, VIII, pp. 75ff., addendum 3 to Chapter 2.[27]

Copenhagen   January 1847

—*JP* V 5969 (*Pap.* VII² B 270) *n.d.*, 1846–47

From draft of version III of "The Book on Adler":

For

the Preface.

In this way I am separated from this book. It is, which will seem [strange] to many, it is actually an upbuilding book—for the one who understands it; and, which will seem even stranger to many, on behalf of my little bit of renown I ask no more than to have written the book, since in connection with it there is an element of good fortune that is seldom offered, since seldom, perhaps, has a person by going the wrong way come as opportunely as Mag. Adler has for me.—*Pap.* VIII^2 B 20 *n.d.*, 1847

From draft of "A Cycle of Ethical-Religious Essays":

The preface to "A Cycle of Ethical-Religious Essays"[28] that was not used.—*Pap.* IX B 9 *n.d.*, 1848

From draft of "A Cycle":

IX
B 10
308

Preface[29]

This entire book was written before, some of it even a long time before, the European crisis of the present year.[30] This is for historical information, but in other respects it is a matter of indifference [*Ligegyldighed*], all in proportion to the extent to which the book contains something of what may be called the equal validity [*Lige-Gyldighed*] of *truth* for all ages, because then the crisis cannot detract but rather adds, can only make publication even more a duty.

May I also give, quite directly, a little watchword concerning what the one who has been able and has wanted to see has undoubtedly seen at the basis of my entire work as an author viewed as a whole, a watchword concerning, *ut ita dicant* [so as they say], my program as author (which, to be sure, does not come first, as is customary, but last): my position and purpose were and are unchanged. The crisis has only helped me to understand it better, while it perhaps will also help me to be understood better than before or at least to become more passionately misunderstood. The question is not about one house of representatives, or two, or ten, nor about the setting up [*Nedsættelse*] of committees or about the appointing [*Opsættelse*] of cabinet ministers. I daresay there are questions about these things, continually repeated questions from thousands and thousands about them; indeed, there is actually no question about anything else. But, see, all this is what the age demands, not what it needs, at least not in a deeper sense; the tragedy is precisely that the age demands what it does not need; all this is therefore partly foolishness, a waste of time, at least in some cases, and partly—oh, the earnestness of these earnest times!—a craving for entertainment. No, in the idea, viewed essentially, there are questions or there is *the question* about Christianity and about Christianity proper—about Christianity, that it is what is needed, about Christianity proper, that it is what has been abolished, that a so-called or rather a fallen Christendom openly or more surreptitiously, at one moment by attack and the next by defense, has abolished it. Governance has now lost patience, will not tolerate it any longer but, radically as it teaches, will make it radically clear how self-contradictory all this is that people, general assemblies, balloting or bombarding, find acceptable as a surrogate for religiousness.

IX
B 10
309

That is why the crisis itself as manifested up to now is only the introduction [*deleted:* belongs in the account book, not in the main ledger], because a new era will not begin until we have come so far that we understand what *the question* is about. Europe as a whole, with the mounting momentum of passion, has *worldly* [*deleted:* in worldly brazenness or worldly confusion,] lost its way in problems that can be answered only *divinely*, that only Christianity can answer and—lest anyone be tempted to hail and acclaim what I have to say—has long since answered. With the introduction of the fourth estate, i.e., all people, to want to solve the problem of *equality* [*Lighed*] of all people in the medium of worldliness—that is, in the medium of which the essence is difference [*Forskjellighed*]—yes, even if all travel in Europe ceased because one would have to wade in blood, and all cabinet ministers became sleepless in order to ponder, and even if ten [*changed from:* a hundred] cabinet ministers lost their minds every day, and every next day ten [*changed from:* a hundred] new ones began where the others left off and also lost their minds—there still would not be essentially one step of progress. An obstruction to it is eternally posited, and eternity's border mocks all human efforts, mocks the presumptuousness toward its sublimely glorious rights, that temporality wants to explain in a temporal [*deleted:* and worldly] way that which in temporality must be an enigma and which only eternity can and will explain. The question is a religious question, a Christian question, and, to repeat, has long since already been answered. Obtain eternity for us again, the view of eternity at every moment, its earnestness and its blessedness, its relief; obtain eternity for every individual again, and a blood bath will not be needed and the cabinet ministers can also be allowed to keep their respective minds. Alas, but to extinguish the fire, the spontaneous combustion occasioned by the friction of the worldliness, in order to get relief, that is, in order to obtain eternity again, it might well be that a blood bath and bombardments will be needed and also that *en passant* many a cabinet minister will lose his mind.

No one knows how long this convulsive seizure will take. But one need not be a great *psychologist* to know how difficult it is to overcome this worldly and earthly commonsensicality when, as is the case with the present generation, people have a superstitious belief in its saving and happiness-producing power, how difficult it therefore is and how complicated it can become in the transition—to relinquish the understanding in order to make the leap into the religious. Worldly commonsensicality is all too entrenched in the worldly person, or he in it; it is with it as with a molar—it takes several attempts and violence to budge it or to take the life and power from it, which is only all too frightfully tenacious of life. Neither does one need to be a great *dialectician* to discover that to worldly passion it can deceptively look as if it were possible to bring about equality between persons in worldliness if only one remains indefatigable in calculating and computing. In any case the finite dialectic will be able to make an unbelievably great number of combinations. The constant refrain will become: treachery, treachery. No, when it is done in another way, when one subtracts a little *here*, adds a little *there*, and then divides equally the more that is there, without forgetting the difference there, collated with the difference here, and there and here and here and yonder and up and down—then it must necessarily be possible to find the equality [*Lighed*], the divisor, the monetary standard for human-likeness [*Menneske-Lighed*] in worldliness, that is, in difference, the equality for the *worldly* human-likeness, that is, for the—different—equality. The system sought for the pure human being, in the same way the modern age now seeks for the equal human being—because in worldliness we are all distorted or distortions, that is, relativities. Worldliness is an enormous variegated composite of more and less, a little more and a little less, much, some, a little, etc., that is, worldliness is difference. But the understanding in the service of worldliness continually insists on imagining that it nevertheless can figure it out and get equality in worldliness. Every new combination then becomes—yes, in the now obsolete style it would probably become a new section—now in the "*styli novi*" it becomes a new government administration.

IX
B 10
311

And when this new administration goes or is violently ousted, will it then be acknowledged that the trouble was not due to the accidental errors and deficiencies in this combination but that essentially something entirely different was needed—namely, religiousness? No, that will not be done. There will promptly be in the offing a new combination and a new government administration, which by having shuffled the relativities kaleidoscopically in some other way imagines that it has found what has been sought. And people will say, almost in total unison, "Certainly not," to the way the former administration wanted it; it cannot be done, but if only the calculation is done correctly, then it must work out—and so there is a new administration, which does less for the bartenders, more for the candlemakers, and then again takes more from the property owners and advances the proletariat, taxes the clergymen equally with the parish clerks, and in general makes equals of a stoop-shouldered watchman and a crooked-legged journeyman blacksmith. In many ways the age will be reminiscent of the time of Socrates (except that it is much more passionate and violent, since it is a sophistry of tangibility and violence), but there will be nothing reminiscent of Socrates.

In the midst of all this, this series of paragraphs or this series of administration changes, the human race will become more and more confused, just as a drunken man, the more violently he storms around, gets more intoxicated, even though he does not get more to drink. And when the preliminary, the convulsive seizure, has run its course, the human race will be so exhausted from sufferings and loss of blood that this matter of eternity might at least be allowed to receive consideration.

[*Deleted:* October 1848]

This is my view or conception of the age, the view of an insignificant person who has something of the poet in his nature, in other respects is a thinker, but—yes, how often I have repeated this, to me so important and crucial, my first statement about myself—"without authority."—*Pap.* IX B 10 *n.d.*, 1848

From draft of "A Cycle":

IX
B 11
312

Preface

This entire book was entirely written before, some of it even a long time before, the European world-historical crisis of the present year. This is for historical information, in other respects a matter of indifference [*Ligegylde*], all in proportion to the extent to which the book contains something of what may be called the equal-validity [*Lige-Gyldighed*] of *truth* for all ages. Yet in any case the book has not been rendered obsolete by the crisis; it has not exactly lost but instead has rather gained by means of the crisis, which makes its publication even more a duty.

[*Essentially the same as* 228:25–230:19 (*Pap.* IX B 10, pp. 308⁸-310²).]

In the idea, viewed essentially, everyone who in confidence with God knows that he truly believes in Christianity has already more than conquered, despite all the world's confusion and rebellion. [*Deleted:* We also have more than conquered.] He acknowledges only one superior force, that of the one who is able to pray more inwardly, with more fear and trembling, than he has been; but such a one is not his enemy, he is his powerful ally. Every opposition, that of capabilities, of talents, of numbers, viewed in the idea, is already *essentially* overcome, no matter if he *incidentally* really comes to or may come to suffer for it. Incidentally, because in a *worldly way* a great commotion is made about sufferings; one suffers in order to be victorious, and then perhaps is not victorious at all. *Christianly* one has in advance already been more than victorious. Therefore one does not suffer in order to be victorious, but instead because one has been victorious, which gives a person precisely the desire to put up with everything and raises one above the sufferings; since one has been victorious, one of course can easily put up with a little suffering. In a worldly way, stressed in uncertainty, one must wait for what follows after suffering, whether the victory follows now. Christianly there is nothing to wait for; in faith the victory was given long ago. One learns this from the prototype. His last words in the suffering were not: Wait just a little and you will see that my cause is victorious. No, he said: It is finished. What? The suffering. But then is he not speaking at all about the victory? No, why should it occur to him—he indeed knew from eternity that he had been victorious.

IX
B 11
313

October 48
—*Pap.* IX B 11 October 1848

Deleted addition to preface (Pap. IX B 11) *to* "A Cycle":

This preface is, as stated, an anticipation. The book was written about two years ago, with the exception of one essay,[31] which is from the end of last year. Inasmuch as this preface is dated October 1848 and since the spring of '48, when "Christian Discourses" was published, I have worked out several short works, these are in fact older than this preface, although they will be published later. But they could not be published before the present book, which they presuppose, would be published. On the other hand, the preface to this book will be understood better after the publication of those works.—*Pap.* IX B 12 *n.d.*, 1848

From draft of "A Cycle":

IX
B 20
316

Preface

[*Essentially the same as 232:19–29* (*Pap.* IX B 11, p. 312).]

And yet this is only the preliminary. But probably neither I nor scarcely anyone now living will experience more, because in all likelihood the convulsive seizure will go on for a longer time, perhaps a considerable period of years, [*deleted:* because it is still a low estimate to estimate forty years for the convulsive seizure].

IX
B 20
317

[*Essentially the same as 230:20–232:16* (*Pap.* IX B 10, pp. 310–11)]

And then, when the preliminary, the convulsive seizure, has run its course and the *political* administrations are out, then the human race will no doubt be so exhausted from sufferings and loss of blood that this matter of eternity might at least be allowed to receive consideration, even though at first it will incite the passions again and give them new powers. There will be a reaction (opposite to that of the Reformation); what looked like and imagined itself to be political will explain itself as a religious movement. In order to recover eternity, blood will again be required, but blood of another kind, not that of battle victims slain by the thousands, no, the more costly blood, of the single individuals—of the martyrs, these powerful dead who are able to do what no living person who has people slaughtered by the thousands is able to do, what these powerful dead were themselves unable to do when alive, but are able to do only when dead: to compel a raging crowd to obedience, precisely because this raging crowd in disobedience was permitted to put the martyr to death. The proverb says: He laughs best who laughs last; but truly he also conquers best who conquers last, therefore not the one who conquers by putting to death—uncertain victory!—but he who conquers by being put to death—O eternal, certain victory! And this sacrifice, the sacrifice of obedience—wherefore God looks, well pleased, upon the obedient one who brings himself as a sacrifice, while he heaps wrath upon the disobedience that puts the sacrifice to death—this sacrifice, this victor, is *the martyr*, for truly not everyone who is put to death is a martyr!—*Pap.* IX B 20 *n.d.*, 1848

From draft of the preface to "A Cycle":

[*Essentially the same as 234:19–36 (Pap.* IX B 20, p. 317).] But   IX
B 22
319
the martyr is the ruler.

Until now, tyrants (in the form of emperors, kings, popes, Jesuits, generals, diplomats) have been able to rule and govern the world at a crucial moment, but from the time the fourth estate is established—when this has had time to establish itself in such a way that it is properly understood—it will become manifest that only martyrs are able to rule the world at the crucial moment. That is, no human being will any longer be able to rule the generation at such a moment; only the divine can do it, assisted by those unconditionally obedient to him, those who are also willing to suffer, but they are indeed the martyrs. In an older order, when the crucial moment was past, an orderly secular government took over, but from the moment the fourth estate is established, it will be seen that even when the crisis is over, the governing cannot be done *secularly*. No matter how much work and responsibility are connected with it, to rule secularly, to be a ruler in a secular way, is an indulgence, and therefore is based upon and is possible only in proportion to this: that the far, far greatest number of people either are so completely unaware that they are not part of (political) life or God-fearing enough not to want [*deleted:* to be part of it] to bother themselves with it. As soon as the fourth estate is established, governing can be done   IX
B 22
320
only divinely, religiously. But religiously to rule, religiously to be the ruler is to be the suffering one; religiously to rule is suffering. Many a time these suffering ones (the rulers) will naturally, if they dared entirely to have their way, wish themselves far away and say good-bye to the generation, in order either to spend their lives in the solitude of contemplation or to enjoy life, but when in fear and trembling they consider their responsibility to God, they dare not. People regard it as good fortune to be chosen to be the ruler secularly; but to be chosen to be the ruler religiously is instead like a punishment, humanly speaking, in any case a suffering, humanly speaking, the very opposite of an advantage, humanly speaking.

Displeased and discontented with the state, the Church, and

everything related to them (art, science, scholarship, etc. etc.), the generation, if it were allowed to have its way, would disintegrate into a world of atoms, whereby the advance would nevertheless be made that God now comes to be related to individuals neither through abstractions nor through representative individuals but becomes the one who, so to speak, takes it upon himself to bring up the generation's countless individuals, becomes himself the schoolmaster, who watches over everyone, each one individually. Here thinking halts. The shape of the world would resemble—well, I do not know to what I should compare it—it would resemble an enormous Christiansfeldt,[32] and then the two most powerful opponents would be present, contending with each other over the interpretation of this phenomenon—*communism*, which would say: This is secularly right; there must be no distinction whatever between persons; wealth and art and science and scholarship and government etc. etc. are of evil; all people should be alike as workers in a factory, as the inmates in a workhouse, dressed alike, eating the same food (made in one enormous pot) at the same stroke of the clock, in the same measure, etc.—*pietism*, which would say: This is Christianly right; there must be no distinctions between persons; we should be brothers and sisters, have everything in common; wealth, position, art, science, scholarship, etc. are of evil; all people should be alike as once was the case in the little Christiansfeldt, dressed alike, praying at specified times, marrying by drawing lots, going to bed by the clock, eating the same kind of food out of one big dish in a definite rhythm, etc.

IX
B 22
321

This is my view or conception of the age, the view of an insignificant person who has something of the poet in his nature, in other respects is a kind of thinker, but—yes, how often I have repeated this, to me so important and crucial, my first statement about myself—"without authority."[33]—*Pap.* IX B 22 *n.d.*, 1848

Deleted in version II; see 25:3:

Note. Authority does not mean advancing at the head of an army—that is powerlessness; or at the head of the public—that is

powerlessness; or to be armed. No, authority lies in the few unchanged, unshakable words: I am called by God. Then, if it
comes to that, the authoritative one can be hog-tied; it makes no
difference either way.—*Pap.* VIII^2 B 7:1c *n.d.*, 1847

Deleted in version III, See 27:2–14:

Neither when I began as an author did I have nor later did I
acquire any authority, just as I do not have any particular significance for my serious age either—well, unless it could be that I
have gained it with the help of my trousers,[34] which to such an
eminent degree have created a sensation and have attracted the
special interest of a serious, cultured public. It is like witchery
in mid-nineteenth century, as in a thousand-and-one-nights
story—a pair of old gray trousers casts everything else into oblivion. And witchery it is, because no one knows why it is. And not
only that, but the next thing is just as bewitched. Those serious,
zealous censors who in the name of a serious public[35] with Ca-
tonian rigor appeal to the demands of the times in regard to—
trousers—have frequently occupied themselves with mine.
Sometimes they have found them too short, sometimes too long,
alas, and the trousers are the same old gray ones. Such a factual
event really has its significance. It is an incident that on the whole
superbly characterizes the public's judgment, and it also has its
significance (which is why it deserves to be immortalized a little)
as a contribution to the history of the age, in order to see what
especially occupied the Copenhagen public. What has filled the
moment, say the wise men of the age, lives eternally; when my
writings have long been forgotten, my trousers, although long
ago worn out, will live eternally.

Here the introduction should really end, but I nevertheless
wish to add a word. Not without distress, not without sadness, do
I write this review. I would prefer not to write it if I did not have
to fear that Magister Adler's writings, which now have been so
highly (and obtusely) praised in *Nordisk Kirketidende*,[36] will attract
attention to themselves, and in that case he must necessarily
cause great confusion in the religious sphere simply because he
has a certain brilliance, and the majority by no means have the

VII^2
B 235
27

VII^2
B 235
28

competence to distinguish *inter et inter* [between one and the other]. The sadness and distress are due, in my opinion, to the conditions in the country. In a little country like Denmark, there naturally can be only a few who have the time and opportunity to occupy themselves exclusively with the spiritual; and in turn, of this small number, there naturally can be only a few individuals who actually have the ability and who also very decisively grasp that this spiritual occupation is assigned to them as their one and only occupation. But it is also all the more important that such an individual, precisely because the limited conditions hardly contain a swift corrective, hold himself in check with the most rigorous discipline, that he not grasp a brilliant confusion instead of what is true. Magister Adler is such an individual. Perhaps he can easily create something of a sensation, perhaps attract the admiration of a few ignorant people, perhaps acquire some adherents. But nothing is gained thereby; on the contrary, great harm is done because the conditions are so limited. And even if by his writings, through the provision of a multitude of brilliant expressions, he has enriched the fund of brilliance that in so many ways is accumulating in our age, that is only a drop in the bucket compared with confusing the all-important concepts upon which the whole of Christianity depends. There is also in the intellectual world a burning voluptuousness, a dangerous seduction of brilliance, that precisely by the play of the multiplicity conceals a total murkiness. Although every author now has a responsibility, it nevertheless seems that an author in a major literature, such as the German, for example, has less responsibility because he causes less harm by quickly disappearing in the crowd. [37]It seems to me that Magister Adler ought to deal with this; I have at least sought to make it clear to myself in the consciousness of being such an individual. It is certain that in a minor literature, simply because it is minor, tasks of a special kind can be carried out that could not succeed at all in a major literature, where one author displaces another, but it is also certain that the responsibility is all the more serious. Where there are plenty of springs, it is not so dangerous that one is muddied, but in a little country where there are scarcely more than one in each direction, it is a matter of great responsibility to muddy it oneself. And just as I am so little a friend of hangers-on and copy-cats, of coteries and alliances, which again thrive best in a little country but also do irremediable harm, it would naturally give me so much joy if in the religious sphere there were still a few other individuals who on their own account, perhaps from a to-tally different point of view, worked for the reclamation of this sphere. But so far Adler has been of no benefit. There is no con-cept that he has explained, no new categorical definition that he has provided, no older and accepted one that he has revived in renewed dialectical acuteness. Thus he himself has been of no benefit in a decisive sense, and in a way he has delayed me. Since he lies within the religious sphere, and since he *pro virili* [with all his might] confuses, and since the conditions of the country are limited, I have considered it my duty to interrupt my own work in order to correct somewhat the thinker in whom I would have preferred to see a superior or a co-worker, yet, note well, on his own account.—*Pap.* VIII^2 B 9:1b-c *n.d.*, 1847

Deleted in version III; see 257:31–258:31:

Let us now consider Magister Adler. In him one at least finds none of this eminent ministering reflection. How did he conduct himself with his revelation-fact? Well, he proclaimed it. But this dialectical thought that this could also become the most dreadful misfortune—this seems completely foreign to him. Now, it is certainly true that his cause proved to be a failure, his example sufficiently deterring; but that was not what he deserved, and he very likely had not expected it, but instead, most unwisely, the very opposite.

Has Adler himself resigned his office in order to accommodate the established order in that way? No, he remained in his office and acted as if nothing had happened until the state Church took some steps, and then he sought to remain in his position, al-though one still cannot charge him with all the chicaneries that generally are usable on such an occasion. Has he done anything to prevent if possible the dubious results for the established order from his example? No, nothing at all. Without having under-stood himself, without having in the least thought, so it seems, about all the difficult issues he has raised by his *assertum* [claim] of a revelation, he has haphazardly rushed in upon the established order with his alarming fact. It is from him that one should seek and find information about all such things; he has instead left it up to the established order to explain all these difficulties. In an age when one has learned from Hegel that the relation of conscience in the individual is a form of evil, and that to bring greetings from God is foolishness, in a confused age when it can be hard enough for the few competent ones to exercise a little restraining force and defend the pathos of the sacred and the venerable—in such an age to blaze away with an immaturity that stands in the closest and most disastrous relation to the highest—this is terrible! That until now one fortunately can say of him that he has not caused very much harm is certainly not to his credit; it is because he has been completely ignored. And yet even in this way he has done harm enough, since the religiousness in our age is by no means so great and so earnest that it is desirable that mockery and light-mindedness acquire such a prize as Adler.

—*Pap.* VIII^2 B 14 *n.d.*, 1847

From draft of version I; see 238:29–239:17:

And if it were not the case that Mag. Adler had so far been entirely ignored, he might already have caused much harm. Perhaps it would have been best to have let him remain at that, but now he has been reviewed in *Kirketidenden*.[38] On the whole, I myself feel how odd the whole thing is that I write, about an author who until now has not been read very much, an extensive inquiry that very likely will not be read either.

In margin: He has so far not been of benefit; he has delayed me.—*Pap.* VII^2 B 248:11 *n.d.*, 1846–47

From draft of version I; see 247:7–15:

Therefore the profound is the opposite of externality; a person who lives only externally is likely to have a tendency to anticipate his future with grand words, promises, etc.; the profound person does just the opposite and hides the principal machinery with which he actually operates. He perhaps usually seems like one who operates with one horsepower, and basically the machine is of the first magnitude.—*Pap.* VII^2 B 252:1 *n.d.*, 1846–47

Version I of Chapter I (Pap. VII^2 B 235, pp. 30–73—less pp. 33–53, 66–67, shifted to Addendum I), replaced in the text, pp. 28–35, by version III (Pap. VIII^2 B 13,15):

Chapter I

VII^2
B 235
30

The Historical Situation

The collision of Magister Adler as a teacher in the state Church with the established order; his dismissal, the state Church's complete justification;[*39] *the special individual in particular and what must be required of him.*

[*Essentially the same as 28:8–29:17.*]

By his revelation-fact, by the new doctrine,* by being under the direct impulsion of the Spirit, Magister Adler must himself readily have become conscious of being placed as a special indi-

VII^2 VI
B 235 B 2
31 3:

*Note. That Magister Adler has said something later about there being nothing new in his doctrine makes no difference. By his conduct he declared it in the highest and strongest terms; it is a fact that the type remained set in the printing house, because he presumably expected that his *Sermons* would immediately require a new printing. That he later incidentally says that it is not something new,[40] just as he, who by his conduct obviously aimed at a sensation, later took a certain humorous turn—such things would no doubt be able to provide an opportunity for a pettifogging journalist to confuse everything. In my opinion, there is nothing more corrupting than these careless transitions and alterations. A man should know what he wants and stand firm; if he changes, he should do it officially. Otherwise everything is easily confused; then with the aid of an anachronism a journalist benefits a man precisely by means of that in which he went astray. One pretends that he had not said it at different times; one turns the last into the contemporary, authentic interpretation, and look, the man who precisely by the doubleness marks himself as unstable becomes a hero and consistent—the state and the state Church, however, are brought into a predicament. But Magister Adler has never solemnly (which by reason of the relation of the spheres must be: penitently) revoked what he has said in the most solemn way. On the contrary, he has allowed the first statement to stand and then loquaciously said this and that about its not being anything new and about its not being exactly a revelation either but in a way some remarkable something or other. Yet more about that in the proper place. But with regard to ambiguous phenomena, one cannot often enough counter the ambiguous, which, precisely when it is not kept together, is as if intended to confuse.

VII^2
B 235
32

vidual completely outside the universal, completely *extra ordinem* [outside the order] as an *extraordinarius*. To want to be in the service of the established order under such conditions is a self-contradiction, and to demand of the established order that it should keep him in service is actually to want to make a fool of the established order, as if it were something so abstract that it could not concentrate with energetic consciousness on what it is and what it wants. To want to be in the service of the established order and then to want to serve that which aims precisely at the very life of the established order is just as unreasonable as if someone wanted to be in a man's service and yet openly acknowledged that his work and diligence were to serve this man's enemy. No man would tolerate that, and the reason one thinks that the universal should be able to tolerate it is that one has a fantastic-abstract idea of the impersonality of the universal, and a fantastic conception of livelihood, according to which the universal must support every graduate. When the army is drawn up facing the established order, then wanting to be in the ranks and to be a *stipendiarius* [receiver of a stipend] but wanting to stand turned the opposite way cannot be done; the moment they are to march (as soon as life stirs), it will be apparent that one is walking the opposite way. Therefore the extraordinary has to step out of the ranks. His importance demands it as does also the earnestness of the universal, because an extraordinary is too important to *be together* in the ranks, and the earnestness of the universal requires agreement and uniformity in the ranks, demands to see who the extraordinary is or to *see* that he is the extraordinary. In this *discrimen* [distinctive mark] the extraordinary will acquire his *competence* [validity]: on the one side to be the lowly one, almost a prodigal son, standing marked in this way as an individual in a special sense, standing marked as a poor Per Eriksen in comparison with the universal, so that no sagacious person would dare to be his friend or even walk with him on the street, so that his friend, if he was sagacious, would swear that he did not know this man,[41] so that "those who passed by would shake their heads" (see Matthew 27:39)—and nevertheless to be the one from whom something new is to come (see Matthew 27:39). This is the painful crisis, but neither will it be easy to

VII²
B 235
33

become an extraordinary. [*Pap.* VII² B 235, pp. 33–53, *shifted to Addendum I.*]

[42]In the terrible responsibility that the true extraordinary must continually bear in mind (since he does not have a conclusion once and for all, he has not become divinity's fully authorized proxy once and for all,* but he must make inquiries every day), there is also the concern that when he assumes the position *extra ordinem* his example can inveigle others, weak, unstable, light-minded, inquisitive people, to want to attempt something similar also, so that consequently his example can become a trap, a temptation. In other words the concern that usually plagues busy, gadding people—to get some copycats, some adherents who agree with him, to get a society established that has its own seal—that concern he does not know. In this regard he is quite frivolously facetious; he does not have even the sagacity that cows have; when a cow stampeding wants to make an attempt in the extraordinary, it first looks to see whether it is gaining sympathy among the public or among all the cows in the field—if not, it sensibly sticks its tail between its legs.[43] The true extraordinary knows how to make sport of vanity and conceitedness, but the terrible thing, whether he has harmed another person, whether he occasioned any person light-mindedly to want to try his hand at what involves the heaviest responsibility of the singular—this terrible thing he understands in a radical way.[44] In a time of movement such as ours, when symptoms of wanting to be a little extraordinary are epidemic, he must with fear and trembling especially keep watch on his terrible responsibility. Therefore precisely here he will in turn make his position as forbidding as possible for others, as unappealing and untempting as possible. For that reason he also desires tough opposition. If the light-minded merely see that enduring something is becoming a bit earnest, they soon fall away; yes, they even change into an opposition to the extraordinary. Light-mindedness would flippantly like to take the extraordinary as a playmate; if it perceives

VII²
B 235
53

VII²
B 235
54

*Note. This is certainly nonsense. A king may very well appoint a highly trusted minister once and for all, inasmuch as the minister is perhaps considerably more competent than the king, but God does not find himself in this situation.

that this cannot be done, it concentrates its childish anger against
him. But every extraordinary unconditionally owes it to the established order first of all by some profound step to transform, if
possible, his extraordinariness into aversion, lest his example do
harm, become a trap. And a true extraordinary in our day (after
reflection and sensibleness have developed so enormously) must
be informed about everything possible, know the dangers and
irregularities. That a man in our age could have a revelation may
not be unconditionally denied, but the entire apparent conduct
of such a chosen one will be essentially different from all the
former ones to whom something similar happened.

A true extraordinary must continually have the qualifications
of his age at his service; thus in our day he must have eminent
disposal over what is the distinctive feature of our age: reflection
and sensibleness. The essential observable difference between a
man in our age to whom a revelation has been imparted and a
man in a former age will be that the former undertakes this extraordinariness with a highly developed composure. Ours is a
reflecting age; it is inconceivable that divine Governance itself is
not aware of this. The chosen one's reflection will not destroy for
him the extraordinary, the revelation—no, but he must have all
the circumspection of reflection at his service the moment he
places himself and his revelation into the context of the age. He
must dialectically know dangers and irregularities of which the
chosen one in former times had no inkling. A chosen one in an
age of reflection must be a unity of being one called by a revelation (and it must stand unswervingly firm for him that it was
and is a revelation) and of being the greatest maieutic of the age.
His gifts and ethical development regarding the latter do not at
all make him *worthy* to be chosen by God—no, in relation to
God's call there is no worthiness worth talking about, but that he
has these gifts and is ethically developed in this way is his apparent distinctive feature.

Now, it is certainly true that the whole Magister Adler affair
had a most unfortunate outcome, so that his example certainly
became forbidding enough, but this is not to his credit. In this
regard he has done nothing to aid the universal, and he probably
did not expect the outcome to be so unfortunate, he who even
[*deleted:* had left the type set up at the press] had made arrange-

ments so that the second edition could come out more quickly. Suppose, then, that having a revelation had made, as they say, a splendid showing; suppose it had become the demand of the times, suppose it had been a success; and then suppose that through Magister Adler's example the universal had been saddled with a little reserve battalion of hysterical women and neurotic students and erudites who refused to take the final examinations, also a few droll chaps who sit in a parsonage and indulge in caprices*—each of whom had tried his hand at improving his status by having a revelation.

*[45]*Note*. It is true that in a parsonage fixed ideas can be developed superbly. If one may even say that life in a big city actually stifles the highest, then it also has the good side that it contains a constant corrective that prevents extravagances. One becomes so accustomed to hearing all this about the age as an age of movement, that the times demand one thing today and tomorrow the opposite, that a brand-new system is imminent—one becomes so accustomed to hearing this that it makes no more impression on one than cursing makes an impression on a sailor. One becomes as accustomed to the vortex of newspapers as to evening prayers—to be sure, one would think that it could not be good to read something so shocking and stimulating at night that it could easily make a person sleepless, but one becomes so accustomed to it that one sleeps sweetly and peacefully. This is how it is in the city. It is different, however, when a theological graduate, full of the superficiality of the city, becomes like a new bottling sent out to a parsonage—then it can easily and quietly become earnest fantasy. Wonderful. Ordinarily just to mention the phrase "a rural pastor" makes one spontaneously think of a modest but calm and contented life out in a quiet landscape where the mill goes klip klap klip klap,[46] where the stork stands on the roof the long summer day, where in the evening the pastor sits "paternally happy [*Faderglad*]" in the arbor with his wife, happy with his life, happy in his modest but meaningful work. When the one who is employed at the big theater in the capital, where energies are lavishly squandered, sometimes wishes for a little recreation, he spontaneously thinks of visiting a rural pastor. Out there, so he thinks, there is rest, there is no prying, thoughtless crowd, there is no bravo-shouting and noise, there one hears no cannonade—from amusement parks;[47] out there everything is quiet yet so smiling, everyone tends to his own business and yet there is harmony, there everything is very small and yet very beneficent, there meals are very plain and yet very tasty, there work is to be done and yet is such a blessing, there the pastor's wife is a domestic sage for the parish and the pastor a spiritual counselor for the congregation. Alas, but sometimes it is otherwise. There is now, for example, Pastor Damkier;[48] he is in a village parsonage—and thinks that there is an enormous stirring in the Danish state Church; indeed, "in seventy years there has not been such a stirring in the Danish Church," says the pastor. One notices at once that this is no "man from the country" who is speaking; one must rather say that it is a man from the

VII[2]
B 235
57

VII²
B 235
57

With the help of imagination I will now purely dialectically venture a little plan that can possibly show what Adler could have done, or I will lift him entirely into reflection. If he had been the true extraordinary, then what he would have found

VII²
B 235
58

necessary to do would of course have become much more profound than a lowly ministering critic can think up. It would have become something much more profound; profundity, then, is really the deep *existential* carrying out of an idea that is directly

VII²
B 235
59

related to God. [52]Nowadays people think that it is very glorious if someone is so fortunate as to be struck by a profound *thought*, to make a profound remark, now and then *horis successivis* [hour by hour] to compile something profound that in every other hour one existentially denies. No, just as perseverance (in contrast to the flaring illusion of the moment) is the true virtue, so also profundity is not an utterance, a statement, but an existing. Profundity is the metaphorical, transferred expression that indicates how many feet a person's existing draws [*stikke*] in the same sense as this is said of a ship. But the ship is not said to draw so and

---

capital city who has become fantastical out in the country. The pastor thinks that it is a hymnbook affair that is producing this enormous movement. But the whole thing is fantasy. At the moment there is no movement in the Danish Church worth mentioning, but there certainly are a few journalists to whose interest, in the same sense as it is to the interest of attorneys that there are court cases, it is to publicize it—in order that if possible there could come to be a little stirring; and thus there are a few gullible people who, like the soap maker in *Egmont*,[49] spread the rumor further. Generally one must, insofar as one wishes to form the correct opinion concerning the movement in an age, use considerable caution with regard to the press. The press is often guilty of a *petitio principii* [begging of the question] in its tactics; it pretends to be reporting a factual

VII²
B 235
58

situation and aims to produce it. There is something that the journalist wants to promote, and perhaps there is no one at all who thinks about it or cares about it; what does the journalist do then? In lofty tones he writes an article about its being a need deeply felt by everyone, etc. His newspaper perhaps has wide circulation, and now we have the game under way. That is, the article is read, discussed; another paper perhaps proceeds to write against it; there are polemics and a sensation is created—"I have found it; I see Aars"[50]—that is, now the stirring is there, *quod erat demonstrandum* [that which was to be demonstrated]. Dialecticians call this behavior a *petitio principii*; one demonstrates that this or that is factual—by making it factual. This hymnbook affair is a purely simulated movement. A committee is set aside [*hensat*], not to mention "set up" [*nedsat*]; it has met, now it meets no more. One appeal after the other has been reso many feet deep in the sense of a probe that one sticks [*stikke*] into something momentarily, but it is the decisive qualification in relation to the ship's entire and daily existence that it draws so and so many feet. Or to illustrate the same thing in another way: the more extensions a telescope has, the better it is, and thus also the more extensions a person has before the secret of his innermost life is reached, the more deeply he draws. [53]The profound mind is not an esthetic qualification with regard to genius but is essentially an ethical qualification, and for that very reason it must be for everyday use by the one who is really to be called profound, yet not so it becomes conspicuous, since the conspicuous is again an esthetic qualification. Let us think of ships: when two ships are sailing together, whatever difference there may be with regard to how many feet they draw is not seen—no, they both are sailing.

It is now assumed here that Adler actually has had a revelation,* that for him it is certain and stands immovably firm that

---

ceived—indeed, it reminds one of the wonders of antiquity, where thousands of people were used to drag together masses of stone for the pyramids: in the same way these appellants harness themselves to drag the committee ahead. But despite all this, despite the many teams, the committee gets nowhere; the whole thing ends up in a little bit of a pamphlet. Of course the many appeals, although factually real, are indeed a fiction. It is a party that wants to have a new hymnbook. Now, the party could have agreed to submit one appeal—and this would not have signified much, or rather nothing at all; it would have been like a demonstration of the correctness of a hypothesis that needs no demonstration. When a party wants to have a new hymnbook, the demonstration begins first by having appeals come from others instead of from the party. This has not happened; on the contrary, something else has happened. The party has divided itself into five or six appeals; thus there are indeed five or six appeals. That means something. In a village parsonage this may very well look like an enormous stirring in the state Church—and the little morsel of a first pamphlet may very well seem to be a prodigious, gigantic work, the equal of which the Danish state Church has not seen in seventy years. It depends so very much on the place from which one sees something—from a basement entrance a low little house looks like a tower. No, only one man is needed; he writes a new hymnbook in three months without needing committees or appeals. The mistake is that many want to be included. Descartes so beautifully says somewhere that something great is never achieved by an association.[51]

*Note. Generally it can occur only to very obtuse people to deny flatly that another person has had a revelation when he himself unalterably says it. As

VII²
B 235
59

it was a revelation, so that from this moment on his life is placed under divine arrest. The question then is about the ministering reflection with which he assumes this extraordinary thing,* with which he places it into the context of the established order. The critic can become admirably involved in this deliberation, and by this ministering reflection the chosen one in our day will, as stated, be recognized as different from any chosen one in former times. The essential they have in common is what is decisive, is the revelation-fact, the gracious favor; the apparent difference is the reflection, which the chosen one in our day must have, for

there is nothing new in the world, but neither is there any uniform, merely copying repetition. The revelation-fact is the fixed element, but the reflection is the broker. In daily life it certainly does not occur to the broker to indulge in the foolish fancy that he owns all the money that passes through his hands. Alas, no, the money belongs to the financier, but the broker is the servant. But here we must remember that in regard to what religiously is the highest the broker is not a sagacious businessman of the finite; on the contrary, his task, or reflection's task, will be to prevent the

---

stated, with regard to such an *assertum* [assertion], one must, if one has a little sense oneself, either believingly submit to it or leave it in abeyance and restrain oneself in skeptical reserve. Then there is still a third possibility, when one, as will be seen in this book about Adler, sees oneself in a position to make it clear *e concessis* [on the basis of the other's premise] that the man himself does not really believe that he has had a revelation. This is very far from being a flat denial by an outsider; on the contrary, it is rather the opposite; it is the person concerned who helps to inform against himself.

In margin: *Note. Even in connection with occurrences of being chosen in times past there is still a suggestion of self-determination. For example, when Moses says, "How should I be able to go to Pharaoh? If you want to send someone, then send someone else."[54] Here self-determination even raises an objection. Overexcitement, insanity, the daimonic certainly can imprison a person in their power by an assault of the sudden in a dreadfully sudden way, but God cannot be assumed to want forcibly to misuse a person against his nature. There must be an agreement between God and the chosen one; the humble words must be heard, "Behold, I am the handmaid of the Lord,"[55] the humble words, "Speak, Lord, for your servant hears."[56] But this is indeed like an expression of agreement or the expression of composure. This is how it is and must have been at every time; its further development in a ministering reflection is something else.

extraordinary from really becoming that, that is, from becoming confused with something else, so that, for example, the extraordinary does not in an utterly wrong way make a success in the world etc. It never occurs to the wine-tapster that the sumptuous deliciousness of the wine is his creation; no, he knows that it is nature's beneficent gift, but the wine-tapster understands how to let it ferment, how to draw it off and bottle it in such a way that through the handling the wine becomes the fine wine it is, does not lose anything, and does not acquire any aftertaste.

Dialectically Adler would now have perceived immediately that the divine gift of grace has the *discrimen* [distinctive mark] of danger, that what is intended as the greatest blessing for others can become the greatest corruption for them through irresponsible and uncircumspect association. At the same moment as he would have taken possession of the gift of grace, he would have, at the same moment, inclosed himself, closed up with it and closed off from everyone else so that no uncircumspect utterance, no dialectical uncircumspection would ruin the whole thing in loquacity; but the extraordinary would take time to settle in the pause (*in pausa*[57]) of silence. "One does not put a new patch on an old garment or new wine into an old wineskin, lest the hole become larger and the wineskin burst"[58]—and the very same thing will happen if by uncircumspect treatment in hasty busyness the absolutely new point of departure is muddled into the old—in that case it only does harm instead of good. At the same moment the ministering reflection would immediately teach him silence,* the silence in which he with a holy resolve

VII²
B 235
62

*Note. In the later books, to be sure, Adler did come around to the silence principle, yet again without the attainment of a decisive expression for this qualitatively essential change. Moreover, it comes somewhat late. God knows what it is now that he really has to be silent about after having promptly blurted out the highest—or perhaps more correctly, more than he has within. There is something curiously effeminate about Magister Adler. One can almost always count on it that a girl, when faced with a big decision, will make the wrong one in the decisive moment, but then gradually she is changed and finally comes to the right one, and then deludes herself into believing that she did so at the beginning. On the whole, Magister Adler may be regarded as a good example of the maundering in the dialectical sense that is so common in our day. One jumbles one thing into another, gives up one system as it is called and goes

had dedicated his life to belong solely to this extraordinary (just as the mother devotes herself by wanting to be only for the sake of the child), and the silence by which for the time being he prevented every communication to any other person, lest something wrong be communicated or in a wrong way.

But this extraordinary must nevertheless be communicated; it must be introduced into the situation of actuality and the established order. Silence must not abort it as a fetus is aborted. But no impatience! There is a nervous tremor that in trembling impatience can neither hold onto something nor beneficially give up something—let us not be deceived by it. Everyone who knows what it is truly to be resolved knows very well that one can persevere and hold fast to a resolution. A man may be so situated in life that he calmly has said to himself before God: The way I am taking is bound to lead me to the stake—and nevertheless he calmly goes forward, step by step. But impatience says: The sooner the better,* and nervous impatience, bordering almost on

VII²
B 235
63

---

further, but at no point does one ever come to any decisive determination, why one gave up the old and why one accepted the new; no accounting is ever arrived at with regard to the responsibility in changing oneself this way. —But the later Adler as an adherent of the silence principle will be discussed in detail in the appropriate place. Here it must be kept in mind only because in connection with ambiguous phenomena one must keep a sharp lookout; ambiguity speculates—in confusing.

In margin: *Note. The necessary slowness is also a cross, which the chosen one has to bear with faith and humility. When the angel had announced to Mary that she would give birth to a child through the Spirit[59] —well, the whole thing was certainly a miracle—why, then, should this child take nine months like other children? Why could it not happen immediately, since she had indeed comprehended and accepted that this birth was a miracle. In other words, let us not make Mary a compound of two natures: an earthly and an earthly-minded woman who finds it quite in order that it takes nine months and the believing Mary who humbly understands that this birth was a miracle. No, she understood that it was a miracle; but why should it then nevertheless in a certain way be in the order of nature? Yes, here is the cross. Nervous impatience becomes confused by the extraordinary and cannot in faith and humility come to itself. That the miraculous must give itself time, only humility is able to bear as Mary did. I wonder if Mary, after receiving the announcement, did not remain the same quiet, humble woman; I wonder if she got busy asking what time it would be, when the month would end—out of fear that it would be annulled.

insanity, says: If only it does not vanish again, if only the pressure within me does not cease, so the dreadful thing would have to be said of me: The children are near to the birth, and there is no strength to give birth (Isaiah 37:3). But it is certainly also terrible to give birth to wind because of sheer busyness. Here it is not a matter of animal sluggishness, whereby an utterly worldly, an almost merely vegetating person can let time go by. The one who has ever served an idea and has ever been deeply moved by the eternal knows very well that this collision of the eternal and the temporal in the moment, in the present, is a dreadful tension that can all too easily become sleeplessness, and all too easily insanity. He knows also that with regard to this moment it seemed as if all would be lost if this moment was not used. But he knows also that there is a remedy for this symptom: faith. If someone with holy resolution has decided to sacrifice his life and then in nervous impatience goes ahead and throws his life away and is executed, the sooner the better—has he been of any benefit, and has he then actually kept his resolution? The point is simply that reflection and time not be allowed to shake his resolution; but, on the other hand, rather than foolishly having it happen right away today, there is another remedy; this remedy is faith, is humility, is daily dedication. And it is then also only in a very overwrought or sensuously excited imagination that the eternal takes on, not symptomatically for a single moment but continually, a likeness to that to which the eternal is most opposed: the sensuous eternal moment. Here, as with the thirst of that rich man burning in hell,[60] the point is: seize it, seize it, seize it while it is foaming—oh, despair, in the next moment it is over. Pick the flower, pick the flower—oh, despair, in the next moment it is withered. How terrible if someone in that frame of mind makes the mistake of wanting to treat the eternal in the same way!

So, then, the extraordinary must be communicated, must be placed into the context of the established order, and the chosen one, the special individual, must take the blow, as it is said, the terrible blow: to be a paradox, whereby he indeed gives the blow. Dialectically there is a doubleness here: that the blow actually, in a qualitative-dialectical decisive sense, becomes the blow,

VII²
B 235
64

and on the other hand that the established order is dealt with as leniently as possible. No more than God is a God of confusion[61] is the chosen one called to confuse—and then to run away from it. He is to love the established order and therefore be willing to sacrifice himself. Just as one handles silver nitrate [*Helvedessteen*, hellstone] with extreme caution (not in order not to use it but to use it properly), has it wrapped in something so that no one comes in direct contact with it, so one must be careful about dedicating oneself to be the special individual lest anyone be harmed by a direct relation to him. The person called is also the one who sacrifices himself. What in him, if he is the true extraordinary, is eternal truth, a divine gift of grace, in any other person, in a direct relation only to the extraordinary, is pandering, untruth, perdition.

When we now proceed further along this road, the aforementioned profound task must lie here: that the person called must first make himself almost repugnant. In one sense the extraordinariness of the gracious gift resembles silver nitrate, although in another sense it is heaven's blessing. The special individual is not directly the extraordinary either; he is not the extraordinary until the thought intervenes that he is paradoxical. This dialectic can be rendered in such a way that the special individual first makes himself the repugnant one, so that no one would wish to be like him, no one could wish to be as he is. In this pain lies, among other things, his self-sacrifice and the reconciliation with the established order that he in his love for it must bring.* That busybodies and fools and windbags prefer something else in order to

---

*Note. The same thing *happened* to the chosen one in the past. He became an abomination, was sacrificed, but the difference is that he did not by any ministering reflection become aware in advance that this was bound to happen, to say nothing of hastening the crisis himself. This happened to the chosen one in the past because this is grounded in existence's own dialectic between the universal and the special individual. When he is the special individual and wants to hold firmly to this, he must become sacrificed whether he will or not; if he will not, then he must become unfaithful to his call. According to existence's own dialectic, this is how it must happen; but precisely because his reflection has not foreseen this, the conflict in existence that he brings about will also cause great confusion in which many will be lost, and for this he still bears a kind of responsibility.

get something to spread and something to mimic, that confused extraordinaries who detest discipline and restraint disdain this and would rather let themselves and others have a fling as *fratres et sorores liberi spiritus* [brothers and sisters of the free spirit][62]— does not matter. A true, legitimate advocate for the established order will judge differently. He will not deny the possibility that there can be something new to bring, but neither will he deny that the caution described here certainly borders on the greatest possible. [*Pap.* VII² B 235, pp. 66–67, *shifted with minor changes to Addendum I, pp. 162:14–163:18.*]

But how, then, does one make oneself repugnant? Let us first recapitulate. The chosen one has had a revelation; this stands firm; he has inclosed himself within himself with this fact. Not a word has betrayed anything, not a look; and neither is his silence conspicuous, since that of course betrays something. No, he is just like other people, talks like other people about what is happening—therefore no one can know that he is silent. A person can be silent in two ways: he can be absolutely mum, but then the silence is suspicious, or he can talk about everything else possible, and then it can occur to no one that he is silent. And yet the extraordinary has happened, and there lives a person who with a life dedicated in holy resolution works in complete silence. If God has favored him with his confidence, he (even if he is well aware of how hard it must be for God to have to deal with a lowly human being, even if this lowly human being is doing his utmost) will not insult God in the least way by turning his confidence into loose talk and gossip, into something that is to be blurted out. Let there be no impatience! But there is a nervous "Confess, confess."* And in a spiritual sense there is a condition that physically resembles that of one who is incontinent. Paul was silent for three years. Nervous impatience can be due to the individual's lack of the power to endure, his having become like a broken bowl, or to his having been shocked into despairing

VII²
B 235
66

VII²
B 235
67

VII²
B 235
68

---

*Note. This cry: "Confess, confess," which is or was Adler's slogan and interjection, has for me at least an alarming ambiguity. It is also reminiscent of the shout to a guilty person: Confess, confess; ease your mind by confessing. It is also reminiscent of the harrowing phenomena of a particular kind in the sphere of the daimonic: involuntary self-denunciation.[63]

anxiety, or to a kind of forced penitence that wants to make up, by a scrupulous confession, for what has been neglected and to mortify oneself by exposing oneself to possible ridicule. There is the not-so-rare confused revivalist who, with a strange religious egotism, seeks to misuse other people by getting them to ridicule him, which in intention can be just as tyrannical as when a tyrant wants to misuse people by having them drudge, like slaves.

So how is he to make himself repugnant when this, note well, must be done in such a way that he does not thereby cause harm, so that he does not go ahead and make the religious repugnant but makes himself repugnant? The confused revivalist serves the religious egotistically and thus makes it repugnant and himself important; the true extraordinary serves the religious humbly and therefore makes himself repugnant. The extraordinary, if he is the true extraordinary, of course must in an eminent sense know what I, who am only a lowly ministering critic, am not so poorly informed about: how undermined our age is in a religious sense—while busy people hold general assemblies about trivialities, and while the thunder of cannons summons to amusements. When that is the case, it must not be difficult to find in the sphere of the daimonic the blackened clothing that could make him repugnant. Let us remember well what was said previously: in the whole world there is still no one aware of what has happened with the extraordinary any more than this pen is that I am holding in my hand, or the inkwell into which I dip it, yet without obtaining the thoughts from it.

VII²
B 235
69

Adler could then *mir nichts und Dir nichts* [without further ado] have resigned, said that the whole matter of his being a pastor was merely a passing notion, something he only wanted to try; and he could have seen to it that this would become the authentic interpretation. He thereby would at least have done everything he was capable of doing so that his example would not tempt others. To want to be out of the ordinary in that way, that is, by instability and lack of character, by deficiency in earnestness and firmness—no one could want that, least of all none of the better contemporaries who have their lives in the established order and serve the established order. Caution in handling a strong medicine teaches one first to make it possible that the strong remedy can be used without doing harm, and only then does one use it. When extraordinariness is represented temptingly as a brilliant distinction, such an example can have a harmful influence on the perhaps usually faithful adherents of the established order; if nothing else, then by making them a little impatient about their position. On the other hand, by temporarily weakening the impression of himself by self-sacrifice, Adler would have made it possible that he could be singled out as a special individual without carrying anyone along with him.

During all this, the compass by which he steered would of course have to remain unaltered, without deviating a point in inwardness, but by daily holy dedication he would have to renew himself in his originality—while every better person would turn away in indignation and disgust from such effeminate conduct as playing at being a pastor—this he himself would have evoked lest any better person be harmed by being smitten with his extraordinariness. Yes, if one suffers from nervous impatience, it is certainly easier to get it out, the sooner the better—even though a few people also go to rack and ruin, even though the unstable are led into temptation, what is the harm in that in comparison with the extraordinary that one has to communicate?*

VII[2]
B 235
70

---

*Note. Adler directly acknowledges this viewpoint in later books and builds himself up by analogies to nature or flatly immoral views: "The star is a star even if it also burns some mosquitoes"; "When the singer sings beautifully, then the song is beautiful, even though he drank beforehand"; "If a messenger boy, a faithful messenger boy, must get to a specific place at a specific time, he may very well knock over a few people on the way" (see *Theolog. Studier,*[64] p. 88, note). It can never occur to impatience to discipline itself to understand that the way in which victory is won is just as important as the victory. It is understandable that a worldly hero, a Napoleon, a desperate general, can be of the opinion that, whatever it costs, one must be victorious; but to want to serve the religious with such categories or with such an attitude is a deplorable confusion. If a legion of angels should be necessary, God surely has it available,[65] but he refuses to use it, not to mention, as they say, if it should be necessary to waste and disturb the lives of some people—no, that this should be necessary God surely cannot understand. God does not need anything at all in order to be victorious; he is from eternity to eternity the strongest. This may be why he has so much time and composure to concern himself solely with the way in which he is victorious. People seem to forget this; they think that God is in a predicament, is unsure of victory, and in that case one must not be too scrupulous about the

Then Adler (since his unconditional silence for the time being gave him unconditional leisure for the time being) could perhaps have produced a poetical presentation in which he would have described a daimon who knew our age's lack of religiousness and knew the Christendom of our age—a daimon who, sent out by the devil in order to show what Christendom was, in order to scoff at it, himself became a pastor, he who in his heart was not only a heathen but a Mephistopheles. Gone are the days when the devil fought against Christendom; then there were actual heroes of faith. Now he found it not even worth the trouble, so sure was he that basically he had been victorious. He amused himself merely by having one of his emissaries become a pastor, not in order to seduce the Christians, ah, no, that was not necessary, but in order to scoff at the Christendom that had become a titular style. So this daimon became a pastor without any difficulties, since the epigram consisted precisely in that. Then he resigned, when the evil spirit had sufficiently amused himself over it. —This was an attempt to screw extraordinariness down even lower. Every better person would be nauseated by something so repugnant.

During all this, the compass by which Adler steered would naturally have to remain unaltered, without deviating a point in inwardness. Obviously this method is slow; it is easier to blurt out immediately. It is, however, terrible to work silently with all one's might this way, in a certain sense against oneself*—what if

---

ways and means. If a father is properly aware of his paternal superiority, he will be all the more carefully concerned about the *way* in which he gets the child to obey. But mediocre parents practically fight with their children; naturally they must in every way see to getting the child to obey blindly, in every way, even if the child would be spoiled by learning to obey blindly in that way.

*Note. To be sure, this is only in a certain sense. Earthly and worldly busyness might also say that Christ worked against himself by coming in a lowly form. If he had come in a magnificent procession, if he had seen to it that who he was had been proclaimed on the street corners and had paraded[66] with drums and trumpets—he certainly would have had a great throng of followers in a hurry—every mountebank likes to do that. *Mundus vult decipi* [The world wants to be deceived][67]—therefore a mountebank always makes a hit, because he wants to deceive and consequently wants what the times demand. In order to prevent this, the truth is compelled, in the earthly and worldly sense of busyness, to work against itself.

one died beforehand and there was no one who knew a single word about it, no one who knew any more about it than my pen knows, or the inkwell into which I dip it, yet without obtaining the thoughts from it! It is very moving when Hamlet in the moment of death almost despairs over the thought that the enormously strenuous hidden life he has lived in the service of the idea would be understood by no one, indeed, no one would get to know it;[68] but if Hamlet goes soft in death, he could indeed have spoken in life, that is, let the whole thing slip out. Yes, it is indeed dreadful when such a person of inclosed reserve thinks of the busyness round about him, which has scarcely five minutes to waste on understanding the richness of thought in a prodigious work. But if Hamlet shudders, and if this shuddering gains the upper hand, then it is vanity. There is a remedy for all nervous impatience: it is faith, humility. The God in whose service the chosen one has dedicated himself, the God who has been called upon every day for witness and aid—he knows it, indeed everything; he surely is not a busy trifler![69] And then what more is needed? Then if death comes and puts a period in a wrong place—no, death simply cannot put a period in a wrong place, because it certainly cannot happen without God's will.

Then when Adler had made himself repugnant in this way and thereby secured himself against any better person's being able to be tempted by his example, well, then humble before God he could have beaten his breast and said: Now the first thing has been done; the sacrifice to the universal has been made. Humanly speaking, I am diminished; no one will be led astray by my example, and I am not importunate toward God either and do not summarily make his cause mine. No, despite all my work I also annihilate myself—then the honor is God's.

Let us recapitulate now and see what Adler has done and bear in mind the words of Paul as a motto: "All that is done is done for upbuilding; whether someone speaks in tongues or he prophesies, he does it for upbuilding."[70] In these words is contained the requirement for composure and the ethical responsibility that no one should chaotically think that it is a person's, to say nothing of a chosen person's, task to be like a troll-witch.

Has Adler himself resigned his office in order to accommodate the established order in that way? No, he remained in it and

VII²
B 235
72

VII²
B 235
73

acted as if nothing had happened until the state Church took
some steps, and then he sought to remain in his position, although one still cannot charge him with all the chicaneries that
generally are usable on such an occasion. Has he done anything
to hinder and if possible to prevent all his example's dubious
consequences for the established order? No, nothing at all. Without having understood himself, without having in the least
thought, so it seems, about all the difficult issues he has raised by
his *assertum* [claim] of a revelation, he has haphazardly rushed in
upon the established order with his alarming fact. It is the special
individual's business to be very exactly informed about everything related to his difficulty; he has instead left it up to the established order to explain all these difficulties. Like that customs
clerk who wrote so that no one could read it, he perhaps has
thought that his business was only to write, his colleagues' to
read[71]—in the same way he has thought that it was his business
to hurl a firebrand into the established order and the established
order's to take care of the consequences. In a tottering age when
unfortunately the rising generation is initiated almost from childhood into all sorts of doubt, in a tottering age when it can be hard
enough for the few competent ones to exercise a restraining
force, to defend the pathos of the sacred and the venerable—in
such an age to blaze away with an immaturity that stands in the
closest and most disastrous relation to the highest is extremely
irresponsible, to put it mildly. That until now one fortunately
can say of him that he has not done very much harm is certainly
not to his credit; it is because he has been completely ignored.
And yet even in this way he has done harm, since the religiousness in our age is by no means so great and so earnest that it is
desirable that mockery and light-mindedness acquire such a prize
as Adler is.—*Pap.* VII[2] B 235, pp. 30–33, 53–73 *n.d.*, 1846–47

Note deleted in version III; see 41:4:

Without impatience, but not without sadness, I would like to
give expression here to my sad situation as an author. Since I
have practically no readers, I never know what I dare to assume.
Yet I reasonably ought to be able to assume that one has read my

earlier published books before becoming involved with this one. If one does not want to do that, it seems even more reasonable that one would at least completely refrain from discussing me. But it is really extremely indefensible for a person, without having become acquainted with the whole development, to stir the whole thing into confusion with the aid of a newspaper article, also by bringing the matter before people who have neither the time nor the opportunity for copious and strenuous thought, who therefore find it quite easy to understand a reviewer's hasty nonsense, while I with my big and copious books am abandoned.—*Pap.* VIII^2 B 9:5a *n.d.*, 1847

Note deleted in version III; see 42:37:

    I see that Johannes Climacus[72] was reviewed in one of the issues of Scharling and Engelstoft's *Tidsskrift*.[73] It is one of the usual two-bit reviews, written in "very fine language" with periods and commas in the right places. A theological graduate, or some such graduate who on the whole is thoroughly incompetent in discussion, copies more or less the table of contents and then adds his criticism, which is something like this: Johannes Climacus is certainly justified in the way in which he emphasizes the dialectical, but (yes, now comes the wisdom) on the other hand one must not forget—mediation. Historically, Johannes Climacus began after mediation; Hegel was already dead some years before *Fragments* was published. J. C. no doubt knows just as much about mediation as such a theological graduate. In order, if possible, to force his way out of the spell of mediation, constantly battling against it, J. C. decisively brought the issues to their logical conclusion through the effort of a qualitative dialectic (something that not every theological graduate or other graduate or two-bit reviewer can do), and then the book is reviewed in this way—that is, with the help of a laudatory reviewer's bungling the book is ruined, annulled, scrapped. And the reviewer even becomes self-important: for the reviewer to stand loftily over the author in this way looks almost like superiority—with the help of a wretched stock phrase. Since he copies with a suspicious anxiety, the reviewer is so insignificant that he would

VII^2
B 235
81

VII^2
B 235
82

scarcely be able to write a review if the book was taken away from him, and a reviewer like that becomes very important at the end. But this is the way an author must work; he must use his time and energy, he must take pains to push the issue to its logical conclusion, and then along comes a laudatory review and assists in making the issue and the book into the same old hash. And the author is not read, but the reviewer calls attention to him; the review is read, and the reader must involuntarily believe the review because it is laudatory—the review that by way of praise has annihilated the book. *Mundus vult decipi* [The world wants to be deceived].[74] But this comes about because being a genuine author has become sacrificing existence and because an intermediate staff of fiddlers has been formed (two-bit reviewers), whose trade flourishes. And since we are accustomed to the coarsest, most boorish guttersnipe tone in the papers, a reviewer presumably thinks that when, as a bonus, he is so nice as to praise the book—he has a right to reduce it to gossip. Johannes Climacus most likely would say, "No, thank you, may I ask to be abused instead; being abused does not *essentially* harm the book, but to be praised in this way is to be annihilated, insofar as this is possible for the reviewer, the nice, good-natured, but somewhat obtuse reviewer." An author who really understands himself is better served by not being read at all, or by having five readers who really read him, than by having, with the help of a good-natured reviewer, this only too widespread confusion about mediation spread further with the help of the author's own book—which was written specifically to battle against mediation. But the conception of being an author in our day has been distorted in an extremely immoral way.—*JP* V 5944 (*Pap.* VIII² B 9:5b) *n.d.*, 1847

VII²
B 235
83

Deleted in version III: continuation of Pap. VIII² B 9:5b:

VII²
B 235
83

Since so many who have no essential qualification at all for being authors (no essential idea to communicate, no essential call, no ethically conscious responsibility) nevertheless become authors, to be an author becomes among men a kind of distinction akin to what adorning oneself is among women: the main point and purpose of writing are to become noticed, recognized, praised. Such an adornment-author has nothing to tell the reader; like someone taking an examination, he writes in order to enjoy the social esteem for having a degree or for being an author; he writes to show that he is skilled in fine writing. It is no trick, of course, for almost anyone to form an estimate of him, because despite being an author, he stands entirely *au niveau* [on the level] with the majority. The untruth, then, consists in this, that such a producer of fine writing and a candidate up for examination is called an author, but as a result of this untruth people are pampered into regarding an author as someone who writes in order to be acknowledged, or probably to be acknowledged even with praise. Should it not be conceivable that an author would write in order that the truth he has to communicate may be understood? In that case, he in no way benefits by being acknowledged, even with praise, by someone who misunderstands. Not so with the examinee; he has nothing to communicate. If he in fact detects that the examiner does not understand him at all, if only the examiner nevertheless says *prae caeteris* [praiseworthy above others], the examinee is pleased as Punch, and one can hardly blame him for that. It is, however, really odd that to be an author should be anything like that [*deleted*: and even more odd that the examiner in relation to the author is not a professor but some literary bungler in a newspaper]. If, with regard to being an author, it were conceivable that a person could become one without writing, could purchase this dignity just as one buys a title and yet, note well, actually enjoy something of a reputation—then a great many of the authors of our generation would perhaps stop writing. And if, without writing, one could earn the money one earns by writing, then many other contemporary authors would undoubtedly refrain from writing, and we would see how many genuine authors we had.—*Pap.* VIII² B 9:5c *n.d.*, 1847

VII²
B 235
84

Deleted in version III; see 43:25:

Note. In *Fragments*[75] this dialectic of contemporaneity is set forth: that in the strict sense an immediate contemporary is not a contemporary, and that for this very reason someone who lives 1800 years later may just as well be able to be a contemporary.

                                    —*Pap.* VIII² B 9:5d *n.d.*, 1847

Deleted in version III; see 49:7–9:

VII²
B 235
90

Note. Yet this in turn contains a little ironic revenge. The art in life does not consist in promptly taking an outright negative position when a man says something extraordinary about himself. Furthermore, this is a hasty denial, since no one can promptly know whether it was still not possible here, unless one assumes

VII²
B 235
91

that nothing extraordinary exists at all. No, it is courteous and fitting and sensible to believe the man for the time being, and if what the man said about himself proves not to be true, then this same behavior is *eo ipso* ironic.—*Pap.* VIII² B 9:5g *n.d.*, 1847

Deleted in version III; see 49:11:

. . . . . by virtue of any of my views or theories to want to deny directly the possibility that Adler may have had a revelation. No, but Adler's later attitudes and later writings adequately established that he himself does not really believe it, although he still has not, repenting, felt prompted to revoke his first statement.

                                    —*Pap.* VIII² B 9:5h *n.d.*, 1847

Deleted in version III; see 50:2:

Very likely, without any essential Christian presupposition, he has gone ahead and become a pastor—then suddenly he is in a crisis, doubly dangerous because he has in such a solemn way already given himself out to be a Christian, since he has taken it upon himself to be a Christian pastor. As if with one blow the essentially Christian suddenly emerges within him; in this strenuous situation he produces the most varied expressions of diversified Christian orthodoxy and of heresy all mixed together. What others know by reading and experience is extorted out of him, as it were, bursts out primitively, but altogether confusedly. But it certainly is within him primitively, since at the time he unquestionably had not read the least thing in the areas of stricter orthodoxy or pietism.—*Pap.* VIII² B 9:5i *n.d.*, 1847

Deleted in version III; see 50:12:

Despite the frightful reprimands he has received, despite all the harm he undoubtedly would have done if he fortunately had not been ignored, it is at least my opinion that much hope for him remains. As a theological graduate he undoubtedly has lived in the delusion that the meager theological knowledge required of the examinee in the final theological examination was Christianity. When the essentially Christian moved him, he got into the strange situation of knowing about it in a certain sense, but by means of a nomenclature. He hastily seizes upon the strongest expressions to describe what has happened to him—and so we have his revelation. But this much is also certain, that he, however long he lives or whatever he produces, is duty-bound to revoke his first statement or step into the character of it and annul what lies between.—*Pap.* VIII² B 9:5l *n.d.*, 1847

Deleted in versions II and III; see 52:22:

. . . . . , the words about which he himself, according to an oral statement, thinks that the voice in which they are said is important and decisive[76]

—*Pap.* VIII² B 7:6 *n.d.*, 1847

Deleted in versions II and III; see 54:17:

. . . . . and his confusion is nevertheless, despite the burned *Logic*, the fruit of his acquaintance with Hegelian philosophy and logic.

—*Pap.* VIII² B 7:6 *n.d.*, 1847

Deleted in versions II and III; see 58:39:

But in the preface such a hope has its significance, because, so says the public, in the preface a hope is very nice. Since, unfortu-

VII²
B 235
92
VII²
B 235
93

nately, there are only a few really avid readers and inquiring minds, but all the more inquisitive ones, an author can never better curry the favor of the public than by maintaining a sort of private sewage connection with the crowd, who must have something to talk about when they meet for tea etc. But it is not so easy to chatter about a book and a real piece of work, but that the author hopes at some time etc., that one personally knows from the author that he is concentrating etc., that one personally has seen a little chapter of it and heard him say that he hoped etc.—all this is of great interest to all inquisitive people. The author's wife flatly demands, as a marital perquisite, that she, on the evening of the same day her husband puts his pen to paper in order to begin, be permitted to be interesting at a party by telling people: My husband is writing a big book, and he hopes etc. A fortnight later the sisters-in-law, the brother-in-law, also demand to be able to be interesting by having seen some of it. Then finally an honorable cultured public, which considers itself as being in a relationship by marriage or in an even closer connection with the author, also demands this cozy, interesting, private intimacy, that between the public and the author it must be as between Klister and Malle, that they know each other completely and say tickle, tickle, tickle to one another.[77]—*Pap.* VIII^2 B 7:6 *n.d.*, 1847

From draft of version I; see 68:5:

As is well known, that the horses once bolted with Pascal made an extraordinarily deep impression and had decisive consequences for his life.[78]—*Pap.* VII^2 B 257:9 *n.d.*, 1846–47

Deleted in versions II and III; see 68:14:

It goes better, however, to exegete this way when the exegete is removed from Paul by the distance of eighteen hundred years; but in relation to what one has oneself solemnly claimed to have experienced two years ago, what one to the joy of humanity has made known to all, to exegete in this manner really betrays a considerable degree of confusion.—*Pap.* VIII^2 B 7:6 *n.d.*, 1847

From draft of version I; see 70:20–71:6:

. . . But what was it now that the ecclesiastical superior had
asked him about—would he admit that he had been in an excited
and confused state of mind when he wrote the preface and the
sermons? And when one has begun in an excited state, it can be
altogether proper to hope for a certain perfectibility* . . ..

*In margin: *Note.* The whole matter of Adler's perfectibility is
just another one of those unfortunate reminiscences from the
colleges. If only Adler had been a layman, since it is one of his
various misfortunes that his fervor has no relation to his poor
theological capacities. Christianity is a revelation—1700 years
later they begin really to develop the theory that it must be perfectible—after all, the many hundred years do amount to something; but to experience a revelation in one's own life and then
to go through this exegetical course concerning what one has
oneself experienced, that is really comical—*JP* III 3203 (*Pap.*
VII² B 257:12) *n.d.*, 1846–47

VII²
B 257:12
288

VII²
B 257:12
289

Deleted in versions II and III; see 70:24:

In that case there can be meaning in hoping for a better future,
for a significant perfectibility. Even in connection with a purely
human endeavor, it usually holds for all more competent persons
that the first is still the best, the first of enthusiasm, of resolve, of
falling in love, and also of the dialectical first estimate of a matter.
And it holds above all when one has begun with a revelation.
—*Pap* VIII² B 7:6 *n.d.*, 1847

Deleted in versions II and III; see 71:2:

See, those exegetes and dogmaticians who invented the theory of perfectibility were not only third parties in relation to the
one favored by the revelation but were even third parties at a
distance of sixteen to seventeen hundred years. Paul was not contemporary with them; therefore, when they began their volatilizing, he could say: No, it was and is and remains a revelation.
—*Pap* VIII² B 7:6 *n.d.*, 1847

From draft of version I; see 71:25–27:

If he would say, for example: Jesus has neither appeared to me nor commanded me to write down these words—but I have been in a confused and overstrained state. For me, however, that moment has had a decisive meaning; so I may say of myself that I have been rescued in a marvelous way—well, then the matter is something else. Honor to the person who humbly but frankly admits about himself that he had to be rescued in a marvelous way.* But in Adler's first and decisive statement (in the preface to *Sermons*), there was not one word about being saved and rescued—there he was the one called by a revelation to whom a new doctrine was entrusted. Now to leave the first in abeyance and to give the reply the appearance of being an explanation is a total confusion. The reply is no explanation but a qualitatively new statement; the explanation does not explain the first statement but explains that the first is something else. If, for example, someone should explain what a circle is and he then explains that it is a square, this is no explanation; it is a new statement. When I explain something, I certainly assume no change in the nature of that which I am explaining. No, that which is to be explained remains unchanged; through the explanation, however, what it is becomes clear. When someone says that by a revelation a new doctrine has been communicated to him according to Jesus' own dictation, and one asks him what he means by that, requests his explanation, and he explains that he means by this that he is saved in a marvelous way, then he is not explaining what is asked about but is producing a new story.

In margin: *Note. It is another question whether it is proper to make that kind of personal confession (above all one must not create a fantastical effect).—*Pap.* VII² B 257:13 *n.d.*, 1846–47

Deleted in versions II and III; see 71:37:

To one who is educated, not to say confused, only by Hegelian dialectic, according to which everything becomes approximately one and the same, it may seem that the overture does not go too far, although it completely annihilates the qualitative distinction. Such a dialectician can live very well in the delusion that: (a) to be called by a revelation and to have received a doctrine; (b) to be rescued in a marvelous way; (c) to have had an enthusiastic moment—that such things are one and the same, and therefore one can serve the ecclesiastical superior with whichever of these expressions one thinks best. Anyone who has any religious discipline at all is well informed about the qualitative difference and knows that the last so-called explanation takes us completely out of the sphere of the religious into the esthetic sphere.—*Pap.* VIII^2 B 7:6 *n.d.*, 1847

Deleted in versions II and III; see 76:27:

. . . . . who lyrically is entitled to confuse his surprise, his excitement, his rejuvenation with having something new to bring—particularly a new revelation. Yet he of course finds no occasion to revoke "the replies" in order to stand firm by his first statements that by means of a revelation he has received something new to bring. Nor has he yet found time to reflect on the relation of the replies to the preface to *Sermons*, as well as on the fact that he, if the replies are to remain standing, is obliged to revoke the preface to *Sermons*.—*Pap.* VIII^2 B 7:6 *n.d.*, 1847

Deleted in versions II and III; see 76:40:

Let us repeat. Under the dateline Hasle, June 18, 1843, we have before us a man who is called by a revelation and has received from the Savior himself a teaching that is written down according to his dictation. —Under the date May 10, 1845, we have before us a man who has been rescued in a marvelous way. —Under the date July 5, 1845, we have before us a man who in a moment of enthusiasm has had to help himself with a few reference points. This man is Magister Adler. Yet there is no mention of the various elements in his life. No, it is that element carefully described in the preface to *Sermons*, the element that by means of explanations is explained as being all these different things. Adler does not seem to notice anything; he goes on as if nothing is

his failure to revoke his first statement demonstrates that he is confused.

In the beginning of his work as an author, he was also on another track when he shouted to the whole nation: Confess, confess; when he, to that extent consistent, had the type for his *Sermons* remain set at the press so that the second edition might follow so speedily that if possible not a half-day would be wasted. That *Sermons* did not have a rapid sale was not Adler's fault, but it certainly is his fault that he essentially changes his entire work as an author by attempting even to become humorous instead of continuing to press forward with a call's πληροφορία [full assurance] despite the whole world's indifference. As soon as an author destroys every teleological relation to a surrounding world, he defines himself humorously and can then, for example, become a lyrical author, which Adler has now become. The lyrical quite rightly has no τέλος [goal, end] outside itself; whether one writes a single page of lyrics or writes folios of lyrics makes no difference with regard to defining the direction of his activity. The lyrical author cares only about production, relishes the joy of production, perhaps frequently through pain and great effort, but he has nothing to do with others. The author who acts is especially concerned about having an effect on people; he has neither time nor desire for lyrical self-absorption in producing; he works—in order to, in order to enlighten people, in order to help them onto the right road, etc. One who is called by a revelation must above all be an author who acts. But what does Adler do? He begins with being called by a revelation (therefore with an absolute teleological qualification), and two years later we learn that for a long time already he has settled down as a lyrical poet in carefree remoteness on Bornholm; we learn that from four books, the fruit of—his lyrical leisure. But Adler notices nothing; he continually thinks he is in identity with himself, although he has become so lyrical in the latest books that he even adopts the lyrical-humorous view of silence when he says: Silence is genius.[92] Adler throws no light on how this is to be more specifically understood; he himself scarcely seems to notice that what to him is more or less a phrase contains within itself a whole life-view, yet, note well, the very opposite of what is otherwise

VII²
B 235
152

wrong; but any dialectician easily perceives the dilemma: either all Adler's replies are nonsense, or he must solemnly revoke his first statement. *His excuse may be that he himself actually does not notice anything; in that case what excuses him is identical with the charge against him—that he is confused.—Pap.* VIII² B 7:6 *n.d.*, 1847

Deleted in versions II and III; see 77:12:

. . . . . , that he is so absentminded and confused that in ab-sentmindedness he is even guilty of blasphemies, is so absent-minded that he forgets that he has had a revelation.—*Pap.* VIII² B 7:6 *n.d.*, 1847

Deleted in versions II and III; see 78:11:

Misgivings have been aroused by the way in which he an-nounced that he has had a revelation. On the basis of the suspi-cion aroused, he was suspended; then he was induced to provide additional details, whereby he succeeded in documenting that he was confused—and then he was dismissed. From Adler's dis-missal nothing at all follows for anyone else.—*Pap.* VIII² B 7:6 *n.d.*, 1847

From draft of version I; see 78:14–80:4:

VII²
B 257:22
290

VII²
B 257:22
291

No, because he said this he was suspended for closer inspec-tion, but with the aid of the concessions he tripped himself up. If one does not think that profundity consists merely of profound notions and brilliant remarks, if one assumes, as I do, that pro-fundity has an essential relation to acting, one cannot deny that Bishop Mynster has managed splendidly in a difficult situation precisely by means of his profundity. The point above all is that the blow fell in the right place (right after the concessions) and that the matter acquired no tail, which it cannot possibly acquire, since something could certainly result from Adler's statement about having had a revelation and his dismissal connected with it, but from his concessions nothing could result for any other person.

In margin: The state would of course have had the right to dismiss a man who calmly and coolly appealed to a revelation, since the extraordinary must step out of the ranks;* but I am thinking only of what impression a necessary step such as that could have made on someone weaker, and for that reason I am happy that this is not at all the case with Adler. Moreover, I am convinced that the true extraordinary would voluntarily resign his office.

*and certainly Christianity is built upon a revelation, but it is also restricted by its specific received revelation; it must not build upon the revelation that Mr. Petersen or Mr. Madsen may have, and in any case Mr. Petersen and Mr. Madsen must face the same danger as those who built the Church upon a revelation.—*Pap.* VII² B 257:22 *n.d.*, 1846–47

From version I of Chapter III, replaced in version III by Pap. VIII² B 9:8–10 (version II, *Pap.* VIII² B 7:7, 9, 10, with changes); *see 80–87:*

2.

Adler's Four Latest Books*

VII²
B 235
127

Adler now seems to want to be advanced to or to be satisfied with being a genius. The fundamental confusion is that he nevertheless acts as if nothing had happened and thinks he is in agreement with his first statement (according to which he was one called by a revelation, to whom a doctrine was entrusted). —*The qualitative difference between a genius and an apostle.* —*Even if Adler had no first, regarded only as the author of the four latest books he would be characterized as a confused genius, a verdict already prompted by the form of the books.*

The last words of a man at the moment of dismissal always have a singular worth, always imprint themselves more fixedly in

* *Studier og Exempler, Forsøg til en kort systematisk Fremstilling af Christendommen i dens Logik; Theologiske Studier, Nogle Digte* [Studies and Examples; An Attempt at a Short Systematic Exposition of the Logic of Christianity; Theological Studies; Some Poems].

VII²
B 235
128

memory. Adler's last words (the last in the last letter of July 5, 1845) contained, as the reader remembers, a hope, a beautiful and in any case trustworthily expressed hope, "that in the future, by working out and calmly developing the ideas over a longer time, he would see his way" etc.[79] Immediately after this declaration of hope followed his dismissal, which honorably and with pension—discharged him from his position in the future.

Favored by leisure and by the pension (as an author Adler would probably have had difficulty in obtaining public support on the basis of—competence; but perhaps incompetence may also properly be regarded as a more essential qualification—for support), Adler kept quiet for the period of a year, presumably, as it is said of Ulysses, βυσσοδομευων [pondering deeply].[80] In the early summer of 1846, he altogether unexpectedly appeared in *Adresseavisen*[81] with four new books at one time. Four books at one time! If this practice is introduced more widely, the mint standard for being an author will no doubt thereby be inordinately jacked up. In the future when there is mention of someone's having become an author, one must promptly ask: Of one or of four books—just as pashas are divided into those with one or with three horsetails,[82] and barbers into those with one or three shaving basins.[83] To publish three or four books at the same time is something so striking that an essential author, even if he had them completed, would very likely avoid what can easily attract an altogether wrong kind of attention and what, regarded as a whim, can at most have some fascination the first time it is accomplished, not the first time by the individual but the first time in the little world where one belongs as an author. Nevertheless, in order to do something like that, it holds true of every real author that he must have excellent reasons. Subjectively he must be conscious of a youthful energy that will permit him to accomplish a task that, according to a proper scale, provokes the envy of criticism. Perhaps his *impetus* [impulse] is intensified even by something haphazard, by the sad consciousness that the external benefits in his circumstances will only for a short time allow him to work on such an almost far too great scale. Perhaps his endeavor itself demands the intensive haste in order, if possible, to present at one time, as it were, or in the shortest possible time,

VII²
B 235
129

what would become something different in minor pieces distrib-
uted over a longer time, inasmuch as the individual part would
come to assert an anarchistic independence and the whole would
bear the stamp of the author's haphazard change over the years.

But primarily the four books must objectively have a deeper
purpose—for example, if possible maieutically to cover a specific
terrain on all sides at the same time. It must then be important to
the author of the four books—for him a half-poetic artistic task—
that each book, which *essentially in itself* is different from the others, be kept *characteristically* distinct from the others. The author
must poetically know how to support the illusion, which consists essentially in the special point of departure in the particular
book. By way of the announcement, he himself must see to split-
ting them up, so that the impact of the four books at the same
time actually is a product of the reader's self-activity. Above all,
no one is obliged to know that there are four books at the same
time. Therefore, the art connoisseur, if he discovers in a round-
about way that there is one author, still can have a certain enjoyment in entering into the illusion that there are not four books by
one author but by four authors. Thus, even in *Adresseavisen*, the
one and the same author does not introduce and offer himself as
the author of four books at one and the same time. As a matter
of fact, not long ago such a thing was done in Danish literature[84]
in a more artistic manner; I at least had not expected to have my
memory of that refreshed so quickly—and so parodically. Four
books at one time, one dedicated to his father, all with Adler's
full name, all essentially in the same form and dealing essentially,
at times almost word for word, with the same thing—in short,
four yards from one piece, but each yard separate and with
Adler's full name! There does not appear to be a trace of any
sensible reason for doing four books. If such writing, such an
encompassing production, is to be published, it may as well be
collected in one volume, and if it is separated in publication, it
can just as well be twelve books as four.

Neither is there any sensible reason for the only variety Adler
has attempted and, note well, on the title page of one book by
calling it: An Attempt at a *Short* Exposition, since essentially all
his books are equally long and equally short, inasmuch as they all

(the longest and shortest) fall under the category: *haphazard length*. If, for example, in order to make the variety really conspicuous, Adler had modestly added on the title page of the voluminous *Studier og Exempler: An Attempt* at a *Long* Book, then one would—despite the modesty and the unmistakable effort, which we leave to other critics to encourage—be justified in saying of the book that, despite its length, regarded as a book it is essentially short. What passes itself off as a book cannot as a matter of course, like yard goods, go under the rubric of length and shortness; it must first substantiate its claim to be a book. A book is like the grammatical concept: a sentence. Two lines of a subordinate clause without a main clause is not a short sentence; a whole page of subordinate clauses without a main clause is not a long sentence. Both the former and the latter, regarded as a sentence, have merely haphazard length and therefore are equally long and equally short. In order for something to be called "a *short* exposition," it must essentially have the quality of being rounded off and demonstrate its shortness through an essential rendering of the whole thing in a small space on a shortened or reduced scale. On the other hand, three printer's sheets of paper can very well be lengthy blather, and thirty printer's sheets of blather may very properly be called a short book. In regard to the first production, the author in question may say "that it became so long because he did not have time to make it short"; and in regard to the latter the author in question might say "that it became such a short piece because he did not have a longer time to write inasmuch as he had to publish." If he had had longer time, then the book presumably would have become—yes, here it comes to a halt. Would it have become longer or would it have become shorter?

And now Adler! His hope is "that in the future, by working out and calmly developing the ideas over a longer time etc." Yet, whatever the future, to which Adler can always look, will bring, the person who critically holds to the finished product before him must acknowledge that Adler's books are a unique production, an almost alarming kind of production. When a pastor has successfully arrived at the third part of his sermon and is already so far into it that, according to the familiarity one has with the proportions of ecclesiastical address, one dares to assume with some certainty that he is beginning to run down and is just about to say the Amen—then it can be alarming if, instead of pronouncing the momentous Amen, he suddenly becomes loquacious and adds one sentence after the other, while the intelligent listeners must say that essentially the discourse is over and the Amen has essentially been said. This is an example of the haphazard length, recognizable by its beginning where, viewed essentially, the Amen should be said. There are examples of people who, embarrassed and embarrassing, continue sitting with one for whole hours just because they feel embarrassed about leaving. This perhaps is also the case with such a pastor, so that, after first having been embarrassed by mounting the solemn place, he is now embarrassed about saying Amen and descending. But in any case the sermon that really undertakes to begin where the Amen should be said, like the visit that really begins when the moment comes when one should go— both are examples of the haphazard length, whose mark here is the negative feature of *beginning where one should stop.* But it is essentially the same negative feature *to begin before the beginning,* that is, before the nudge of the ideal conclusion has indicated to one: now you can begin. Thus if a person, without yet having attained sufficient clarity and maturity to write a book, wanted to begin to write the preface to the book (he as yet could not write), this preface would fall under the rubric of haphazard length. And this is exactly the case with Adler as an author—he has begun before the beginning. That "longer time," frequently mentioned and over a longer time, by the proper use of which Adler hopes (this is a present tense in the historical style) "in the future to be able to have the ideas develop in a more appropriate form" etc., must either have not yet arrived, or not been long enough, or not been used properly. Adler has begun before the beginning, and therefore his productions lie within the category of haphazard length. All of the three new books (the fourth contains poetry) are an aggregate of tumultuous aphorisms, the beginning of which is haphazard, the factual range of which is without a τέλος [goal], the possible continuation of which can keep on indefinitely.

To state the contents of the books is of course an impossibility; one can, however, perhaps characterize them by calling to mind

VII²
B 235
132

a poem by Horace, provided it is understood in a singular way: *dum* [meanwhile]* *meam canto Lalagen et ultra terminum vagor curis expeditis* [meanwhile I was singing of my Lalage and wandering carefree far beyond the boundaries of my farm],[85] since more often it is indeed outside the plowed land, on the other side (*ultra terminum*), that Adler, exempt from all author-cares (*curis expeditis*), carefreely wanders around (*vagatur*), humming about his Lalage. Just as a person out in a country region completely gives himself over to his own devices and to the indefiniteness of strolling about, he is now infatuated with one impression, now with another; now he skips for joy, now makes a long leap for the fun of it, now in turn stands still and ponders, now is actually profound, and then in turn rather tasteless and insipid—so it is that Adler wanders around as a reader of the Bible. When a Bible
VII[2] B 235 133 verse appeals to him, he writes something about it and then turns down another street. At times he notices something, perhaps for a particular use later, but this is also included. During all this he still does not forget his Lalage. Depending on who is interpreting the ode, Lalage can mean many different things. I recall from my school days that the rector understood it as life's innocent joys. Adler's Lalage may be understood to mean that doctrine communicated to him (by a revelation), a doctrine that he now interprets, now transcribes, since even though he seems *to have forgotten completely that the doctrine was communicated to him by a revelation*, he still has not forgotten the doctrine, the words, which instead have become much too fixed in his head.

If being called by a revelation must in the highest and deepest sense make a man earnest, then it is indeed strange to see such a person, who in absentmindedness must have forgotten the reve-

**Note*. The word *dum* states the time. When does Adler write these many books? Answer, he writes them: meanwhile. An abstract "meanwhile" such as that states merely the abstract disappearance of time; it is while that "longer time" (by the proper use of which etc.) disappears that Adler writes these many books. Every essential production essentially fills out the time; an authentic author uses one or two or ten years of his life to write a book, but Adler writes—in the meanwhile; while time passes (essentially unused), Adler writes. Within this "meanwhile" a more exact specification of time is not possible; it is impossible to say which he wrote first and which last; they were all written—meanwhile.

lation, just as one may forget one's hat and just as many absentminded people may forget their heads, now carry on like an adventurer in a religious mode, a mystical wandering knight, an itinerant, or like someone who aimlessly takes a constitutional walk in the Bible for the sake of the exercise, or like a person who, essentially disengaged, seeks and finds and seeks and chats—and that man is called by a revelation!

If being called by a revelation must in the highest and deepest sense make a man into a zealous, active servant who in action enters into life as the called worker in the eminent sense, then it is indeed strange to see such a called person (who nevertheless acts as if nothing had happened and as if everything were in order with the identification) transformed into an *otiosus* [man of leisure], who now fiddles around with effeminate work, now with a humorous flourish of his hat *à la* one and another of the pseudonyms reflects on this and that and himself and on what is shocking in the pale countenance of the frightened Jonah,[86] and then in turn is melodiously heard on the erotic reed pipe.

What is particularly important for the understanding of Adler is that in these four latest books *there is no longer any mention of that revelation-fact or of a continued revelation or of the fact that this and that had been written under the direct impulse of the Spirit.* But even if it is assumed that the latter is entirely in order, inasmuch as Adler has not later had a revelation or later found occasion to make a distinction between what is of the Spirit and what is his own, yet surely that revelation-fact in the preface to his *Sermons* cannot be summarily laid aside, just as a girl lays aside her party finery. To be sure, he does frequently come back to the doctrine that was communicated to him, but there is no mention that it was communicated to him by a revelation. He does not argue from it to its divine authority; he does not appeal to this evidence of its truth; he does not on the strength of it assert himself as one who has divine authority. And yet, as was shown in the introduction to this book,[87] that the doctrine was communicated to him by a revelation is decisive, is what categorically shifts the whole matter and the whole relation into a sphere totally different from the one to which Magister Adler together with his doctrine can belong. But it is very amazing that what ordinarily someone who

VII²
B 235
134

has a revealed doctrine to communicate reminds all others about repeatedly—that it is revealed—this Adler himself seems to have forgotten in connection with his revealed doctrine, and I must continually remind him that it is indeed, according to his own statement, a revealed doctrine.

But Adler (the Hegelian, later the apostle) perhaps finds himself, together with his revealed doctrine, in a new stage, and now has stepped out of the immediate (as a revelation is called in Hegelian veiling language) into reflection and now understands the revelation. So he now, in Hegelian fashion, goes further and does not stop with the revelation—with the revelation he himself has had. See, at the time when Christianity entered into the world, it proclaimed itself to be a revelation and has steadily maintained that. But then time passed; randomly and gradually we all became Christians of sorts, and then many centuries later there lives a generation (in geographical Christendom) that presumes to understand and comprehend the revelation. Thus the same revealed doctrine is treated by entirely different people, by a generation that is many centuries removed from that first one. But the very same man who has announced that he has had a revelation must certainly know what is what with regard to the revelation that was granted him—either he must stand firm by it, that it was and is a revelation, and in that case speak and act and write in conformity with it, or he must say that he has now understood and comprehended it. But a little caution—what, indeed, can he have understood? Has he understood that it was no revelation? Then of course he must revoke his first statement. Or if he has better understood what he presumably must have understood originally, since he did say that it was a revelation, then he must indeed maintain it, argue on the basis of it, act in accordance with it, transform his whole existence in relation to it. But someone who claims to be called by a revelation must above all strive most conscientiously for an honest accounting; he may not cast away a revelation as a thief casts away stolen goods when the police are after him—because then he is a deliberate deceiver, which Adler certainly is not. But neither may he allow this matter of the revelation to lie in abeyance unexplained,

VII²
B 235
135

while he, acting as if nothing had happened, turns down a different street—because in that case he is confused.

In the four latest books, *where,* although there is continual
mention of the doctrine, *there is no mention anymore of that revela-*
tion-fact by which it was communicated or of the communication of the
doctrine by a revelation; there is, however, almost to the point of
abomination, mention of *genius, genius* here and *genius* there, that
genius is an inexplicable something, that *nobody can understand ge-*
nius,[88] that *genius is the autodidactic foal,*[89] etc.

We will stop here and look carefully ahead, since it seems
sufficiently clear that the outcome of the whole Adler episode is
that he is a genius. *Quel bruit pour une omelette* [What a fuss over
an omelet]![90] Honor be to the genius; if Adler is a genius, well,
I certainly will not begrudge him that. But to begin with having
had a revelation, if then the *summa summarum* is that this is to be
understood as meaning that he is a genius, that the first statement
is perhaps what is called a bold expression for being a genius—
yes, that is surely a hitherto unheard-of disorder and confusion!
The category genius is certainly completely other than and qualitatively different from having received a doctrine from the Savior through a revelation! To have, if you please, something new
to bring by virtue of being a genius certainly lies within the
sphere of immanence; then the newness can indicate only the
primitivity of the reproduction—is indeed still something other
than and qualitatively different from having received a doctrine
from the Savior through a revelation! We speak of the primitivity
of genius, of its originality, but these qualifications (or this qualification) are certainly not identical with having had a revelation
through which the Savior communicated a doctrine to the one
who was called!

See, a mistaken exegesis and dogmatics have surely played on
Christianity the trick of going ahead and *understanding* the concept of a revelation, or of going ahead and *comprehending* a revelation in approximately this way: a revelation, it is immediacy; it is
genius, something of genius, the new, novelty, originality, primitivity, etc. Adler does just about the same thing, but then he does
a little extra, by which he earns, ironically enough, the merit of

VII²
B 235
136

indirectly making conspicuous the conduct of that exegesis and dogmatics against the Christian revelation. Adler begins by saying that he himself has had a revelation, and thereupon he gives in modern style an exegesis of the concept of revelation—that is, *in action* he gives an exegesis by letting his first statement stand and then becoming a genius, pretending as if there were good sense in this correlation, or as if there were sense in the lack of correlation. [*Pap.* VII^2 B 235, pp. 136–50, *with minor changes, became the text of Addendum II, pp. 173–77.*]

VII^2
B 235
150

VII^2
B 235
151

We now return to Adler and his aforementioned radical transformation, whereby from being one called by a revelation he became a genius, and yet he thinks he is in identity with himself. The one who is called by a revelation must *eo ipso* be teleologically positioned; he is indeed an instrument of God who is to be used to be active. It is otherwise with a genius, who can live humorously in secluded self-satisfaction. From Adler's latest books, it may be concluded that it is this position of humorous self-satisfaction that he now endeavors to occupy. One certainly does produce, perhaps even abundantly, but one requires no reader; if there is someone who wants to read, fine; if there is no one, it makes no difference either, and the author has no more to do with the reader than the nightingale with the listener.[91] Well, now, such a humorous, inactive work as an author is understandable—but Adler, after all, has begun by being called by a revelation, and Adler thinks he is in identity with himself, that is, he does not notice that there is a qualitative, decisive difference between his first statement and his latest. Although a revelation is the paradoxical fact that passes human understanding, one can still understand this much, which is indeed everywhere apparent: that a person is called by a revelation to go out in the world, called to proclaim the Word, to act and to suffer, to the uninterrupted active life as the Lord's messenger. But that a person would be called by a revelation to retain undivided possession of the estate, in active literary *far niente* [idleness] in a remote place to be momentarily brilliant and then to be publisher as well as compiler of the vagaries of his brilliance—this is almost a blasphemous thought. Here again Adler's latest is a refutation of the reality and truth of his first statement, while

contained in the latest books, in which Adler appears as an immediate lyrical genius. But Adler is much too unembarrassed to discover such a contradiction, and of course he actually does not write books any more than he thinks. It may rather be said that he is keeping a pub for witticisms, and therefore it makes no difference that the customers are mixed, indeed, discordant, if only they do not come to blows.

VII²
B 235
153

Silence is inward deepening and the road by which an originality is gained that is more than a substitute for the originality of genius. (A revelation is in a completely different sphere and therefore is not discussed here.) By holding firm to a definite life-impression, a definite single thought, in absolutely silent inwardness, by not wanting to open the slightest communication with any other person (by which one slyly obtains the relative and comparative criterion, the criterion of mediocrity), anyone, provided he is not on the way to losing his mind (since there undeniably is this danger), will *acquire originality*. This is the road of freedom and of self-consciousness and of disciplined passion to what the immediate genius receives in the cradle, or in dreams, or in the moment. It is, namely, far from being the case that reflection, properly understood, stifles genius; on the other hand, rightly used, it is able to acquire originality. The reverse and opposite of this relation of freedom, this slow acquiring, is the direct, the immediate genius (and in a way, then, being called by a revelation, which lies within the sphere of the paradoxical religious). The idea of silence, the whole view of silence as inwardness, is the road of inward deepening to the highest for every human being, whether or not he is originally a genius. This view has found adequate expression in the works of the pseudonymous authors, to which on this matter I therefore refer everyone except Adler, who with this statement, silence is genius, has managed to include in his four latest books an idea that, silent and quiet, utterly annihilates them, which is already droll enough and becomes even more so when one considers that in turn his four latest books annihilate his first statement. Even if it is granted that Adler is a genius, he will still be an immediate genius, but by means of silence it is impossible to become something immediate, just as on the whole it is nonsense to think of a method in relation to immediacy, which is definitely prior to method.

In the four latest books, Adler is only genius, pure, sheer ge-nius—and yet, presumably in his opinion, is in agreement with his first statement. That those words in the preface to *Sermons* (to which Adler continually returns) were communicated to him by a revelation, dictated by the Savior, is forgotten; that *Sermons* (to which Adler frequently refers) was written with Jesus' collaborat-ing grace is forgotten. Adler, presumably in absentmindedness, as a genius has taken over the whole *Wirtschaft* [show]—in absent-mindedness, because if it had happened consciously he of course would solemnly have to revoke his first statement. How far Adler can go in absentmindedness one ascertains further by reading his four latest books; there one comes to see with what frivolousness (which only absentmindedness can excuse) Adler associates with God and Christ, engages, shall I say, in chatter with them and even chatters to them, until finally he is all at sea, like Soldin, who said to Rebecca: Is it I who is speaking[93] . . . . . or is it—alas, and in connection with Adler the following clause will be: or is it Christ? That this is so can again serve to explain in retrospect how it really hangs together with Adler's revelation. In the latest books he poetizes, he introduces God and Christ speaking with each other—this certainly is poetical! When something like this is done with human propriety, there can be no objection to it, but above all it is a matter of not becoming so confused oneself that one does not know what is what. Adler's *Forsøg til en kort systematisk Fremstilling af Christendommen* [An Attempt at a Short Systematic Exposition of the Logic of Christianity] begins as fol-lows: "Before God created the world, he said to Jesus: I can do everything as perfectly as possible etc." God and Jesus are intro-duced speaking and conversing. Yet this certainly was not com-municated to Adler by a revelation! But what is it then? Well, yes, it is a little fictionizing attempt to enliven the exposition. But see, Adler himself quotes this talk later; he argues from it. In several places he says: Then Jesus promised to let himself be born (see 1:c, pp. 14–16)—that is, he speaks about this conversation between God and Christ as something that actually took place

VII²
B 235
154

and to which one can refer, as if those words by Jesus were *ipsis-sima verba* [the very words]. Indeed, somewhere Adler even says:

We must, namely, bear in mind that Jesus said to God etc.,⁹⁴ and then follow some of those fictionized words. Thus, frivolously fictionizing, one first ventures out into spheres where one should rather refrain from fictionizing, and then fixes one's own fiction-izing so firmly in mind that one believes it is actuality. In this way a frivolous person can also easily have a revelation. He needs only to grope around capriciously for a time with a fantastic notion of a revelation. Then finally it probably becomes so fixed in him that he has had a revelation that he fictionizes that he has had a revelation, and then this fictionizing becomes fixed as an actual-ity—until something new becomes fixed.

But while Adler treats his own fictionizing as if it were actual-ity, he inversely treats the New Testament in an equally frivolous way in that he does not treat it as an actuality. He does otherwise, however, say many a beautiful word about the Bible, and there-fore that behavior again indicates precisely a confused state of mind. With a strange, fantastical willfulness he sometimes usurps the Bible's words and makes them his own* without quotation marks; indeed, there are passages where he in this frivolousness begins to identify himself with Christ. An aphorism begins with words by Christ in the first person: I say unto you. These words have no quotation marks; there is no hint that they are from the Bible, which would be especially important since they are in the first person. To these words (which are in the first person) the next sentence is directly attached, which likewise is in the first person but is Adler's words. A reader ordinarily must simply as-sume, and Adler has led every reader to assume, that it is he who is speaking in the whole aphorism, that the *I* in the first sentence is the same *I* as in the second and third sentences. Yet the first *I* is Christ, and the second *I* is Adler.

As the author of the four latest books, as a genius (*let us for a moment forget the total confusion that is implicit in the misrelation be-tween Adler's first and last statements, or, to express it more precisely, in*

---

*Note. Such conduct in the relation between author and author is called plagiarism; in the relation between an author and Christ, it becomes blasphemy.

his total ignoring of this misrelation), Adler is a confused genius, who has his life and thinking in the momentary. His own existence explains nothing by which another person could order his life according to his guidance, and there is no esthetic or religious concept that he has developed in such a way that through him it has gained new clarity or is thought with true originality. On the contrary, he touches on the most diverse things and confuses almost everywhere. Yet profound remarks cannot be denied him, but unconditional profundity certainly can, if the explanation we gave at the very beginning of this book is on the whole correct, that profundity is related to coherence and continuity. And even in his profound remarks, there is a certain uniformity; for the most part they are all tailored to the same pattern. Having understood a thought is like being able to decline a paradigm: if one can decline the paradigm, one can also decline all the words that follow it. If one has understood a thought, one can seem to make many profound remarks by using it in many "examples," and yet the many are only repetitions and, to refer again to the simile, one is not justified in saying of oneself that one has learned many declensions because one can decline the many words that follow one declension. It is the same with having understood one thought; lest the repetitions become boring, one must add a poetic element that makes the rendition of the example esthetically valuable in itself. But Adler has no time for that—he who according to his own authentic interpretation (see paragraph 1) has nothing new to bring—he who lives in lyrical leisure! In form, he himself admits, he has been harmed, he who must endeavor to achieve something with the help of the form,[95] since he has not had or does not have anything new to bring (the content).

A particular thought Adler rides is the old Hegelian one that the concept flips over,[96] except that it is brought more into the category of the ironic. This thought is expressed in my dissertation (about irony) in this way: irony makes the phenomenon manifest.[97] How this is to be understood more explicitly, how it takes place, is frequently explained and demonstrated by the pseudonymous writers. The ironic subtlety consists, by means of transforming itself into nothing with negative-acting

VII[2]
B 235
157

consistency, in bringing the counter phenomenon into the awkward situation of not having anything else to do but to disclose
itself.* At first glance and to obtuse people it may look as if irony
were the loser, whereas precisely in the subtlety it is the victor,
aided by the flipping over of the concept, and while in the eyes
of irony the very evidence of its victory is that obtuse people
believe that it has lost; irony can never become popular. How
many contemporaries did not regard Socrates as a dunce who in
no way could compete with the Sophist, who could show him
up with a vengeance. So what did Socrates do? With proper
ataraxia he related himself in his ignorance with negative consistency, and he thereby caused the Sophist to dish out his wisdom
more and more. But see, the concept had flipped over; the Sophist ended up betraying his obtuseness precisely by his abundant
wisdom. The Sophist thought, and all obtuse people are of the
same opinion, that the more he talked the more he manifested his
wisdom. Socrates in all subtlety ventured to be of another opinion, but he did not say it directly; that would have helped the
Sophist. He suppressed it and thereby helped the Sophist to continue to strengthen Socrates all the more in his opinion that the
Sophist was letting himself be carried away.

VII²
B 235
158

In this way, by means of negative-acting consistency, an ironist can transform *an attacker, an accuser,* into a person who, without
knowing it, talks only about himself, *denounces himself,* his own

In margin: *Note. The Danish language has some *verba neutra* [intransitive
verbs] that in combination with prefixes signify an outcome adverse to what the
root word means—for example, *at forløbe sig, at forsee sig, at forhaste sig, at fortale
sig, at forsnakke sig* [to let oneself be carried away, to offend, to be over-hasty, to
give oneself away, to say too much]. Now, irony helps a person to that end, but
by what means and how? By relating itself negatively and indirectly. Imagine a
mutual relation between two people, of whom one is an ironist. The ironist
now makes himself into nothing and relates himself altogether negatively, and
he thereby indirectly helps the other to let himself be carried away [*at forløbe sig*].
This "himself," this reflexive pronoun conceals the irony. The man lets himself
be carried away. Consequently he himself does it, but he does it with the negative help of the ironist. The man is of the opinion that he has another person to
deal with, but through the subtlety of the ironist the man has only himself to
deal with, since he indeed lets *himself* be carried away.

insignificance, wretchedness, etc. The attacker, the accuser, likewise all obtuse people, are of the opinion that the more he is carried away the more he harms the poor ironist, while the latter in all subtlety modestly ventures to be of another opinion. Ironic subtlety culminates in the cunning with which one brings a person to talk about himself, to denounce himself, to disclose himself, just when in his own view he is not talking about himself at all, yes, has even forgotten himself. It is one thing to get to know a person's inner being when he in confidence opens himself, and it is something else ironically to get his attention diverted to another point just at the moment one in his every word is conversing with his inner being. When a man says something extraordinary about himself, it is ironically correct to believe him (the negative consists in not directly opposing him, flatly denying it vehemently) in order in that way, aided by his naïveté, to get it disclosed that it is untruth, to get the lie wormed out of him. Naïveté apparently relates itself affirmatively in order to bring out the denial. It is easy to see how the concept flips over. With his naïveté the ironist makes the boaster uncircumspect—and then he is trapped. When a person has essential ethical self-control, proper ataraxia, and mastery in dialectics, he will be able to make manifest any dialectically entangled and ambiguous phenomenon whatever, not exactly for all, because irony is and remains unpopular, and an ironist who is understood by everybody is *eo ipso* not an ironist, but a joker.

But enough of that. What is strange is that all such things can still have the interest of surprise for Adler. To me he seems like a child who is so delighted at being able to do a trick that he keeps on doing it and cannot get it into his head that there very likely are others who are able to do it. Adler dwells long on the profundity that the law let itself be carried away when it condemned Christ.[98] The law did not take care to see who Christ was, that he was the innocent one; it let itself be carried away, and this was its downfall. Well, yes, that means the concept flipped over: the law ended up doing wrong and thereby condemned itself precisely when it condemned Christ. A second and more difficult question, which Adler does not take up, is whether

VII²
B 235
159

this whole conception of the relation between the law and Christ does not have a touch of utterly unchristian frivolousness, because it ignores very decisive dogmatic qualifications regarding Christ's sacrificial death and that Christ came to the world *in order* to suffer and die. But I cannot enter into this further in this context; I shall, however, merely add a remark with regard to the flipping over of the concepts. The Platonic dialectic was already aware that the concepts flip over (μεταβολή, μεταβάλλειν εἰς τὸ ἐναντίον [change, change into the opposite]).⁹⁹ In Hegel the matter became confused because he, with his enormous authority, forced the illusion upon people, so to speak, obliged them to believe that it is the concept *itself* that with immanent necessity flips over.¹⁰⁰ Irony has the merit of being aware of the *transition*, inasmuch as it is aware of its drollery or its ingenuity. The qualitative dialectic (which specifically protests the immanent necessity) is in the first place actually in harmony with the category of *the leap*,¹⁰¹ a category that, as could be expected, Adler botches.

VII²
B 235
160

Among Adler's profound remarks there are also at times reminiscences of others, and in a way it can be entirely in order for Adler to return so often to the thesis and to defend the thesis that theft is altogether permissible in the world of the mind.¹⁰² Well, everyone has his own opinion about that; I do not deny that I have the opposite opinion. But again what is strange is that Adler, he who has a revelation to appeal to, is the one who arrives at this thesis. A revealed doctrine is certainly something that the person who is called cannot have borrowed from others, and so far there surely is no one who has stolen anything from Adler. If, on the other hand, Adler considers himself guilty of intellectual theft, or innocent, inasmuch as this theft is in his opinion permissible, then it seems singularly awkward that the one who is placed above all other people by a revelation pinches a little from the poor. But Adler nevertheless may perhaps be doing himself an injustice if he has suspected himself, since theft in the world of the mind is so far from being permissible that it is impossible, because in the world of the mind, and only in that world, there is absolute security of property rights. Only insignificant and poorly developed people think that thoughts can be stolen. Why? Because such people have a material conception of thoughts.

If one regards Adler as a confused genius (who neither *qua* thinker nor *qua* artist is master of himself and in the voluptuousness of producing touches on the most heterogeneous things) and one wishes to define *his genius* more particularly, totally, and essentially, then one must say: it is *dizziness*. This is not to deny that the particular aphoristic expression and remark may even be profound. An intoxicated man is certainly able to say good things, but his essential genius is intoxication. I shall now illustrate this dizziness with some examples from Adler's latest books, although I ask the reader not to forget the main point, which further illustrates how dizzy he is: that the one who propounds esthetic-dizzy views that are wholly reminiscent of paganism and of a worldly life-view, that he passes himself off not only as an orthodox Christian but even claims to have had a revelation from the Savior. It is simple dizziness to hold esthetic-dizzy views, but it is dizziness to the second power also to want to be a Christian in the eminent sense and to want to improve the understanding of the essentially Christian by means of esthetics.

VII²
B 235
161

Dizziness, as has been pointed out with physiological correctness, occurs when the eyes have no fixed point upon which to rest. Therefore one becomes dizzy by looking down from a high tower, because the gaze plunges down and finds no boundary, no limitation.[103] For a similar reason one becomes dizzy at sea, because everything is continually changing so that again there is no boundary and limitation. A physician has somewhere explained that what the French soldiers died of in Russia was *seasickness*, caused by there being nothing before the eyes in the infinite expanse. Thus when a person notices that he is becoming dizzy, he can stop it by fixing his eyes upon something particular. For example, if a person who gets dizzy by riding down a hill will undertake to be the driver, he most likely will not become dizzy. The definite way in which he, responsible as the driver, is compelled to pay attention to the reins will prevent the dizziness. So it is with physical dizziness. What is dizzying is the expanse, the infinite, the unlimited, the indeterminable, and the dizziness itself is the senses' lack of restraint. Indeterminableness is the basis of dizziness but is also a temptation to give in to it. Indeterminableness is admittedly certainly against human nature, and it is not only science that according to Aristotle abhors the unlimited,[104] not only ethics that abhors ambiguity, but just because indeterminableness is against nature it is also tempting. Thus the dialectic of dizziness contains the contradiction of wanting what one does not want, what one shrinks from, while this shrinking nevertheless only deters—temptingly. Therefore the remedy for dizziness is limitation; and in the spiritual sense all discipline is limitation. Just as the person who physiologically has a tendency to become dizzy is right in avoiding for the time being great open spaces and is right in making his way alongside buildings in order that the multiplicity can help by means of a relative standard, so the person who spiritually suffers from dizziness must seek to set limits for himself. The boundary is not only the beautiful in the Greek sense but rescuing in the ethical sense.

In the spiritual sense, dizziness can be twofold. It can be occasioned by a person's going so far astray in the infinite that nothing finite can have continuance for him, that he can find no criterion. This kind of dizziness is most likely due to an excess of imagination, and one could, insofar as one, if anything, metaphorically places dizziness in relation to the eye, perhaps call it *single-sighted dizziness*. The second kind of dizziness is occasioned by an abstract dialectic that, since it abstractly sees everything double, sees nothing at all. This kind of dizziness could be called *double-sighted dizziness*. Rescue from all dizziness in the spiritual sense is essentially to be sought in the ethical, which by a qualitative dialectic disciplines and sets limits, establishes the individual and the tasks.

Adler suffers particularly from the first kind of dizziness. As a dialectician he was shaped mainly by Hegel, whose system has no ethics,[105] and whose dialectic, far from being existential, is a kind of fantasy-view. From the dizzy heights of Hegelian metaphysics, Adler plunges headlong down into the religious and now discovers, if you please, orthodoxy, but, note well, outside the ethical. When this relation is abandoned, one may say that dizziness must necessarily set in.

As an example of Adler's dizziness,* *I will first cite* his doctrine of
the moment,[106] which he admittedly propounds nowhere but di-
gresses toward at every moment. Briefly, it goes like this: seize
the moment; it depends on the moment; in the next moment it
is too late, and then you will end up wandering your whole life
like the Wandering Jew. Throughout Adler's latest books there
runs a pagan desperate joy over having himself seized the moment, and a desperate anxiety merely at the thought—what if he
had not seized it? For Adler the moment is neither more nor less
than what luck was in paganism, except that he is the sort of
fellow who combines this dialectic with the essentially Christian,
so that then in a lucky moment he was called by a revelation from
the Savior and was entrusted with a doctrine. Thus the game of
chance has at its disposal not only, as in the past, wealth, honor,
power, the most beautiful girl, etc., but to receive a revelation is
also a game of chance.

"The moment," regarded as an issue, is undeniably a very
difficult task, since it has to deal with the dialectical relation between the temporal and the eternal.[107] The eternal is the infinite
value, and yet this is to be made commensurable with temporality, and the contact is—in the moment. Yet the moment is nothing. Thinking halts here at the most terrible contradiction, at the
most exhausting of all thoughts, which, if it is to be held fast for
long at the most extreme point of exhaustion, must lead the
thinker to madness. To erect a house of cards on a table is not
difficult, but to have to erect an enormous building (and the
eternal is indeed the infinite value) or in so doing to have to
understand that an enormous building can be erected on what is
smaller than the sharp corner of a card, upon a foundation that is
nothing (because the moment as such does not exist, is merely
the boundary between the past and the future, is when it has
been)—is certainly a terrible contradiction. If the imagination is
permitted to run wild, then paganism's teaching about luck and
fate emerges, or the unchristian doctrine of election by grace in

---

*What I here and immediately following must briefly explain belongs under
the issues that the pseudonyms have clarified in such a way that I can refer
people to them—but not to Adler, that would certainly be too late.

the desperate sense. To be saved by the desperate election by grace,[108] which dialectically is just like fate, is the most unblessed of all felicities. In a certain sense, the desperate election by grace posits the most dreadful split in humanity, and in another sense it makes the whole human race unblessed, because it is unblessed to be excluded and cast out, unblessed to be saved in this manner. To be saved, to be happy, and to know that all others are not and not able to be that, that one has not had and in all eternity will not have a condition in common with them, that one has no fundamental fellowship with them; to be saved and know that one has no word to shout to others, no highest and final comfort that is common to all—indeed, what human heart could bear this blessedness! If that verse in Scripture: "Call upon the Lord while he is near"[109] were to be understood with regard to the second, as if the Lord were a passing traveler who in the next second would be far away, if that verse were to be understood so enigmatically with regard to the second that no one knew or could know when the moment is—who then would dare to venture to preach about it, and how inconsiderate it is that it is preached on once each year (*anno redeunte* [recurring each year])! Nor is it to be understood with a nervous anxiety, and it cannot possibly be understood Christianly in the same way as the text about the sick people who lay beside the pool at Bethesda, that whoever came first was saved. The Gospel specifically reports that the sick man who for many years had continually come too late nevertheless was healed.[110] This is the Gospel, the good news that the cruelty of fate and the fortuity of luck and that wild play of forces are abolished, that first and foremost the salvation of the soul is offered to everyone, whether he is sound in body or not. Who would not have to despair if the soul's salvation were also a matter of coming first, if such were Christianity; and who would not have to be in a desperately dizzy state as a Christian to raise up paganism again!

VII²
B 235
165   What, then, can halt this dizziness, which actually results because a person stands still in fantasy and does not earnestly grasp any task for his life, and therefore he becomes like a galvanic frog that twitches for a moment? What can resist this dizziness; what can constrain that desperate overwrought state of the moment?

The ethical. When at every moment of one's life there is work and a task, when often enough there unfortunately is serious concern that one has not attended to one's work as one should— then there is not time to indulge in fantasy or to abandon oneself to fantastical speculation on the moment and on the dialectic that it is all and is nothing. The ethical and the religious that contains the ethical resist with all their might lest we be enveloped in the hopelessness of paganism—and where indeed does paganism show its hopelessness more than in its theory of luck! The ethical knows nothing and wants to know nothing about luck and despair and the differences, about someone's being a genius, about someone's receiving the lamp, about someone's coming first, about someone's winning in the lottery. Ethics is bored with all this anecdotal blather; it shrinks from the horrors of those times when fantasy haunted the childhood of the human race and played its baleful game of chance. Ethics will have to do only with the universal human tasks—and for that very reason has power over the luck of the moment, which is a horror. Even to the most desperate person, even to the one who forfeited the most, the ethical and the ethical-religious dare to shout: The moment is *still* there. The ethical cannot be fooled any more than God can be mocked;[111] it knows very well how, with qualitative dialectic, to make the moment valid as *decision*. But it will not worry a person to madness, nor madly make him happy with a game.

As an *example* of Adler's dizziness, *reference can be made also to his conception of Abraham*, to whom he often returns in verse and prose.[112] Here he warms up the old idea that it was an evil spirit, the devil, that suggested to Abraham the idea of sacrificing Isaac. Now with this explanation, as was shown in *Fear and Trembling*,[113] the only gain is that the difficulty comes again in a later place: how in that case one explains that the Church can think of making Abraham the father of faith and God's friend, since he himself must have discovered later that it was a temptation to which he yielded, which is why he must not be represented as the father of faith, but perhaps as the originator of repentance. But Adler is original. He assumes, as was said, that it was the devil who gave Abraham the idea, but see, God thought so well of this

VII²
B 235
166

idea, because it was bold and brave and great* (and suggested by the devil), that he prevents it from being carried out but makes Abraham his friend—and in this way Abraham becomes the father of faith.[114] Thus it has gone so far that not only do we human beings presumably not know exactly the difference between good and evil, that evil can become so impressive that we confuse its greatness with its goodness, but also so far that God himself sits and fools around with it. Then one flatters him just as one does a little miss of sixteen years who only wants the lover to do something great, indeed, she even falls head over heels in love with a robber chieftain.

But when one has no ethics, when one makes do with the quantitative dizziness of the esthetic and the disinterestedness of metaphysics, then one surely can arrive at such terrible results. And yet it is even more terrible that the one who understands Abraham in this way has had a revelation from *the Savior* and received a doctrine. For the sake of accuracy, one is almost compelled to ask Adler whether in relation to Christ it was not with him as it presumably was with Abraham in relation to our Lord, whether it was not an evil spirit (and it was indeed at the very time Adler had the revelation that he discovered that an evil spirit existed; see the preface to *Sermons*[115]) that prompted him to fictionize that he has had a revelation, and that Christ then found it so brave that he etc.

As an example of Adler's dizziness, *reference can finally be made to the recklessness with which he thinks that the great thing, the individual's spirited and bold idea, must have the right to assert itself even if a little wrong is done by it, even if some people also go to rack and ruin because of it.* In order to defend this view, he continually appeals to natural analogies, that the sun remains just as magnificent even when

*Note. If what Adler wanted to say was that the greatness of the worldly heroes, of those celebrated by the poets, is often a dubious *confinium* [border territory] between good and evil, that is another matter. But Abraham is indeed a religious hero; he is not worldly great, but great precisely because of purity and piety. Whether God could have forgiven Abraham for acting upon the devil's suggestion, whether God could have been pleased with Abraham's repentance, is again another matter. But to have God immediately fall for the great idea (from the devil) and for Abraham in this way, without having any repentance come between, is more or less blasphemy.

it also scorches some creatures[116] etc., very much *à la* Don Juan, who "also has philosophy" and in defense of his life also appeals to the sun: "Round about it (the sun) ladyloves die and are born, and it does not pay attention to the corpses of its sacrifices."[117] And of course D. Juan remains just as bold for all that, the sun just as magnificent, since magnificence, boldness, etc. are not exactly ethical qualifications. Anyone who has merely a very modest and bourgeois concept of the ethical knows very well that nature is a very mediocre analogy to the ethical, that wanting to live *à la* nature is precisely wanting to live unethically, also that by way of such analogies one finally arrives at the Neronic: to burn down Rome—but that was a proud and magnificent sight. Nature is indifferent to the distinction that to ethics is everything: the distinction between good and evil.

Ethical sobriety, which is the opposite of Adler's dizziness, consists essentially in this, that a person's striving reproduces itself exactly in the dialectic of the means.[118] Then the means that he uses, then the way in which he fights for his idea, then the slightest thing he allows himself in actualizing the idea are just as important to him, absolutely just as important, as what is being fought for and worked for. Think, for example, of the rigorousness of the orthodox Fathers of the Church, of Augustine's rigorous teaching about truth, that no one is allowed to save even one's chastity by an untruth,[119] and why not? Because untruth is more unchaste than a physical violation to which no concupiscence assents. One thinks of Pythagoras, praised by antiquity for his purity, the reduplicated consistency with which he followed his principle. But a Don Juan, a Napoleon, a Nero, in short, all impetuous individualities, they acclaim analogies to nature—and then Adler, to whom, however, a new doctrine is entrusted by a revelation from the Savior—a new doctrine perhaps—and yet it is not that either—but from the Savior!

In the four latest books, then, Adler is a confused genius, and the *summa summarum* of what he says first and last is that he is to be regarded as confused. Having in the main established this conception of him, as has now been done by showing the amazing misrelation between the first statement (being called by a revelation and having received a doctrine from the Savior) and the last

VII²
B 235
168

(being a genius of sorts), also that this seems to have escaped
Adler altogether—one can, in order to illustrate his confused
state further, take a look at the externals of the books, which no
doubt will be sufficient for most people to make a judgment of
Adler. It cannot be denied that one feels very strangely uncom-
fortable in looking through his four latest books a little. To an
extraordinary degree he has emancipated himself from every re-
striction as an author, from every requirement for order, from
every consideration for the reader. It is difficult to assume that
this is supposed to be art, a maieutic tactic. I have, however,
assured the denial of this by showing the total confusion in the
essentials.

Adler not infrequently treats the reader like a child to whom
one assigns a lesson. For example, he prints the identical scripture
passage, which is six lines long, in its entirety three times on two
pages.[120] Now, it certainly cannot be denied that every Scripture
passage has the excellent quality of always deserving to be read—
which is why everyone surely ought to own a Bible and read it
again and again. But to fill a big book by having the same Scripture passage printed so often in such a small space is still somewhat strange. He sometimes treats the reader just like a child in
another manner also. It is well known that as an assignment in
composition in the mother tongue one sometimes uses disconnected single words from which the pupil is to form a coherent
statement. In the same way Adler throws out very abrupt, at
times meaningless little clauses,[121] perhaps to give the reader an
opportunity to practice producing and working out a coherent
statement. In other places he seems to go on as if the reader did
not exist at all, that is, as if what he wrote were not intended to
be printed but from time to time was jotted down in a notebook
and was printed by mistake.

But of course I wish to be brief about all such things. It is of
very little concern to me to deal esthetically with his books; my
only essential concern is his revelation-fact and his relation to
that. I shall, however, make one more comment that belongs
here, one that in my opinion characterizes Adler essentially. In
reading his four latest books, one gets a suspicion and an idea (and

it is impossible to escape this impression) that Adler really does not think but instead must have the habit of putting himself into an excited mood. He seizes upon a very simple expression, a brief saying; he then unthinkingly disconnects it; he connects it, again unthinkingly, with something else but continues to repeat it[122] until this monotonous repetition anesthetizes him and brings him into an excited state, so to him it seems as if there must be something profound in it. But what it is concerns him very little; his only concern is to enter into this excited state. One cannot help imagining Adler pacing back and forth and continually repeating the same simple clause, perhaps aiding the fantastic effect by changing his voice and gesticulating until he has hexed himself into a kind of intoxication, so he senses a strange, solemn buzzing in his ears. But this is not thinking.

VII²
B 235
170

If a man wanted to put himself in a ceremonial mood and then paces back and forth and continually says: 7—14—21, 7—14—21, 7—14—21, this monotonous repetition would act like a magic formula, act like a strong drink on a neurotic person; to him it would seem that he had come in contact with something extraordinary. Then if someone else to whom he communicated his wisdom were to say to him: But what is this 7—14—21 all about, he would no doubt answer: It depends upon what voice you say it in, and you must keep on saying it for a whole hour, and in addition you must gesticulate—then you will surely discover that there is something.

If someone wrote on small slips of paper short sentences such as: "He left the castle"; "He drew the knife"; "I may have dislocated my hip"[123]—if he then hid all these slips in a drawer and then sometime later, perhaps during solemn rituals, would go and open the drawer, take out a single slip one at a time, and uninterruptedly repeat what was written on it, he would finally get into a fantastical state and it would seem to him that there was something extraordinarily profound in it. In other words, through chance and through the play of chance combinations that it encourages, the abrupt has something tempting for the imagination. Who has not experienced this! When in rummaging around in old papers one perhaps finds short statements such

as these, the whole context of which has been forgotten, there is
something enjoyable about it, a moment of abandonment to this
play of the imagination. Then when that is over, one burns the
papers. Adler does it differently; he publishes them. And probably he can also get a reader to devote himself to this game so that
he, too, can amuse himself with it for a moment. But in this way

VII²
B 235
171

one becomes an author in only a very improper sense. Instead of
wishing and asking the reader to keep his mind quiet in order to
reflect on the thought that is communicated, as an author usually
does, Adler would rather recommend that his reader put himself
into ecstasy, since the more tense one can be the more whimsi-
cally the abrupt works. In a way it would be quite consistent if
Adler, by analogy with magicians and conjurers, recommended
and prescribed certain rituals, that at the stroke of twelve at night
one should get up, then walk around the room three times, then
take the book and open it (just as the simple folk do to find their
fortunes in the Bible), then read the single passage, first in a soft
voice, and then let the voice rise to its peak, and then again
downward (just like Per Degn with sol-mi[124]) until the voice
becomes quite soft, then walk around the room seven times in a
figure eight, and then see if there is not something in the passage.
The fantastical effect of the abrupt is essentially supported by
mime and pantomime; on the other hand, it is disturbed by the
composure and coherence of thinking. And yet there is hidden,
as it were, a rich depth of unfathomable profundity in the abrupt,
whereas a clear, coherent, carefully prepared lecture is quite simply just what it is. In magic and conjuring formulas, the effect is
due to the mysteriousness of the abrupt, the mysteriousness of
the meaningless, and is aided by the mime and the pantomime—
the witch comes riding on a broomstick, dances three times
around, etc. If someone could get a lot of people to believe that
he possessed a secret wisdom, and he then wrote abrupt sentences on small slips of paper; if in addition he rented all the
scenery used at the lottery drawing, the big awning, the wheel of
fortune, a company of soldiers, a government official to whom
arms would be presented as he stepped out on the balcony—then
when he, to soft festive music blended with some rolling surges,

VII²
B 235
172

made the wheel turn and the festively decked-out boy drew a

ticket and the contents were read aloud—at least a few women would faint on the occasion.

What is said here about Adler's desire to bring himself into a state of excitement contains no exaggeration at all, because I am by no means tempted to exaggeration in regard to Adler. It is not said that his books betray something of this kind all the way through, but there are enough passages that do. In my opinion, just as it would be indefensible if someone wrote something like this last and then nothing more about Adler, it would, it seems to me, also be equally indefensible if a truthful perception of his confusion did not find its place in a more extensive examination of him.

But, as stated, his books do not concern me directly; my examination essentially deals only with that revelation-fact of his, and with how he himself understands himself in this, that such a thing has happened to him, or with his not understanding himself in it. His books are used for only one definite purpose. If I were to deal with them purely esthetically and directly, I would give myself the pleasure of acknowledging, as officially as possible, what my judgment is, that one can really learn something from them or, to express myself very precisely, that I really have learned something from them. To be sure, usually a reviewer thinks in a superior way that although he cannot learn anything from the author he can still recommend the books to the public, since the public is not as eminently wise as the reviewer and therefore can certainly learn something. But such is not the case here. People in general will unquestionably, indeed, unconditionally, only be able to be harmed by reading Adler's books, because he confuses totally. But the person who has what he lacks, dialectical clarity about the spheres and the totality, he and only he will truly be able to learn something from the particular brilliant, lively, upbuilding, stirring, and at times profound expressions. He and only he, self-assured, without losing more than he gains, will have pleasure from what Adler at times succeeds in doing purely stylistically, even though as a stylist he has no original merit at all. Strangely enough, it is a more common opinion that it is easier to read aphorisms than coherent writing. But this is not at all the case, because in order to benefit from aphorisms

VII²
B 235
173

a person must himself energetically possess a coherent view in which he understands himself. It is this that Adler lacks; he does not understand himself when the requirement is made according to a recognized criterion. In this regard I cannot bargain. Just as I believe that I cannot be accused of enviously clipping the coin with which I as reviewer pay the sacred tribute of admiration to the extraordinary ones, neither will I inversely bargain, but I will admit with pleasure that, measured by another, a slack requirement, he looks a good deal better, and also that, evaluated by a reviewer who is just as good a dialectician as he himself is, he will of course come off with flying colors.—*Pap.* VII^2 B 235, pp. 127–36, 150–73 *n.d.*, 1846–47

Note deleted in version III; see 87:18, 286:21:

It is really sad to see that Adler, instead of attending to his own affairs (having had a revelation, having received a revealed doctrine, together with what follows from that), engages in copying the pseudonymous writers, who are as diametrically opposite to him as possible. I have also noted that A. continually enjoins that theft in the world of the mind is entirely permissible, or, as he says somewhere in the big book,[125] in the world of the mind it should be as at a fire, where one takes another's clothes, which of course would be acceptable only if it is permissible to assume that there is always fire in the world of the mind. Let everyone have his opinion on that; I, however, certainly have a different opinion, that theft in the world of the mind is not only not permissible, but actually impossible, and that therefore it is a necessity that the thief comes to grief. Be that as it may, but if it can be done in any way at all, then the person involved must not denote his beginning so qualitatively as by having had a revelation. Suppose stealing could be done, suppose A. was conscious of having pilfered a little—it is not easy to imagine a more sorrowful and terrible confusion than that of the one who has had a revelation and has a revealed doctrine and engages in pilfering a little from others, engages in literary petty larceny.—*Pap.* VIII^2 B 9:10b, *n.d.*, 1847

From version I, replaced in version III by Pap. VIII² B 9:11 (*version II, Pap.* VIII² B 7:11); *see 88–90:*

Appendix to Chapter III

Recapitulation

The reader will recall that continually throughout this whole book the argument is only *e concessis*. It is nowhere directly denied that Adler has had a revelation; on the contrary, it is assumed, since he himself says it, but in this way he is aided in trapping himself in a self-contradiction.

1. In order to illustrate the presence of confusion, Adler's replies to the ecclesiastical authority's questions are utilized. The dilemma may be stated here as follows: *either* all his separate replies are nonsense, *or* in themselves they contain essentially the revocation of his first statement (that he has had a revelation and has received from the Savior a new doctrine). If the latter is assumed (that the revocation is in his replies), then the confusion is this, that he is not in earnest about the revocation but acts as if nothing has happened or himself notices nothing, lets the replies have meaning and reality, which they have only insofar as they are the revocation of the first statement.

The argumentation within the dilemma was this. In the replies Adler identifies himself in such a way with what was printed first (the preface to *Sermons, Sermons, Studies*) that in the common and ordinary sense he must be regarded as the author of them—but if he is the author in this way, then he has indeed had no revelation, then Christ has indeed not dictated anything to him, then he has not been only an instrument. —Adler authentically acknowledges that he does not have anything new; on the contrary, like every ordinary Christian he keeps to Scripture, proclaims Jesus, appeals to the words of Scripture as proof texts for what he says—but in that case the first statement about the revelation etc. is essentially revoked. —Adler hopes that later he will be able to present the doctrine (what was revealed and dictated by the Savior) better; consequently he hopes for the perfectibility of the doctrine. But this hope is altogether meaningless, yes, blasphemous, if that doctrine is not Adler's own; and if it is his own,

VII²
B 235
174

then of course he has had no revelation by which the doctrine was communicated to him by the Savior.

2. Next, in order to illustrate the confusion and the glaring self-contradiction in Adler (for the contradiction is certainly glaring and the confusion precisely this, that Adler acts as if nothing had happened), consideration was given to his four latest books. Instead of what one would be justified in expecting if Adler did not continue to be in a confused state, instead of the fruit of composure—*either* information about how he understood himself in the extraordinary that had happened to him *or* revocation—one finds that he has now settled down to rest in the view that he is a genius. This can readily be granted to him, especially here, where we have nothing whatever to do with such things. But as soon as his four latest books are put together, in the sense of earnestness, with his first statement (the revelation and the revealed doctrine), the dilemma appears: **either** the four latest books (even if their incidental content is ever so excellent), *considered totally and as books by Adler*, are to be regarded as nonsense, **or** there is also contained in them essentially the revocation of his entire first statement. If the latter is assumed, then the confusion consists in this, that Adler acts as if nothing had happened and is not in earnest about the revocation. The metamorphosis from apostle to becoming a genius is so decisive, so qualitative, and in addition so reversed that least of all in the world can it be ignored or treated as if it were nothing. In civil matters, on the whole in the world of the finite, it can very well happen that a man begins all over again even more than once and without any fuss lets the past be forgotten, that a man changes his profession, tries his luck in a new career, and without any fuss lets the past be something bygone and forgotten. But if a man thinks that this can be done also in the world of the spirit, this opinion is enough to demonstrate that he is confused; and anyone who lives that way is actually confused. In the world of the finite, the randomness of the changes may be all right, it may be true as the proverb says: *variatio delectat* [change pleases], but in the world of the spirit continuity is not only joy but is spirit itself—that is, continuity is spirit, and not to respect continuity qualitatively is to have one's life outside the sphere of the spirit, either in the

VII²
B 235
175

sphere of worldliness or in the sphere of confusion. Continuity is not sameness, in continuity there is also change, but the continuity is that every change is made dialectically in relation to the preceding. When the change is qualitative (as from apostle to genius), then continuity's final expression is the revocation of the first, which in turn, insofar as one has communicated the first, is required to be communicated officially. In the world of the spirit, fabulousness is confusion, and equally so the absentmindedness that does not notice that the change is qualitative. To the same degree to which one has ventured further out, even to claiming to have had a revelation, to the same degree the fabulousness or absentmindedness is more dubious.

In Adler, however, the confusion becomes still greater because in his new position in life as a private lyrical genius he— ingenious, exegeting, paraphrasing, etc.—continues to relate himself to that doctrine (communicated to him, according to his first statement, by a revelation from the Savior). His absent- mindedness and confusion are made only more clearly manifest by his having completely forgotten that this doctrine has been communicated to him by a revelation from the Savior.

VII²
B 235
176

If, then, in the future there is to be earnestness and meaning in Adler's life as an author, he must *either* revoke his first statement and be content with what he is in his four latest books, if these are considered without relation to his first statement, *or* he must cancel his latest as a defection from his idea and his call, solemnly acknowledge, something he by his explanatory bungling has confused, that he has had a revelation and has received from the Savior a new doctrine, and then act, speak, and write by virtue of that (not in the role of a private lyrical genius). If, however, he, acting as if nothing has happened, continues to leave both parts in abeyance, he demonstrates thereby that he is in a confused state of mind.

In a confused state of mind. By this it is in no way to be understood that he is what is called insane, something that only an impudent busybody in life can think. No, by this it is to be understood that he, lacking education in Christian concepts, lacking moral respect for qualitative definitions of concepts, is to such a degree not master of himself and his thoughts that he, through confusion in his thinking, can even *bona fide* [in good faith] utter blasphemies.—*Pap.* VIII² B 9:11 *n.d.*, 1847

Sketch of chapter IV, version I; see 91–132.

Chapter IV.

A Psychological View of Adler as a Phenomenon and as a Satire on Hegelian Philosophy and Our Age.—*Pap.* VII² B 265:1

A theological graduate (with ordinary personal qualifications), without Christianity, a Hegelian, becomes a pastor. —The collisions. (only preaching, confessing the dying—and himself not a Christian)—*Pap.* VII² B 265:2

The explosion.
the striking step of burning the manuscripts.
the frequent disappointment in such striking steps.
—*Pap.* VII² B 265:3

The good in A. is *inwardness*
(to be developed)—all must be traced to this
even the good in his style.
—*Pap.* VII² B 265:4

The dubiousness in A.
is *in toto* a basic misrelation between his inwardness
and his religious knowledge and intellectual
cultivation. —If he had been a layman,
it certainly would have gone better.—*Pap.* VII² B 265:5

1. that he confuses his subjective change—with having had a revelation. The kind of illusion to be found frequently—for example, in the erotic area. (the truth in: that everyone who actually falls in love can be said to discover erotic love.) (something different with the concept: a revelation).

Here Hegelianism has helped him into this mistake. Hegel explains a revelation as immediacy. Hegelianism tends toward what Feuerbach has expressed: to make theology into anthropology.[126]—*Pap.* VII^2 B 265:6

The concept "revelation" has essentially an objective meaning, cannot be used subjectively about originality in the individual, newness in him, primitivity.—*Pap.* VII^2 B 265:7

2. when he is to defend himself on the occasion of the ecclesiastical authority's question, he resorts to Hegelianism and its volatilizations. (the epigrammatic in this—on Hegel and on Adler).—*Pap.* VII^2 B 265:8

3. Now he obviously needs quiet. But instead reflection plays a trick on him, so that yet again he becomes productive in the wrong place. —here lie the four latest books—he has not become quiet, but becomes productive about: not yet having become quiet.—*Pap.* VII^2 B 265:9

Hegelian philosophy has helped him into this confusion too (see a slip of paper marked C [304 (*Pap.* VII^2 B 266:28)]). The satirical on Hegelian philosophy, which shows up superbly in a situation like this, and on A.—*Pap.* VII^2 B 265:10

He is an epigram on present-day Christendom
    that he became a pastor when he was a pagan
    and was dismissed when he had come closer
    to becoming a Christian.—*Pap.* VII^2 B 265:11

He gives the impression of a pagan who has become a Christian and therefore does not explain the issue of our age: to become Christian when one is that. —One would not think that A. had been brought up in Christianity. —The sad insight such an

VII²
B 265
302

event gives into what is commonly understood by being brought up in Christianity, by having had a Christian upbringing. —How in antiquity upbringing was referred to as a decisive factor in a person's life; nowadays upbringing is thought to be nothing.

—*Pap.* VII² B 265:1–12 *n.d.*, 1846–47

From draft of version I; see 117:5–18:

His first statement about himself, that he has had a revelation, may be explained by this misrelation, and all his later [writings] only throw more light on this, that is, since they show that he— after it has been made obvious that by his "reply" he has only a very slipshod idea of what a revelation is, and least of all the Christian concept (from which it in turn follows that he cannot possibly understand himself in having had a revelation)— consigns the revelation to oblivion and in the role of a lyrical genius begins a new productivity about everything else possible.

—*Pap.* VII² B 268 *n.d.*, 1846–47

From draft of version I; see 129:31–130:56:

But to view it as an element is not by any means to get out of it, and on the contrary he must first get out of it before there can be talk of viewing it as an element. On the whole, the ethical turns everything around and says: The main thing is to act, to strive, to get out of a wrong condition; at best there can be conceded *nebenbei* [alongside]: a little half-hour to view the particular preceding as an element in his life. Adler is ensnared in self-reflection, but in addition he is so far from having something else that can help him out of it that inside he has precisely the Hegelian reminiscences that must strengthen him in the idea that this is even profundity and the highest wisdom.

On the whole it is incredible what confusion Hegelian philosophy has brought about in personal life—the lamentable result of a philosopher's being publicly a hero and privately a philistine and a pedant.

Some astonishing examples are found among the philosophers after Hegel who have appropriated the Hegelian method. Such a philosopher writes a new book, and he becomes conscious of it as an element within the striving forward that began with his first book. But that is not enough; he becomes conscious of his whole striving (which does not yet exist) as an element in the whole philosophical striving after Hegel, and that in turn as an element in Hegel, and Hegel as an element in the world-historical process from antiquity through China, Persia, Greece, Judaism, Christianity, the Middle Ages.

But this baleful desire to view as an element has become a fixed idea whereby people become self-important, at times even in such a way that in new confusion they exclude future elements. The view of ethics: to strive, to be in the future—and of metaphysics: to view everything as an element—battle with each other in a life-and-death struggle. Every living person, if he is not utterly thoughtless and absentminded, must choose decisively; but if he chooses the metaphysical, then spiritually understood he commits suicide.—*Pap.* VII² B 266:28 *n.d., 1846–47*

From draft of version I; see 132:4–7:

But a traveling scholar in almost the confused sense, a lyrically excited dithyrambic—well, in a way he may be right about having broken with Hegel, but when he then proceeds to get himself wedged fast in reflection and then in addition wants to become fully conscious that his present state is an element in his life's development—then he really gets Hegelian philosophy into hot water, by which it is not served at all.—*Pap.* VII² B 266:29 *n.d., 1846–47*

Heading and text of chapter IV, section 5, in version III replaced in version IV by Pap. X⁶ B 55; see 132:8–133:19:

5.

VII²
B 235
218

[127]**Magister Adler as an Epigram on the Christendom of the Present Age**

How Magister Adler indirectly satirizes Hegelian philosophy (in that he strikingly breaks with it but still unconsciously connives with it, and then by way of the muddled state of his life places Hegelian philosophy in situations where it is bound to manifest itself as self-contradictory as it is) has been pointed out several times; that he can serve also as an epigram on Christendom of the present age will in conclusion be indicated and utilized.

Magister Adler was of course born, brought up, and confirmed, a native of geographical Christendom—consequently he was a Christian (just as all are Christians of sorts). He became a theological graduate—and was a Christian (just as all are Christians). He becomes a Christian pastor, and only now he has the singular experience that through a life-impression he comes into a more earnest contact with the decision: to become a Christian. Just when he, by being religiously shaken, undeniably has come closer to becoming a Christian than ever in all the time he was a Christian, precisely then he is dismissed. And his dismissal is entirely legitimate, because now the state Church first has the opportunity to become aware of the nature of his Christianity. [128]But the epigrammatic aspect still remains: that he as a pagan becomes a Christian pastor, and that he, when he had come somewhat closer to becoming a Christian, is dismissed.

By a single event such as this, one undeniably has an opportunity to get a glimpse into what this must mean that we all are Christian of sorts. One begins to suspect whether these many Christians in geographical Christendom are not an illusion. This certainly is not said to pass judgment—may all such external busyness be far from me. Whether the individual on his own might not be able to learn something about himself from this whole event with Magister Adler is another matter. To be sure, this is my opinion, and while I am dubious about whether Magister Adler can in the stricter sense actually be called a Christianly awakened person, it appears to me that his life's crisis must be able to have something awakening for everyone, whatever the outcome amounts to otherwise. [129]That is, if Magister Adler is not an awakened person, if he is not called by an awakening to be a teacher who can help the age, then his life's event can still be a memento for geographical Christendom.

Perhaps this is not the case; I know nothing and want to know nothing; but let us imagine that many just go on living as Chris-

VII²
B 235
219

tians and actually are pagans, inasmuch as existence, the surrounding world, has transformed itself into a huge illusion that again and again and in every way strengthens them in the notion that they are Christians. Let us imagine these many people later in life, each one as the founder . . . .—*Pap.* VII² B 235, pp. 218–19 *n.d.*, 1846–47

On folder with manuscript of "A Cycle," *No. VI:*

The last part of that on Adler can become a separate little essay:

Adler's name is to be suppressed. . . .
—*Pap.* X⁶ B 56 *n.d.*, 1849

What I have written about Adler[130] perhaps could be published separately under the title: "A Literary Review," and the longer preface[131] to "A Cycle of Ethical-Religious Essays" could be used here.—*JP* VI 6334 (*Pap.* X¹ A 90) *n.d.*, 1849

From draft of version I; see 133:12:

Yet it is undeniable that whereas at one time in the world to become a Christian was a decision from which most people shrank back, nowadays to be a Christian of sorts is like an enchantment, in which one is strengthened in so many ways that a special kind of awakening that can tear one out of illusions may very well be needed, if one is ensnared in them, and show one that a person can even become a Christian pastor although he is ensnared in a delusion about being Christian and is essentially only a pagan.

Deleted in margin: Thus Adler's significance for the contemporary age consists not so much in the crisis or what he can have become through the crisis as in what he through the crisis indirectly makes manifest and indicates: how in geographical Christendom one can be a Christian of sorts and even become a Christian pastor without having the least impression of Christianity.
—*Pap.* VII² B 266:30 *n.d.*, 1846–47

From draft of version I; see 141:33–142:6:

In every Christian country where Christianity has so perme-
ated all relations in such a way that everyone as a matter of course
(that is, without the decision of inwardness) is a Christian, the
main point first and last is to pose the issue: to become Christian,
and this issue is not to be confused with theological disputations.
On this matter, however, I can refer to Johannes Climacus's
Concluding Postscript.—*Pap.* VII² B 266:34 *n.d.*, 1846–47

From draft of version II; see 142:38:

Addendum.

Mag. Adler's four latest books, a literary
monstrosity, which undoubtedly must be explained as
the result of a fixed idea.

Presented
by
S. Kierkegaard.

This presentation is, of course, purely esthetic, since it deals only
with Adler's four latest books as an isolated performance in
which there is no discussion of having had a revelation. The presentation therefore ventures also to indulge in the comic. . . .
—*Pap.* VIII² B 7:18 *n.d.*, 1847

VII¹
A 150
97

From the Book on Adler.

. . . . . There are examples in Adler of a style in an uncon-
trolled form no doubt familiar (esthetically and artistically) to
Frater Taciturnus, since he, himself using a completely different
style, has Quidam of the imaginary construction[132] express himself in this stylistic form. To construct rhetorically upon a condi-
tional clause and then have the main clause amount to nothing,
an abyss from which the reader once again shrinks back, as it
were, to the antecedents; to plunge into a tentative effort as if
this wealth were inexhaustable and then the very same second

discontinue it, which is like the trick of pulling up short at full gallop (most riders fall off—usually one first breaks into a gallop and then into a trot); to be at the head of a cavalry of predicates, the one more gallant and dashing than the other, to charge in, and then swerve; the leap in modulation; the turning to the concept in one single word; the unexpected stop etc. Just as the voice of all passionate peoples, all southern peoples (the Jews, for example) continually breaks, just as every passionate person talks in this manner, so is it also possible to produce this effect stylistically.

But this would take me much too far afield, and how many are there, after all, who have any intimation of how prose can be used lyrically—and of the task I am committed to, to produce in prose a stronger lyrical effect than in verse—if people would only learn how to read and to insist on thought in every word, whereas verse always has a little padding. So I cut this short; it would concern only authors anyway. In this respect, all of the pseudonyms have an unqualified linguistic value in having cultivated prose lyrically. It is clear that Adler, too, has learned something from them, but what his flattering reviewer says in the *Kirketidende*,[133] that he began just about the same time as the pseudonyms,[134] is not true, for he began after them, and the style of his four latest works is markedly different from that of his sermons, where he had not as yet been so strongly influenced. On the other hand, what his reviewer says about the presence of passages in Adler (four latest books) thoroughly reminiscent of the pseudonyms[135] is true, but I see nothing meritorious in that, neither in copying another nor in forgetting that by having had a revelation of one's own one has entirely different things to think about than language exercises.—*JP* V 5939 (*Pap.* VII[1] A 150) *n.d.*, 1846

Deleted in version III of Addendum I; see 149:13:

Magister Adler certainly is not to be accused of cunning; assuredly his entry into the service of the state Church was utterly without guile. It is something entirely different, which is seen to

VII[1]
A 150
98

VII[2]
B 235
39

be evident from the crisis; he has not somewhat light-mindedly chosen to become a pastor, perhaps did so only in consideration of and reliance upon having passed the theological examination. This will be elucidated later, since in this regard Adler as a phenomenon manifests how complicated everything has become because Christendom has become a title; thus in a *Christian* country, where *all are Christians*, it can happen that one can even become a theological graduate, indeed, become a Christian pastor—without ever having come in contact with the self-examining question whether one is oneself a Christian, inasmuch as the latter is self-evident, just as it is self-evident that one is a human being.

Then he was pastor—and only now occurred the event that was bound to place him as the special individual *extra ordinem* [outside the order]. The collision is there, for it is easy to see that Adler was so situated, and only for the sake of more clarity will I very briefly indicate—*Pap.* VIII² B 9:14d–e *n.d.,* 1847

VII²
B 235
40

What holds true of the apostles, who were very simple men of the poorest class (since in this very way their *authority* was all the more strongly accentuated; they were nothing at all in themselves, not geniuses, not councilmen or state governors, but fishermen—therefore all of their *authority* was from God), holds true also of the poor Greek of the New Testament. Earlier, Socrates had considered it improper to use the brilliant speech prepared by a young man for his defense, because he, as he said, had grown too old for childish things.[136] How much more unsuitable for God to employ elegant Greek!—*JP* I 182 (*Pap.* VIII¹ A 225) *n.d.,* 1847

Authority does not mean to be a king or to be an emperor or general, to have the power of arms, to be a bishop, or to be a policeman,* but it means by a firm and conscious resolution to be willing to sacrifice everything, one's life, for one's cause; it means to articulate a cause in such a way that a person has made up his mind about needing nothing and fearing nothing. This recklessness of infinity is authority.** True authority is present when the truth is the cause. The reason the Pharisees spoke without authority, although they were indeed authorized teachers, was precisely that their talk, like their lives, was in the finite power of seventeen concerns.

In margin: *that is, it is the concept of authority in immanence, not the paradoxical concept: authority.

In margin: **the one with authority, therefore, always appeals to the conscience, not to the understanding, intelligence, profundity—to the human being, not to the professor.—*JP* I 183 (*Pap*. VIII^1 A 416) *n.d.*, 1847

From version I (Pap. VII^2 B 235, p. 144); see 180:30:

Note. One or another reader perhaps recalls that I have always used this expression about myself *qua* author, that I am *without authority*, and have used it so emphatically that it *has been repeated as a formula in every preface*. Even though as an author I have had no benefit, I have at least done everything finitely possible not to confuse the highest and the holiest. I am a poor individual human being. If I am, as some think, a bit of a genius, about that I would say: Let it go hang. But an apostle is in all eternity qualitatively just as different from me as from the greatest genius who has ever lived and from the most obtuse person who has ever lived.—*Pap*. VII^2 B 235, p. 144 *n.d.*, 1846–47

From version III; see 180:30:

[137]*Note*. But perhaps some reader recalls that Magister Kierkegaard has [*changed later to:* I have] always used the expression about himself [myself] *qua* author that he is [I am] *without authority* and used it so emphatically that it *is repeated as a formula in every preface*.[138] Authority is a specific quality either of an apostolic calling or of ordination. To preach is precisely to use authority, and that this is what it is to preach has simply been altogether forgotten in our day when, to be sure, every theological graduate knows, even in a didactic review, how to instruct Magister

Kierkegaard [me], since he [I], O fortunate age, is [am] the only theological graduate who is not informed with regard to what obviously has occupied him [me] from his [my] *Two Upbuilding Discourses* (1843) up to the present moment.—*Pap.* VIII² B 9:17 *n. d.*, 1847

A book could be written
Clues to Illuminate the Modern Religious Confusion
in
Aphorisms
Perhaps this form (glimpses) would be most illuminating; a rigorous development of certain concepts that the age has completely forgotten might be nourishing for the sickness: didacticism. In any case, I may do it myself sometime, or perhaps my successor.

Then what is found in these journals would be used. Concerning *authority*, the relationship between God and man, the mission in present-day Christendom, etc.—*JP* V 6081 (*Pap.* VIII¹ A 445) *n.d.*, 1847

Instructions

First of all, publish a book of essays. For this the book on Adler can be used as I arranged it formerly. And then a new one will be added: How Was It Possible That Jesus Christ Could Be Deprived of His Life.* This essay must come out, as well as the two about the collision between the universal and the single individual and about the relation between a genius and an apostle, before I begin on the doctrine of sin.[139] —*JP* V 6114 (*Pap.* VIII¹ A 562) *n.d.*, 1848

In margin of Pap. VIII¹ A 562:

N.B. *If this essay is to be pseudonymous, I must add it as an addendum; then the title will be "Essays" by S. K., with an addendum.—*JP* V 6115 *(Pap.* VIII¹ A 563) *n.d.,* 1848

It was really fortunate that I finally did publish that little arti-cle,[140] thereby remaining true to myself to the last, so that my life may not become a detriment rather than a benefit.

If I had died without doing it, I am convinced that in the horrible irresponsible confusing of concepts in our day some would have stepped forward and gabbled something about my being an apostle. Good God, instead of being of benefit for hold-ing the essentially Christian in a position of honor, I would have ruined it. What a charming kinship for the apostle: that a person like me was also an apostle. What a charming fruit of my life to help establish the masterful category: also a kind of apostle and the like.

From the very beginning I have kept an Argus eye on that confusion, that horrible confusion. In such a chatty age as ours, which flirts with everything—if it merely spots someone some-what different from the clergy—oh, then the creation of confu-sion lies so close at hand. Did not Magister Adler aspire to this? I have worked against this with fear and trembling. To that end my continual use of the phrase: without authority; to that end the essay on the difference between a genius and an apostle.[141] But all that still would not have helped—but now an article about an actress. . . .—*JP* VI 6220 (*Pap*. IX A 189) *n.d.*, 1848

It is curious that today in Arndt's *True Christianity*[142] I read a line that is just like my description of the confusion of our age, but the author probably did not mean the same by it as I. It reads (p. 225): *Wenn anders das Haupt und nicht die Füsse im Lande regieren* [If otherwise the head and not the feet rule the land]. It reminds me very much of the postscript[143] to the second essay[144] in "A Cycle of Ethical-Religious Essays."—*JP* VI 6264 (*Pap*. IX A 338) *n.d.*, 1848

From draft of "A Cycle of Ethical-Religious Essays":

No. I.[145]

Something on What Might Be Called
"Premise-Authors." . . .

[*No. II.*[146]

*The Dialectical Relations: the Universal,
the Single Individual, the Special Individual.*]
Addendum I [*changed to:* No. II.] . . .

[*No. III.*

*Does a Human Being Have the Right to Let Himself
Be Put to Death for the Truth?*] . . .

[*No. IV.*[147]

A Revelation in the Situation of the Present Age.] . . .

No. V.[148]

A Psychological Interpretation of Magister Adler as a
Phenomenon and as a Satire upon Hegelian Philosophy
and the Present Age. . . .

[*No. VI.*[149]

The Difference between a Genius and an Apostle. . . . .

Addendum II, changed to:] No. VI. . . . .
—*Pap.* IX B 1–6 *n.d.*, 1848

Deleted addition in draft of version IV; see 156:31:

IX
B 8
306

Note. And now in 1848 we have gotten enough of the new, but when all is said and done perhaps precisely this is the new that this new age has brought—that it needs the old as no earlier age ever did, and this is undeniably something new indeed!—that it needs, and this is undeniably true, needs as no other age ever did, "those basically honest men who with godly resignation under-

IX
B 8
307

stood it as a task: not to invent anything new but with life and soul to be faithful in the established order." This holds true with regard to the religious and holds true also—something I other- wise regard as no concern of mine—with regard to the political.

Now in 1848 it has been made radically obvious, something that the few who could see and assess also saw, that the error of the previous age was truly not that the government misused power, but exactly the opposite, that it did not dare to use its power; in short, the error was that there was no governing. Now it is certainly obvious that what, politically understood, is needed, what is necessary, is contained in one simple word: government. [*Deleted:* Thus if—to speak in biblical terms—if the government were now to send judges, they would have to have orders opposite to what the judges had in the past; their orders and instructions would have to be to this effect: With all power to assist the government so that, if possible, there could be governing. Already just prior to 1848, there was a reformer with a polemical aim at the king, the government, etc.—in my opinion, something ludicrous. But now it has certainly become as evident as possible that a true reformer, comparable to earlier true reformers, must take the opposite position. Precisely for that reason, just before 1848 it became so cheap to be such a reformer, because, by being at the head of the "crowd" the "reformers" possessed the power and—yes, it is the most ludicrous thing one can imagine—*reformingly* attacked the weaker (the government), and—reformingly attacked the best there was, and reformingly with the aid of—the "crowd," which became regarded as the good and the true.

October 1848
—*Pap.* IX B 8 October 1848

From draft of "A Cycle"; *see 188:37:*

Not to be used.
[*In margin:* For essay No. II.[150]]
Postscript for one who has read the essay
October 1848

IX
B 24
321

This essay, as stated in the preface [*changed from:* like the whole collection], was written before, some of it long before, the events that have now changed the shape of Europe.[151] If with regard to the past it was possible to say justifiably that there was a lack of

IX
B 24
322

action everywhere, it seems now, however, as if action enough has been taken. But it only seems so. Anyone who has a mature idea of what it is to act will easily see on closer inspection that all over Europe there has been what amounts to no action at all, that everything that has happened disintegrates into events, incidents, or insofar as something does occur, into something enormous, but without any acting personality who knows definitely beforehand what he wants, so that afterward he is able to say definitely whether what he wanted has occurred or not.

In France, for example; a republic like that really has no place in history, and unconditionally not under the rubric "action"; it finds its place better in an advertising paper under "Lost and Found." The same in the rest of Europe. Everything everywhere is an event, in many places an aping that even regarded as aping is not action, because again it is not an individual who apes something foreign and now in his own country is acting—no, the aping quite correctly consists in a kind of commotion that arises, God knows how—and then something happens. But there is no one steering, no one acting, no one who could truthfully say: I wanted this and that, and now what I wanted has occurred or it has not occurred.

Therefore the change or the incursion of the new must, once it has commenced, begin with an untruth; people must take a few days to fool one another into thinking that what occurred is what they wanted. Just as it is somewhat awkward for the particular individual to become something "one fine morning," God knows how, and thus he must see to assisting himself with various untruths, that what he has now become he has wanted from his earliest childhood etc. etc.; just as for the one who in an overexcited moment at a ball becomes engaged to a girl he does not know at all, scarcely knows who she is, it becomes a need and a temptation, out of shame, to begin with a little untruth about his having loved this girl from his earliest childhood and having proposed to her once before etc. etc.—so also the generation finds itself in the predicament of having to give finishing touches with [*deleted:* a little] untruth in order to get history running again.

IX
B 24
323

After all, they still have a little remnant of a conception of what it means to be a free rational being. In order to rescue this conception, they have to fabricate that what has occurred is what they wanted to occur—unless in the Hegelian manner they assume that it has occurred by necessity. But that the upheaval occurs and has occurred in such a way is again the old evil, this shoving responsibility away from oneself, forced, to be sure, into something big on such a scale that finally existence must assume the paternity for what occurs in the world of free rational beings, somewhat as in nature, so that these upheavals are to be regarded meaninglessly and inhumanly as natural phenomena, and thus revolutions and republics arise in quite the same sense as there is cholera.

As far as the present essay is concerned, it is my hope that in his reading the reader will continually have had the impression that it is ethical-religious and has nothing to do with politics, that it ethically-religiously investigates how a new point of departure is procured in relation to an established order, that it comes to pass in such a way *that the point of departure is* **from above**, *from God, and the formula is this paradox, that an individual is used.* Humanly speaking, an individual, in comparison with the established order (the universal), is obviously infinitesimal, nothing; therefore it is a paradox that an individual is the stronger one. The explanation of this paradox can be only that it is God who uses him, God who hides behind him; but in turn God is seen for this very reason, just because the relation is a paradox. When there are hundreds of people, God is not seen; then what happens is explained as the direct result of the activity of hundreds of people, but the paradoxical constrains (insofar as it is possible to constrain freedom) one to become aware of God, of his being involved.

Politically, the whole thing, even when it comes to a decision, goes more easily, less paradoxically, more directly. Politically, one has nothing to do with God, no inconvenience from his having to be involved; *the point of departure is* **from below**, *from that which is lower than the established order,* since even the most mediocre "established order" is still preferable and superior to the flabbiest of everything flabby—the crowd. Nowadays, *si placet* [if you please], efforts are made in the states to bring about this irrationality, the existence of a prodigious monstrosity with many heads or, more correctly and accurately, a thousand-,

IX
B 24
324

according to the circumstances, a hundred-thousand-legged monstrosity, the crowd, an irrational enormity, or an enormous irrationality, that nevertheless has physical force, the force of the shout and uproar, also an amazing virtuosity in making everything commensurable with the hands raised to vote or with the decision of fists lifted up for a brawl. This abstraction is an inhuman something whose power is certainly enormous, but whose enormous power cannot be defined humanly but can be more accurately defined as the power of a machine, that it has the power of so and so many horses—the power of the crowd is always horsepower.

This abstraction, whether it is called the public, or the majority, or the crowd, or, meaninglessly, the people, this abstraction is used politically for movement. Just as in *Gnavspil*[152] and other party games, something is put up for which the game is played, so this abstraction is the stake for which the political game is played. Truth and the like, God in heaven etc., death, judgment, and much more, politics regards in about the same way as one finds it boring to play cards for nothing. No, cards must be played for money, and the political game must be played for the crowd, to see who can get the most *à tout prix* [at any price] on his side, or the most who with their feet go over to his side.

When one of the players sees that he has obtained the most, he hurries one evening to push forward at the head of this enormity.[*] Or more accurately, there are not even any players—this is still perhaps too much a qualification of personality—the whole thing is a game in which there nevertheless are no players, like a talk although there is no one speaking, like ventriloquism. But this is certain, one evening, or possibly many evenings in succession, an enormous crowd is on its feet, surely for the organism of the state a very precarious situation that is comparable only to flatulence. This crowd of people finally becomes embittered by the friction and now demands—or, more accurately, it does not demand, it does not itself know what it wants—it merely assumes its menacing stance in the hope that something will surely happen, in the hope that the weaker party (the established government, the ruler) will perhaps become so

[*]*In margin*: that sings freedom songs, patriotic hymns, etc.

alarmed that he will go ahead and do what neither the crowd nor the stronger ones at the head of the crowd—and the brave ones (if there are any)—have the courage to declare in specific words. Therefore, to be the stronger party is not to act but, by way of an abstract possibility, by sounds of nature, to alarm the weaker party into doing something—just as Louis Philippe[153] departed in alarm and by running away gave France a republic, or brought France into a condition out of which it became a republic (indeed, who would have thought it!). In alarm the king goes ahead and does something, and what the king does the crowd of people idolizes, maintaining that it is really the crowd that has done it.

Whereas the single individual, who in truth relates himself to a religious movement, must guard and fight with all his might and utmost power lest the terrible thing should happen that this enormous abstraction would want to help him by going with its feet over to his side (since winning with the help of this is, from a religious point of view, helping untruth to win), whereas the religious individual must therefore suffer indescribably under the weight of his responsibility and his doubly reflected struggling solitariness (since he struggles alone but also to be allowed to be alone in a life-and-death struggle)—thus it goes much more easily for the political hero, and most easily of all when there is not even so much as a political hero. But if there is such a one, he takes care only to make sure of these thousands before he ventures anything, and when he has made sure of them, then he ventures—that is, then he still does not venture anything, since in a physical way he is by far the strongest and he strives in a physical way.

IX
B 24
326

But that is why almost every political movement is, instead of progress to the rational, a retrogression to the irrational. Even a mediocre government that still is organic is better than the meaninglessness that such an abstraction governs the state. The existence of this abstraction in the state (like a noxious fluid in the human organism) ultimately puts an end to a rational state. Wherever this abstraction is enthroned, there really is no governing. Obedience is given only to the one whom people themselves have established, somewhat as the idol-worshiper idolizes and worships the god he himself has fashioned—that is, people obey themselves, people idolize themselves. With the cessation

of the rational state, statecraft becomes a game. Everything revolves around getting shoes on the crowd, and then getting it on
one's side, voting, making noise, carrying torches, and armed,
regardless, altogether regardless, of whether it understands anything or not.

Since this is the present situation and since everything these
days is politics, it will not surprise me if the majority will find that
the present essay treats of nothing and is preoccupied with difficulties that do not even exist. Well—so it is; it does in fact treat
of God and of the God-relationship in the single individual.

—*Pap.* IX B 24 *n.d.*, 1848

From final copy of "Two Ethical-Religious Essays":

Two Ethical-Religious
Essays
by
H. H. . . .
Deleted in margin: end of 1847
—*Pap.* X⁵ B 9:1a *n.d.*, 1849

On folder with ms. of "A Cycle," *old No. V, new No. VI:*

[*Deleted:* The Dialectical Relations: the Universal, the Single
Individual, the Special Individual

and]

A Psychological Interpretation of Mag. Adler as a Phenomenon, as a Satire on Hegelian Philosophy and the Present Age.
written in '46
—*Pap.* X⁶ B 52:1 *n.d.*, 1849

On folder with ms. of "A Cycle," *old No. V, new No. VI:*

If that about Adler should be published, it could have as the
main title:
A Kind of Literary Review.
—*Pap.* X⁶ B 52:2 *n.d.*, 1849

On folder with ms. of "A Cycle," old No. V, new No. VI:

Deleted: Both essays could be published together and simply called: Two Ethical-Religious Essays.
They were written in '46.
—*Pap.* X⁶ B 52:3 *n.d.*, 1849

On folder with ms. of "A Cycle," old No. V, new No. VI:

I have considered the possibility of making the last section of that on Adler into a separate little essay; in that case what is requisite lies here.

Moreover, there is here a possible little preface[154] to the whole essay on Adler.—*Pap.* X⁶ B 53 *n.d.*, 1849

From draft of no. VI in "A Cycle":

Preface

If by a superficial glance a theologian—and this essay is written only for theologians—should arrive at the conclusion that the essay is too large in relation to the man with whom it deals, I nevertheless ask him not to leave the essay unread for that reason. It contains developments of concepts and in my opinion very essential developments of concepts. I could very well have presented these in contrast to the confusion of concepts in our age without including Mag. Adler. But I consider it extremely fortunate to have someone who quite accurately manifests the confusion of the whole age, so one can make the development of a concept into a clinical demonstration. This is why I have applied such a large criterion to Mag. Adler.—*Pap.* X⁶ B 54 *n.d.*, 1849

N.B.   **N.B.**
N.B.

X¹
A 94
72

Great care must be taken now; there must be a new direction.

There are three possibilities open to me. (1) To step forth directly and decisively into the world of actuality in the *character* of the extraordinary, disregarding the fact that I am essentially a poet, that essentially I have related poetically to it (even though I am unusually ethical for a poet in the sense of giving expression to willing to be what is poetized), disregarding the fact that I have an accidental advantage: private means. —This would be false on my part and is therefore an impossibility. (2) To draw back everything poetical in me as a poet and then completely arrange my personal life as a poet, seek a poet-distance in order to avoid any occasion for confusion as to whether I am existentially what is poetized. There would be meaning in that. (3) To seek an appointment,[155] as I originally intended.

But my financial concern,[156] especially in these confused times,[157] has taken a bit out of me. With this advantage I wanted to be able to keep on my feet in spite of all the mistreatment from people and to be approximately what has been poetized, but this concern has gnawed at the dialectical tension in my mind and spirit, and the mistreatment and all the loathsomeness I have put up with has made me a little impatient, to the point where I almost went ahead and declared something about myself (of course still dialectical enough so that I would not say I was that but that I had been that), something which, to be sure, is not untrue but which I have regarded religiously as my duty to keep in self-denial, and therefore in all consistency I cannot disclose what lies behind it, however surreptitiously.

X¹
A 94
73

Deleted: For this reason No. 2 of "A Cycle of Ethical-Religious Essays"[158] (the universal—the single individual—the special individual) cannot come out either. Despite all disclaimers it will be understood as being about me. But it does also contain the explanation of "The Seducer's Diary,"[159] although it probably will not be understood that way, but rather as being about my exposure of myself to the rabble.—*JP* VI 6336 (*Pap.* X¹ A 94) *n.d.*, 1849

N.B.   N.B.

It is absolutely certain that I truly am not "a kind of extraordinary" as he is presented in No. 2.[160] I have never clashed with the established order, have always been basically conservative. In breaking an engagement I have clashed—but as an individual— with something universally human. But this really does not concern any other person; it is not a collision with the historical as an established order, the kind of collision embodying the dialectic of bringing forth something new. But I have never claimed to have that. Moreover, I have done everything lest my example, my collision, should harm anyone, as if there were something great in not getting married.—*JP* VI 6343 (*Pap.* X^1 A 112) *n.d.*, 1849

N.B.   N.B.

N.B.

X^1
A 116
86

"A Cycle of Ethical-Religious Essays," if that which deals with Adler[161] is omitted (and it definitely must be omitted, for to come in contact with him is completely senseless, and furthermore it perhaps is also unfair to treat a contemporary merely psychologically this way), has the defect that what as parts in a total study does not draw attention to itself (and originally this was the case) will draw far too much attention to itself now and thereby to me. Although originally an independent work, the same applies to no. 3,[162] a more recent work.

X^1
A 116
87

But if no. 2[163] and no. 3, which are about Adler, are also to be omitted, then "A Cycle" cannot be published at all.

Besides, there should be some stress on a second edition of *Either/Or.* Therefore either—as I previously thought—a quarto with all the most recent writing or only a small fragment of it, but, please note, a proper contrast to *Either/Or.* The "Three Notes"[164] on my work as an author are as if intended for that, and this has a strong appeal to me.

If I do nothing at all directly to assure a full understanding of my whole literary production (by publishing "The Point of View for My Work as an Author") or do not even give an indirect telegraphic sign (by publishing "A Cycle" etc.)—then what? Then there will be no judgment at all on my authorship in its totality, for no one has sufficient faith in it or time or competence

to look for a comprehensive plan [*Total-Anlæg*] in the entire production. Consequently the verdict will be that I have changed
somewhat over the years.

So it will be. This distresses me. I am deeply convinced that
there is another integral coherence, that there is a comprehensiveness in the whole production (especially through the assistance of Governance), and that there certainly is something else
to be said about it than this meager comment that in a way the
author has changed.

I keep this hidden deep within, where there is also something
in contrast: the sense in which I was more guilty than other men.

These proportions strongly appeal to me. I am averse to being
regarded with any kind of sympathy or to representing myself as
the extraordinary.

This suits me completely. So the best incognito I can choose
is quite simply to take an appointment.

The enticing aspect of the total productivity (that it is esthetic—but also religious) will be very faintly intimated by the
"Three Notes." For that matter, if something is to function
enticingly, it is wrong to explain it. A fisherman would not tell
the fish about his bait, saying "This is bait." And finally, if everything else pointed to the appropriateness of communicating
something about the integral comprehensiveness, I cannot emphasize enough that Governance actually is the directing power
and that in so many ways I do not understand until afterward.

This is written on Shrove Monday. A year ago today, I decided to publish *Christian Discourses*;[165] this year I am inclined to
the very opposite.

For a moment I would like to bring a bit of mildness and
friendliness into the whole thing. This can best be achieved by a
second edition of *Either/Or*[166] and then the "Three Notes." In
fact, it would be odd right now when I am thinking of stopping
writing to commence a polemic in which I do not wish to en-
gage by replying (a polemic that is unavoidable because of no. 1
and no. 2 in "A Cycle"[167]).

Let there be moderation on my part: if someone wants a fight,
then behind this I certainly am well armed.[168]—*JP* VI 6346 (*Pap.*
X¹ A 116) February 19, 1849

N.B.   N.B.

N.B.

x¹
A 117
88

To venture looks different to me this time from the way it did before. Previously I have always been keen on publishing what I had written; now it is a matter of holding back.

x¹
A 117
89

As for "A Cycle of Ethical-Religious Essays," it dates from an earlier period. Its composition is also unusual, because it is the original larger work ["The Book on Adler"] that is chopped into pieces, and the stimulus for the whole work (Adler) is omitted, and a separate essay, No. 3,[169] added. I cannot get myself into it in such a way that I really have a desire to publish it. Moreover, it has been laid aside or put away more than once.

As far as "The Point of View" is concerned, the point there is that it was written entirely in a frame of mind in which I did not expect to live to publish it myself. It is like the confession of a dying man. It is certainly a great benefit for me to have succeeded in writing it, and if I had gone abroad last spring as first planned I very likely would never have lived to get something like that written. For that there had to be altogether different sufferings, and I had to sink into myself more deeply than ever before. In that regard the past summer has been extremely important to me. In that way it was again good that I did not travel. I have achieved a productivity that I otherwise would not have achieved. But as far as "The Point of View" is concerned, this does not mean that it must be published.

The second edition of *Either/Or* and the 3 Notes:[170] this appeals to me. It is totally in character for me to hide the best in inwardness. In the past I have endured being looked upon as a villain, although I certainly was not exactly a villain: so let me as an author also endure seeming to be an oddity, although I am not exactly that. But at that time the circumstances did not torment me so much; so I was tempted to show that I was not a villain but was perhaps just the opposite. With regard to my work as an author, the circumstances have tormented me more, and moreover this is also in another sense a public relationship.

x¹
A 117
90

But I must remember that I now have an additional danger, one that is totally foreign to me: a little bit of security for my

(I must just do it.)

future. I am assuming now that the limit of risking is this: trusting in God, one ventures into the danger about which one nevertheless has the idea that one has the possibility of being able to endure it. Thus I have been and am willing (on the old conditions) to venture into battle with people, their power, their ridicule etc., because I understood myself in the possibility of being able to be victorious by God's help. But I cannot have the other danger at the same time. I am not that strong; here I consider that my venturing is for me a rash act.

My original thought has always been to break off my work as an author and then to seek a minor appointment. Even though as an author I put out money and reaped no profit, I had hoped that I nevertheless would leave it with a kind of honor. It is this, if anything, that has embittered me somewhat, that I have to leave it as one mistreated. It has pained me that my stopping as an author should be interpreted as weakness. This bitterness has possibly influenced me to want to rise a stage higher than I myself had ever imagined. True enough, one must also remember that a person receives his orders only successively and to that extent there could be some truth in the idea that I went further than I had originally thought of doing. But yet it is also a matter of being true to myself.—*Pap.* X^1 A 117 *n.d.*, 1849

N.B.

The beginning of my authorship is indirectly explained in something correlative, the essay "The Dialectical Relations: the Universal, the Single Individual, the Special Individual."[171] The more recent direction is indirectly explained in the essay "Does a Human Being Have the Right to Let Himself Be Put to Death for the Truth?"[172]—*JP* VI 6358 (*Pap.* X^1 A 140) *n.d.*, 1849

N.B.

All the essays (except the one on Adler[173]) in "A Cycle" etc. could well be published. But they are to be published separately, each by itself, or at most two together, and by the pseudonyms

H H, F F, P P.[174] They could then, like guerrillas, accompany the publication of the three books for awakening.[175] But precisely because their role is that of guerrillas, they must appear in doses as small as possible.—*JP* VI 6387 (*Pap.* X^1 A 263) *n.d.*, 1849

. . . Now the two essays are being published: "Does a Human Being Have the Right to Let Himself Be Put to Death for the Truth?" and "The Difference between a Genius and an Apostle," but anonymously. Today, May 5,[176] they were sent to Gjødvad.. . .[177] —*Pap.* X^1 A 302 May 5, 1849

How witty a typographical error can be! In the second of the two essays, instead of "the gift [*Gave*] of being able to work miracles," it read "the inconvenience [*Gene*]."[178]—*JP* VI 6399 (*Pap.* X^1 A 336) *n.d.*, 1849

Just as the Guadalquibir [*sic*] River at some place plunges underground and then comes out again, so I must now plunge into pseudonymity, but I also understand now how I will emerge again under my own name. The important thing left is to do something about seeking an appointment and then travel.

(1) The three ethical-religious essays[179] will be anonymous; this was the earlier stipulation. (2) "The Sickness unto Death" will be pseudonymous and is to be gone through so that my name and the like are not in it. (3) The three works, "Come Here, All You," "Blessed Is He Who Is Not Offended," and "From on High He Will Draw All to Himself" will be pseudonymous. Either all three in one volume under the common title, "Practice in Christianity, Attempt by - - - - - - -," or each one separately. They are to be checked·so that my name and anything about me etc. are excluded, which is the case with number three. (4) Everything under the titles "The Point of View for My Work as an Author," "A Note,"[180] "Three Notes,"[181] and "Armed Neutrality"[182]* cannot conceivably be published.

*See this journal, p. 157 [*Pap.* X^1 A 450].

X^1
A 422
268

X^1
A 422
269

These writings properly remain pseudonymous. Here there is the dialectical tension and tightening with respect to the doctrine of sin and redemption, and then I begin with my own name in a simple upbuilding discourse. But it is one thing for a work of such a dialectical nature to appear pseudonymously and something quite different if it appears over my name, in character, as the finale of the whole effort.

After all, there is no hurry about publishing. But if it is to be in character and as a finale, it must be done as soon as possible, something that has pained me frightfully and that has now become almost an impossibility, because today, June 4, I spoke with Reitzel,[183] who said he dared not take on anything new for publication. On the whole the man has plagued me unbearably with his miseries, which perhaps are exaggerated anyway.

A battle of ideas has taken place here. In actuality the whole matter of publishing with or without my name perhaps would be a bagatelle. But to me in my ideality it is a very taxing problem, that above all I do not falsely hold myself back or falsely go too far but truly understand myself and continue to be myself.

I have struggled and suffered fearfully. Yet one who fights for the "You shall" as I do must also suffer at this point. But yet at times I probably have not been far from pressing this "You shall" in an almost melancholy-frantic way. But now I understand myself. You shall—this is eternally true—but it is not less true and it is also a "You shall" that with God you shall understand your limits and beyond them you shall not go or you shall abandon such desires.

But, gracious God, how I have suffered and how I have struggled. Yet it is my consolation that the God of love will let this be to my good, and in a certain sense it consoles me that I have endured this suffering, because in this very suffering I have become convinced of the way I am to turn.

X¹ A 422 270

My misfortune always has been that it is so difficult for me to take an appointment. My depression, which is almost a quiet derangement, has been a hindrance to me all along, my consciousness of sin, too. This has aided me continually in venturing, for it has assured me that I was at least not being guided by vanity and the like. But now in God's name I must turn in this direction.

Strangely enough, incidentally, I have written so much in journal NB[10] [*Pap.* X[1] A 82–294] and in this journal [NB[11], *Pap.* X[1] A 296–541], but there is on a loose sheet something I have not wished to enter in the journal and that I still really regard as the most decisive and also one of the earliest—I now end with precisely this.[184]—*JP* VI 6416 (*Pap.* X[1] A 422) June 4, 1849

[*In margin*: About F. F.[185]]

F. F. (and consequently I, too) can truthfully say that this book is written with Magister Adler most in mind.—*Pap.* X[1] A 534 *n.d.*, 1849

[*In margin:* the eulogy on Bishop Mynster by F. F.[186]]

This eulogy is given on the presupposition that "state Church," "established Christendom" are valid concepts. That from a Christian standpoint this must be denied is an entirely different matter. But if these concepts are assumed to have reality (and this ought to be assumed in a conception of Bishop Mynster, since it is reasonable, after all, to conceive a man according to his own idea and thought), then he is great and admirable. On the other hand, Bishop Mynster can be attacked only if one attacks those two concepts—*JP* VI 6441 (*Pap.* X[1] A 535) *n.d.,* 1849

The trouble with the "Three Ethical-Religious Essays"[187] is: I do not name Adler, and the whole thing will be understood to be about me, as if I would half insinuate that I myself was the extraordinary; and the confusion will become as disastrous as possible just at that moment. If I name Adler, then I will have the desperate man to deal with, which I by no means want; that is why I altogether gave up publishing the essay about him.

The best thing to do is not to publish them at all.

The third essay[188] perhaps could be published separately.

—*Pap.* X[1] A 544 *n.d.*, 1849

Christianity's first aspect is and must be so appalling that only an absolute *shall* is able to drive a person into it. But this first aspect has been abolished, and Christianity's other aspect has now been taken: mildness—and this is recommended for various reasons, is defended, and so on.

But this will cost the race dearly. Just as a spoiled child, to his own ruin, manipulates his parents into being lenient, so also the race, to its own ruin, has fooled and intimidated those who should command and use authority into not daring to say: You shall.

What the world needs most of all right now is this *You shall*, pronounced with authority. This is the only thing that can give impetus, and he who implores another, "Just speak rigorously to me!" understands what is best for him.

"You shall" has been abolished. In every relationship, even in preaching, the contemporaries are made the authority; the speaker or the individual recommends his cause, his wares, be it raisins or Christianity—but there is no teacher and no assembly of learners, far from it—every assembly is the master, and the individual is the candidate up for examination.—*JP* IV 4893 (*Pap.* X^1 A 625) *n.d.*, 1849

X^2
A 119
91

Christianity and Speculation

[*In margin:* Christianity and speculation]

Christianity is an *existence-communication* [*Existens-Meddelelse*], has entered into the world by the use of *authority. It is not to be an object of speculation*; Christianity is to be kept existentially on the move, and becoming a Christian is to be made more and more difficult.

Take a simple example. An officer says to a disorderly mob: Move on, please—no arguing.

No arguing —why? Because he uses authority.

Is there, then, nothing objective in Christianity or is Christianity not the object of objective knowledge? Indeed, why not? The objective is what he is saying, he, the authority. But no arguing, least of all the kind that, as it were, sneaks behind the back of the authority and finally speculates him away, too, and turns everything into speculation.

How, after all, can a *divine* doctrine enter into the world? By God's empowering a few individuals and overpowering them, as it were, to such a degree that at every moment throughout a long life they are willing to act, to endure, to suffer everything for this doctrine. This, their unconditional obedience, is the form of their authority. They use the authority and appeal to God, but they also support it with their unconditional obedience. If you will not do this amicably, well, then we are prepared to suffer everything, and then we will find out who is the stronger. It is like being at an auction. People want to frighten the one sent from God, show him all the horrors, but he says: I bid nevertheless because my unconditional obedience, in which I myself also am constrained, makes it possible that I can bid so low with regard to enduring everything that you cannot underbid me. He endures, then, and finally he dies. Now he is constraining. Now he constrains the generation and thereby brings the divine doctrine to bear upon the race. His unconditional obedience, which was the support, now transforms itself into an explanation of his having had divine authority, something he himself had said. As long as he is living and striving, he really uses the most unconditional obedience, because he cannot get a willing ear for his divine authority; but then he dies, and now the authority has all the greater effectiveness.

The two small pieces by H. H. are very instructive.—*JP* I 187 (*Pap.* X² A 119) *n.d.*, 1849

X²
A 119
92

Real self-redoubling [*Selvfordoblelse*] without a constraining third factor outside oneself is an impossibility and makes any such existing [*Existeren*] into an illusion or imaginary constructing.

Kant was of the opinion that a human being is his own law (autonomy)—that is, he binds himself under the law that he himself gave himself.[189] Actually, in a profounder sense, this is how lawlessness or imaginary constructing is posited. This is not being

X²
A 396
280

rigorously earnest any more than Sancho Panza's self-adminis-
tered blows to his own bottom were vigorous.[190] It is impossible
for me to be really any more rigorous in A than I am or wish to
be in B. Constraint there must be if it is going to be in earnest. If
I am bound by nothing higher than myself and I am to bind
myself, where would I get the rigorousness as A, the binder, that
I do not have as B, who is supposed to be bound, when A and B
are the same self?

X²
A 396
281

This appears particularly in all religious areas. The transition—
which really is from immediacy to spirit—this dying-away-from
does not get to be in earnest, becomes an illusion, imaginary
constructing, if there is no third factor, the constraining factor
that is not the individual himself.

Therefore all the eminent individualities, the real "instru-
ments," are constrained.

The maxim that I give myself is not only not a law, but there
is a law that is given me by one higher than myself, and not only
that, but this lawgiver takes the liberty of taking a hand in the
capacity of tutor and bringing constraint to bear.

Now if a person is never even once in his lifetime willing to
act so decisively that this tutor can get hold of him, well, then it
happens that he is allowed to live on in self-complacent illusion
and make-believe and imaginary constructing, but this also
means: utterly without grace.

A person can be so rigorous with himself that he is able to
understand that all his rigorousness amounts to nothing; I must
have the help of someone else who can be that rigorousness,
even if he is also mildness.

But to involve oneself with this other one does not mean to
give assurances and give assurances; it means to act.

As soon as a person acts decisively and enters into actuality,
then existence [*Tilværelsen*] can get hold of him and Governance
can bring him up.

It is certainly true that even if a person pampers himself ever so
much, it still can occur to Governance to take him to task [*tage
ham i Skole*]. But Governance does not like to do this; this is
almost anger. What Governance wants is that a person shall believe and believe in Governance. Governance is no friend of this

coddling, this wanting to play at being an autodidact when at the
same time there lives such a remarkable tutor and teacher as our
Lord, to whom he can turn.

X²
A 396
282

But in ordinary human circumstances the fact that I am sent to
school or seek to enter school means that I go here or there,
wherever the teacher lives. Spiritually, this means that I act decisively—and immediately the teacher lives right there. What is it
I want—I want to be brought up to be spirit—and yet I do not
want to act decisively? Nonsense!—*JP* I 188 (*Pap.* X² A 396)
n.d., 1850

Clement of Alexandria

declares that we must substitute the purely human—reflection,
scholarship, etc.—for what the apostles had directly through the
spirit.[191]

Here is where the confusion lies. It looks as if what the apostles
had through the spirit was profundity, speculative intuition—
instead of authority. Thus it is forgotten that Christianity is the
existential.

Simply because Clement of Alexandria must have room for
scholarship, he indirectly and without knowing it remodels "the
apostle" so that "the apostle" tends to become a qualification of
genius,[192] however lofty a place is to be assigned to genius.—*JP*
IV 3861 (*Pap.* X⁴ A 110) *n.d.*, 1851

Three Ethical or Ethical-Religious
Essays

by.
[*deleted:* F. F.]
M. M.
—*Pap.* X⁶ B 57:1 *n.d.*, 1851–53

Contents

No. 1. Something on What Might Be Called "Premise
Authors."

No. 2. The Dialectical Relations: the Universal, the Single
     Individual, the Special Individual.
No. 3. A Revelation in the Situation of the Present Age.
                —*Pap*. X[6] B 57:3 *n.d.*, 1851–53

Preface

This little book,[193] which will essentially be able to interest
only theologians, was written in '46 and '47.
                  [*deleted:* F. F.] M. M.
            —*Pap*. X[6] B 57:2 *n.d.*, 1851–53

For the three ethical-religious essays by F. F.[194]
     see journal NB. p. 266 [*Pap*. X[1] A 535 [195]]
   The eulogy on Bishop Mynster that is in No. II[196] [*same as Pap*.
X[1] A 535] . . ..
                —*Pap* . X[6] B 60 *n.d.*, 1851–53

See journal NB.[12] p. 1 [*Pap*. X[1] A 544[197]].

   The trouble with the publication of the three essays is:
     If I do not name Adler, then everything is understood to be
     about myself, as if I would smuggle in the idea that I myself
     am the extraordinary, and the confusion would become
     most disastrous. If I name Adler, I will have the desperate
     man to deal with, which I by no means want; it was for that
     reason that the whole work was chopped into pieces at that
     time.
   [*In margin:* Essay No. 3[198] could perhaps be published separately.]
                —*Pap*. X[6] B 61 *n.d.*, 1851–53

For the three ethical-religious essays.
          See journal NB.[12] p. 1 [*Pap*. X[1] A 544[199]]
   Perhaps there could be added to the preface:
   The more knowledgeable person will easily perceive one or
another specific phenomenon has occasioned these essays; he

will then also easily discover what it may be. But in part it is then really the occasion in only the most rudimentary sense; in part the phenomenon was not very gratifying, and finally it is for the most part indeed forgotten; therefore I will not even name it here in the preface.

(It was Adler.)

—Pap. X^6 B 62 n.d., 1851–53

Regarding the Three Ethical-Religious Essays

Perhaps only the first two are to be published. The title will then be: Two Ethical-Religious Essays by P. P. (not F. F.), edited by S. Kierkegaard.

Then perhaps the postscript to No. 2^{200} could be used. . . .

—Pap. X^6 B 63 n.d., 1853

N.B. If, instead of bearing the author-signature M. M.,[201] the three ethical-religious essays[202] should have a proper pseudonym, I would call the author Emanuel Leisetritt, a pseudonym I perhaps could use, if not here, if I should ever again have need for a pseudonym.—*JP* VI 6838 (*Pap.* X^5 A 93) *n.d.*, 1853

For
"Three Ethical Religious Essays"[203]

The passage about Bishop Mynster[204] goes out! It is the right thing to do, something I had concluded repeatedly while I was still thinking of some way to be able to keep it, because after all I do have this melancholy devotion to the old man.

Inasmuch as the three religious essays were formerly intended to be published anonymously, I thought that perhaps this passage could be kept, since a pseudonym is indeed not myself. I also thought that since it says in the preface, which indeed is the truth, that the treatise predates 1848, it could be done, because 1848 and the following time have so starkly exposed Bishop M. that I cannot defend speaking this way after that time.

Now he is dead.[205] Once again I am thinking of those three essays and that passage, whether it now could remain or whether it could remain with a footnote by me that it predates 1848, that after that time I did not dare allow a pseudonym to speak this way about Bishop Mynster. But a note such as that would, after all, have exactly the effect opposite to the aim of that passage: to extol Bishop M.

Consequently: it goes out.

March 1, 1854

—*Pap.* XI³ B 1 March 1, 1854

The Passage on Mynster that Certainly Goes Out

. . . [pp. 152:6–153:34 (*Pap.* VII² B 235, pp. 43:8–45:10²⁰⁶)]
—*Pap.* XI³ B 2 *n.d.,* 1854

XI³
B 4
6

For the "Three Ethical-Religious Essays"

[*In margin:* Not to be used.]

Postscript by S. Kierkegaard

March 1855

This little piece by the pseudonym will contribute to a more truthful understanding of me, even if in another sense it makes it

XI³
B 4
7

more difficult to understand me. Yet this difficulty belongs to the true understanding; I am not very directly understandable and will never be understood by those who want to have everything direct.

The longer I live, [*changed from:* Just as Socrates speaks about his having a daimon, so] I am more and more convinced that there must be something daimonic in my nature, an ideality that makes me, in whatever different situation I have been, never to have related myself directly in the situation. No, everywhere the situation has been thus: I myself have used my powers to create the difficulties, the opposition, to which I then have related myself; frequently I have not myself realized that I did this but only afterward understood that I had done it.

This is the way I also understand it now, that I—the very one who has proceedings against the established order, my true task—that I for a long time have provided the most adequate defense of the established order, have directed my whole dialectic toward those who occupy themselves with wanting to attack it. Consequently, instead of directly relating myself to my task— to attack the established order, promptly beginning there, and probably also directly establishing contact with what opposition there was—I have begun the very opposite, have worked against myself by defending what nevertheless should end with being attacked, and have worked against myself by placing myself in a contentious relation to the opposition, which viewed directly might be said to be on the same side as I am.

Once again, by publishing this little essay now I am creating for myself an opposition. That is, this little piece presents what ideally must be required of the one who is to take on the business of opposing the established order—and that is myself. But in such a characterless age as ours, where in every respect the ideals have been lost, there is of course absolutely no ideal conception of what is required of the one who wants to fight against the established order. This I could then utilize so as to become regarded, at an extremely low price, as something big in the capacity of opposition. It is absolutely certain, because, just as it is certain that Bishop Mynster by no means had sufficient ideality to be able to defend the established order—the ideality I alone was capable of demonstrating—it is just as certain that today there is not a single person who has the ideality to demonstrate the ideality for being the opposition.

So what am I doing in publishing this little piece? In a way I am arming the contemporary age against me by playing into its hands an ideality that otherwise did not exist for it. And in this way I once again have the formula for my existence: I have never in relation to anyone related myself directly in the situation, but basically to myself, since the opposition, which makes my cause difficult, indeed dangerous, comes from me; I myself first arranged it.—*Pap.* XI³ B 4 March 1855

XI³
B 4
8

For the three ethical-religious essays

Postscript by S. Kierkegaard

April [*deleted:* 3] 1855

By publishing these three essays I intend to do the ecclesiastical established order the service of lifting up the requirement for wanting to reform into the highest ideality, something neither the late secularly sagacious master, Bishop Mynster, was able to do, nor the present half-experienced bungler, Bishop Martensen, is able to do. In this way I am defending the established order. Viewed in the idea, this is the only true defensive method. Anyone whom the truth engages and whose only interest is that *it* must be victorious cannot wish to defend an established order in any other way. To defend an established ecclesiastical order by means of wanting to put a wax rose on God and pulling the wool over people's eyes, thus by wanting to make fools of both God and human beings, to defend an established ecclesiastical order by means of optical illusion is Christianly a crime and can indeed occur only to those for whom truth is something one leaves in abeyance, a chimera, a fantasy, and on the other hand profit, possession of worldly power, secure enjoyment are the most important—in this way I certainly have never defended the established order.—*Pap.* XI³ B 6 April 1855

SELECTIONS FROM
ADLER'S WRITINGS

Nogle Prædikener [*Some Sermons*]
Copenhagen: 1843, pp. 3–4, 20, 26:

Preface

In December of last year, I had almost completed a work that I had wanted to call "Popular Lectures on Subjective Logic." It was my own thought that had immersed itself in itself and with a superficial knowledge of the Bible had undertaken to explain creation and Christianity.

One evening I had just given an account of the origin of evil; then I perceived as if in a flash that everything depended not upon thought but upon spirit, and that there existed an evil spirit. That same night a hideous sound descended into our room. Then the *Savior* commanded me to get up and go in and write down these words: **The first human beings could have had an eternal life, because when thought joins God's spirit with the body, then life is eternal; when the human being joins God's spirit with the body, then the human being is God's child; so Adam would have been God's son. But they sinned. Thought immersed itself in itself without the world, without the body. It separated the spirit from the body, the spirit from the world. And when the human being himself, when thought itself separates the spirit from the body and the spirit from the world, the human being must die and the world and the body become evil. And what becomes of the spirit? The spirit leaves the body. But God does not take it back. And it becomes his enemy. And where does it go? Back into the world. Why? It is angry with the world, which abandoned it. It is the evil spirit. And the world itself created the evil spirit.**

Then Jesus commanded me to burn my own works and in the future to keep to the Bible.

As for the sermons from no. VI to the end, I know that they were written with Jesus' collaborating grace, so that I have been only an instrument.

Hasle, June 18, 1843

20   IV

Maundy Thursday
Luke 22:14–21

————————

Prayer*

O God, our Father in heaven! God of omnipotence and love, Father of power, of grace, look down upon us with mercy and compassion for your Son, Jesus Christ's sake, and enlighten us with your Holy Spirit. . . .

26   . . . Man's body had become sinful, the world had become sinful, and the whole world should have been punished; all flesh was corrupted and had fallen to the evil spirit, to the torture of hell. . . .

Skrivelser min Suspension og Entledigelse vedkommende
[*Papers Concerning My Suspension and Dismissal*]

Published by A. P. Adler

Copenhagen: 1845, pp. 3–7, 14–24:

3   In order that the public can be informed about how the final decision concerning my dismissal was reached, I have had the following letters printed.

*This prayer was given to me by Jesus' collaborating grace.

On January 19, 1844, Dean Steenberg wrote to me as follows:

His Right Reverend Dr. Bishop Mynster wrote to me the 9th of this month as follows:

"The Royal Danish Chancellery on January 4 wrote to me as follows:

"After Your Reverence last August 12 had communicated to this council your thoughts on the occasion of the book *Nogle Prædikener* by A. P. Adler, *Magister Artium*, pastor of the Hasle and Ruthsker parishes, and after this council on August 29 had   4
requested Your Reverence to try to persuade Pastor Magister Adler to apply through the Dean of Bornholm for a temporary release from the office entrusted to him, Your Reverence, in your favor of August 16 to the undersigned, has reported that Pastor Magister Adler could not be persuaded to apply for a release from the office, and furthermore that he—as is verified by the work published by him later, *Studier ved A. P. Adler, M. A., Pastor til Hasle og Ruthsker Menigheder*—is in such a condition that the conduct of a pastoral office can no longer be entrusted to him.

"Because of this, the Chancellery should herewith duly apply to Your Reverence to suspend the aforesaid Pastor Adler immediately and make the necessary arrangements for the temporary filling of the office until the final determination, of which a detailed report is awaited, can be made.

"In accordance with this resolution by the Royal Danish Chancellery, may I duly request that Your Reverence suspend Pastor Adler from his office immediately and please arrange for the office to be temporarily filled, as is customary in cases of vacancies, by the rotation of the pastors concerned until the   5
more definite determination, which should be made as soon as possible."

In accordance with this order assigned to me, the Herr Magister is herewith suspended from the office hitherto entrusted to you as pastor in the Hasle and Ruthsker parishes, and in addition

I must request you to send me all the pertinent records and documents of the office.

    Rønne, January 19, 1844

                    Steenberg

On January 23, 1844, I wrote to Bishop Mynster as follows:

Since the Chancellery resolution communicated to me orders only my suspension and does not give the slightest hint that any provision for further proceedings is being considered, I herewith appeal to Your Reverence to request a consistory court to be arranged.

    Hasle, January 23, 1844

                    Respectfully,
                    A. Adler

---

6   Furthermore, in January 1844 the Hasle and Ruthsker parishes sent the following communication to the Royal Danish Chancellery:

           To the Royal Danish Chancellery

With sadness we have learned that our beloved Pastor Magister Adler, in accordance with the resolution of the Royal Danish Chancellery, has been suspended from his office. We do not know what has occasioned this suspension, but we do know, and we wish to have the high council made aware, that we all are well satisfied with Magister Adler and desire to keep him. We feel that a sincere Christian spirit pervades all his discourses and sermons, and with regard to his other relations to us, they are on the whole as good as can ever be wished between a pastor and his parish.

    Hasle and Ruthsker, January 1844

                    Most humbly yours,
                    [116 signatures]

On February 16, 1844, Dean Steenberg wrote to me as follows:

I have to inform you that until further notice Chaplain Christian Ørsted has been appointed by his R. R. Bishop Mynster, with the consent of the Royal Danish Chancellery, to administer, on his own responsibility, the Hasle and Ruthsker incumbency, at a salary of 500 rix-dollars, which is to be provided by Your Reverence.

    Rønne, February 16, 1844

Respectfully,
Steenberg

On April 29, 1845, Dean Steenberg wrote to me as follows: 14

Since it is now more than a year since Herr Magister was suspended from your office as pastor of the Hasle and Ruthsker parishes and it will be necessary that a final determination be made with regard to the aforesaid office, may I, in accordance with instructions from the Bishop of the diocese, officially request you to favor me with your explanation:

Do you acknowledge having been in an excited and confused state of mind when you wrote and published your *Sermons* and so-called *Studies*?

Do you perceive that it is fanatical and wrong to expect and to follow such presumably external revelations as, for example, those you described in the preface to your *Sermons*?

Do you acknowledge that in your aforesaid printed writings there appear several false and according to Christian doctrine deviating statements, such as that "the earth was not originally good" (thus presumably not created by God), or that "the sexual instinct is the evil spirit and came into the world through the evil spirit"?

Do you admit that in your aforesaid writings there are many

expressions that are offensive, shocking, or highly inappropriate, such as what is said on page 99 of *Sermons*, that witches
should be burned, or on page 112 about Origen; in *Studies*, pp.
63f., "if a son does not believe in Jesus, the father may as well
break his neck, and if the father himself does not believe, he
may as well cut his throat," or on pages 165 and 170 about
Esau and Jacob, and much more?

Rønne, April 29, 1845

Respectfully,
Steenberg

On May 10, 1845, I sent Dean Steenberg the following explanations:

In a letter of April 29 this year, in accordance with instructions
from the Bishop of the diocese, Your Reverence requested my
explanation

1. Do I acknowledge . . . ?
2. Do I perceive . . . ?
3. Do I acknowledge . . . ?
4. Do I admit . . . ?

My explanations of the above-mentioned four points are as
follows:

to 1. Since I can show meaning and coherence in what I have
written in my *Sermons* and *Studies*, I do not acknowledge
having been in an excited and confused state of mind when
I wrote and published them.

to 2. By my having written in the preface to my *Sermons* "that
Jesus commanded me in the future to keep to the Bible";
by my having preached him, by my having quoted the
words of Scripture as proof texts, it must be obvious to
which Gospel and to which revelations I keep and have
taught others to keep. But that there was a rescue in marvelous ways—as I have described in the preface to *Ser-*

mons—is for me a fact that I cannot deny. Even if my *Sermons* and *Studies* are regarded only as a child's first babbling, lisping, imperfect voice, I nevertheless believe that the words testify that an event through which I was deeply moved by faith did occur.

to 3. With regard to the statement: that the earth was originally not good, allow me to note that by "earth" is here suggested the raw, unformed mass (ὕλη ἄμορφος [amorphous matter]) that first received life and was put in order by God. Allow me to cite II Peter 3:5: They deliberately ignore that by the word of God heavens existed long ago, and the earth appeared out of water and by means of water. Hebrews 1:10: You, Lord, did found the earth in the beginning, and the heavens are the work of your hands (here a distinction also seems to be made between the earth, which was like an unformed mass and was established by God, and the heavens as the works of his hands). Isaiah 45:18: For he says, the Lord, who created the heavens, he the God, who formed the earth and made it, he established it, did not create it a chaos, he formed it to be inhabited. Genesis 1–2: In the beginning God created the heavens and the earth. And the earth was without form and void. See *Sermons*, p. 115.   19

With regard to the statement: "The sexual instinct is the evil spirit, and it came into the world through the evil spirit," allow me to note: that from the outset in the preface to *Sermons* and all through *Sermons* and *Studies* I have set forth in many ways how the evil spirit came into existence as a result of the sin of humankind, that by the above-mentioned statement I cannot possibly have intended to identify the sexual instinct entirely with the evil spirit. The meaning of the above-mentioned statement is approximately this: that the sexual instinct became dominant in humankind and obtained power over all human beings through the evil spirit, who came into the world and incites people to evil. With regard to this connection between the sexual instinct and evil, allow me to cite

20 woman's punishment in Genesis 3:18—that in Mosaic law [Leviticus 12:2–8] the woman was regarded as unclean after giving birth and must undergo purification—that Jesus, in whom a human being is rightly born, so in him God was pleased with human beings, was conceived by the Holy Spirit. Furthermore, allow me to cite Matthew 19: 10–12, where Jesus, just after a previous discussion about marrying, says: There are eunuchs who have made themselves eunuchs for the sake of the kingdom of heaven, whereby he therefore suggests that the sexual instinct is abnormal in God's kingdom. It is also in regard to this that I have quoted the passage about Origen, *Sermons*, p. 112.

Incidentally, I am far from "forbidding marrying," since it is precisely my view that Jesus, conceived by the Holy Spirit, is justice, justification for human beings with regard to how human beings really should be born, and that he as woman's lineage has brought the law to the world: The woman's lineage is the birth of the human being (see Paul: born of a woman, born under the law).

to 4. When *Sermons*, p. 99, says, "For one can achieve nothing with witches. They must be burned," according to which nonbelievers in the foregoing and subsequently are called

21 bewitched by the evil spirit, so here the phrase "be burned" alludes to the eternal fire, to the nonbelievers' damnation.

When in *Studies*, pp. 63f., after justification by Jesus is briefly mentioned, it says, "Therefore—if your son does not believe in Jesus, you may just as well break his neck; for he shall be ransomed by a lamb. And if you yourself do not believe in him, you may just as well cut your throat, for Jesus is the congregation's head and it is his body. And when a person here separates the head from the body, the person is dead"—then this is the strong expression that I believed I was able to use without danger, since the only result could be that people would hear the necessity, the indispensability, and the importance of faith strongly expressed. If one is oneself deeply moved by faith, is it any

wonder that one uses a strong expression about one's innermost, strongest feeling? The fault is at least excusable:
that one seized a too strong expression to extol what is
dearest to one. Incidentally, the first of the above-mentioned expressions was formed according to Exodus 13:12.

I cannot deny that in Esau and Jacob I find a typological   22
meaning parallel to history, and when one considers how
difficult it is to express such subjects, one must excuse it
that the truth—this I readily confess—has often required
beauty as a sacrifice.

In addition, allow me to note here that on the whole the
content of *Studies* has not been used in my sermons and
discourses. Only a few main points on which I have been
able to move most freely have been used. Only one sermon
is found printed verbatim in *Studies*, namely, Study 25.
Even though it is well-known to the high authorities, I
nevertheless cannot omit at this same opportunity to mention that my parishes have testified "that a Christian spirit
pervades all my sermons and discourses."

Hasle, May 10, 1845

Respectfully,
A. Adler

In order if possible to arrive at an agreement with the authorities, I made, after a conversation with Bishop Mynster, as great an   23
overture as possible when on July 5, 1845, I sent him the following letter:

Prompted by conversation with you, may I be permitted to
add the following to the explanations provided at Your Reverence's request:

1. That I do not insist upon regarding my *Sermons* (or *Studies*) as
    revelations alongside or opposite to Christianity, but I regard
    the words written down in the preface to *Sermons* and my
    frequently recurring dogmatic categories as reference points
    that have been necessary for me in order in the beginning of

the enthusiasm to be able to set the Christian substance securely in a form.

2. That I acknowledge that the unusual, strange, objectionable,
   aphoristic, and abrupt form in which the ideas appear in many
   places in my *Sermons* and *Studies* may reasonably have awakened the misgivings of the high authorities.

3. That in the future, by working out and calmly developing the
   ideas over a longer time, I will see my way to have the Christian content unfold in a form more appropriate and more in
   accord with the specific words of Holy Scripture.

   Copenhagen, July 5, 1845.

Respectfully,
A. Adler

On September 13, 1845, Bishop Mynster wrote to me as
follows:

His Majesty the King on the 26th of the past month has most
graciously sent me the following rescript:

> "Our most affectionate greetings! We herewith let it
> be known that we will have the pastor of the Hasle and
> Ruthskers parishes on our land Bornholm, Herr Magis-
> ter Artium Adolph Peter Adler, honorably discharged
> from the aforesaid office, with such compensation as we
> may see fit to decide more definitely upon a more de-
> tailed representation from our financial deputation.
>
> "You are most humbly to comply accordingly and to
> communicate this to the persons concerned. God be
> with you."

This is hereby officially communicated to Your Reverence.

Copenhagen September 13, 1845.

Mynster

EDITORIAL APPENDIX

ACKNOWLEDGMENTS

Preparation of manuscripts for *Kierkegaard's Writings* in the final editorial phase of the edition is supported by a genuinely enabling grant from the National Endowment for the Humanities and gifts from the Danish Ministry of Cultural Affairs, the General Mills Foundation, and Gilmore and Charlotte Schjeldahl.

The many revised versions of *The Book on Adler* and the absence of a fair copy of the last integral version required close examination of the complicated original manuscripts. This work was made possible by a grant from the Vellux Fond. The Søren Kierkegaard Forskningscentre, Copenhagen, provided good working quarters, and members of the congenial, knowledgeable staff gave helpful counsel on numerous sticky points and larger puzzles.

The translators-editors are indebted to Grethe Kjær and Julia Watkin for their knowledgeable observations on crucial concepts and terminology.

Per Lønning, Wim Scholtens, and Sophia Scopetéa, members of the International Advisory Board for *Kierkegaard's Writings*, gave valuable detailed criticism of the translation. Regine Prenzel-Guthrie and Nathaniel J. Hong, associate editors of *KW*, carefully scrutinized the manuscript. The index was prepared by Nathaniel J. Hong.

Inclusion in the Supplement of entries from *Søren Kierkegaard's Journals and Papers* is by arrangement with Indiana University Press.

The book collection and the microfilm collection of the Kierkegaard Library, St. Olaf College, and Gregor Malantschuk's annotated set of *Kierkegaards Papirer* have been used in preparation of the text, notes, supplement, and editorial appendix.

The manuscript was typed by Karen Rannow, and matters concerning the electronic manuscript were handled by Francesca Lane Rasmus, Nathaniel J. Hong, and Gretchen Oberfranc. The volume was guided through the press by Marta Nussbaum Steele.

NOTES

TITLE PAGE

TITLE PAGE. *Pap.* VIII² B 26.

PREFACE AND INTRODUCTION

1. *Pap.* VIII² B 27 is the preface to version III. For earlier and later prefaces, see Supplement, pp. 226–36 (*Pap.* VII² B 270; VIII² B 20; IX B 10, 11, 12, 20, 22).

2. Both Kierkegaard and Adler held the *Magister Artium* degree, which in the philosophical faculty of the University of Copenhagen was the equivalent of the degree of doctor in the other faculties. In 1854 the *Magister* degree with dissertation was abolished, and those with that degree were declared to be doctors of philosophy.

3. The major part of "The Book on Adler" was written during the summer of 1846. This preface, to version III of the manuscript, was written in November 1847.

4. See I Corinthians 9:26.

5. David Friedrich Strauss, *Das Leben Jesu*, I–II (Tübingen: 1835); Ludwig Andreas Feuerbach, *Das Wesen des Christenthums* (Leipzig: 1843; *ASKB* 488).

6. See Supplement, p. 224 (*Pap.* VIII² B 24).

7. See Supplement, p. 312 (*Pap.* VIII¹ A 562).

8. In version IV ("A Cycle"; *Pap.* IX B 1) the "Introduction" in versions I, II, and III was replaced by: "No. I. Something about What Could be Called 'Premise Authors.'" Additional revisions and extensive deletions were also made. These changes in *Pap.* VII² B 235, pp. 5–29, are incorporated in the present text.

9. See Supplement, pp. 244–47 (*Pap.* VII² B 235, pp. 56–59). See, for example, also *JP* IV 4106; V 5740 (*Pap.* V A 77, 58); *Pap.* VII¹ B 195.

10. A version of a line by Boethius, *The Consolation of Philosophy*, II, 17; See *De consolatione philosophiae Severini Boethii libri V* (Eger: 1758; *ASKB* 431), p. 43; *The Consolation of Philosophy*, tr. W. V. Cooper (New York: Carlton House, n.d.), p. 38. See also Proverbs 17:28.

11. See, for example, *From the Papers of One Still Living*, in *Early Polemical Writings*, pp. 76–84, *KW* I (*SV* XIII 68–76).

12. See Aristotle, *Sophistical Refutations*, 165 a, 171 b; *Aristoteles græce*, I–II, ed. Immanuel Bekker (Berlin: 1831; *ASKB* 1074–75), I, pp. 165, 171; *The Complete Works of Aristotle*, I–II, ed. Jonathan Barnes (Princeton: Princeton University Press, 1984), I, pp. 279, 291. See also *JP* V 5618 (*Pap.* IV A 63).

13. Cf. Plato, *Gorgias*, 464 d; *Platonis quae exstant opera*, I–XI, ed. Friedrich Ast (Leipzig: 1819–32; *ASKB* 1144–54), I, pp. 302–03; *Udvalgte Dialoger af Platon*, I–VIII, tr. Carl Johan Heise (Copenhagen: 1830–59; *ASKB* 1164–67 [I–VII]), III, p. 45; *The Collected Dialogues of Plato*, ed. Edith Hamilton and Huntington Cairns (Princeton: Princeton University Press, 1963), p. 247 (Socrates speaking): "Thus it is that cookery has impersonated medicine and pretends to know the best foods for the body, so that, if a cook and a doctor had to contend in the presence of children or of men as senseless as children, which of the two, doctor or cook, was an expert in wholesome and bad food, the doctor would starve to death."

14. During 1813–18 Denmark suffered a period of debased money. See *JP* V 5725 (*Pap.* V A 3).

15. See Daniel 2:1–6; *JP* V 5325, 5743 (*Pap.* II A 757; V A 71); *Stages on Life's Way*, p. 360, *KW* XI (*SV* VI 337).

16. Here "the moment" is used in the ordinary sense of the momentary. For Kierkegaard's special use of "the moment," see, for example, *The Concept of Anxiety*, pp. 82–91, *KW* VIII (*SV* IV 351–61); *Fragments*, pp. 13–21, 25, 28, 30–31, 51–52, 58–59, 62–64, 111, *KW* VII (*SV* IV 183–90, 194, 196, 198–99, 218, 224–25, 227–29, 272). See Supplement, pp. 251, 289 (*Pap.* VII² B 235, pp. 64, 163).

17. Cf. I Corinthians 9:26.

18. Augustin Eugène Scribe, *Les Premières Amours ou Les Souvenirs d'enfance*, tr. Johan Ludvig Heiberg, *Det Kongelige Theaters Repertoire*, 45 (Copenhagen: 1832), p. 8. See *Either/Or*, I, pp. 231–79, *KW* III (*SV* I 205–51).

19. See Adam Gottlob Oehlenschläger, *Sanct Hansaften-Spil, Digte* (Copenhagen: 1803), p. 238.

20. See, for example, *From the Papers of One Still Living*, pp. 76–84, *KW* I (*SV* XIII 68–75).

21. *Stages on Life's Way*, pp. 185–397, *KW* XI (*SV* VI 175–370).

22. Ibid., pp. 363–64 (340); *JP* II 1280 (*Pap.* II A 23).

23. *Stages*, p. 456, *KW* XI (*SV* VI 424); cf. *JP* V 5678 (*Pap.* IV A 132).

24. See *JP* I 121; II 1624 (*Pap.* I A 105; II A 729).

25. See A. P. Adler, *Nogle Prædikener* (Copenhagen: 1843), p. 3; Supplement, p. 339.

26. See, for example, *Concluding Unscientific Postscript to* Philosophical Fragments, p. 557, *KW* XII.1 (*SV* VII 486).

27. An allusion to Gotthold Ephraim Leibniz's view of "the best of all possible worlds." See *Leibnitzs Theodicee*, tr. Johann Christoph Gottscheden (Hanover, Leipzig: 1763; *ASKB* 619), para. 169–70, pp. 333–39; *Guil. Leibnitii opera philosophica*, I–II, ed. Johann Eduard Erdmann (Hanover, Leipzig: 1763; *ASKB* 619), II, pp. 554–55; *Theodicy* (tr. of *T.* in *Philosophische Schriften*, I–VII, 1875–90), ed. Austin Farrer, tr. E. M. Huggard (New Haven: Yale University Press, 1952), pp. 229–33.

28. For the note deleted in version II, see Supplement, pp. 236-37 (*Pap.* VIII² B 7:1c).

29. For the deleted remainder of the paragraph and the following paragraph, deleted in version III (*Pap.* VIII² B 9:1b-c), see Supplement, pp. 237–39 (*Pap.* VII² B 235, pp. 27–29).

30. The source of this anecdote has not been located.

CHAPTER I

1. The text of Chapter I is version III (*Pap.* VIII² B 13–15). For version I and shifted sections, see Supplement, pp. 241–58 (*Pap.* VII² B 235, pp. 30–33, 53–66, 67–73), and Addendum I, pp. 143–63 (*Pap.* VII² B 235, pp. 33–53, 66–67 [*Pap.* VII² B 9:15, pp. 50–51]).

2. See Supplement, p. 339 (*Prædikener* , p. 3).

3. Ibid., p. 4.

4. See Historical Introduction, note 1.

5. Cf. Matthew 26:74.

6. See Matthew 27:39.

7. In version III of Chapter I (*Pap.* VIII² B 13–15), a long paragraph on Adler was deleted, another step in the deletion of references to Adler. See Supplement, pp. 239–40 (*Pap.* VIII² B 14).

8. *Poetry and Truth*, an allusion to Goethe's autobiography. See p. 102 and note 16.

CHAPTER II

1. The title in version IV (no. IV in "A Cycle") and in version V (no. III in "Three Ethical-Religious Essays"; see Supplement, p. 334 [*Pap.* X⁶ B 57:3]) replaced the earlier title: "The So-Called Revelation Fact Itself as a Phenomenon in the Context of the Whole Modern Development!" The version III text of Chapter II is version I with revisions and deletions.

2. See, for example, *Postscript*, pp. 46–49, *KW* XII.1 (*SV* VII 34–37).

3. See Psalm 90:4; II Peter 3:8.

4. "Spoonerism" is the closest equivalent of the Danish *bakke snagvendt eller snakke bagvendt* (speak backward). The English term comes from William A. Spooner (1844–1930), Warden of New College, Oxford. Examples: "a half-warmed fish" ("a half-formed wish"); "You [a failing student] have tasted two worms, and you will leave Oxford by the first town drain" ("You have wasted two terms, and you will leave Oxford by the first down train").

5. See, for example, *Fragments*, p. 13, 55–59, *KW* VII (*SV* IV 183, 221–24).

6. The Danish text has *usandsynligt* (improbable), instead of a repetition of *sandsynligt* (probable). According to some scholars this is probably a copying or typesetting error, but cf. pp. 39–40.

7. See Luke 23:34.

8. This was done in *Fragments* in a Socratic-Platonic context.

9. An allusion to a poem, "*Ein Weltverjüngungs-Fest* (A Festival of World Renewal)," by Novalis (Friedrich v. Hardenberg), *Geistliche Lieder*, IX, *Novalis*

Schriften, I–III, ed. Ludwig Tieck and Eduard v. Bülow (Berlin: 1826–46; *ASKB* 1776 [I-II]), II, p. 27.

10. Cf. Luke 19:42.

11. See Luke 10:30–37.

12. For deleted note, see Supplement, pp. 258–59 (*Pap.* VIII² B 9:5a).

13. See Plato, *Apology*, 30 d–e; *Opera*, VIII, pp. 130–31; *Dialogues*, pp. 16–17. See also *JP* IV 4265; V 5953 (*Pap.* VII¹ A 69, B 213).

14. For deleted notes, see Supplement, pp. 259–61 (*Pap.* VIII² B 9:5b-c).

15. See Poul Martin Møller, *"Tanker over Muligheden af Beviser for Menneskets Udødelighed, med Hensyn til den nyeste derhen hørende Literatur,"* *Efterladte Skrifter*, I–III (Copenhagen: 1839–43; *ASKB* 1574–76), II, p. 179; *Postscript*, p. 392, *KW* XII.1 (*SV* VII 340).

16. For deleted note, see Supplement, pp. 261–62 (*Pap.* VIII² B 9:5d).

17. On Hegelian mediation, see, for example, *Either/Or*, II, pp. 173–74, *KW* IV (*SV* II 157–58); *Fragments*, p. 12 (*SV* IV 182) and note 18; *Postscript*, pp. 198, 369–81, 395–97, 408–12, *KW* XII.1 (*SV* VII 165–66, 319–30, 342–44, 354–57); *JP* III 3294 (*Pap.* IV A 54).

18. According to the auction catalog (*ASKB*), Kierkegaard had three works by Ludwig Feuerbach, including *Das Wesen des Christentums* (Leipzig: 1843; *ASKB* 488).

19. See John 1:11.

20. See I Corinthians 2:14.

21. See Genesis 5.

23. For deleted lines, see Supplement, p. 262 (*Pap.* VIII² B 9:5h).

24. Hans Ancher Kofo[e]d, *Almindelig Verdenshistorie i Udtog* (Copenhagen: 1813), a widely used and frequently reprinted Danish school book.

25. For the deleted thirteen following lines, see Supplement, pp. 262–63 (*Pap.* VIII² B 9:5i).

26. For the deleted remainder of the paragraph, see Supplement, p. 263 (*Pap.* VIII² B 9:5l).

CHAPTER III

1. The text of Chapter III, §1 in versions II and III (*Pap.* VIII² B 7:4–6, 9:7) is the same as in version I (*Pap.* VII² B 235, pp. 93–127) with eleven deletions.

2. See Supplement, pp. 340–48.

3. A chaplain had been appointed, at a salary amounting to one-half of Adler's salary, to serve Adler's congregation during the period of his suspension.

4. See Supplement, p. 339 (*Prædikener*, p. 3).

5. In a review of Adler's *Populaire Foredrag over Hegels objective Logik* (1842; *ASKB* 383), Hans Friedrich Helweg had encouraged Adler to write a book on subjective logic. See a reference to this in his review of Adler, *Nogle Prædikener*, *Fædrelandet*, 1345, September 3, 1843, col. 10781 fn.

6. See Supplement, p. 339 (*Prædikener*, pp. 3–4).

7. For continuation of the sentence, See Supplement, p. 263 (*Pap.* VII² B 7:6).

8. See, for example, Philipp Marheineke, *Lærebog i christelig Tro og Levnet for tænkende Christne*, tr. Mourits Mørch Hansen (Copenhagen: 1842; *ASKB* 646), pp. 69, 89–90; *Die Grundlehren der christlichen Dogmatik als Wissenschaft* (Berlin: 1827; *ASKB* 644), pp. xviii–xxiii, 15–19, 125–26.

9. See Supplement, p. 344 (*Skrivelser*, p. 17).

10. See Supplement, p. 347 (*Skrivelser*, pp. 22–23).

11. See Supplement, pp. 343–44 (*Skrivelser*, p. 15).

12. See Supplement, p. 348 (*Skrivelser*, pp. 23–24).

13. Hans Friedrich Helweg, "*Mag. Adlers senere Skrifter*," *Dansk Kirketidende*, 45, 46, July 19, 26, 1846. See Supplement, pp. 308–09 (*Pap.* VII¹ A 150).

14. In 1846 Adler published *Nogle Digte, Studier og Exempler, Forsøg til en Kort systematisk Fremstilling af Christendommen i dens Logik* and *Theologiske Studier* [*ASKB* 1502; *U* 11, 13, 12].

15. For lines deleted in versions II and III, see Supplement, pp. 263–64 (*Pap.* VIII² B 7:6).

16. See Supplement, p. 348 (*Skrivelser*, pp. 23–24).

17. Adler, *Studier*, p. xxiv.

18. See Supplement, p. 343 (*Skrivelser*, p. 15).

19. Ibid.

20. See Supplement, pp. 344–45 (*Skrivelser*, pp. 17–18).

21. *Prædikener*, pp. 3,4.

22. See Supplement, p. 264 (*Pap.* VII² B 257:9).

23. For lines deleted in versions II and III, Supplement, p. 264 (*Pap.* VIII² B 7:6).

24. See Supplement, p. 348 (*Skrivelser*, pp. 23–24).

25. For lines deleted in versions II and III, Supplement, p. 265 (*Pap.* VIII² B 7:6).

26. See Supplement, p. 265 (*Pap.* VII² B 257:12).

27. For lines deleted in versions II and III, Supplement, p. 265 (*Pap.* VIII² B 7:6).

28. For continuation of the paragraph in a draft of version I, see Supplement, p. 266 (*Pap.* VII² B 257:13).

29. See Supplement, p. 347 (*Skrivelser*, p. 23). For lines deleted in versions II and III, see Supplement, pp. 266–67 (*Pap.* VIII² B 7:6).

30. See Supplement, p. 347 (*Skrivelser*, p. 23).

31. See *JP* IV 4773 (*Pap.* II A 34) on Shakespeare, *King Lear*, IV, 6, 100–01.

32. See, for example, *Postscript*, pp. 228–32, *KW* XII.1 (*SV* VII 192–95).

33. At the time there was street lighting, but only when according to the almanac there was no moonlight. The determination was made by a magistrate. The "magistrate's moonlight" was inferior to the light of the moon. See, for example, *Politivennen*, 1145, December 9, 1837.

34. P. 59.

35. For the lines deleted in versions II and III, see Supplement, p. 267 (*Pap.* VIII² B 7:6).

36. Cf. *Fear and Trembling*, p. 69, *KW* VI (*SV* III 118); *Anxiety*, p. 10, *KW* VIII (*SV* IV 282).

37. For the lines deleted in versions II and III, see Supplement, pp. 267–68 (*Pap.* VIII² B 7:6).

38. For the lines deleted in versions II and III, see Supplement, p. 268 (*Pap.* VIII² B 7:6).

39. See *Fragments*, p. 6 and note 12, *KW* VII (*SV* IV 177).

40. See Supplement, pp. 340–41 (*Skrivelser*, pp. 3–4).

41. For the lines deleted in versions II and III, see Supplement, p. 268 (*Pap.* VIII² B 7:6).

42. With reference to the remainder of the paragraph and the following two paragraphs, see Supplement, pp. 268–69 (*Pap.* VII² B 257:22).

43. For the sections in Chapter III §2 in version I (*Pap.* VII² B 235, pp. 127–36, 150–73) replaced in version II (*Pap.* VIII² B 7), which is retained in version III (*Pap.* VIII² B 9:8) except for the ending (*Pap.* VIII² B 9:9–10), see Supplement, pp. 269–98. For the section moved from version I (*Pap.* VII² B 235, pp. 136–50) to Addendum II, see pp. 173–77.

44. See p. 278, note 91.

45. For deleted note, see Supplement, p. 298 (*Pap.* VIII² B 9:10b).

46. Plutarch recounts that when a soldier commanded Archimedes to come to Marcellus, Archimedes said he wanted to finish working on some geometrical figures, whereupon the soldier killed him. Plutarch, *Marcellus*, 19, *Lives*; *Plutarks Levnetsbeskrivelser*, I–IV, tr. Stephan Tetens (Copenhagen: 1800–11; *ASKB* 1197–1200), III, pp. 283–84; *Plutarch's Lives*, I–XI, tr. Bernadotte Perrin (Loeb, New York: Macmillan, 1914–26), V, pp. 486–87.

47. For version I of the Appendix to Chapter III, see Supplement, pp. 299–302 (*Pap.* VII² B 235, pp. 173–76).

CHAPTER IV

1. Chapter IV in versions I, II, and III became no. V in version IV ("Cycle") and the section headings were changed to Chapters I–V. The present text is version III, essentially the same as version I, with incorporation of changes in version IV, particularly in section 5. See note 57 below. For draft of Chapter IV, see Supplement, pp. 302–04 (*Pap.* VII² B 265).

2. See *Irony*, p. 214 fn., *KW* II (*SV* XIII 294); *Stages*, p. 56, *KW* XI (*SV* VI 57).

3. See, for example, Hegel, "*Ueber: Aphorismen über Nichtwissen und absolutes Wissen in Verhältnisse zur christlichen Glaubenserkennisz* . . . . Von Carl Friedrich G. . . . . !." *Vermischte Schriften, Georg Wilhelm Friedrich Hegel's Werke,* I–XVIII, ed. Philipp Marheineke et al. (Berlin: 1832–45; *ASKB* 549–65), XVII, pp. 113–16; *Sämtliche Werke. Jubiläumsausgabe* [*J.A.*], I–XXVI, ed. Hermann Glockner (Stuttgart: Frommann, 1927–40), XX, pp. 278–81; *Encyclopädie der philosophischen Wissenschaften, Erster Theil, Die Logik, Werke,* VI, pp. xxi–xxiv; *J.A.* (*System der Philosophie*), VIII, p. 17. The preface is not included in *Hegel's Logic* (tr. of *L.*, 3 ed., 1830; Kierkegaard's ed., 1840, had the same text plus *Zusätze*), tr. William Wallace (Oxford: Oxford University Press, 1975).

4. Twice a week during the winter semester of 1840–41, Adler lectured on speculative logic.

5. Adler, *Populaire Foredrag over Hegels objective Logik* (Copenhagen: 1842; *ASKB* 383).

6. See note 3 above.

7. L'Hombre, a card game, originally Spanish.

8. See Luke 5:10.

9. Kierkegaard had Jonathan Swift, *Satyrische und ernsthafte Schriften*, I-VIII (Zurich: 1756–66; *ASKB* 1899–1906). See *Stages*, pp. 419–20, *KW* XI (*SV* VI 391).

10. See Supplement, p. 339 (*Prædikener*, p. 3).

11. See Supplement, p. 345 (*Skrivelser*, p. 18; *Studier*, pp. iv, 527–28, 543–44).

12. See Supplement, p. 339 (*Prædikener*, p. 3).

13. See Supplement, p. 340 (*Prædikener*, p. 4).

14. Cf. *Either/Or*, I, pp. 3–6, *KW* III (*SV* I v–viii).

15. Johann Arnold Kanne (1773–1824), German philologist and mythologist. See *Pap.* I C 5. Kierkegaard had a number of Kanne's works (*ASKB* 588–92).

16. Goethe, *Aus meinem Leben. Dichtung und Wahrheit, Goethe's Werke. Vollständige Ausgabe letzter Hand, I-LX* (Stuttgart, Tübingen: 1828–42; *ASKB* 1641–68 [I-LV]), XXV, p. 67; *The Autobiography of Goethe*, I-II, tr. John Oxenford (London: Bell, 1881), I, pp. 216–17:

> This uncertainty of taste and judgment disquieted me more and more every day, so that at last I fell into despair. I had brought with me those of my youthful labours which I thought the best, partly because I hoped to get some credit by them, partly that I might be able to test my progress with greater certainty; but I found myself in the miserable situation in which one is placed when a complete change of mind is required,—a renunciation of all that one has hitherto loved and found good. However, after some time, and many struggles, I conceived so great a contempt for my labours, begun and ended, that one day I burnt up poetry and prose, plans, sketches, and projects all together on the kitchen hearth, and threw our good old landlady into no small fright and anxiety by the smoke which filled the whole house.

17. Cf. I Peter 2:16.

18. Cf. *JP* IV 4542, 4545 (*Pap.* VIII¹ A 165; IX A 363).

19. See Aristotle, *Poetics*, 1447 a; Bekker, II, p. 1447; *Works*, II, p. 2316.

20. See Psalm 139:1–18.

21. See Luke 10:42.

22. See Matthew 4:4.

23. See Deuteronomy 30:14.

24. See *Anxiety*, p. 86, *KW* VIII (*SV* IV 356); *Christian Discourses*, p. 74, *KW* XVII (*SV* X 78).

25. Cf. Luke 12:16–20.

26. A saying attributed to the Greek Cyrenaic philosopher Aristippus (c. 435–356 B.C.). See Horace, *Epistles*, I, 1, 19; *Q. Horatii Flacci opera* (Leipzig: 1828; *ASKB* 1248), p. 224; *Horace Satires, Epistles and Ars Poetic*, tr. H. Rushton Fairclough (Loeb, Cambridge: Harvard University Press, 1978), pp. 252–53: " . . . bend [*subiungere*] the world to myself [*mihi*], not myself [*me*] to the world."

27. Cf. Luke 10:42.

28. See, for example, *Stages*, pp. 444, 445, 470, 471, 477, *KW* XI (*SV* VI 414, 415, 437, 438, 443); *Postscript*, pp. 140, 204, 232, 288, *KW* XII.1 (*SV* VII 114, 171, 195, 246); *JP* II 1142, 1402 (*Pap.* X^4 A 114; X^2 A 494).

29. See Hebrews 3:7; Luke 12:20.

30. In "The Boasting Traveller," Aesop tells of a character who claims to have made an extraordinary leap on the island of Rhodes. A bystander replies, "*Hic Rhodos; hic salta* [Here is Rhodes; leap here]." *The Fables of Aesop*, ed. Thomas Bewick (New York: Paddington, 1975), p. 59.

31. See John 4:21.

32. See Philostratus, "*Leben des Apollonius von Tyane*," IV, 25, *Heldengeschichte*, Flavius Philostratus, the Elder, *Werke*, tr. Friedrich Jakobs, I–V (Stuttgart: 1819–32; *ASKB* 1143), III, pp. 379–81; *Philostratus The Life of Apollonius of Tyance*, I–II, tr. F. C. Conybeare (Loeb, Cambridge: Harvard University Press, 1960), I, pp. 406–09:

> "As such," replied Apollonius, "you must regard this adornment, for it is not reality but the semblance of reality. And that you may realise the truth of what I say, this fine bridge is one of the vampires, that is to say of those beings whom the many regard as lamias and hobgoblins. These beings fall in love, and they are devoted to the delights of Aphrodite, but especially to the flesh of human beings, and they decoy with such delights those whom they mean to devour in their feasts." And the lady said: "Cease your ill-omened talk and begone"; and she pretended to be disgusted at what she heard, and no doubt she was inclined to rail at philosophers and say that they always talked nonsense. When, however, the goblets of gold and the show of silver were proved as light as air and all fluttered away out of their sight, while the wine-bearers and the cooks and all the retinue of servants vanished before the rebukes of Apollonius, the phantom pretended to weep, and prayed him not to torture her nor to compel her to confess what she really was. But Apollonius insisted and would not let her off, and then she admitted that she was a vampire, and was fattening up Menippus with pleasures before devouring his body, for it was her habit to feed upon young and beautiful bodies, because their blood is pure and strong.

33. See pp. 15–17.

34. With reference to the remainder of the paragraph, cf. Supplement, pp. 308–09 (*Pap.* VII^1 A 150).

35. See, for example, *Irony*, pp. 291–92, *KW* II (*SV* XIII 362); *Two Ages*, p. 66, *KW* XIV (*SV* VIII 62); *JP* I 790; II 1235 (*Pap.* I A 197; II A 281); Adler, *Studier*, pp. 449, 459. See Marcus Vitruvius Pollio, *Vitruvius on Architecture*, I–II,

tr. Frank Granger (Loeb, Cambridge: Harvard University Press, 1970), IX, 9–
10, II, pp. 203–05:

> Hiero was greatly exalted in the regal power at Syracuse, and after his victo-
> ries he determined to set up in a certain temple a crown vowed to the im-
> mortal gods. He let out the execution as far as the craftsman's wages were
> concerned, and weighed the gold out to the contractor to an exact amount.
> At the appointed time the man presented the work finely wrought for the
> king's acceptance, and appeared to have furnished the weight of the crown
> to scale. However, information was laid that gold had been withdrawn, and
> that the same amount of silver had been added in the making of the crown.
> Hiero was indignant that he had been made light of, and failing to find a
> method by which he might detect the theft, asked Archimedes to undertake
> the investigation. While Archimedes was considering the matter, he hap-
> pened to go the baths. When he went down into the bathing pool he ob-
> served that the amount of water which flowed outside the pool was equal to
> the amount of his body that was immersed. Since this fact indicated the
> method of explaining the case, he did not linger, but moved with delight he
> leapt out of the pool, and going home naked, cried aloud that he had found
> exactly what he was seeking. For as he ran he shouted in Greek: heureka
> heureka.
>
> Then, following up his discovery, he is said to have taken two masses of
> the same weight as the crown, one of gold and the other of silver. When he
> had done this, he filled a large vessel to the brim with water, into which he
> dropped the mass of silver. The amount of this when let down into the water
> corresponded to the overflow of water. So he removed the metal and filled
> in by measure the amount by which the water was diminished, so that it was
> level with the brim as before. In this way he discovered what weight of silver
> corresponded to a given measure of water.
>
> After this experiment he then dropped a mass of gold in like manner into
> the full vessel and removed it. Again he added water by measure, and discov-
> ered that there was not so much water; and this corresponded to the lessened
> quantity of the same weight of gold compared with the same weight of silver.

36. See *JP* V 5922 (*Pap.* VII¹ A 50).

37. Israel Joachim Behrend (d. 1821), a well-known Copenhagen character
about whom many anecdotes were told. See *Postscript*, p. 108, *KW* XII.1 (SV
VII 87–88); *JP* 140 (*Pap.* II A 571); Lauritz Nicolai Bjørn, *Dumriana eller Indfald,
Anecdoter og Characteertræk Claus Dumrians Levnet* (Copenhagen: 1829), pp. 5–6;
Jakob Davidsen, *Fra det gamle Kongens Kjøbenhavn*, I–II (Copenhagen: 1880–81),
I, pp. 364–69.

38. See *Postscript*, pp. 555–61, *KW* XII.1 (*SV* VII 484–90).

39. With reference to the following two paragraphs, see Supplement, p. 304
(*Pap.* VII² B 268).

40. Cf. I Corinthians 2:9. See, for example, *Fragments*, p. 36. *KW* VII (SV IV
203).

41. See, for example, Philipp Marheineke, *Zur Kritik der Schellingschen Offenbarungsphilosophie* (Berlin: 1843; *ASKB* 647), pp. 7–22, especially pp. 21–22.
42. See, for example, Hegel, *Die Phänomenologie des Geistes, Georg Wilhelm Friedrich Hegel's Werke. Vollständige Ausgabe*, I-XVIII, ed. Philipp Marheineke et al. (Berlin:1832–45; ASKB 549–65), II, pp. 36–37; *Sämtliche Werke. Jubiläumsausgabe [J.A.]*, I-XXVI, ed. Hermann Glockner (Stuttgart: Frommann, 1927–40), II, pp. 44–45; *The Phenomenology of Mind* (tr. primariliy based on P.G., 3 ed., 1841; Kierkegaard had 2 ed., 1832), tr. J. B. Baillie (New York: Harper, 1967), pp. 105–06; *Encyclopädie, Werke*, VI, pp. 46–47; *J. A.*, VIII, pp. 84–85; *Hegel's Logic*, p. 37:

> Philosophy, on the contrary, does not deal with a determination that is nonessential, but with a determination so far as it is an essential factor. The abstract or unreal is not its element and content, but the real, what is self-establishing, has life within itself, existence in its very notion. It is the process that creates its own moments in its course, and goes through them all; and the whole of this movement constitutes its positive content and its truth. This movement includes, therefore, within it the negative factor as well, the element which would be named falsity if it could be considered one from which we had to abstract. The element that disappears has rather to be looked at as itself essential, not in the sense of being something fixed, that has to be cut off from truth and allowed to lie outside it, heaven knows where; just as similarly the truth is not to be held to stand on the other side as an immovable lifeless positive element. Appearance is the process of arising into being and passing away again, a process that itself does not arise and does not pass away, but is *per se*, and constitutes reality and the life-movement of truth. . . . Judged by that movement, the particular shapes which mind assumes do not indeed subsist any more than do determinate thoughts or ideas; but they are, all the same, as much positive and necessary moments, as negative and transitory. In the entirety of the movement, taken as an unbroken quiescent whole, that which obtains distinctness in the course of its process and secures specific existence, is preserved in the form of a self-recollection, in which existence is self-knowledge, and self-knowledge, again, is immediate existence.

> To speak of thought or objective thought as the heart and soul of the world, may seem to be ascribing consciousness to the things of nature. We feel a certain repugnance against making thought the inward function of things, especially as we speak of thought as marking the divergence of man from nature. It would be necessary, therefore, if we use the term thought at all, to speak of nature as the system of unconscious thought, or, to use Schelling's expression, a petrified intelligence. And in order to prevent misconception, "thought-form" or "thought-type" should be substituted for the ambiguous term thought.
> From what has been said the principles of logic are to be sought in a system of thought-types or fundamental categories, in which the opposition be-

tween subjective and objective, in its usual sense, vanishes. The signification thus attached to thought and its characteristic forms may be illustrated by the ancient saying that "νοῦς [mind] governs the world", or by our own phrase that "Reason is in the world"; which means that Reason is the soul of the world it inhabits, its immanent principle, its most proper and inward nature, its universal.

43. Horace, *Epistles*, I, 10, 24; *Opera*, p. 239; Loeb, pp. 316–17.

44. Ibid., I, 18, 71; p. 253; pp. 374–75.

45. See supplement, p. 348 (*Skrivelser*, p. 23).

46. Ludvig Holberg, *Den Stundesløse*, I, 4; *Den Danske Skue-plads*, V, no pagination; *The Fussy Man, Four Plays by Holberg*, tr. Henry Alexander (Princeton: Princeton University Press for the American-Scandinavian Foundation, 1946).

47. A sixty-year-old perpetual student character in a musical comedy by J. L. Heiberg. See *Recensenten og Dyret*, 3, *Skuespil af Johan Ludvig Heiberg*, I-VII (Copenhagen: 1833–41; *ASKB* 1553–59), III, pp. 201–02. He can, he says, produce testimonials to his almost having taken the Latin law examination, and he quotes in Italian an adage (which he had learned from Madame Voltisubito, an equestrian): "*Chi va piano, va sano* [slow but sure]."

48. See, for example, *Two Ages*, pp. 98–99, *KW* XIV (*SV* VIII 91–92); *JP* I 146 (*Pap.* IV A 161).

49. See Supplement, p. 348 (*Skrivelser*, pp. 23–24).

50. Ibid.

51. See Supplement, p. 288 (*Pap.* VII^2 B 235, p. 162) and note 105.

52. See p. 43 and note 15.

53. See Supplement, pp. 304–05 (*Pap.* VII^2 B 266:28).

54. See *JP* I 1030 (*Pap.* IV A 164).

55. See *Postscript*, p. 146, *KW* XII.1 (*SV* VII 119).

56. See Adler, *Studier*, p. xv.

57. In a later (1849) restructuring of "A Cycle," most of Chapter V, "A Psychological View of Adler as a Phenomenon and as a Satire on Hegelian Philosophy and the Present Age," was omitted (sections 1–4 in version I). The last part (section 5 of Chapter IV in version I) of Chapter V in "A Cycle" became a new Chapter VI in version IV, with a new title "An Inoffensive Satire on Established Christendom" and new opening paragraphs (*Pap.* X^6 B 55). References to Adler were omitted in the new title and in the three new paragraphs. Kierkegaard then considered publishing Chapter II of "A Cycle," "The Dialectical Relations: the Universal, the Single Individual, the Special Individual" and the old Chapter V together as "Two Ethical-Religious Essays" (*Pap.* X^6 B 52:1,3). A second possibility was the separate publication of the old Chapter V on Adler under the title "A Kind of Literary Review" (*Pap.* X^6 B 52:2). A third possibility was the separate publication of the new Chapter VI, "An Inoffensive Satire" (*Pap.* X^6 B 53), in which "Adler's name is to be suppressed" (*Pap.* X^6 B 56). None of these publication ideas was carried out. Therefore in

version IV the new Chapter VI of "A Cycle" constitutes the latest version of section 5 of Chapter IV of "The Book on Adler."

For the replaced version, see Supplement, pp. 305–07 (*Pap.* VII² B 235, pp. 218–19). See also Supplement, pp. 320–21 (*Pap.* X⁶ B 52:1–3, 53, 54).

58. At one time Kierkegaard considered using this Latin sentence as the title of a book. See *JP* V 5813–18 (*Pap.* VI A 55–59, 61).

59. For continuation of the paragraph, see Supplement, p. 307 (*Pap.* VII² B 266:30).

60. With reference to the remainder of the section, see Supplement, p. 307 (*Pap.* X⁶ B 56).

61. See, for example, *Fragments*, pp. 95–97, *KW* VII (*SV* IV 258–60); *Postscript*, pp. 366–67, *KW* XII.1 (*SV* VII 317–18); *JP* I 452 (*Pap.* V A 10).

62. See *JP* III 3309 (*Pap.* VII¹ A 152).

63. See Plato, *Phaedrus*, 229 d-230 a; *Opera*, I, pp. 130–31; *Dialogues*, p. 478 (Socrates speaking):

> For my part, Phaedrus, I regard such theories [a scientific account of how Boreas seized Orythia from the river] as no doubt attractive, but as the invention of clever, industrious people who are not exactly to be envied, for the simple reason that they must then go on and tell us the real truth about the appearance of centaurs and the Chimera, not to mention a whole host of such creatures, Gorgons and Pegasuses and countless other remarkable monsters of legend flocking in on them. If our skeptic, with his somewhat crude science, means to reduce every one of them to the standard of probability, he'll need a deal of time for it. I myself have certainly no time for the business, and I'll tell you why, my friend. I can't as yet "know myself," as the inscription at Delphi enjoins, and so long as that ignorance remains it seems to me ridiculous to inquire into extraneous matters. Consequently I don't bother about such things, but accept the current beliefs about them, and direct my inquiries, as I have just said, rather to myself, to discover whether I really am a more complex creature and more puffed up with pride than Typhon, or a simpler, gentler being whom heaven has blessed with a quiet, un-Typhonic nature.

See also *Fragments*, pp. 37–39, *KW* VII (*SV* IV 204–06); *Postscript*, p. 161, *KW* XII.1 (*SV* VII 133).

64. See *Diogenes Laertius*, II, 5, 31; *Diogenis Laertii de vitis philosophorum*. I-II (Leipzig: 1833; *ASKB* 1109), p. 75; *Diogen Laërtses filosofiske Historie*, I-II, tr. Børge Riisbrigh (Copenhagen: 1812; *ASKB* 1110–11), I, p. 70; *Stages*, p. 316, *KW* XI (*SV* VI 295); *Postscript*, p. 386, *KW* XII.1 (*SV* VII 334); *Two Ages*, p. 10, *KW* XIV (*SV* VIII 10); *The Sickness unto Death*, pp. 42–43, *KW* XIX (*SV* XI 155); *Works of Love*, p. 232, *KW* XVI (*SV* IX 222); *The Moment*, *KW* XXIII (*SV* XIV 225–27); *JP* IV 4267 (*Pap.* VII¹ A 193).

65. With reference to the remainder of the paragraph and the following sentence, see Supplement, p. 308 (*Pap.* VII² B 266:34).

66. See, for example, *JP* I 454 (*Pap.* V A 26).

67. Version II of Chapter IV included an appendix (*Pap.* VIII² B 7:18–19), a discussion of Adler's four latest books. The appendix was omitted in version III. See Supplement, pp. 308–09 (*Pap.* VIII² B 7:18; VII¹ A 150).

ADDENDUM I

1. In version III of "The Book on Adler," the major revisions of Chapters I, III, and IV included the shifting and revision of parts to constitute, with additions, two addenda: "The Dialectical Relations: the Universal, the Single Individual, the Special Individual" and "The Difference between a Genius and an Apostle." The text of Addendum I is basically version I (*Pap.* VII² B 235, pp. 33–53, 66–67), with revisions in version III (*Pap.* VIII² B 9:13–15) and in version V (*Pap.* X⁶ B 58 and XI³ B 2–3). The concluding pages are *Pap.* VIII² B 12, an extensive revision of version I (*Pap.* VII² B 235, pp. 54–55. 59–72) and additions. The entire restructuring of material, with revisions and additions, is according to version IV (*Pap.* IX B 2). Deletions and revisions in version IV (*Pap.* IX B 2, 3b) and in version V (*Pap.* X⁶ B 58 and XI³ B 2–3) are given in the text or in the notes.

2. Cf. Adam Gottlob Oehlenschläger, "*Skattegraveren*," *Oehlenschlägers samlede Digte*, I–III (Copenhagen: 1803), III, p. 28.

3. See Ludvig Holberg, *Peder Paars* (Copenhagen: 1798; *ASKB U* 67), II, 1, p. 139; *Peder Paars*, tr. Bergliot Stromsoe (Lincoln: University of Nebraska Press, 1962), pp. 69–70.

4. Socrates.

5. See Acts 5:9; *Irony*, p. 261, *KW* II (*SV* XIII 335).

6. For the deleted paragraph and a reference to Adler (*Pap.* VIII² B 9:14d, e), see Supplement, pp. 309–10 (*Pap.* VII² B 235, pp. 39–40).

7. Presumably a reference to the laws of Charondas (5 c. B.C.). See *Diodors von Sicilien historische Bibliothek*, I–IV, tr. Julius Friedrich Wurm (Stuttgart: 1827–29: *ASKB* 1105–08), XII, 17, II, p. 867. See also *Ludvig Holberg, Niels Klims Underjordiske Reise*, IV, tr. Jens Baggesen, *Jens Baggesens danske Værker*, I–XII (Copenhagen: 1827–32; *ASKB* 1509–20), XII, pp. 222–23; *Journey of Niels Klim to the World Underground*, tr. James I. Mc Nelis, Jr. (Lincoln: University of Nebraska Press, 1960), p. 37:

> At length we came to the royal city of Potu, which for beauty and magnificence might vie with any. The buildings there are more numerous and extensive than at Keba, and the streets wider and more commodious. The Forum, which was the first place we were brought to, was filled with numbers of merchants and surrounded every way with shops of artists and tradesmen. But I saw with some astonishment in the middle of the Forum a certain criminal with a halter about his neck, and a large company of grave and elderly trees standing round him. Upon my asking what was the matter, and for what crime he deserved hanging, especially as I thought no crime here

was capital, it was told me that this offender was a projector who had advised the abolition of a certain old custom; that those who stood round him were the senators and lawyers, who then and there examined the projector's scheme, so that if it should appear that it was a well-digested thing, and salutary to the commonwealth, the offender was not only absolved, but rewarded; but if injurious to the public, or if the projector by the repeal of this law appeared to have glanced at his own advantage, he was presently to be hanged as a disturber of the realm.

8. Homer, *Iliad*, II, 204; *Homers Iliade*, I–II, tr. Christian Wilster (Copenhagen: 1836), I, p. 23; *Homer The Iliad*, I–II, tr. A. T. Murray (Loeb, Cambridge: Harvard University Press, 1976–78), I, pp. 64–65.

9. Cf. *Upbuilding Discourses in Various Spirits*, p. 341, *KW* XV (*SV* VIII 416); "What Does the Fire Chief Say?" The Moment *and Late Writings*, *KW* XXIII (*SV* XIV 231–34).

10. The remainder of the long paragraph (pp. 152:6–153:34; *Pap.* VII² B 235, pp. 43⁸–45¹⁰) with reference to Bishop Mynster was revised in version IV ("A Cycle," *Pap.* IX B 2:1–4) and in version V ("Three Ethical-Religious Essays," no. II, *Pap.* X⁶ B 58), and in a later (1854) revision of version V (*Pap.* XI³ B 2–3) was deleted entirely, along with the following paragraph.

11. See Galatians 2:9.

12. See Jac[k]ob Peter Mynster, "*(Forerindring) ved tredie Oplag,*" *Prædikener*, I–II (Copenhagen: 1826, 1832; *ASKB* 228), I, p. ix.

13. Cf. Titus 1:7.

14. Attributed to the Greek lyric poet Cleobulus (7 c. B.C.). See Diogenes Laertius, *Lives of Eminent Philosophers*, I, 91, *Diogenis Laertii de vitis philosophorum*, I–II (Leipzig: 1833; *ASKB* 1109), I, p. 43; *Diogen La rtses filosofiske Historie*, I–II, tr. Børge Riisbrigh (Copenhagen: 1812; *ASKB* 1110–11), I, p. 41; *Lives of Eminent Philosophers*, I–II, tr. R. D. Hicks (Loeb, New York: Putnam, 1925), I, p. 95. See also *JP* III 2592 (*Pap.* IV A 237).

15. See Document VI, "School Testimony," by Michael Nielsen, principal of Borgerdyds School, which Kierkegaard attended, *Letters*, p. 7, *KW* XXV.

16. See Supplement, pp. 314–15 (*Pap.* IX B 8).

17. The quotation has not been located in Luther's works listed in *ASKB*. See Martin Luther, *Tischreden*, 3007, *Dr. Martin Luther's sämmtliche Werke*, I–LXVII (Erlangen, Frankfurt am Main: 1826–63), LXII, p. 470; *Table Talk*, ed. and tr. Theodore G. Tappert, *Luther's Works*, I–LV, ed. Jaroslav Pelikan and Helmut T. Lehmann (Philadelphia: Fortress; St. Louis: Concordia, 1958–75), LIV, p. 111. See *Self-Examination*, p. 24, *KW* XXI (*SV* XII 314).

18. See Plato, *Apology*, 25 a–b; *Opera*, VIII, pp. 116–17; *Dialogues*, p. 11 (Socrates speaking to Meletus):

> Well, let me put another question to you. Take the case of horses. Do you believe that those who improve them make up the whole of mankind, and that there is only one person who has a bad effect on them? Or is the truth just the opposite, that the ability to improve them belongs to one person or

to very few persons, who are horse trainers, whereas most people, if they have to do with horses and make use of them, do them harm? Is not this the case, Meletus, both with horses and with all other animals? Of course it is, whether you and Anytus deny it or not. It would be a singular dispensation of fortune for our young people if there is only one person who corrupts them, while all the rest have a beneficial effect.

19. See *JP* V 5885 (*Pap.* VII[1] A 27).

20. Luke 16:9.

21. An allusion to the statement by Archimedes about a fulcrum and lever. See Plutarch, "*Marcellus,*" 14, *Lives*; *Plutark's Levnetsbeskrivelser*, I-IV, tr. Stephan Tetens (Copenhagen: 1800–11; *ASKB* 1197–1200), III, p. 272; *Plutarch's Lives*, I-XI, tr. Bernadotte Perrin (Loeb, Cambridge: Harvard University Press, 1968–84), V, p. 473: "Archimedes, who was a kinsman and friend of King Hiero, wrote to him that with any given force it was possible to move any given weight; and emboldened, as we are told, by the strength of his demonstration, he declared that, if there were another world, and he could go to it, he could move this." See also, for example, *Either/Or*, I, p. 295, *KW* III (*SV* I 266); *Repetition*, p. 186, *KW* VI (*SV* III 221); *JP* I 117; *JP* V 5099 (*Pap.* I A 8, 68).

22. See Aristotle, *Physics*, 199 a-b; *Aristoteles graece*, I-II, ed. Immanuel Bekker (Berlin: 1831; *ASKB* 1074–75), I, p. 199; *The Complete Works of Aristotle*, I-II, ed. Jonathan Barnes (rev. Oxford tr., Princeton: Princeton University Press, 1984), I, pp. 339–40:

> If then, it is agreed that things are either the result of coincidence or for the sake of something, and these cannot be the result of coincidence or spontaneity, it follows that they must be for the sake of something; and that such things are all due to nature even the champions of the theory which is before us would agree. Therefore action for an end is present in things which come to be and are by nature.
>
> Further, where there is an end, all the preceding steps are for the sake of that. Now surely as in action, so in nature; and as in nature, so it is in each action, if nothing interferes. Now action is for the sake of an end; therefore the nature of things also is so. Thus if a house, e.g., had been a thing made by nature, it would have been made in the same way as it is now by art; and if things made by nature were made not only by nature but also by art, they would come to be in the same way as by nature. The one, then, is for the sake of the other; and generally art in some cases completes what nature cannot bring to a finish, and in others imitates nature. If, therefore, artificial products are for the sake of an end, so clearly also are natural products. The relation of the later to the earlier items is the same in both. . . .
>
> It is plain then that nature is a cause, a cause that operates for a purpose.

23. See Aristotle, *Generation of Animals*, 769 b-773 a; Bekker, I, pp. 769–73; *Works*, I, pp. 1190–96.

24. See I Corinthians 1:23.

25. See *Fragments*, p. 10 and note 13, *KW* VII (*SV* IV 181).

26. See *JP* II 2263 (*Pap.* II A 404).

27. See Luke 5:36–37.

28. See Luke 1:26–35.

29. Luke 16:24–26.

30. See I Corinthians 14:33.

31. See Hans Lassen Martensen, *Mester Eckart. Et Bidrag til at oplyse Middel-alderens Mystik* (Copenhagen: 1840; *ASKB* 649), pp. 12–14.

32. An allusion to the Tivoli amusement park, which was opened in 1843.

33. Attributed to Pope Paul IV but found earlier in Sebastian Brandt, *Narren-schiff*. In Danish translation the line is part of the title of a frequently performed drama by Augustin E. Scribe, *Puf, eller verden vil bedrages*, tr. Nicolai C. L. Abra-hams, *Det Kongelige Theaters Repertoire*, 167, (Copenhagen: 1849; *ASKB* U101). See for example, *Irony*, pp. 253–54, *KW* II (*SV* XIII 328); *Stages*, p. 340, *KW* XI (*SV* VI 318); *JP* V 5937–38; VI 6680 (*Pap.* VII¹ A 147–48; X³ A 450).

34. Cf. *JP* V 5900 (*Pap.* VII¹ A 113).

35. For a contemplated postscript to version IV of Addendum I as no. II in "Cycle" (1848), see Supplement, pp. 315–20 (*Pap.* IX B 24). For two forms of a contemplated postscript to version V of Addendum I as no. II in "Three Ethical-Religious Essays" (March and April 1855), see Supplement pp. 336–38 (*Pap.* XI³ B 4, 6).

ADDENDUM II

1. See Historical Introduction, pp. xiv–xvii. Addendum II is the one part of the Adler manuscript that Kierkegaard published, the second essay in *Two Ethi-cal-Religious Essays* (May 19, 1849). In *Essays* (*SV* XI 95–98) the text of version I (*Pap.* VII² B 235, pp. 136–41) was used with some changes, and the manu-script of *Pap.* VII² B 235, pp. 141–50, with a few changes, was used as the printing copy of *Two Essays* (*SV* XI 98³⁵-107⁶). The last three pages, section 3 (*Pap.* VIII² B 9:18; *SV* XI, pp. 107:7–109), replaced text dealing with Adler (*Pap.* VIII² B 7:9–10).

2. See *JP* V 5181 (*Pap.* I A 328).

3. In Greek the word means "one who is sent."

4. The following nine pages were used as the printing manuscript for the essay. See note 1 above.

5. See Supplement, p. 310 (*Pap.* VIII¹ A 225).

6. See Supplement, p. 327 (*Pap.* X¹ A 336).

7. With reference to the following three paragraphs, see Supplement, pp. 310–11 (*Pap.* VIII¹ A 416).

8. See *Anxiety*, p. 59, *KW* VIII (*SV* IV 329).

9. See Psalm 51:12.

10. With reference to the following note, see Supplement, pp. 311–12 (*Pap.* VII² B 235, p. 144; *Pap.* VIII² B 9:17).

11. See the prefaces in *Eighteen Discourses*, pp. 5, 53, 107, 179, 231, 295, *KW*

V (*SV* III 11, 271; IV 7, 73, 121; V 79); *Three Discourses on Imagined Occasions*, p. 5, *KW* X (*SV* V 175). See also Corsair *Affair*, Supplement, p. 173, *KW* XIII (*Pap.* VII¹ B 38); *On My Work*, in *Point of View*, *KW* XXII (*SV* XIII 494).

12. See Ephesians 2:19.

13. See, for example, *Sickness unto Death*, pp. 99, 117, 126, 127, *KW* XIX (*SV* XI 210, 227, 235, 237).

14. See Matthew 7:29.

15. See Matthew 28:18.

16. See Plato, *Phaedo*; *Opera*, I, pp. 472–618; Heise, I, pp. 1–175; *Dialogues*, pp. 41–98.

17. An allusion to Nicolai Frederik Severin Grundtvig (1783–1872), Danish pastor, poet, and politician. See, for example, *JP* V 5752, 5753 (*Pap.* V A 94, 95).

18. See I Corinthians 4:13. The part of the manuscript of *The Book on Adler* used as the printing copy for part of "The Difference between a Genius and an Apostle" (*Two Ethical-Religious Essays*, in *Without Authority*, pp. 96- 105, *KW* XVIII (*SV* XI 98–107) ends here. The remainder is version IV of Addendum II (*Pap.* VIII² B 7:9–10, 9:18) and is the same as the closing paragraphs of the essay.

19. II Corinthians 6:10.

20. See Philippians 4:7.

21. For a contemplated postscript, see Supplement, pp. 315–20 (*Pap.* IX B 24).

SUPPLEMENT

1. See Adler, *Den isolerede Subjectivitet i dens rigtigste Skikkelser*, pp. 7–9, 13–14, 18–20. This was Adler's dissertation, defended June 25, 1840.

2. Ibid., p. 5.

3. Ibid., pp. 19–20.

4. Ibid., p. 4; Johan Ludvig Heiberg, *"Det logiske System. Første Afhandling, indeholdene Paragrapherne 1–23,"* *Perseus*, 2, August, 1838 (*ASKB* 569), p. 11.

5. See note 1 above.

6. See J. L. Heiberg, *"Det logiske System,"* *Perseus*, 2, pp. 1–45.

7. Ibid., p. 3.

8. Ibid., p. 43.

9. See Hegel, *Wissenschaft der Logik*, I, *Die objektive Logik, Georg Wilhelm Friedrich Hegel's Werke. Vollständige Ausgabe*, I-XVIII, ed. Philipp Marheineke et al. (Berlin: 1832–45; *ASKB* 549–65), III, p. 114; *Sämtliche Werke. Jubiläumsausgabe* [*J.A.*], I-XXVI, ed. Hermann Glockner (Stuttgart: Frommann, 1927–40), IV, p. 124; *Hegel's Science of Logic* (tr. of *W. L.*, Lasson ed., 1923; Kierkegaard had 2 ed., 1833), tr. A. V. Miller (New York: Humanities, 1976), p. 111:

Determinateness thus isolated by itself in the form of *being* is *quality*—which is wholly simple and immediate. *Determinateness* as such is the more universal term which can equally be further determined as quantity and so on. Because of this simple character of quality as such, there is nothing further to be said about it.

10. Adler, *Populaire Foredrag over Hegels objective Logik* (Copenhagen: 1842; *ASKB* 383).

11. Plutarch, *Concerning Talkativeness*, 17; *Plutarchs moralische Abhandlungen*, I-V, tr. Johann Friedrich S. Kaltwasser (Frankfurt am Main: 1783; *ASKB* 1192–96), IV, p. 471; *Plutarch's Moralia*, I-XVI, tr. Frank Cole Babbitt et al. (Loeb, Cambridge: Harvard University Press, 1967–84), VI, p. 445:

> And we must be careful to offer to chatterers examples of this terseness, so that they may see how charming and how effective they are. For example: "The Spartans to Philip: Dionysius in Corinth." And again, when Philip wrote to them, "If I invade Laconia, I shall turn you out," they wrote back, "If."

12. Adler, *Studier og Exempler* (Copenhagen: 1846; *ASKB U* 11), pp. 70–71.
13. See Addendum I, pp. 143–72.
14. See *Fragments*, pp. 87–110, *KW* VII (*SV* IV 251–71).
15. See Supplement, p. 339 (*Prædikener*, p. 3).
16. See Supplement, pp. 340–48 (*Skrivelser*).
17. See p. ix and note 13.
18. See Supplement, p. 339 (*Prædikener*, p. 3).
19. *The Concept of Irony, with Continual Reference to Socrates* (1841); *KW* II (*SV* XIII).
20. See "'Guilty?'/'Not Guilty?'" *Stages*, pp. 185–397, *KW* XI (*SV* VI 175–370).
21. See Supplement, pp. 308–09 (VII¹ A 150).
22. See note 36 below.
23. See Supplement, p. 221 (*Pap.* VII¹ B 218).
24. See *Postscript*, pp. 617, 619, KW XII.1 (*SV* VII 537, 539).
25. Abraham à St. Clara (Ulrich Megerle) (1644–1709), Augustinian monk and writer. Kierkegaard had *Abraham à St. Clara's Sämmtliche Werke*, I-XXII (Passau, Lindau: 1835–54; *ASKB* 294–311).
26. Georg Christoph Lichtenberg, *Ideen, Maximen und Einfälle*, I-II (Leipzig: 1831; *ASKB* 1773–74), I, p. 122. See also *JP* V 5245, 6099 (*Pap.* II A 124; VIII¹ A 655).
27. *Johann Gottlieb Fichte's sämmtliche Werke*, I-VIII, ed. Immanuel Hermann Fichte (Berlin: 1845–46: *ASKB* 492–99), VIII, pp. 75–76:

> Der Leser will doch ohne Zweifel ein richtiges Urtheil über die Producte der Kunst und der Wissenschaft, auf das er sich auch verlassen könne. Wer kann denn nun, und wer soll diese Urtheile fällen? Doch wohl die ersten Meister in jedem Fache der Kunst und der Wissenschaft?
> Wenn nun zuvörderst der einige grösste Meister in einem Fache—denn es ist doch wohl nicht anzunehmen, dass die Grossen wie Pilze aus der Erde

wachsen—etwas schriebe, wer soll denn diesem sein Urtheil fällen? Wer soll gegenwärtig in der Kunst über Goethe, wer sollte zu seiner Zeit in der Philosophie über Leibnitz, wer sollte, als Kant mit seiner Kritik der reinen Vernunft hervortrat, über Kant urtheilen? Ueber den letzten etwa die Garve, die Eberharde? Nun, sie haben es gethan, und es ist darnach. Diesen Fall aber abgerechnet: sollten denn die grössten Meister die Geneigtheit haben, dieses Richteramt über die Schriften zu übernehmen; sollten sie nicht etwas Besseres thun können, das dem gemeinen Wesen noch erspriesslicher sey?

[The reader, however, undoubtedly wants a correct judgment about the products of art and scholarship that he could depend upon. Who, now, is able to and should pass these judgments? Should that not be the prime masters in each field of art and scholarship?

If now first of all the one greatest master in a field—for surely it can hardly be assumed that the great ones appear on the scene as plentifully as mushrooms emerge from the soil—would write something, who should pass judgment on that? Who in our time should in the field of art pass judgment on Goethe, who in Leibnitz's time should have passed judgment on his philosophy, who when Kant came forward with his Critique of Pure Reason should have passed judgment on Kant? On the latter, perhaps Garve, Eberhard? Well, they did it, and the judgment is accordingly. But regardless of this case: if the greatest masters deigned to assume this office as judge of the writings, should they not be able to do something better that would benefit the general public even more?]

28. See Supplement, pp. 313–14 (*Pap.* IX B 1–6).

29. The so-called "longer preface." See *JP* VI 6334 (*Pap.* X^1 A 90).

30. In France, the July Revolution of 1830 was followed by the February Revolution of 1848. In that year there were also revolutions in Germany. In Denmark, the revolutionary spirit found expression in an enormous demonstration at Christiansborg Palace on March 21, 1848. King Frederik VII (King Christian VIII had died January 28, 1848) agreed to the dissolution of the ministries. Thereupon the March government, the Moltke-Hvidt government, was formed and Frederik VII declared that he now regarded himself as a constitutional monarch.

In addition to the internal unrest in Denmark, there was the external threat from Prussia. In the context of the old Slesvig-Holsten issue, Prince Frederick of Augustenburg put himself at the head of a provisional government proclaimed at Kiel in March 1848. A Danish army subdued the rebels as far as the Eider River. A new national assembly of Germany decided to incorporate Slesvig, and a Prussian army under Wrangel drove the Danes back and entered Jutland. On August 26, 1848, an armistice was signed in Malmø and the government of the two duchies was entrusted to a commission composed of two Prussians, two Danes, and a fifth member by consent of the four. War was renewed between March and July 1849, and a second armistice was signed between Prussia and Denmark. Germans in the duchies increased their army under General Willesen. The Danes trapped Willesen's army at Idsted on July 23, 1849. In July 1850 Prussia concluded a treaty with Denmark and gave up claim to the duchies. In London, May 8, 1852, the leading European powers signed a treaty concerning the succession after Frederik VII, and there was no further outbreak until his death in 1863. From 1848 on, the financial situation of the country was precarious and inflation rampant.

31. "Does a Human Being Have the Right to Let Himself Be Put to Death for the Truth?" no. III of "A Cycle," eventually published as no. I of *Two Ethical-Religious Essays.*

32. A small Danish town in southern Jutland, founded by a colony of Moravian Brethren (*Herrnhuter Brüdergemeinde*).

33. See Historical Introduction, *Without Authority*, p. ix and note 1, *KW* XVIII.

34. See Corsair *Affair*, "trousers," p. 318.

35. Presumably a marginal note here, later clipped from the page. See Supplement, pp. 308–09 (*Pap.* VII[1] A 150).

36. Hans Friedrich Helweg, "*Mag. Adlers senere Skrifter* (*Nogle Digte, Studier og Exempler,* and *Forsøg til en kort systematisk Fremstilling af Christendommen i dens Logik*)," *Dansk Kirketidende,* 45, 46, July 19, 26, 1846.

37. With reference to the remainder of the paragraph, see Supplement, p. 240 (*Pap.* VII[2] B 248:11).

38. See Supplement, p. 237 (*Pap.* VII[2] B 235, p. 27).

39. The wide marginal side of the manuscript sheet has been removed. The asterisk in the text presumably refers to a heading: "The Dialectical Relations: the Universal, the Single Individual, and the Special Individual." See Addendum I, p. 143.

40. See Adler, *Studier og Exempler,* pp. VII, XVII, XXIV-XXV.

41. See Matthew 26:74.

42. For revision of pp. 243–57, see Addendum I, pp. 163–72.

43. See *JP* II 1287; V 5841 (*Pap.* I A 83; VI A 104).

44. See, for example, *JP* I 624; V 5646 (*Pap.* V A 47; IV A 87).

45. With reference to the following note, cf. *Pap.* VII[1] B 195.

46. See "*Von dem Machandelboom,*" *Kinder- und Haus-Märchen. Gesammelt durch die Brüder Grimm,* I-III (2 ed., Berlin, 1819–22; *ASKB* 1425-27), no. 47, I, p. 236; "The Juniper Tree," *The Complete Grimm's Fairy Tales,* tr. Margaret Hunt, rev. James Stern (New York: Pantheon, 1972), p. 226.

47. Presumably a reference to the Copenhagen amusement park Tivoli, which was opened in August 1843.

48. Jacob Rasmus Damkier (1810–1871), who for a time after 1840 participated in negotiations about a new hymnbook.

49. See Johann Wolfgang v. Goethe, *Egmont,* II, 1; *Goethe's Werke. Vollständige Ausgabe letzter Hand,* I-LX (Stuttgart, Tübingen: 1828–42; *ASKB* 1641-68 [I-LV]), VIII, pp. 199–200; *Goethe's Works,* I-V, tr. Hjalmar H. Boyesen (Philadelphia: George Barrie, 1885), II, p. 202.

50. Holberg, *Peder Paars* (Copenhagen: 1798; *ASKB U* 67 [*n.d.*]), IV, 1, p. 308; *Peder Paars*, tr. Berglivt Stromsoe (Lincoln: University of Nebraska Press and American-Scandinavian Foundation, 1962), p. 145.

51. See René Descartes, *Discourse on Method; Opera philosophica. Editio ultima*, I–III (Amsterdam: 1678; *ASKB* 473), II, p. 7; *A Discourse on Method and Selected Writings*, tr. John Veitch (Everyman, New York: Dutton, 1951), p. 9:

> I was then in Germany, attracted thither by the wars in that country, which have not yet been brought to a termination; and as I was returning to the army from the coronation of the emperor, the setting in of winter arrested me in a locality where, as I found no society to interest me, and was besides fortunately undisturbed by any cares or passions, I remained the whole day in seclusion, with full opportunity to occupy my attention with my own thoughts. Of these one of the very first that occurred to me was, that there is seldom so much perfection in works composed of many separate parts, upon which different hands had been employed, as in those completed by a single master. Thus it is observable that the buildings which a single architect has planned and executed, are generally more elegant and commodious than those which several have attempted to improve, by making old walls serve for purposes for which they were not originally built.

52. The remainder of the paragraph, with slight changes, was used in Addendum I. See pp. 164–65.

53. With reference to the remainder of the paragraph, see Supplement, pp. 240–41 (*Pap.* VII^2 B 252:1).

54. See Exodus 4:13.

55. Luke 1:38.

56. I Samuel 3:9.

57. A reference to the marking of a long vowel in Hebrew. See *Fragments*, p. 80, *KW* VII (*SV* IV 244); *JP* II 2263 (*Pap.* II A 404).

58. See Matthew 9:16–17; Luke 5:36–37.

59. See Luke 1:26–35.

60. See p. 167 and note 29.

61. See p. 168 and note 30.

62. A mystical-pantheistic sect of the thirteenth and fourteenth centuries. See Hans Lassen Martensen, *Mester Eckart. Et Bidrag til at oplyse Middelalderens Mystik* (Copenhagen: 1840; *ASKB* 649), p. 12 (ed. tr.): ". . . their pantheistic spiritualism seemed to many to have manifested itself as a false antinomianism that placed itself not only above the precepts of the Church but above morality itself. The religious genius proclaimed the emancipation of the flesh because Spirit was not bound by any externality."

63. See *Anxiety*, pp. 123–29, *KW* VIII (*SV* 391–96).

64. Adler, *Theologiske Studier* (Copenhagen: 1846; *ASKB U* 9).

65. See Matthew 26:53.

66. Danish: *ride Herredage ind*, an old Danish expression for the festive open-

ing of the supreme court and earlier for the opening of the assembly when it convened as the court. In Kierkegaard's time the ceremony took place before the courthouse on Nytorv in the vicinity of the Kierkegaard home.

67. See p. 171 and note 33.

68. See Shakespeare, *Hamlet*, V, 2, 349–59; *William Shakspeare's Tragiske Værker*, I–IX, tr. Peter Foersom and Peter Frederik Wulff (Copenhagen: 1807–25; *ASKB* 1889–96), I, p. 175; *Shakspeare's dramatische Werke*, I–XII, tr. August Wilhelm v. Schlegel and Ludwig Tieck (Berlin: 1839–41; *ASKB* 1883–88), VI, pp. 142–43; *The Complete Works of Shakespeare*, ed. George Lyman Kittredge (Boston: Ginn, 1936), p. 1193:

> *Hamlet.* O, I could tell you—
> But let it be. Horatio, I am dead;
> Thou liv'st; report me and my cause aright.
> To the unsatisfied.
> *Horatio.* Never believe it.
> I am more an antique Roman than a Dane.
> Here's yet some liquor left.
> *Hamlet.* As th'art a man,
> Give me the cup. Let go! By heaven, I'll ha't.
> O good Horatio, what a wounded name
> (Things standing thus unknown) shall live behind me!
> If thou didst ever hold me in thy heart,
> Absent thee from felicity awhile,
> And in this harsh world draw thy breath in pain,
> To tell my story.

69. Danish: *Stundesløs*, the title of a comedy by Ludvig Holberg, also the characterization of the main character.

70. See I Corinthians 14:26; II Corinthians 12:19.

71. See *Postscript*, p. 191, *KW* XII.1 (*SV* VII 159).

72. Johannes Climacus, pseudonymous author of *Fragments* and *Postscript*. The review was of *Fragments*.

73. Johan Frederik Hagen (under the pseudonym 80), *Theologisk Tidsskrift*, Ny Række, IV, 1 (vol. X), May 1846, pp. 175–82. *Pap.* VII^1 A 158 on this review is essentially the same as *Pap.* VII^2 B 235, pp. 81–83.

74. See p. 171 and note 33.

75. See *Fragments*, pp. 55–71, *KW* VII (*SV* IV 221–34).

76. See *Postscript*, pp. 24–25 fn., *KW* XII.2 (*Pap.* VI B 29, p. 110 fn.).

77. See J. L. Heiberg, *De Uadskillelige*, 10, *Skuespil af Johan Ludvig Heiberg*, I–VII (Copenhagen: 1833–41; *ASKB* 1553–59), IV, p. 258.

78. See "*Leben des Blaise Pascal*," by Gilberta Perier (his sister), in Blaise Pascal, *Pascal, Gedanken über die Religion und einige andern Gegenstände*, I–II, tr. Karl Adolf Blech (Berlin: 1840; *ASKB* 712–13), I, p. 33 fn.

79. See Supplement, p. 348 (*Skrivelser*, pp. 23–24).

80. Homer, *Odyssey*, 17.66; *Homers Odyssee*, I–II, tr. Christian Wilster

(Copenhagen: 1836), II, p. 64; *Homer the Odyssey*, I–II, tr. A. T. Murray (Loeb, Cambridge: Harvard University Press, 1976), II, pp. 156–57.

81. *Adresseavisen*, 137, June 12, 1846.

82. In Turkey at one time, the officials were distinguished by the insignia of one, two, or three horsetails. See *Either/Or*, I, p. 22, *KW* III (*SV* I 6).

83. At one time in Denmark, the sign of three basins indicated that the barber was a member of the privileged guild of barbers or was an individual privileged barber.

84. *Three Upbuilding Discourses, Philosophical Fragments, The Concept of Anxiety*, and *Prefaces* (by Kierkegaard, Johannes Climacus, Vigilius Haufniensis, and Nicolaus Notabene respectiveley) were published June 8–17, 1844.

85. Horace, *Odes*, I, 22, 10–11; *Q. Horatii Flacci opera* (Leipzig: 1828; *ASKB* 1248), p. 24; *Horace The Odes and Epodes*, tr. C. E. Bennett (Loeb, Cambridge: Harvard University Press, 1978), pp. 64–65.

86. See Adler, *Studier*, pp. iii–iv.

87. Pp. 18–20.

88. See Adler, *Studier*, pp. 65, 180–81, 207–08, 209, 214–15, 317, 320, 441, 492.

89. Ibid., pp. ix, xxi fn., 465, 467; *Theologiske Studier*, p. 9; *Forsøg*, p. 24.

90. Attributed to the poet Jacques Desbarreaux (1602–1674), who, having ordered an omelet on a fast day, threw the omelet out the window to console the innkeeper, who interpreted a sudden thunderstorm as a punishment for his offense.

91. See Adler, *Theologiske Studier*, p. 88 fn.

92. See Adler, *Studier*, p. 257.

93. Abraham Soldin, bookseller on Grønnegade, Copenhagen, was notorious for his absentmindedness. Once when a customer entered the bookstore, Soldin was standing on a ladder searching for a book. Imitating the voice of Soldin, the customer said a few words to the bookseller's wife. Turning on the ladder, Soldin said, "Rebecca, is it I who is speaking?" See *Anxiety*, p. 51, *KW* VIII (*SV* IV 322); *Postscript*, p. 167, *KW* XII.1 (*SV* VII 138).

94. See Adler, *Forsøg*, p. 2 fn.; *Studier*, p. 2.

95. See ibid., p. xv.

96. See *Fragments*, p. 6, *KW* VII (*SV* IV 177).

97. See *Irony*, pp. 247–54, *KW* II (*SV* XIII 322–29).

98. See, for example, Adler, *Forsøg*, pp. 33 fn., 38–39 fn. 2; *Theologiske Studier*, p. 19; *Studier*, for example, pp. 126, 144, 212, 259, 406.

99. See, for example, Plato, *Sophist*, 254 d–255 a; *Opera*, II, pp. 320–23; *Dialogues*, p. 1000:

> STRANGER: Now, among the kinds, those we were just now discussing— existence itself and rest and motion—*are* very important.
> THEAETETUS: Quite so.
> STRANGER: And observe, we say that two of the three will not blend with one another.

THEAETETUS: Certainly.

STRANGER: Whereas existence can be blended with both, for surely they both exist.

THEAETETUS: Of course.

STRANGER: So they make three in all. And each one of them [existence, motion, rest] is *different* from the other two, and the *same* as itself.

THEAETETUS: That is so.

STRANGER: But what do we mean by these words we have just used— "same" and "different"? Are they a pair of kinds distinct from those three, though always necessarily blending with them, so that we must consider the forms as five in all, not three? Or, when we say "same" or "different," are we unconsciously using a name that belongs to one or another of those three kinds?

THEAETETUS: Possibly.

STRANGER: Well, motion and rest at any rate cannot be [identical with] difference or sameness.

THEAETETUS: Why not?

STRANGER: Neither motion nor rest can be [identical with] anything that we say of both of them in common.

THEAETETUS: Why?

STRANGER: Because motion would then be at rest, and rest in motion, for whichever of the two [motion or rest] becomes applicable to both [by being identified with either sameness or difference, which *are* applicable to both] will force the other [rest or motion] to change to the contrary of its own nature, as thus coming to partake of its contrary.

100. See Hegel, *Geschichte der Philosophie*, II, *Werke*, XIV, pp. 232–35; *J.A.*, XVIII, pp. 232–35; *The History of Philosophy*, II, pp. 63–66.

101. On this important concept in Kierkegaard's thought, see, for example, *Fragments*, p. 43, *KW* VII (*SV* IV 210); *Anxiety*, pp. 17 fn., 30, 111–13, *KW* VIII (*SV* IV 289, 303, 379–80); *Postscript*, pp. 93–106, *KW* XII.1 (*SV* VII 74–85); *JP* III 2338–56; VII, p. 56.

102. See, for example, Adler, *Theologiske Studier*, p. 29 fn.; Supplement, p. 298 (*Pap*. IX B 9:10b).

103. See, for example, *Anxiety*, p. 61, *KW* VIII (*SV* IV 331).

104. See, for example, Aristotle, *Physics*, 207 a; Bekker, I, p. 207; *Works*, I, pp. 352, 353; *Metaphysics*, 994 a, b; Bekker, II, p. 994, *Works*, I, pp. 1570, 1571:

> The infinite turns out to be the contrary of what it is said to be. It is not what has nothing outside it that is infinite, but what always has something outside it. This is indicated by the fact that rings also that have no bezel are described as infinite, because it is always possible to take a part which is outside a given part. The description depends on a certain similarity, but it is not true in the full sense of the word. This condition alone is not sufficient: it is necessary also that the same part should never be taken twice. In the

circle, the latter condition is not satisfied: it is true only that the next part is always different.

Thus something is infinite if, taking it quantity by quantity, we can always take something outside. On the other hand, what has nothing outside it is complete and whole. For thus we define the whole—that from which nothing is wanting, as a whole man or box. What is true of each particular is true of the whole properly speaking—the whole is that of which nothing is outside. On the other hand that from which something is absent and outside, however small that may be, is not "all". Whole and complete are either quite identical or closely akin. Nothing is complete which has no end and the end is a limit.

. . . Consequently, also, it is unknowable, *qua* infinite; for the matter has no form. (Hence it is plain that the infinite stands in the relation of part rather than of whole. For the matter is part of the whole, as the bronze is of the bronze statue.) If it contains in the case of sensible things, in the case of intelligible things the great and the small ought to contain them. But it is absurd and impossible to suppose that the unknowable and indeterminate should contain and determine.

Evidently there is a first principle, and the causes of things are neither an infinite series nor infinitely various in kind. For, on the one hand, one thing cannot proceed from another, as from matter, *ad infinitum*, e.g. flesh from earth, earth from air, air from fire, and so on without stopping; nor on the other hand can the efficient causes form an endless series, man for instance being acted on by air, air by the sun, the sun by Strife, and so on without limit. Similarly the final causes cannot go on *ad infinitum*,—walking for the sake of health, this for the sake of happiness, happiness for the sake of something else, and so one thing always for the sake of another. And the case of the formal cause is similar. For in the case of an intermediate, which has a last term and a prior term outside it, the prior must be the cause of the later terms. For if we had to say which of the three is the cause, we should say the first; surely not the last, for the final term is the cause of none; nor even the intermediate, for it is the cause only of one. It makes no difference whether there is one intermediate or more, nor whether they are infinite or finite in number. But of series which are infinite in this way, and of the infinite in general, all the parts down to that now present are alike intermediates; so that if there is no first there is no cause at all.

At the same time it is impossible that the first cause, being eternal, should be destroyed; for while the process of becoming is not infinite in the upward direction, a first cause by whose destruction something came to be could not be eternal.

Further, the *final cause* is an end, and that sort of end which is not for the sake of something else, but for whose sake everything else is; so that if there is to be a last term of this sort, the process will not be infinite; but if there is no such term there will be no final cause. But those who maintain the infinite series destroy the good without knowing it. Yet no one would try to do anything if he were not going to come to a limit. Nor would there be reason in the world; the reasonable man, at least, always acts for a purpose; and this is a limit, for the end is a limit.

105. See, for example, *Stages*, p. 231, *KW* XI (*SV* VI 218); *Postscript*, p. 119, *KW* XII.1 (*SV* VII 98).

106. See Adler, *Studier*, p. 324, 421; *Theologiske Studier*, pp. 29, 32.

107. See *Anxiety*, pp. 82–85, *KW* VIII (*SV* IV 351–54).

108. See Adler, *Studier*, pp. 98, 100, 305, 339, 354, 364–67; *Forsøg*, p. 31 fn.

109. See Isaiah 55:6.

110. See John 5:2–9; Adler, *Theologiske Studier*, pp. 27, 28–29.

111. See Galatians 6:7.

112. See, for example, Adler, *Digte*, pp. 33–41; *Studier*, pp. 74–77, 91, 120–21, 128, 152.

113. See *Fear and Trembling*, p. 30, *KW* VI (*SV* III 82).

114. See Adler, *Studier*, p. 17; *Digte*, p. 40.

115. See Supplement, p. 339 (*Prædikener*, pp. 3–4).

116. See Adler, *Studier*, p. 344.

117. Wolfgang Amadeus Mozart, *Don Juan*, tr. Laurids Kruse (Copenhagen: 1807), I, 5, p. 14. The scene is not found in *Don Giovanni*, tr. Ellen H. Bleiler (New York: Dover, 1964).

118. See, for example, *Upbuilding Discourses in Various Spirits*, pp. 141–43, *KW* XV (*SV* VIII 231–33).

119. See Augustine, *De mendacio*, VII; *Sancti Aurelii Augustini hipponensis epis-copi Opera*, I-XVIII (Bassano: 1797–1807; *ASKB* 117–34), VIII, col. 1770–71.

120. See Adler, *Studier*, pp. 105–06.

121. Ibid., pp. 88, 364–65.

122. Ibid., pp. 105, 106, 121–23, 137–39, 148–51.

123. Ibid., p. 121; *Forsøg*, p. 45 fn.

124. See Holberg, *Erasmus Montanus*, I, 4, *Den Danske Skue-Plads*, I-VII (Copenhagen: 1788; *ASKB* 1566–67), V, no pagination; *Comedies by Holberg*, tr. Oscar James Campbell and Frederic Schenck (New York: American-Scandinavian Foundation: 1935), p. 127.

125. Adler, *Theologiske Studier*, p. 29.

126. See Ludwig Andreas Feuerbach, *Das Wesen des Christenthums* (Leipzig: 1843; *ASKB* 488), p. xiii; *The Essence of Christianity*, tr. George Eliot (New York: Harper, 1957), p. xxxvii: "The true sense of Theology is Anthropology." See also *Postscript*, p. 579, *KW* XII.1 (*SV* VII 505).

127. With reference to the heading and the following text, see pp. 132–33 (*Pap.* X^6 B 55).

128. With reference to the remainder of the paragraph, see Supplement, p. 305 (*Pap.* VII^2 B 266:29).

129. With reference to the following sentence, see Supplement, p. 307 (*Pap.* VII² B 266:30).

130. "A Cycle," No. V. See Supplement, p. 314 (*Pap.* IX B 5).

131. See Supplement, pp. 234–36 (*Pap.* IX B 20, 22).

132. See *Stages*, pp. 195–397, *KW* XI (*SV* VI 185–370).

133. See Supplement, p. 237 (*Pap.* VII² B 235, p. 27) and note 36.

134. Ibid.

135. Ibid.

136. See *For Self-Examination*, pp. 9–10, *KW* XXI (*SV* XII 301–02).

137. See p. 180. Note replaced by SV XI 101. The pronominal changes represent the alternation in various versions between pseudonymous publication and signed publication.

138. See the prefaces in *Eighteen Upbuilding Discourses*, pp. 5, 53, 107, 179, 231, 295, *KW* V (*SV* III 11, 271; IV 7, 23, 121; V 79); *Three Discourses on Imagined Occasions*, p. 5, *KW* X (*SV* V 175). See also Supplement, Corsair *Affair*, p. 173, *KW* XIII (*Pap.* VII¹ B 38); *On My Work as an Author*, in *The Point of View*, *KW* XXII (*SV* XIII 494).

139. See, for example, *JP* V 6110 (*Pap.* VIII¹ A 558).

140. *The Crisis and a Crisis in the Life of an Actress*, by Inter et Inter, *Fædrelandet*, 188–91, June 24–27, 1848; with *Christian Discourses*, *KW* XVII (*SV* X 319–44).

141. See Supplement, p. 312 (*Pap.* VIII¹ A 562) and note 139.

142. Johann Arndt, *Sämtliche geistreiche Bücher vom wahren Christenthum* (Tübingen: *n.d.*; *ASKB* 276).

143. See Supplement, pp. 315–20 (*Pap.* IX B 24).

144. See Addendum I, pp. 143–72.

145. A revision of version I, *Pap.* VII² B 235, pp. 5–16.

146. Addendum I in version III, a revision of *Pap.* VII² B 235, pp. 33–53.

147. A revision of version I, *Pap.* VII² B 235, pp. 74–90.

148. A revision of version I, *Pap.* VII² B 235, pp. 176–230.

149. Addendum II in version III, but without later changes (see p. 180 fn., Supplement, pp. 311–12 [*Pap.* VII² B 235, p. 144; VIII² B 9:17a] and p. 188 end).

150. Essay II in "A Cycle" is Addendum I in version III of *Adler*, "The Dialectical Relations: the Universal, the Single Individual, the Special Individual." See Supplement, p. 314 (*Pap.* IX B 2) and note 146.

151. See Supplement, p. 228 (*Pap.* IX B 10) and note 30.

152. For other references to the Danish game, see *Fear and Trembling*, p. 100, *KW* VI (*SV* III 147); *Fragments*, p. 22, *KW* VII (*SV* IV 191).

153. Louis Philippe (1773–1850), King of France (1830–48), came to power in The July Revolution of 1830 and abdicated during the revolution in February 1848. He fled ignominiously to England, where he died two years later.

154. See Supplement, p. 321 (*Pap.* X⁶ B 54).

155. See, for example, *JP* VI 6418 (*Pap.* X¹ A 424).

156. In the later years of his life, Kierkegaard became more stringent about

his expenses. He divided what he had into units that were placed in the custody of his brother-in-law Henrik Ferdinand Lund of the National Bank. Shortly before his death he drew out the last portion. See, for example, *JP* V 5881 (*Pap.* VII¹ B 211).

157. See Supplement, p. 228 (*Pap.* IX B 10) and note 30.

158. See note 150.

159. *Either/Or*, I, pp. 301–445, *KW* III (*SV* I 273–412). The essay is an explanation in the sense that the Seducer is a negative instance of the extraordinary.

160. See note 150.

161. Chapter IV of *Adler* and No. V in the original plan of "A Cycle." See Supplement, pp. 314, 307 (*Pap.* IX B 5; X¹ A 90).

162. Essay No. III in "A Cycle" and essay no. I in *Two Essays*, "Does a Human Being Have the Right to Let Himself Be Put to Death for the Truth?" See Supplement, p. 314 (*Pap.* IX B 3).

163. See note 150.

164. The "Three Notes Concerning My Work as an Author" intended as appendixes to "The Point of View" were (1) "Concerning the Dedication to 'that Single Individual,'" (2) "A Word on the Relation of My Work as an Author to 'That Single Individual,'" and (3) "Preface to the 'Friday Discourses.'" Eventually No. 3 was omitted. A shortened version of No. 3 was used as the preface to *Two Discourses at the Communion on Fridays* (1851).

165. Published April 26, 1848.

166. Published May 14, 1849.

167. See Supplement pp. 313–14 (*Pap.* IX B 1, 2).

168. See *Armed Neutrality*, in *Point of View*, *KW* XXII (*Pap.* X⁵ B 107).

169. See note 162 above.

170. See note 164 above.

171. See note 150 above.

172. See note 162 above.

173. See note 161 above.

174. Only one of the pseudonyms was used: H. H., the pseudonymous author of *Two Ethical-Religious Essays* (May 19, 1849), *KW* XVIII (*SV* XI 55–91).

175. The three parts of *Practice in Christianity*, eventually published September 27, 1850.

176. Kierkegaard's thirty-sixth birthday.

177. Jens Finsteen Gi(j)ødvad (1811–1891), journalist, editor of *Fædrelandet*, and Kierkegaard's middleman between him and the printer and the bookseller of the pseudonymous works.

178. *Tvende ethiske-religieuse Smaa-Afhandlinger* (Copenhagen: 1849, p. 70) has *Gave* (gift). The typographical error (*Gene*, inconvenience) must have been in the page proofs. Cf. *Either/Or*, I, p. 20, *KW* III (*SV* I 4).

179. In version V there were the three essays (I, II, IV in "A Cycle") remaining after the withdrawal of *Two Ethical-Religious Essays* (III, VI) and the omis-

sion of one on Adler (V). These three essays were given the title "Three Ethical-Religious Essays." See Supplement, pp. 313–14, 333–34 (*Pap.* IX B 1,2,4; X⁶ B 57:3).

180. "The Accounting" in *On My Work as an Author*.

181. See note 164 above.

182. See note 168 above.

183. Carl A. Reitzel (1789–1852), Copenhagen bookseller and publisher.

184. See *JP* VI 6418 (*Pap.* X¹ A 424).

185. See Supplement, pp. 326–27 (*Pap.* X¹ A 263) and note 174.

186. See note 196 below.

187. See Supplement, p. 327 (*Pap.* X¹ A 422) and note 179.

188. "A Revelation in the Situation of the Present Age," No. 3 in version V, "Three Essays," No. IV in version IV, "A Cycle," and most of chapter II in version I (VII² B 235, pp. 74–90). See note 179. See Supplement, p. 314 (*Pap.* IX B 4).

189. See Immanuel Kant, *Critique of Practical Reason*, tr. Lewis White Beck (Indianapolis: Bobbs-Merrill, 1956), pp. 46–51.

190. See Miguel de Cervantes, *Don Quixote*, II, ch. 71; *Den sindrige Hervemands Don Quixote af Mancha Levnet og Bedrifter*, I-IV, tr. Charlotte Dorothea Biehl (Copenhagen: 1776–77; *ASKB* 1937–40), IV, pp. 338–42; *Don Quixote*, tr. John Ormsby, ed. Joseph R. Jones and Kenneth Douglas (New York: Norton, 1981), pp. 813–16.

191. See Friedrich Böhringer, *Die Kirche Christi und ihre Zeugen, oder Kirchengeschichte in Biographien*, I¹⁻⁴-II¹⁻⁴ (Zürich: 1842–58; *ASKB* 173–77 [I¹⁻⁴-II¹⁻³]), I¹, p. 82.

192. Cf. Addendum II, pp. 173–88; *Two Ethical-Religious Essays* in *Without Authority*, pp. 91–108, *KW* XVIII (*SV* XI 93–109).

193. See Supplement, p. 333 (*Pap.* X⁶ B 57:1).

194. See note 179 above.

195. See Supplement, p. 329.

196. "The Dialectical Relations," essay II in partial version IV, "A Cycle," Addendum I in version III, and essay 2 in partial version V, "Three Ethical-Religious Essays" by F. F. or M. M.

197. See Supplement, p. 329.

198. See Supplement, p. 314 (*Pap.* IX B 3).

199. P. 329

200. See Supplement, pp. 315–20 (*Pap.* IX B 24).

201. See Supplement, p. 333 (*Pap.* X⁶ B 57:1).

202. See note 179 above.

203. Ibid.

204. See pp. 152–53.

205. Bishop Mynster died January 30, 1854

206. See note 204.

BIBLIOGRAPHICAL NOTE

For general bibliographies of Kierkegaard studies, see:

Jens Himmelstrup, *Søren Kierkegaard International Bibliografi*. Copenhagen: Nyt Nordisk Forlag Arnold Busck, 1962.

International Kierkegaard Newsletter, ed. Julia Watkin. Launceton, Tasmania, Australia, 1979–.

Aage Jørgensen, *Søren Kierkegaard-litteratur 1961–1970*. Aarhus: Akademisk Boghandel, 1971. *Søren Kierkegaard-litteratur 1971–1980*. Aarhus: privately published, 1983.

Kierkegaard: A Collection of Critical Essays, ed. Josiah Thompson. New York: Doubleday (Anchor Books), 1972.

Kierkegaardiana, XII, 1982; XIII, 1984; XIV, 1988; XVI, 1993; XVII, 1994; XVIII, 1996.

Bruce H. Kirmmse, *Kierkegaard in Golden Age Denmark*. Bloomington: Indiana University Press, 1990.

François H. Lapointe, *Sören Kierkegaard and His Critics: An International Bibliography of Criticism*. Westport, Connecticut: Greenwood Press, 1980.

Søren Kierkegaard's Journals and Papers, I, ed. and tr. Howard V. Hong and Edna H. Hong, assisted by Gregor Malantschuk. Bloomington: Indiana University Press, 1967.

For topical bibliographies of Kierkegaard studies, see *Søren Kierkegaard's Journals and Papers*, I-IV, 1967–75.

INDEX

prose: graduate student's, 225; lyrical, 309
prototype: Christ as, 233
pseudonym: 80 (Johan Frederik
Hagen), 374
public, 12; and apostle, 188; and author, 14, 17, 22, 264; Copenhagen, 237; cultured, 159, 264;
discussion, 146–47; and genius,
188; and individual, 149; and reviewer, 297
public opinion, 243; and the extraordinary, 163; and the individual,
23, 24, 43, 147
puddling. *See* analogy
Pythagoras, 293

qualitative change. *See* change
qualitative dialectic. *See* dialectic,
qualitative
qualitative difference: God and
human being, 181–83
quality: and quantity, 214
quantity: and quality, 214

reader: and Adler, 278, 294, 296–97;
and author, 14, 226, 258–60, 279,
309; and critic, 226; slow, 221
reality: and existence, 211
redoubling, 118–19, 130, 170, 180;
self-, 331
reference points, 72, 74, 76, 347
reflection, 127, 170; and Adler, 304–
05; and age, 244; and basic principles, 145; as broker, 248; and originality, 280; and revelation, 30–35,
84
reform, 229–31, 234
reformation: and the individual,
158
Reformation, the, 234
reformer, 148–49, 151, 157–58; ap-
proach of, 159; and 1848, 315
Reitzel, Carl A., 328, 381
religion: absentmindedness, 103,
109; and critics, 21; and culture,

134–40; and distance, 107–8; inwardness and, 108–10; and the
moment, 104–06; subjectivity
and, 99, 104
religiousness A and B, 113
repetition, 81, 219, 283, 293; mes-
merizing, 219, 295
repugnance: and the extraordinary,
168–70, 172
rescue, 66, 71
resolution, 166–67, 251, 310
responsibility: and the extraordinary,
243
results: the age's concern for, 49
revelation, 17; in the age, 244; and
authority, 32; and Christian scholarship, 84–85; and communication, 53, 278; concept of, 119,
122, 130, 222, 277, 303; and contemporaneity, 44; denying, 247–
48; and doctrine, 54, 66; and exegesis, 71, 278; and genius, 86,
277; and historical distance, 103,
123; and livelihood, 33–34; and
modern age, 77; and Paul, 26; and
perfectibility, 68, 265; and reflection, 30–35, 84; state Church judging, 77–79
revelation-fact: and Adler, 18–19,
23, 28, 29, 45, 51; and authority,
32; confused with awakening or
enthusiasm, 60; — faith event, 68,
99; — reference points, 72, 74,
76; — rescue, 66, 71; confusing
content and source, 72–73; and
critic, 19–22, 31; earnestness of,
16, 25–26; perfecting, 68–71; and
loquacity, 22; revocation of, 57,
58, 60, 63–65, 69–71, 73, 76,
80, 83
reviewer, 259–61; harming books,
259–60; Kierkegaard as, 237, 298;
and public, 297
revolutionary: and state Church,
145
Rhodes, 108, 360

ADVISORY BOARD

KIERKEGAARD'S WRITINGS